HISTORICAL VIEWPOINTS

Volume Two: Since 1865

HISTORICAL VIEWPOINTS

Volume Two: Since 1865

NOTABLE ARTICLES FROM AMERICAN HERITAGE

The Magazine of History

Editor
JOHN A. GARRATY
Columbia University

American Heritage Publishing Co., Inc. New York

Harper & Row, Publishers, Incorporated
New York, Evanston and London

© 1970 by Harper & Row, Publishers, Inc.
All articles have appeared in American Heritage, The Magazine of History, some under different titles.
All rights reserved.
Library of Congress Catalog Card Number: 78–105689
SBN: 8281-0090-X

Introduction

*T*here are almost as many kinds of history as there are historians. In addition to the differences between political history and the social, economic, and cultural varieties, the discipline lends itself to such classifications as analytical, narrative, statistical, impressionistic, local, comparative, philosophical, synthetic, and many others. Often the distinctions between one and another kind of history are overemphasized. No one can write good political history without some consideration of social, economic, and cultural questions; narrative history requires analysis to be meaningful; impressionistic treatments of past events are, in a way, statistical histories based on very tiny samples. Nevertheless, the types exist and serve different purposes. Each focuses on part of the total human experience and sees it from a particular perspective; each, when well done, adds its own contribution to the total record. It is therefore foolish to argue that any kind of historical approach is inherently better than all the others. Some are perhaps more generally useful (that is, more interesting to a wider segment of the population) or more suggestive at a particular time and place than others, but the distinctions are like those between a miniature and a mural, a sonnet and an epic poem. No one would suggest that "The Moonlight Sonata" was a waste of Beethoven's time because he was capable of producing the *Choral* symphony, or that Mozart should not have written "Eine Kleine Nachtmusik" because he had within him *Don Giovanni,* and in the same way a monograph or an article of twenty pages can be as well worth doing and as satisfying to read as Edward Gibbon's *Decline and Fall of the Roman Empire*.

The most useless and confusing distinction commonly drawn between varieties of history is that separating "scholarly" from "popular" history. These terms came into existence during the latter half of the nineteenth century. Before that time, all history was popular in the sense that those who wrote it, viewing themselves as possessors of special information acquired through scholarship or through having observed firsthand the events they described, aimed to transmit that knowledge to anyone interested in the subject. But when history became "scientific" and professionalized, historians began to write primarily for other historians. They assumed that nonspecialists had no interest in their work or were incapable of understanding it, and even argued that to write history for the general reader was to prostitute one's talents. Therefore, although with many notable exceptions, the best-trained and most knowledgeable and intelligent historians tended to forswear the task of transmitting their scholarly findings to ordinary readers.

Of course popular history continued to be written and read, but most of it was produced by amateurs, and thus its quality varied greatly. The scholarly prejudice against "popularizers" had a solid basis in fact. Too often popular history was—and still is—shallow, error-ridden, out-of-date before publication, a mere rehash of already written books, an exasperating mixture, as one critic has said, of "something we all knew before" and "something which is not so." Much of it was written by journalists and novelists who often lacked the patience, the professional skills, and the knowledge of sources that are as necessary for the writing of good history as narrative power, imagination, and lucidity of style.

It was chiefly with the hope of encouraging professional historians to broaden their perspectives that, beginning in the 1930's, a group of historians led by Professor Allan Nevins of Columbia University began to think of founding a general circulation magazine of American history. Their aim was a magazine in which solidly researched and significant articles would be presented in a way that would interest and educate readers who were not professional students of the past. Nevins himself, one of the great historians of the twentieth century, epitomized the combination these men sought to produce. He was a prodigious scholar, author of dozens of learned volumes, and trainer of literally hundreds of graduate students, but he was also a fluent and graceful writer whose work was widely read and appreciated. Nevins' books won Pulitzer Prizes as well as academic renown.

The example provided by Nevins and a few other outstanding historians of his generation, such as Samuel Eliot Morison, undoubtedly influenced the gradual revival of concern for popular history that has occurred in recent times on the part of professional academic scholars. So did the increasing sophistication of the general reading public, which made it less difficult for these experts to write this type of history without sacrificing their intellectual standards. In any case, in 1954 the Nevins group—the Society of American Historians— joined the American Association for State and Local History in sponsoring the hard-cover magazine they had envisioned: *American Heritage*.

The success of *American Heritage* was rapid and substantial. It achieved a wide circulation, and a galaxy of the best professional historians began to publish in its pages. Its articles, at their best, have been authoritative, interesting, significant, and a pleasure to read. They have ranged over the whole course of American history from the pre-colonial era to the present, and have dealt with every aspect of American development from politics to painting and from economics to architecture.

The present selection from among the hundreds of essays and book excerpts that have appeared in *American Heritage* since 1954 does not pretend to offer "the best" of these articles, although any such collection would undoubtedly include many of those I have chosen. It seeks rather to provide a balanced assortment of articles to supplement and enrich general college courses in American history. Keeping in mind the structure of these courses and the topics they tend to emphasize, I have reprinted here articles which, in my opinion, will add depth and breadth to the student's understanding.

This is—by definition—popular history, but it is also history written by experts. The articles differ in purpose and approach. Some present new findings, some re-examine old questions from a fresh point of view, others magisterially distill and synthesize masses of facts and ideas. From the total the reader may extract, along with the specifics of the individual essays, a sense of the variety and richness of historical literature. He will observe how forty-odd historians (and not all of them academic scholars) have faced the task of presenting knowledge not to other historians alone but to an audience of intelligent and interested general readers. Since most of the students enrolled in college history courses are not specialists—even those who intend to become professional historians stand at the very beginning of their training—this approach seems to me ideally adapted to their needs. Many, though by no means all, of the subjects treated in these essays have also been covered in articles in professional historical periodicals, often written by the same historians. But as here presented, without sacrifice of intellectual standards, the material is not so much easier to grasp as it is more meaningful. Details are clearly related to larger issues; historical characters are delineated in the round, not presented as stick figures or automatons; too much previous knowledge is not assumed. I once read the draft of an essay on the history of the Arabs which contained the sentence, "The life and philosophy of Mohammed are well-known," and which then went on to other less universally understood topics. Such essays no doubt have their place, but that place is not in collections designed for beginners, whatever the subject.

Finally, I believe that at least some of the essays I have included here illustrate the truth that history is, at its best, an art as well as a science. After all, the ancients gave history its own Muse, Clio. From reading the following pages, I hope and expect that students will come to realize that history is a form of literature, that it can be *enjoyed*, not merely assimilated. Even those who see college history courses exclusively as training grounds for future professionals surely will not object if their students enjoy these readings while they learn.

John A. Garraty
Columbia University
August, 1969

Contents

RECONSTRUCTION AND THE NEGRO

James G. Randall and
R. N. Current

How Lincoln
Would Have
Rebuilt the Union

What would Lincoln have done after the Civil War had he not been assassinated? The sainthood that his foul murder brought to him distorted for decades his actual views. He was pictured as both the Great Emancipator of the blacks and as the binder of the nation's wounds, the man who, "with malice toward none," would have treated the former slaveholders with Christlike compassion. That he could not have been both an ardent champion of Negro rights and the forgiving friend of the former rebels eventually became clear, but a full understanding of his attitudes was only slowly uncovered by historians.

One of the historians who did most to throw light on Lincoln's policies was the late James G. Randall, whose four-volume Lincoln the President *is a model of lucid and painstaking scholarship. When Randall died before completing the last volume of this work, Richard N. Current, now professor of history at the University of North Carolina at Greensboro, took on the task of finishing it. In the following essay Randall and Current discuss Lincoln's approach to reconstructing the Union. As they admit, no one can say with total assurance how Lincoln would have acted if he had not been killed, or what the result would have been. But they demonstrate beyond argument that his policy was carefully thought out and based on close observation of conditions in the South.*

*I*n his annual message to Congress, delivered in December of 1863 in fulfillment of the provision of the Constitution requiring that the President shall "give to the Congress Information of the State of the Union," Lincoln addressed himself to the question of reconstruction. He did not deal in quibbles or generalities, but came up with a plan. Anyone who knew Lincoln would have known that his design for a restored Union would not be hateful and vindictive. It would not rule out the very spirit of reunion. His view had never been narrowly sectional. Born in the Southern state of Kentucky of Virginia-born parents, moving thence to Indiana and Illinois, he was part of that transit of culture by which Southern characteristics, human types, and thought patterns had taken hold in the West and Northwest. Though he was antislavery and of course antisecession, he was never anti-Southern.

He had said in his first inaugural: "Physically we cannot separate," and on various later occasions he had returned to this theme. As he wrote in his annual message of December 1, 1862, to "separate our common country into two nations" was to him intolerable. The people of the greater interior, he urged, "will not ask where a line of separation shall be, but will vow rather that there shall be no such line." The situation as he saw it, in "all its adaptations and aptitudes . . . demands union and abhors separation." It would ere long "force reunion, however much of blood and treasure the separation might cost."

Thus Lincoln's fundamental adherence to an unbroken Union was the point of departure for his reconstruction program. One could find, in the earlier part of his presidency, other indications bearing upon restoration. In an important letter to General G. F. Shepley, military governor of Louisiana (November 21, 1862), he advised strongly against what came to be known as "carpetbagger" policy. He did not want "Federal officers not citizens of Louisiana" to seek election as congressmen from that state. On this his language was emphatic: he considered it "disgusting and outrageous . . . to send a parcel of Northern men here as representatives, elected, as it would be understood (and perhaps really so), at the point of the bayonet."

While in this manner disallowing the idea of importing Northern politicians into a Southern state as pseudo-representatives in Congress, he also repudiated the opposite policy of Fernando Wood of New York which would accept Southerners in Congress prematurely—that is, before resistance to the United States was ended and loyalty assured. To mention another point, he had, in considering the formation of the new state of West Virginia, expressed his view that, in the pattern of the Union, only those who were loyal—i. e., who adhered to the United States—could be regarded as competent voters.

To these points—the indispensable Union, loyalty, and the unwisdom of carpetbaggism—one must add Lincoln's fundamental policy of emancipation and his non-vindictiveness in the matter of confiscation. Taking these factors together the historian has, before December, 1863, the ingredients of the President's reunion program.

In announcing that program on December 8, 1863, Lincoln issued two documents: a proclamation, and a message to Congress. In his proclamation, having the force of law, he set forth the conditions of a general pardon and the terms of restoring a Southern state to the Union. In his accompanying message he commented upon his plan, telling more fully what was in his mind and defending his course by reason and persuasion. The offer of pardon (with stated exceptions) and restoration of rights (except as to slaves) was given to anyone in a seceded state who would take and keep a simple oath. Phrased by the President, this oath constituted a solemn pledge to support the Constitution of the United States "and the union of the States thereunder." The oath-taker would also swear to abide by and faithfully support all the acts of Congress and all the proclamations of the President relating to slaves unless repealed, modified, or declared void by the Supreme Court.

So much for the oath, with pardon and restoration of rights. The next element in the proclamation was re-establishment of a state government. This again was intended to be simple and practical. Whenever, in a seceded state, a number not less than one tenth of those voting in 1860, should re-establish a republican government, such a government, according to Lincoln's proclamation, would "be recognized as the true government of the State."

Turning from the proclamation to the simultaneous message, we find Lincoln setting forth the reasons and conditions of his policy. In this he addressed himself to various questions that he knew would arise. What about the oath? Why the ten per cent? What about state laws touching freedmen? Why preserve the state as it was? How about state boundaries? Why was the President assuming the power of reconstruction as an executive function? He started with the obvious unwisdom and absurdity of protecting a revived state government constructed from the disloyal element. It was essential to have a test "so as to build only from the sound." He wanted that test to be liberal and to include "sworn recantation of . . . former unsoundness." As for laws and proclamations against slavery, they could not be abandoned. Retaining so far as possible the existing political framework in the state, as Lincoln saw it, would "save labor, and avoid confusion." He did not, of course, mean by this that the system in any state was to be permanently frozen for the future in unchangeable form.

As to the specific formula of ten per cent, he said little; yet his simile of a rallying point held the key. The important object was to get a movement started. Acceptance of an initial electorate of ten per cent did not signify that Lincoln was favoring minority rule. It was not his thought that any minority should usurp the rights of the majority. Within his pattern of loyalty, Union, non-dictatorial government, and emancipation, he was putting the formation of any new state government in the hands of the loyal people of the state. Government by the people was to him fundamental, but as a practical matter some loyal nucleus was essential; else time would pass, precious time, and nothing would be done.

In J.E. Baker's 1864 cartoon,
Andrew Johnson, who was
a tailor as a young man, and
Lincoln, the railsplitter,
labor to reunite the Union.

The whole situation, of course, was abnormal. All beginnings, or rebeginnings, are difficult, especially rebuilding after or during a war, taking up the shattered pieces of a disrupted social and political order and putting them partly together so that ultimately they could be fully restored. Lincoln was willing to accept informality in order to accomplish the main practical purpose which he considered imperative. He was unwilling to throw away the cause while futilely waiting for perfection. Reconstruction, as he saw it, was a matter of stages. His "ten per cent plan" was easy to criticize. Yet it was the first step.

Lincoln would take his first step in the most available manner. A few states could be rebuilt and restored. This was to be done during the war, indeed as an important factor in waging and ending the war. Let people see that Lincoln did not intend an ugly and vindictive policy, and Southerners themselves, the President hoped, would set their own houses in order. Let one or two states do this; they would serve as examples for others as the armies advanced and national authority was extended. In time of war, prepare for peace, was Lincoln's thought. On the other hand, let the months pass, and let the Southern people witness only carpetbaggism, Federal occupation, and a repressive attitude as to the future, and victory itself would lose much of its value. It was Lincoln's intent that policy associated with victory should envisage willing loyalty while leaving free play for self government.

Lincoln's plan of reunion was greeted with a mixed response. The Washington *Chronicle*, regarded as a Lincoln "organ," naturally praised the President's announcement. The editor noted that the President gave out his statement in a setting of military and naval success : our armies victorious, our navy in control of Southern coasts, our cause strengthened by increased friendship of foreign nations. His generous offering of pardon was interpreted by the *Chronicle* as evidence of his kindness and sympathy toward the people of the South.

An English gentleman friendly to the United States wrote : "We have just received the news of President Lincoln's message, accompanied with his amnesty; also the message of . . . [Jefferson] Davis. The two documents coming together are doing an immense amount of good for the right cause."

It is doubtful how many readers made the comparison of the two messages, but those who did must have noted a marked difference of tone. In general spirit Lincoln's message of December 8, 1863, was notable for its absence of war-engendered hatred toward the South, ending as it did on the note of "freedom disenthralled." In appealing for reunion the President was holding out the hand for genuine renewal of friendly relations. This attitude, however, was not reciprocated by the Confederate President. Though perhaps the comparison should not be overstressed, one finds quite the opposite note in the message (December 7, 1863) of Jefferson Davis to his Congress. After a depressing account of Confederate military reverses and of discouraging condition in foreign affairs and finance, the Southern Executive threw in bitter denunciations of the "barbarous policy" and "savage ferocity" of "our enemies." At one point he referred to them as "hardened by crime." (There were, of course, those in the North, though not Lincoln, who were saying equally hateful things of the South.) That enemy, wrote Davis, refused "even to listen to proposals . . . [of peace] of recognizing the impassable gulf which divides us." This expression, the orthodox attitude of Confederate officialdom, must be remembered along with Lincoln's other problems. If anyone doubted why the President, in his reconstruction plans and his wariness toward "peace negotiations," realized the hopelessness of expecting high Confederate officials to consider a peaceable restoration of the Union, the reading of this message of Davis would have been enough to dispel such doubt.

It was obvious from the start that the President's plan would not have smooth sailing, but on several fronts steps were taken to make it known and put it into operation. Army officers were instructed to take copies of the proclamation and distribute them so as to reach soldiers and inhabitants within Confederate-held territory. Aid and protection was to be extended to those who would declare loyalty. On the occasion of raids into enemy territory a number of men were to be detailed "for the purpose of distributing the proclamation broadcast among rebel soldiers and people, and in the highways and byways."

On the legal or prosecuting front the effect of the pardon policy was explained in an instruction from the office of the attorney general of the United States to district attorneys throughout the country. It was made known that the "President's pardon of a person guilty of . . . rebellion . . . [would] relieve that person for the penalties" of that crime. District attorneys were therefore directed to discontinue proceedings in United States courts whenever the accused should take the oath and comply with the stated conditions.

Such a statement would make it appear that the transition from a kind of rebellious guilt to complete relief from penalty was easy, automatic, and practically instantaneous, but it soon became evident that the matter was not so simple as that. Lincoln found that he had to make a distinction in applying his offer of pardon in return for the oath. What about Confederate soldiers held by Union authorities as prisoners of war? On this point the President issued a letter clarifying the proclamation, declaring that his pardon did not apply to men in custody or on parole as prisoners of war. It did apply, he explained, to persons yet at large (i.e., free from arrest) who would come forward and take the oath. It was also explained that those excluded from the general amnesty could apply to the President for clemency and their cases would have due consideration.

What it amounted to was that Lincoln himself was generous in the application of his pardon both to soldiers and civilians, and the same was true of the attorney general's office; but army officers were not prepared, in return for the oath, to deliver prisoners nor give up penalties for offences of various sorts, such as violation of rules of war. No one statement applies. Some enemies held as prisoners, on establishing loyalty, were discharged from custody by the President on assurance of good faith by three congressmen. This showed, as in many cases, that Lincoln's general rules were subject to individual exceptions.

With a scorn of fine-spun theories and an urgent wish to get ahead with the job of reconstruction, the President proceeded, so far as possible, to make restoration a reality whenever, and as soon as, any reasonable opportunity offered in the seceded South.

In Lincoln's plan of reconstruction the effort in Louisiana was of vital importance. From the time that New Orleans fell to Union arms on May 1, 1862, the President saw, in terms of Federal occupation, an early opportunity to make reconstruction a wartime reality. Let Louisiana be restored, he thought, let this be done in a reasonable manner with Washington approval, let it be seen that the plan would work, and other states would follow. To go into all the details of the Louisiana story, treating its complications month by month, would be a tedious process. It will be convenient to reduce this elaborate Louisiana story to four successive phases:

First Phase in Louisiana: Military Rule Under Butler and Shepley. The first phase was that of army rule under General B. F. Butler. Immediate adjustments were of course necessary from the moment when New Orleans, largest city of the South, together with a large portion of Louisiana, came under the Union flag. Governmental officials in the occupied region, including merely local functionaries in city or parish, were now under Federal authority—not in terms of any deliberation as to procedure by Congress or the Executive, but simply by the fortunes of war. Where men in local office stood ready to co-operate with the occupying power, they had a good chance of being retained; if un-cooperative, they were dismissed. For a time the mayor and council of New Orleans were continued in office subject to General Butler's authority with some relaxation of military pressure, but this situation did not last long. Within a month the mayor was deposed and imprisoned, and George F. Shepley, acting closely with Butler, took over mayoral functions. Then in June, 1862, Shepley became military governor of Louisiana; soon afterward he had the rank of brigadier general.

This was military occupation, and of course it was intended only as a temporary condition. It amounted to martial law which has been defined as the will of the military commander; this meant that the sometimes eccentric will of General Butler was paramount. If nothing offered in the form of a re-established and recognized state government, the abnormal and temporary regime would continue.

It thus came about that Federal rule in Louisiana, the first step toward what Lincoln regarded as restoration of loyalty and normal conditions, got off to a bad start. The name of ''Beast Butler'' became a hated byword in the South, with far-reaching complications in Federal-Confederate relations; it came as a considerable relief when President Lincoln removed him from his Louisiana command on December 16, 1862. His successor, as commander of the military forces stationed in Louisiana and Texas, was Major General Nathaniel P. Banks, with Shepley retaining his position as ''military governor of Louisiana.''

Under Butler little or nothing had been done toward wartime governmental reconstruction in the state, but this problem, dear to Lincoln's heart, was tackled under the President's urging during the Banks-Shepley regime.

A careful study of these matters reveals a problem as to top executive leadership locally applied—that is, the difficulty of achieving effectiveness in a particular area in terms of policy developed in Washington. Lincoln was President; he was the Chief; he made the appointments and formed decisions; presumably he would choose men to put his policies into operation. Yet so unpredictable were events and so complicated was the situation as to politicians' maneuvers that those who supposedly should have carried out Lincoln's purposes promoted their own factional and contrary schemes in such manner as to jeopardize the President's best laid plans.

George F. Shepley was a case in point. He had been a Maine Democrat, an appointee of Pierce and later of Buchanan as district attorney, and a supporter of Douglas in 1860. These factors in his background did not militate against him in Lincoln's view—the President often appointed Democrats—nor should they have been a drawback to successful service in Louisiana's reconstruction. There was, however, the further fact that Shepley became a Butlerite and a Radical; remaining after Butler's removal, he played the Radical game at a time when it was hoped that a more Lincolnian policy would be inaugurated. Thus Shepley stood as an obstacle to Lincoln's efforts to allay factionalism and to promote speedy and liberal restoration.

Toward the end of the Butler-Shepley period an election was held within the Union lines on December 3, 1862, for members of Congress from Louisiana. Two men of different outlook were elected: B. F. Flanders from New Hampshire, who was to become an instrument of the Radical faction; and Michael Hahn, a citizen of Louisiana born in Bavaria, who was more in tune with Lincoln's purposes. When the question of admitting these gentlemen as members of the House of Representatives was brought before that body (February 9, 1863) a species of dog fight ensued, a forerunner of the rough treatment in store for Lincoln's whole reunion program. Few were ready for frontal attack and sidestepping was more in evidence; the result was confusion, unrelated motions, and postponement. Finally, on February 17, 1863, the House voted, 92 to 44, to seat Flanders and Hahn. By that time that particular Congress, the Thirty-seventh, was about to pass out of existence.

Second Phase: Shepley and Durant versus Banks. In the next phase, while Banks was in top command in Louisiana with Shepley as military governor—i. e., governor as to civil affairs under military authority—certain groups in the state got to work, though at cross purposes, to seize control of the process of state remaking. It turned out to be a period of bickering and futility, a time of bitter disappointment to the President. Taking over the rebuilding task and attempting to do it in his own way, Governor Shepley proceeded to make a registry of voters, appointing T. J. Durant, a Radical like himself, as commissioner of registration. An oath of allegiance was required (this was before the presidentially prescribed oath of December 8, 1863) and the registration of whites who would take the oath was ordered. It was Durant's idea that ten loyal men in a parish, if no more could be registered, would be a sufficient basis for an election. This was a period when Banks was preoccupied with military command in the Port Hudson and Texas areas, while Shepley was also absent from Louisiana, spending a large part of the summer of 1863 in Washington. Lincoln approved the Shepley-Durant registration and wanted it pushed.

The President was trying to keep himself in the background, to avoid seeming to dictate, and to let things work themselves out as a Louisiana movement. Yet he soon found that a jurisdictional dispute or confusion as to control was spoiling everything. Shepley as military governor and Durant, his appointee, were claiming "that they were exclusively charged with the work of reconstruction in Louisiana," while Banks had "not felt authorized to interfere" with them. In a letter of December 16, 1863, Banks advised the President that he was "only in partial command," adding: "There are not less than *four* distinct governments here claiming . . . independent powers based upon instructions received directly from Washington, and recognizing no other authority than their own."

Though this unfortunate situation was due in large part to the activities of Radical groups, another factor may have been a bit of inadvertence on the part of the burdened President: he had supposed all the time that Banks was in chief command but had not made that point sufficiently clear. He now wrote a strong letter to Banks (December 24, 1863) with a fourfold repetition of the main theme: You are master. The President was seriously annoyed at the frustration and delay. Shepley, he wrote, was to "assist" Banks, not to "thwart" him. The desirable object, of course, was to have unity among pro-Union men and leaders, but a serious obstacle to such unity was the attitude of Shepley and his considerable faction. It became increasingly apparent that these Radicals were unwilling to co-operate with the man whom Lincoln had placed in chief authority and whom he had plainly designated as "master." Treating delay and factionalism as if things of the past, Lincoln wrote to Banks: "Give us a free State reorganization of Louisiana in the shortest possible time."

Third Phase: The Louisiana Constitution of 1864. Under Lincoln's spurring Banks went into action. In January and February of 1864 he issued proclamations for two kinds of elections: an election for governor under the old Louisiana constitution of 1853, and an election of delegates to a convention to make a new state constitution. In his proclamations, copies of which he sent to the President, Banks declared that officials then to be chosen were to govern unless they tried to change Federal statutes as to slavery. Voters were required to take the oath of allegiance to the United States.

Lincoln continued to prod and encourage. Proceed "with all possible dispatch," wrote the President. "Frame orders, and fix times and places for this and that. . . ." Recognition of the death of slavery in Louisiana was causing less difficulty than might have been expected. While the planter class wanted to keep the institution, they were in the minority; the majority of the people were ready to accept emancipation.

Both of the elections were a success from the standpoint of Banks and of Lincoln. Not that Lincoln considered the outcome perfect, but the whole point of Lincoln's policy was that he was not expecting perfection. He wanted steps to be taken, a "free" government set up; modifications and improvements could come later. The vote for state officials was held on February 22, 1864. In a total of 11,411 votes (over a fourth of the normal peacetime vote of Louisiana) Michael Hahn, the moderate Union candidate acceptable to Banks and Lincoln, received 6,183 votes and was elected; Flanders, candidate of the anti-Banks

Radical element, received 2,232 votes; J. Q. A. Fellows, nominated by the proslavery conservatives, received the disturbingly large vote of 2,996.

Next came the problem of constitution remaking. By Banks's proclamation an election was held on March 28, 1864, by which delegates were chosen (not a distinguished lot, but they represented the people rather than officials or politicians) to form a new instrument of government. From April to July the convention labored. Among its main acts was to abolish slavery by a vote of seventy to sixteen. Negro suffrage, then a new question and a difficult one, came harder. After voting it down, the convention reconsidered; it then "empowered" the legislature to grant the vote to colored persons; by the constitution it was provided that a militia be enrolled without distinction of color.

On September 5, 1864, the people of Louisiana voted to ratify the constitution (6,836–1,566); members of Congress were then chosen by popular election, after which the legislature set up under the new constitution chose two senators. If and when these men should be admitted by Congress—a big "if"—reconstruction for Louisiana, so far as essential political structure was concerned, would be complete. In the matter of preliminary steps—shaping up the situation so that Congress could act—the work of the executive branch for this pivotal state was done.

Fourth Phase: Trouble in Congress. Much water was to pass over the mill before one could know what Congress would do as to admitting Louisiana according to Lincoln's plan. The Radical clique in Louisiana had opposed the measures taken in 1864 looking toward a new state government. This element made a break with the Lincoln Administration, denounced the new constitution as null and void, and proceeded to make their influence felt in Congress. The Radical element in Congress was working strongly against Lincoln's program in any case, and it was no surprise that the decision of the solons at Washington concerning Louisiana reorganization was negative. A long period of Federal occupation and troublous abnormality was to ensue. There were a number of uneasy years after Lincoln's death before the state was, one should not say restored, but outfitted with a carpetbag government. After that there was to be further delay—nearly a decade—before that unworkable carpetbag regime collapsed.

As in Louisiana, so in other regions of the Confederate South, Lincoln did his best to promote reorganization measures so that state governments could supersede Federal military rule, but wartime conditions made for obstruction and progress was slow. In Tennessee, where secession had been strongly resisted and where Union victories came in February and April of 1862, it might have seemed that a choice opportunity was offered for early restoration of civil government under unionist auspices. The pro-Confederate regime in Tennessee was brief; it extended only from May 7, 1861 (legislative ratification of the military league with the Confederacy) to March 3, 1862, when Lincoln appointed Andrew Johnson military governor of the state, a period of ten months.

Johnson's attitude had been demonstrated by "violent opposition to slavery and secession" and by retention of his seat in the United States Senate. His unionism was unassailable, but he could only perform the functions of civil government on an emergency basis and Lincoln's hopes for instituting a more permanent and regular regime were repeatedly deferred. There was heavy fighting in 1862 and 1863. Guerrilla warfare, raids by Forrest, agitation among discordant pro-Union elements, puzzlement as to what was "regular" by the old code of the state (nothing could be strictly regular in those war times), lack of popular interest when elections were held, complications as to soldier voting and military influence, divided leadership as between Nashville and Washington—these were among the factors that caused continual delay.

Not until February, 1865, was an election held in Tennessee which had importance in terms of popular voting for fundamental state reorganization. After that there loomed, as always, the serious obstacle of congressional opposition. Tennessee was not to be admitted to the Union until 1866. Yet as early as September 11, 1863, Lincoln had written to Governor Johnson: "All Tennessee is now clear of armed insurrectionists." Insisting that "Not a moment should be lost" in "reinaugurating a loyal State government," the President insisted, as in Louisiana, that prudent steps be taken without delay. Discretion was left with Johnson and "co-operating friends" as to ways and means, with the presidential injunction that the reinauguration should not be allowed to slip into the hands of enemies of the Union, "driving its friends . . . into political exile." "It must not be so," wrote Lincoln. "You must have it otherwise."

In September, 1863, Andrew Johnson said to his people: "Here lies your State; a sick man in his bed, emaciated and exhausted . . . unable to walk alone. The physician comes. Don't quarrel about antecedents, but administer to his wants . . . as quickly as possible. . . . This is no . . . metaphysical question. It is a plain, common sense matter, and there is nothing in the way but obstinacy." Johnson's simile of the sick man and his suggestion as to the ineptness of those administering to him could have covered a great deal more territory than Tennessee.

Events of 1863 and early 1864 in Arkansas proceeded with little difficulty so far as that commonwealth itself was concerned. It was a sparsely settled state, with 435,000 inhabitants in 1860, of whom 111,115 were slaves. Illinois, of comparable area, had nearly four times the population. It was chiefly in the southeastern part, in the plantation area near the Mississippi River, that slaveholding was concentrated. Throughout most of the state there were few slaves, in the northern portion hardly any. People of the Ozark mountain region had little in common with the few cotton-growing magnates. To the vast majority of the people the abolition of slavery would produce no serious reordering of their lives and economy.

The state had avoided secession until swept away by the post-Sumter excitement; when secession was adopted it was done reluctantly. Even after secession, considerable Union sentiment remained.

According to a contemporary account, pertaining to the situation in 1863, "Citizens of distinction came forward to advocate the Union cause; among others, Brig.-Gen. E. W. Gantt, of the Confederate army, once held as a prisoner of war." The shift of General Gantt from Confederate to Union allegiance was, as he said, part of a popular movement; Union sentiment, he noted, was "manifesting itself on all sides and by every indication." For many who were of like mind with Gantt the open declaration of loyalty to the Federal government, especially after the Confederate surrender of Vicksburg, came naturally. It was like snapping out of an abnormal situation.

Military events provided a considerable impulse toward Union reorganization, especially the Union victories at Vicksburg and Port Hudson, and the Helena-Little Rock expedition of General Frederick Steele, U. S. A., against Sterling Price, C. S. A., which resulted in Confederate evacuation of Little Rock on September 10, 1863. With this Confederate reverse a large part of the state was brought under Union control.

Lincoln kept in touch with Arkansas affairs, notifying General Steele that he, as in the case of Banks in Louisiana, was "master" of the reorganization process. "Some single mind," wrote the President, "must be master, else there will be no agreement in anything." He had ample reason to realize the truth of this statement.

The pattern of the Arkansas movement reveals much as to Lincoln's plan in practical operation. Sentiment developed in meetings, with Union resolutions, in large parts of the state. Delegates were chosen in such meetings (by no more and no less authority than is usual in such popular movements under the stress of abnormal conditions) for a "convention" designed to make a new regime constitutional and legal. Lincoln encouraged the holding of the convention, welcoming it as a fulfillment of his plan as announced in December, 1863. On January 20, 1864, he indicated that the reorganization emanated from citizens of Arkansas petitioning for an election, and directed Steele to "order an election immediately" for March 28, 1864. When, on counting the votes for a Union-minded governor and for changes in the state constitution, the number should reach or exceed 5,406 (that being ten per cent of the Arkansas vote of 1860), Lincoln directed that the governor thus chosen should be declared qualified and that he should assume his duties under the modified state constitution. (As a minor detail, when it was found that the Union convention in Arkansas was planning the election for March 14, not March 28, the President quickly acquiesced in the convention plan.)

In the President's mind a milestone had been reached in Arkansas affairs with that election of March 14. By an overwhelming majority (12,179 to 226) the voters, having qualified by taking the Federal oath of allegiance, approved those changes in the state constitution which abolished slavery, declared secession void, and repudiated the Confederate debt. Isaac Murphy, already installed as provisional governor by the convention, was now elected governor by "more than double what the President had required." On April 11 the new state government under the modified constitution was inaugurated at Little Rock. The reconstructed legislature chose senators (William M. Fishbach and Elisha Baxter); three members of Congress had already been chosen in the March election.

Obstruction in House and Senate prevented the admission of these representatives and senators, and for long years Arkansas remained outside the pale so far as Congress was concerned. Lincoln's view, however, both as to practical matters and as to his own function in promoting them, was shown in his executive measures to get these important steps taken, and in his advice to Steele (June 29, 1864) that, despite congressional refusal to give these solons their seats at Washington, the new state government should have "the same support and protection that you would [have given] if the members had been admitted, because in no event . . . can this do any harm, while it will be the best you can do toward suppressing the rebellion."

A different type of situation presented itself in Florida, where the reconstruction effort was of a minor sort. Military accomplishment, so evident in Louisiana, Tennessee, and Arkansas, was lacking in this detached area, which was off the main line of strategy and unpromising as a field in which to commit any considerable body of troops. Aside from holding a few coastal points and maintaining the blockade, the United States paid little attention to the region of the St. John's, the St. Mary's, and the Suwannee. The only sizable engagement in the state during the war was the ill-starred "battle of Olustee," in the northeast corner, a short distance inward from Jacksonville, where a minor Union force under General Truman Seymour, U. S. A., was defeated by somewhat superior numbers, with advantage of defensive position, under General Joseph Finegan, C. S. A. This engagement, February 20, 1864, was the futile anticlimax of an army-navy expedition of Seymour, a subordinate of General Quincy A. Gillmore who was in command of the "Department of the South" with headquarters at Hilton Head, S. C.

Under these circumstances, though Union sentiment was held to be widespread in the state, the small-scale efforts to restore Florida were subject to the taunt that their motive was to give a plausible basis for sending pro-Lincoln delegates to the coming Republican convention; even the Seymour expedition was derided as a feature of the political campaign of 1864.

From Lincoln's standpoint the approach to reconstruction in Florida was like that in other Southern areas. On January 13, 1864, he wrote Gillmore advising that the general was to be "master" if differences should arise; in this letter the President urged that restoration be pushed "in the most speedy way possible," and that it be done within the range of the December proclamation. To handle some of the details John Hay was sent to Florida "with some blank-books [for recording oaths] and other blanks, to aid in the reconstruction." This trip of Hay's (February-March 1864) was not a brilliant success and the sum-total of the Florida gesture for reconstruction was far from impressive. Florida's "delegates," chosen by a few in Jacksonville, did turn up at the Republican convention in June, 1864, but not until after the war did the commonwealth proceed to the making of a new state constitution within the range of the Union; readmission to the Union— i.e., inauguration of carpetbag government—occurred in 1868; restoration of home rule—the throwing off of Radical Republican control— was deferred to 1877.

Small though it was, there was more in the Union effort in Florida than at first met the eye. One could treat the Seymour, or Gillmore-Seymour, expedition of 1864 as a sorry military enterprise, or as a disappointing phase of Lincoln's reconstruction plan, but in a realistic study one needs to enlarge the scope of inquiry. The episode must also be viewed in its relation to such subjects as the use of Negro troops (in which there was creditable performance), maneuvers in the pro-Chase sense, the opening of trade, and what has been called "carpetbag imperialism." In a detailed study George Winston Smith has pointed out that grandiose schemes or experiments were conjured up in connection with the Florida effort. There was, for example, the "extravagant plan" of Eli Thayer of Kansas emigrant fame—a well-intentioned plan to set up "soldier-colonists" and create model communities on the most approved New England pattern. The plan reached "only the blueprint stage," but it reveals much as to Yankee enterprise in the deep South. There was also injected into the wartime Florida scene the "machinations" of Lyman K. Stickney, "the most notorious of the early Florida carpetbaggers," who operated under Secretary Chase in the enforcement of a congressional act for collecting the Federal direct tax in the South. This law, writes Smith, was a "move to confiscate the real property of southern landholders" and was so administered as to become "an instrument of predatory corruption in Florida."

These factors need to be borne in mind in judging Lincoln's approach to reconstruction. It was a complicated problem of many facets, with idealistic motives combined with profit-seeking greed. Lincoln tried to keep restoration on the main track and keep it unmarred, but it was part of the history of the time—the prelude to the "Gilded Age"—that debased and uninspiring maneuvers would creep in. Florida was only an example. When one remembers such influences, he can realize with fuller force the significance of Lincoln's rejection of the whole drive and tendency toward carpetbaggism.

. . . In Lincoln's planning for a restored Union he kept his eye constantly on a highly important factor, that of unionism in the South. Of course it could have been said by critics that Lincoln was not bothering with the opposition, that he was requiring an oath of Union allegiance as a prerequisite for the right to vote on any state reorganization, and that he was thus stacking the cards in his favor, working only with friends of the Union. This seemed the more striking because of his willingness to depend on a Union-minded minimum of ten per cent (of 1860 voters) for the initial steps of reconstruction.

Yet on closer study it will be seen that success for any reunion movement was dependent upon popular support in the state. Always at some point there had to be an election, a popular choice of a constitutional convention to remake the state constitution, and a vote for state officials and members of Congress. People who voted in these initial elections had to take the Union oath; but no one was to be coerced into taking it, and if the number of oath-takers was too insignificant, the plan would not get very far. Lincoln was starting with a loyal minority, but the quality and extent of that minority was never unimportant. Furthermore, the President was planning for peace, for the long years ahead after the war ended.

At all times the President felt assured that his plan would work for the whole South. He could hardly have proceeded with such confidence unless he genuinely believed that unionists in the South were, for the long run and for normal times, in the majority. In fact the validity of Lincoln's basic political philosophy depended upon self rule by the people. To impose a government upon an unwilling state—even a benevolent government—would have been contrary to this fundamental philosophy. There was a risk involved in Lincoln's scheme but it was a calculated risk. When there would come the hazard of an election, that would not merely mean that people should vote because of having sworn allegiance. It meant that such allegiance was expected to prove justified in the type of government set up, the working out of labor adjustment, the choice of well disposed officials, the installing of honest government, and the like.

If these things went wrong even after the initial steps had been taken in compliance with the President's plan, the broad policy would fail. Lincoln's feeling of assurance that it would not fail must have been based on more than wishful thinking. It is therefore of importance to look into the matter and find the basis for this assurance—in other words, to discover some of the evidences of unionism in the South which were known to the President. To give the whole body of such evidence is obviously impracticable, but a few items may be mentioned with the understanding that they were typical of a large and impressive total.

There was the element of war-weariness in the South; people were sick and tired of the continued slaughter. A captured Union general, the famous Neal Dow, wrote to Lincoln from Libby Prison, Richmond, on November 12, 1863: ''. . . I have seen much of Rebeldom, behind the curtain, and have talked with a great many soldiers, conscripts, deserters, officers, and citizens. The result of all is, to my mind, that . . . the masses are heartily . . . anxious for its [the war's] close on any terms. . . .'' He went on to mention numerous Confederate desertions, soldier infirmities, general debility, the worthlessness of conscripts, depreciation of the currency, flour at $125 a barrel, and ''everything in the provision line . . . [bearing] a corresponding price.''

In Virginia the attitude of intelligent and patriotic unionists was typified by Alexander H. H. Stuart. Though not active against secession during the war, he had been fundamentally opposed to it as inexpedient. Stuart defined his wartime attitudes as follows:

''During the war, I abstained from all participation in public affairs, except on two or three occasions when I was called to address public meetings to urge contributions for the relief of the suffering soldiers and the prisoners going to as well as returning from the North.

"My age relieved me from the obligation to render military service, and all the assistance I gave to the Confederate cause was by feeding the hungry and clothing the naked and nursing the sick Confederate soldiers, and making myself and urging others to make liberal donations for their relief."

Another prominent Virginia unionist was the distinguished lawyer John Minor Botts. He had strongly opposed Southern Democratic disunionists, and, though disapproving also of abolitionists, had given support to the efforts of John Quincy Adams in the matter of anti-slavery petitions presented to Congress. When Lincoln was a Whig member of Congress from Illinois, Botts was a Whig member from Virginia (1847-49); indeed many of his views were similar to Lincoln's. Both in 1850 and in 1860 he was an earnest opponent of secession, his opposition to Jefferson Davis and to Governor Henry Wise of Virgina being especially marked. He greatly regretted the secession of his state in 1860, which he had tried to prevent. During the war he was so far out of sympathy with the Confederate government that he was arrested and confined for some months in jail. For the most part, however, he spent the war years in retirement. His later career showed the steadfastness of his Union loyalty.

The fact that certain Southern areas had never left the Union was, of course, significant. That was true of Kentucky. It was remarked that the mountainous districts of that border state were "with very few exceptions . . . thoroughly union." The same observer noted derisively that in the central part of the state "most of the large slave holders, . . . the gamblers . . . all the decayed chivalry . . . all the fast & fashionable ones & nearly all the original Breckinridge Democrats are bitter to secessionists."

Unionist voices were audible throughout the unhappy South. A clear sign of the times in Louisiana was the editorial of the *True Delta* of New Orleans (February 5, 1864) praising Lincoln, comparing him to Washington and Jackson, and favoring his re-election. In Mississippi a local judge wrote: "I have *first, last and all the time,* been a Union man." Secession, he reported, had been put over without the people understanding what was involved. In another report from Mississippi it was indicated that there were "thousands . . . who desire most ardently the restoration of the United States."

In North Carolina peace movements were rife and it was reported early in 1864 that troops from the Old North State were deserting rapidly and extensively from the Confederate service. In the previous year a group of North Carolina citizens had presented a petition to the President, asking him to "order an election day for this district for the purpose of electing a representative for the next Congress." These petitioners represented themselves as "loyal to the Constitution of our country anxious that it should be perpetuated."

As to Alabama it was predicted that if the question of returning to the Union were submitted to a vote, the people would "vote aye, *five to one.*" The President was given the following assurance: "Could you know how deep and universal is the returning love for the union among the people of Ala & Geo you would discharge your great responsibilities with a hymn of joy in your heart.''

These evidences, and more of the same, were available to Lincoln. Since his day further material has come to light tending to reveal the extent of Union sentiment in seceded states. Naturally, men and women of Union sympathies in the South found existing conditions difficult for any expression of loyalty in active, organized form. Yet their restricted attitude was significant as they maintained a kind of passive resistance, avoided voluntary measures against the government at Washington, opposed the Confederate draft, carried provisions and medicines to Union soldiers, contributed money for the welfare of blue-coats, attended boys in hospitals, and performed other friendly acts for Federal troops. Such acts incurred persecution, and the Southern unionist moved often in an atmosphere of scorn and hostility not unaccompanied by threats and acts of personal violence. Of course, in various respects he was compelled to act against his will when it was a matter of serving as conscript, subscribing to a Confederate loan, contributing cotton, paying taxes, or performing labor. Since Southern wartime history has been largely remembered and recorded in Confederate terms, these details are still somewhat obscure; at least their full force is not generally recognized.

No history of Lincoln, however, can ignore them. His reports from the South were a vital element in policy making. When he made his broad appeal in December, 1863, offering pardon, prescribing his simple oath, and opening the way for new state governments by genuine Southern effort looking toward peace with freedom and union, he had reason to know, at least in large part, the kind of support and fulfillment upon which he could count. His sense of his own function as leader was strengthened by his realization that Southern unionism did not signify willingness to accept the program and regime of congressional Radicals. On the contrary, such union-mindedness was oriented in Lincolnian terms. In taking on the responsibility of launching and promoting reconstruction, Lincoln saw an opportunity which needed to be seized while its most fruitful results were yet possible. . . .

The many-sided problem of reconstruction was a subject of continual debate in the North from 1863 on. After reaching a furious pitch in the summer of 1864, the debate had been toned down during the final weeks of the presidential campaign, to be renewed fitfully and shrilly as the final military victory approached. Lee's surrender brought the issue to a climax again. Then, temporarily at least, Lincoln and the Radicals found themselves even farther apart than before.

For a while, in early April, 1865, he seemed willing to readmit the Southern states on terms more generous than those he had announced in his ten per cent plan and in his amnesty proclamation of December, 1863. But the Radicals were prepared to demand terms even more rigorous than those they had embodied in the Wade-Davis bill, which Lincoln had refused to sign in July, 1864.

With a new sense of urgency the Radicals began to consult with one another and to speak out. On the day after Appomattox, in Washington, General Butler made a speech in which he recommended, on the one hand, that the leaders of the rebellion should be disfranchised and disqualified for public office and, on the other, that the masses including the Negroes should be given immediately all the rights of citizenship. The next evening, in Baltimore on court duty, Chief Justice Chase dined with Henry Winter Davis and other Maryland Radicals, then wrote a letter to the President. "It will be, hereafter, counted equally a crime and a folly," Chase said, "if the colored loyalists of the rebel states shall be left to the control of restored rebels, not likely, in that case, to be either wise or just, until taught both wisdom and justice by new calamities."

That same evening, April 11, Lincoln made his own, last contribution to the public debate when he addressed the crowd gathered on the White House grounds. After a few congratulatory words on Grant's recent victory, he proceeded to defend at some length his own reconstruction view.

The problem, as he saw it, was essentially one of re-establishing the national authority throughout the South. This problem was complicated by the fact that there was, in the South, "no authorized organ" to treat with. "Nor is it a small additional embarrassment that we, the loyal people, differ among ourselves as to the mode, manner, and means of reconstruction." He had been criticized, he said, because he did not seem to have a fixed opinion on the question "whether the seceded States, so called," were "in the Union or out of it." He dismissed that question as "a merely pernicious abstraction" and went on to declare: "We all agree that the seceded States, so called, are out of their proper practical relation with the Union; and that the sole object of the government, civil and military, in regard to those States is to again get them into that proper practical relation."

He had been criticized also for setting up and sustaining the new state government of Louisiana, which rested on the support of only ten per cent of the voters and did not give the franchise to the colored man. He confessed that the Louisiana government would be better if it rested on a larger electorate including the votes of Negroes—at least "the very intelligent" and those who had served as soldiers. "Concede that the new government of Louisiana is only to what it should be as the egg is to the fowl, we shall sooner have the fowl by hatching the egg than by smashing it?" The loyalists of the South would be encouraged and the Negroes themselves would be better off, Lincoln argued, if Louisiana were quickly readmitted to the Union. An additional ratification would be gained for the Thirteenth Amendment, the adoption of which would be "unquestioned and unquestionable" only if it were ratified by three fourths of *all* the states.

What Lincoln said of Louisiana, he applied also to the other states of the South. "And yet so great peculiarities pertain to each state; and such important and sudden changes occur in the same state; and, withal, so new and unprecedented is the whole case, that no exclusive, and inflexible plan can safely be prescribed as to details and colatterals." (Virginia was not mentioned.) In concluding, Lincoln said enigmatically that it might become his duty "to make some new announcement to the people of the South. I am considering, and shall not fail to act, when satisfied that action will be proper."

In Washington and throughout the country the speech aroused much speculation about Lincoln's undisclosed intentions, and it provoked mixed feelings about his general approach to reconstruction. The editor of the Philadelphia *Public Ledger* noted that the President had indicated his "feelings and wishes" rather than his "fixed opinions," then commended him for his lack of "passion or malignancy" toward the late rebels. The Washington correspondent of the Cincinnati *Gazette* believed that Lincoln's position was generally approved except among the Radical Republicans, who were saying that the rebel leaders must be punished and the rebel states subjected to "preliminary training" before being restored to their rights as members of the Union. "The desire of the people for a settlement—speedy and final—upon the easiest possible terms, will, it is believed, sustain the President in his policy foreshadowed in his speech."

Whatever the people might have approved, it was again made clear to Lincoln, when the Cabinet met on the morning of April 14 (with General Grant present), that some of his own advisers would not approve a settlement upon easy terms. Secretary Stanton came to the meeting with a project for military occupation as a preliminary step toward the reorganization of the Southern states, Virginia and North Carolina to be combined in a single military district. Secretary Welles objected to this arrangement on the grounds that it would destroy the individuality of the separate states. The President sustained Welles's objection but did not completely repudiate Stanton's plan. Instead, he suggested that Stanton revise it so as to deal with Virginia and North Carolina separately, and that he provide copies of the revised plan for the members of the Cabinet at their next meeting.

Before the Cabinet meeting adjourned, Lincoln said he was glad that Congress was not in session. The House and the Senate, he was aware, had the unquestioned right to accept or reject new members from the Southern states; he himself had nothing to do with that. Still, he believed, the President had the power to recognize and deal with the state governments themselves. He could collect taxes in the South, see that the mails were delivered there, and appoint Federal officials (though his appointments would have to be confirmed, of course, by the Senate). He knew that the congressional Radicals did not agree with him, but they were not in session to make official objection, and he could act to establish and recognize the new state governments before Congress met in December. He did not intend to call a special session before that time, as he told the Speaker of the House, Schuyler Colfax, later on the day of that final Cabinet meeting, as he was leaving to go to Ford's Theater.

When, in December, 1865, the regular session of Congress finally began, Andrew Johnson had been President for nearly eight months. At first, in the days of terror following Lincoln's assassination, Johnson talked like a good Radical. He also acted like one when he ordered the arrest of Jefferson Davis and other Confederate leaders on the charge of complicity in the assassination. But Johnson and the Radicals soon disagreed on reconstruction. During the summer he succeeded in the restoration of state governments according to a plan which required them only to abolish slavery, retract their ordinances of secession, and repudiate their debts accumulated in the Confederate cause. In December the Radicals in Congress refused to seat the Senators and Representatives from these restored states. After checking Johnson's program, the Radicals proceeded to undo it, while impeaching the President. Eventually they carried through their own program of military occupation, similar to the one Stanton had proposed at the Cabinet meeting of April 14, and they undertook to transfer political power from the old master class to the freedmen, as Chase and other Radicals long had advocated.

Whether Lincoln, if he had lived, would have done as Johnson did, is hard to say. Certainly Lincoln would not have hounded Jefferson Davis or other Confederate officials (but, then, the presupposition here is that there would have been no assassination to seem to justify it). To his Cabinet in April he had indicated his hope that there would be no persecution, no bloody work, with respect to any of the late enemy. "None need expect he would take any part in hanging or killing those men, even the worst of them," Welles paraphrased him. "Frighten them out of the country, open the gates, let down the bars, scare them off, said he, throwing up his hands as if scaring sheep."

As for the restoration of state governments, it is impossible to guess confidently what Lincoln would have done or tried to do, since the very essence of his planning was to have no fixed and uniform plan, and since he appeared to be changing his mind on some points shortly before he died. In the states already being reconstructed under his program of December, 1863, he doubtless would have continued to support that program, as he did to the last. In other states he might have tried other expedients.

Whether, if Lincoln had lived and had proceeded along Johnson's lines, he would have succeeded any better than Johnson, is another "iffy" question, impossible to answer. It seems likely that, with his superior talent for political management, Lincoln would have avoided the worst of Johnson's clashes with Congress. Yet he could scarcely have escaped the conflict itself, unless he had conceded much more to the Radicals than Johnson did.

Another poser is the question whether Lincoln's approach to peace, if he had lived and had carried it through, would have advanced the Negro toward equal citizenship more surely than did the Radical program, which degenerated into a rather cynical use of the Negro for party advantage. One is entitled to believe that Lincoln's policy would have been better in the long run for Negroes as well as for Southern whites and for the nation as a whole.

David Donald

Why They Impeached Andrew Johnson

The story of Presidential Reconstruction begun by Randall and Current in the last essay is completed in this one by Professor David Donald of Johns Hopkins University. Lincoln's approach to restoring the Union was cautious, practical, thoughtful—humane in every sense of the word. Because of his assassination, however, the evaluation of his policy has to be a study in the might-have-beens of history. The Reconstruction policy of his successor, Andrew Johnson, superficially similar to Lincoln's, was reckless, impractical, emotional, and politically absurd. While historians have differed in evaluating his purposes, they have been in unanimous agreement that his management of the problem was inept and that his policy was a total failure.

Professor Donald's essay provides an extended character study of Johnson, and it is not an attractive portrait. Donald believes that Johnson "threw away a magnificent opportunity" to smooth and speed the return of the Confederate states to a harmonious place in the Union. But he also shows how difficult Johnson's task was and to how great an extent southern white opinion was set against the full acceptance of Negro equality. Donald, a former student of James G. Randall, is best known for his revision and expansion of Randall's The Civil War and Reconstruction, *and for his own Pulitzer Prize winning* Charles Sumner and the Coming of the Civil War, *the first part of a soon-to-be-completed biography of the Massachusetts senator.*

Reconstruction after the Civil War posed some of the most discouraging problems that have ever faced American statesmen. The South was prostrate. Its defeated soldiers straggled homeward through a countryside desolated by war. Southern soil was untilled and exhausted; southern factories and railroads were worn out. The four billion dollars of southern capital invested in Negro slaves was wiped out by advancing Union armies, "the most stupendous act of sequestration in the history of Anglo-American jurisprudence." The white inhabitants of eleven states had somehow to be reclaimed from rebellion and restored to a firm loyalty to the United States. Their four million former slaves had simultaneously to be guided into a proper use of their new-found freedom.

For the victorious Union government there was no time for reflection. Immediate decisions had to be made. Thousands of destitute whites and Negroes had to be fed before long-range plans of rebuilding the southern economy could be drafted. Some kind of government had to be established in these former Confederate states, to preserve order and to direct the work of restoration.

A score of intricate questions must be answered: Should the defeated southerners be punished or pardoned? How should genuinely loyal southern Unionists be rewarded? What was to be the social, economic, and political status of the now free Negroes? What civil rights did they have? Ought they to have the ballot? Should they be given a freehold of property? Was Reconstruction to be controlled by the national government, or should the southern states work out their own salvation? If the federal government supervised the process, should the President or the Congress be in control?

Intricate as were the problems, in early April, 1865, they did not seem insuperable. President Abraham Lincoln was winning the peace as he had already won the war. He was careful to keep every detail of Reconstruction in his own hands; unwilling to be committed to any "exclusive, and inflexible plan," he was working out a pragmatic program of restoration not, perhaps, entirely satisfactory to any group, but reasonably acceptable to all sections. With his enormous prestige as commander of the victorious North and as victor in the 1864 election, he was able to promise freedom to the Negro, charity to the southern white, security to the North.

The blighting of these auspicious beginnings is one of the saddest stories in American history. The reconciliation of the sections, which seemed so imminent in 1865, was delayed for more than ten years. Northern magnanimity toward a fallen foe curdled into bitter distrust. Southern whites rejected moderate leaders, and inveterate racists spoke for the new South. The Negro, after serving as a political pawn for a decade, was relegated to a second-class citizenship, from which he is yet struggling to emerge. Rarely has democratic government so completely failed as during the Reconstruction decade.

The responsibility for this collapse of American statesmanship is, of course, complex. History is not a tale of deep-dyed villains or pure-as-snow heroes. Part of the blame must fall upon ex-Confederates who refused to recognize that the war was over: part upon freedmen who confused liberty with license and the ballot box with the lunch pail; part upon northern antislavery extremists who identified patriotism with loyalty to the Republican party; part upon the land speculators, treasury grafters, and railroad promoters who were unwilling to have a genuine peace lest it end their looting of the public till.

Yet these divisive forces were not bound to triumph. Their success was due to the failure of constructive statesmanship that could channel the magnanimous feelings shared by most Americans into a positive program of reconstruction. President Andrew Johnson was called upon for positive leadership, and he did not meet the challenge.

Andrew Johnson's greatest weakness was his insensitivity to public opinion. In contrast to Lincoln, who said, "Public opinion in this country is everything," Johnson made a career of battling the popular will. A poor white, a runaway tailor's apprentice, a self-educated Tennessee politician, Johnson was a living defiance to the dominant southern belief that leadership belonged to the plantation aristocracy.

As senator from Tennessee, he defied the sentiment of his section in 1861 and refused to join the secessionist movement. When Lincoln later appointed him military governor of occupied Tennessee, Johnson found Nashville "a furnace of treason," but he braved social ostracism and threats of assassination and discharged his duties with boldness and efficiency.

Such a man was temperamentally unable to understand the northern mood in 1865, much less to yield to it. For four years the northern people had been whipped into wartime frenzy by propaganda tales of Confederate atrocities. The assassination of Lincoln by a southern sympathizer confirmed their belief in southern brutality and heartlessness. Few northerners felt vindictive toward the South, but most felt that the rebellion they had crushed must never rise again. Johnson ignored this postwar psychosis gripping the North and plunged ahead with his program of rapidly restoring the southern states to the Union. In May, 1865, without any previous preparation of public opinion, he issued a proclamation of amnesty, granting forgiveness to nearly all the millions of former rebels and welcoming them back into peaceful fraternity. Some few Confederate leaders were excluded from his general amnesty, but even they could secure pardon by special petition. For weeks the White House corridors were thronged with ex-Confederate statesmen and former southern generals who daily received presidential forgiveness.

Ignoring public opinion by pardoning the former Confederates, Johnson actually entrusted the formation of new governments in the South to them. The provisional governments established by the President proceeded, with a good deal of reluctance, to rescind their secession ordinances, to abolish slavery, and to repudiate the Confederate debt. Then, with far more enthusiasm, they turned to electing governors, representatives, and senators. By December, 1865, the southern states had their delegations in Washington waiting for admission by Congress. Alexander H. Stephens, once vice president of the Con-

A Harper's Weekly *cartoon depicts Johnson (left) and Thaddeus Stevens as engineers committed to a collision course.*

federacy, was chosen senator from Georgia; not one of the North Carolina delegation could take a loyalty oath; and all of South Carolina's congressmen had "either held office under the Confederate States, or been in the army, or countenanced in some way the Rebellion."

Johnson himself was appalled, "There seems in many of the elections something like defiance, which is all out of place at this time." Yet on December 5 he strongly urged the Congress to seat these southern representatives "and thereby complete the work of reconstruction." But the southern states were omitted from the roll call.

Such open defiance of northern opinion was dangerous under the best of circumstances, but in Johnson's case it was little more than suicidal. The President seemed not to realize the weakness of his position. He was the representative of no major interest and had no genuine political following. He had been considered for the vice presidency in 1864 because, as a southerner and a former slaveholder, he could lend plausibility to the Republican pretension that the old parties were dead and that Lincoln was the nominee of a new, nonsectional National Union party.

A political accident, the new Vice President did little to endear himself to his countrymen. At Lincoln's second inauguration Johnson appeared before the Senate in an obviously inebriated state and made a long, intemperate harangue about his plebeian origins and his hardwon success. President, Cabinet, and senators were humiliated by the shameful display, and Charles Sumner felt that "the Senate should call upon him to resign." Historians now know that Andrew Johnson was not a heavy drinker. At the time of his inaugural display, he was just recovering from a severe attack of typhoid fever. Feeling ill just before he entered the Senate chamber, he asked for some liquor to steady his nerves, and either his weakened condition or abnormal sensitivity to alcohol betrayed him.

Lincoln reassured Republicans who were worried over the affair: "I have known Andy for many years; he made a bad slip the other day, but you need not be scared. Andy ain't a drunkard." Never again was Andrew Johnson seen under the influence of alcohol, but his reformation came too late. His performance on March 4, 1865, seriously undermined his political usefulness and permitted his opponents to discredit him as a pothouse politician. Johnson was catapulted into the presidency by John Wilkes Booth's bullet. From the outset his position was weak, but it was not necessarily untenable. The President's chronic lack of discretion made it so. Where common sense dictated that a chief executive in so disadvantageous a position should act with great caution, Johnson proceeded to imitate Old Hickory, Andrew Jackson, his political idol. If Congress crossed his will, he did not hesitate to defy it. Was he not "the Tribune of the People"?

Sure of his rectitude, Johnson was indifferent to prudence. He never learned that the President of the United States cannot afford to be a quarreler. Apprenticed in the rough-and-tumble politics of frontier Tennessee, where orators exchanged violent personalities, crude humor, and bitter denunciations, Johnson continued to make stump speeches from the White House. All too often he spoke extemporaneously, and he permitted hecklers in his audience to draw from him angry charges against his critics.

On Washington's birthday in 1866, against the advice of his more sober advisers, the President made an impromptu address to justify his Reconstruction policy. "I fought traitors and treason in the South," he told the crowd; "now when I turn around, and at the other end of the line find men—I care not by what name you call them— who will stand opposed to the restoration of the Union of these States, I am free to say to you that I am still in the field."

During the "great applause" which followed, a nameless voice shouted, "Give us the names at the other end. . . . Who are they?"

"You ask me who they are," Johnson retorted. "I say Thaddeus Stevens of Pennsylvania is one; I say Mr. Sumner is another; and Wendell Phillips is another." Applause urged him to continue. "Are those who want to destroy our institutions . . . not satisfied with the blood that has been shed? . . . Does not the blood of Lincoln appease the vengeance and wrath of the opponents of this government?"

The President's remarks were as untrue as they were impolitic. Not only was it manifestly false to assert that the leading Republican in the House and the most conspicuous Republican in the Senate were opposed to "the fundamental principles of this government" or that they had been responsible for Lincoln's assassination; it was incredible political folly to impute such actions to men with whom the President had to work daily. But Andrew Johnson never learned that the President of the United States must function as a party leader.

There was a temperamental coldness about this plain-featured, grave man that kept him from easy, intimate relations with even his political supporters. His massive head, dark, luxuriant hair, deep-set and piercing eyes, and cleft square chin seemed to Charles Dickens to indicate "courage, watchfulness, and certainly strength of purpose," but his was a grim face, with "no genial sunlight in it." The coldness and reserve that marked Johnson's public associations doubtless stemmed from a deep-seated feeling of insecurity; this self-educated tailor whose wife had taught him how to write could never expose himself by letting down his guard and relaxing.

Johnson knew none of the arts of managing men, and he seemed unaware that face-saving is important for a politician. When he became President, Johnson was besieged by advisers of all political complexions. To each he listened gravely and non-committally, raising no questions and by his silence seeming to give consent. With Radical Senator Sumner, already intent upon giving the freedmen both homesteads and the ballot, he had repeated interviews during the first month of his presidency. "His manner has been excellent, & even sympathetic," Sumner reported triumphantly. With Chief Justice Salmon P. Chase, Sumner urged Johnson to support immediate Negro suffrage and found the President was "well-disposed, & sees the rights & necessities of the case." In the middle of May, 1865, Sumner reassured a Republican caucus that the President was a true Radical; he had listened repeatedly to the Senator and had told him "there is no difference between us." Before the end of the month the rug was pulled from under Sumner's feet. Johnson issued his proclamation for the reconstruction of North Carolina, making no provisions for Negro suffrage. Sumner first learned about it through the newspapers.

While he was making up his mind, Johnson appeared silently receptive to all ideas; when he had made a decision, his mind was immovably closed, and he defended his course with all the obstinacy of a weak man. In December, alarmed by Johnson's Reconstruction proclamations, Sumner again sought an interview with the President. "No longer sympathetic, or even kindly," Sumner found, "he was harsh, petulant, and unreasonable." The Senator was depressed by Johnson's "prejudice, ignorance, and perversity" on the Negro suffrage issue. Far from listening amiably to Sumner's argument that the South was still torn by violence and not yet ready for readmission, Johnson attacked him with cheap analogies. "Are there no murders in Massachusetts?" the President asked.

"Unhappily yes," Sumner replied, "sometimes."

"Are there no assaults in Boston? Do not men there sometimes knock each other down, so that the police is obliged to interfere?"

"Unhappily yes."

"Would you consent that Massachusetts, on this account, should be excluded from Congress?" Johnson triumphantly queried. In the excitement the President unconsciously used Sumner's hat, which the Senator had placed on the floor beside his chair, as a spittoon!

Had Johnson been as resolute in action as he was in argument, he might conceivably have carried much of his party with him on his Reconstruction program. Promptness, publicity, and persuasion could have created a presidential following. Instead Johnson boggled. Though he talked boastfully of "kicking out" officers who failed to support his plan, he was slow to act. His own Cabinet, from the very beginning, contained members who disagreed with him, and his secretary of war, Edwin M. Stanton, was openly in league with the Republican elements most hostile to the President. For more than two years he impotently hoped that Stanton would resign; then in 1867, after Congress had passed the Tenure of Office Act, he tried to oust the Secretary. This belated firmness, against the letter of the law, led directly to Johnson's impeachment trial.

Instead of working with his party leaders and building up political support among Republicans, Johnson in 1866 undertook to organize his friends into a new party. In August a convention of white southerners, northern Democrats, moderate Republicans, and presidential appointees assembled in Philadelphia to endorse Johnson's policy. Union General Darius Couch of Massachusetts marched arm in arm down the convention aisle with Governor James L. Orr of South Carolina, to symbolize the states reunited under Johnson's rule. The convention produced fervid oratory, a dignified statement of principles —but not much else. Like most third-party reformist movements it lacked local support and grass-roots organization.

Johnson himself was unable to breathe life into his stillborn third party. Deciding to take his case to the people, he accepted an invitation to speak at a great Chicago memorial honoring Stephen A. Douglas. When his special train left Washington on August 28 for a "swing around the circle," the President was accompanied by a few Cabinet members who shared his views and by the war heroes Grant and Farragut.

At first all went well. There were some calculated political snubs to the President, but he managed at Philadelphia, New York, and Albany to present his ideas soberly and cogently to the people. But Johnson's friends were worried lest his tongue again get out of control. "In all frankness," a senator wrote him, do not "allow the excitement of the moment to draw from you any *extemporaneous speeches.*"

At St. Louis, when a Radical voice shouted that Johnson was a "Judas," the President flamed up in rage. "There was a Judas and he was one of the twelve apostles," he retorted. ". . . The twelve apostles had a Christ. . . . If I have played the Judas, who has been my Christ that I have played the Judas with? Was it Thad Stevens? Was it Wendell Phillips? Was it Charles Sumner?" Over mingled hisses and applause, he shouted, "These are the men that stop and compare themselves with the Saviour; and everybody that differs with them . . . is to be denounced as a Judas."

Johnson had played into his enemies' hands. His Radical foes denounced him as a "trickster," a "culprit," a man "touched with insanity, corrupted with lust, stimulated with drink." More serious in consequence was the reaction of northern moderates, such as James Russell Lowell, who wrote, "What an anti-Johnson lecturer we have in Johnson! Sumner has been right about the *cuss* from the first. . . ."

The fall elections were an overwhelming repudiation of the President and his Reconstruction policy.

Johnson's want of political sagacity strengthened the very elements in the Republican party which he most feared. In 1865 the Republicans had no clearly defined attitude toward Reconstruction. Moderates like Gideon Welles and Orville Browning wanted to see the southern states restored with a minimum of restrictions; Radicals like Sumner and Stevens demanded that the entire southern social system be revolutionized. Some Republicans were passionately concerned with the plight of the freedmen; others were more interested in maintaining the high tariff and land grant legislation enacted during the war. Many thought mostly of keeping themselves in office, and many genuinely believed, with Sumner, that "the Republican party, in its objects, is identical with country and with mankind." These diverse elements came slowly to adopt the idea of harsh Reconstruction, but Johnson's stubborn persistency in his policy left them no alternative. Every step the President took seemed to provide "a new encouragement to (1) the rebels at the South, (2) the Democrats at the North and (3) the discontented elements everywhere." Not many Republicans would agree with Sumner that Johnson's program was "a defiance to God and Truth," but there was genuine concern that the victory won by the war was being frittered away.

The provisional governments established by the President in the South seemed to be dubiously loyal. They were reluctant to rescind their secession ordinances and to repudiate the Confederate debt, and they chose high-ranking ex-Confederates to represent them in Congress. Northerners were even more alarmed when these southern governments began to legislate upon the Negro's civil rights. Some laws were necessary—in order to give former slaves the right to marry, to hold property, to sue and be sued, and the like—but the Johnson legislatures went far beyond these immediate needs. South Carolina, for example, enacted that no Negro could pursue the trade "of an artisan, mechanic, or shopkeeper, or any other trade or employment besides that of husbandry" without a special license. Alabama provided that "any stubborn or refractory servants" or "servants who loiter away their time" should be fined $50 and, if they could not pay, be hired out for six months' labor. Mississippi ordered that every Negro under eighteen years of age who was an orphan or not supported by his parents must be apprenticed to some white person, preferably the former owner of the slave. Such southern laws indicated a determination to keep the Negro in a state of peonage.

It was impossible to expect a newly emancipated race to be content with such a limping freedom. The thousands of Negroes who had served in the Union armies and had helped conquer their former Confederate masters were not willing to abandon their new-found liberty. In rural areas southern whites kept these Negroes under control through the Ku Klux Klan. But in southern cities white hegemony was less secure, and racial friction erupted in mob violence. In May, 1866, a quarrel between a Memphis Negro and a white teamster led to a riot in which the

JOHNSON'S LOVE FOR THE SOLDIER.

This cartoon is an example of the virulence of the attacks on Johnson by his enemies.

city police and the poor whites raided the Negro quarters and burned and killed promiscuously. Far more serious was the disturbance in New Orleans two months later. The Republican party in Louisiana was split into pro-Johnson conservatives and Negro suffrage advocates. The latter group determined to hold a constitutional convention, of dubious legality, in New Orleans, in order to secure the ballot for the freedmen and the offices for themselves. Through imbecility in the War Department, the Federal troops occupying the city were left without orders, and the mayor of New Orleans, strongly opposed to Negro equality, had the responsibility for preserving order. There were acts of provocation on both sides, and finally, on July 30, a procession of Negroes marching toward the convention hall was attacked.

"A shot was fired . . . by a policeman, or some colored man in the procession," General Philip Sheridan reported. "This led to other shots, and a rush after the procession. On arrival at the front of the Institute [where the convention met], there was some throwing of brick-bats by both sides. The police . . . were vigorously marched to the scene of disorder. The procession entered the Institute with the flag, about six or eight remaining outside. A row occurred between a policeman and one of these colored men, and a shot was again fired by one of the parties, which led to an indiscriminate firing on the building, through the windows, by the policemen.

"This had been going on for a short time, when a white flag was displayed from the windows of the Institute, whereupon the firing ceased and the police rushed into the building. . . . The policemen opened an indiscriminate fire upon the audience until they had emptied their revolvers, when they retired, and those inside barricaded the doors. The door was broken in, and the firing again commenced when many of the colored and white people either escaped out of the door, or were passed out by the policemen inside, but as they came out, the policemen who formed the circle nearest the building fired upon them, and they were again fired upon by the citizens that formed the outer circle.''

Thirty-seven Negroes and three of their white friends were killed; 119 Negroes and seventeen of their white sympathizers were wounded. Of their assailants, ten were wounded and but one killed. President Johnson was, of course, horrified by these outbreaks, but the Memphis and New Orleans riots, together with the Black Codes, afforded a devastating illustration of how the President's policy actually operated. The southern states, it was clear, were not going to protect the Negroes' basic rights. They were only grudgingly going to accept the results of the war. Yet, with Johnson's blessing, these same states were expecting a stronger voice in Congress than ever. Before 1860, southern representation in Congress had been based upon the white population plus three fifths of the slaves; now the Negroes, though not permitted to vote, were to be counted like all other citizens, and southern states would be entitled to at least nine additional congressmen. Joining with the northern Copperheads, the southerners could easily regain at the next presidential election all that had been lost on the Civil War battlefield.

It was this political exigency, not misguided sentimentality nor vindictiveness, which united Republicans in opposition to the President.

Johnson's defenders have pictured Radical Reconstruction as the work of a fanatical minority, led by Sumner and Stevens, who drove their reluctant colleagues into adopting coercive measures against the South. In fact, every major piece of Radical legislation was adopted by the nearly unanimous vote of the entire Republican membership of Congress. Andrew Johnson had left them no other choice. Because he insisted upon rushing Confederate-dominated states back into the Union, Republicans moved to disqualify Confederate leaders under the Fourteenth Amendment. When, through Johnson's urging, the southern states rejected that amendment, the Republicans in Congress unwillingly came to see Negro suffrage as the only counterweight against Democratic majorities in the South. With the Reconstruction Acts of 1867 the way was open for a true Radical program toward the South, harsh and thorough.

Andrew Johnson became a cipher in the White House, futilely disapproving bills which were promptly passed over his veto. Through his failure to reckon with public opinion, his unwillingness to recognize his weak position, his inability to functon as a party leader, he had sacrificed all influence with the party which had elected him and had turned over its control to Radicals vindictively opposed to his policies. In March, 1868, Andrew Johnson was summoned before the Senate of the United States to be tried on eleven accusations of high crimes and misdemeanors. By a narrow margin the Senate failed to convict him, and historians have dismissed the charges as flimsy and false. Yet perhaps before the bar of history itself Andrew Johnson must be impeached with an even graver charge—that through political ineptitude he threw away a magnificent opportunity.

Alan F. Westin

Ride-in:
A Century of
Protest Begins

The last quarter of the nineteenth century—after the federal
government relaxed its pressure on the southern states to deal fairly
with their black citizens—has been called "the nadir" of the history
of the Negro in America after emancipation. Some historians argue
that the low point came somewhat later, during the early twentieth
century, but few would disagree with the thesis that the period in
question was indeed disastrous for American blacks. Although never
really treated decently (in the North as well as in the South), Negroes
had made important gains during Reconstruction; the Fourteenth and
Fifteenth Amendments "guaranteed" their political and civil rights,
and Congress passed stiff laws protecting these rights, including the
Civil Rights Act of 1875, which outlawed discrimination in places of
public accommodation.

After the so-called Compromise of 1877, however, these gains were
gradually stripped away by a combination of southern pressure, northern indifference, and a series of crippling legal interpretations by the
Supreme Court. In this essay Professor Alan F. Westin of Columbia
University, an expert on constitutional history, describes one of the
first and most significant of the Supreme Court decisions of the era,
one which emasculated the Civil Rights Act of 1875. His story reads in
some ways like an account of the civil rights struggles of the 1950's
and 1960's, but with the terrible difference that freedom and justice
were in this instance the losers, not the winners of the fight.

*I*t began one day early in January when a Negro named Robert Fox stepped aboard a streetcar in Louisville, Kentucky, dropped his coin into the fare box, and sat down in the white section of the car. Ordered to move, he refused, and the driver threw him off the car. Shortly after, Fox filed a charge of assault and battery against the streetcar company in the federal district court, claiming that separate seating policies were illegal and the driver's actions were therefore improper. The district judge instructed the jury that under federal law common carriers must serve all passengers equally without regard to race. So instructed, the jury found the company rules to be invalid and awarded damages of fifteen dollars (plus $72.80 in legal costs) to Mr. Fox.

Immediately there was sharp criticism of the Fox decision from the city and state administrations, both Democratic; the company defied the court's ruling and continued segregated seating. After several meetings with local federal officials and white attorneys co-operating with them, Louisville Negro leaders decided to launch a full-scale "ride-in." At 7 P.M. on May 12, a young Negro boy boarded a streetcar near the Willard Hotel, walked past the driver, and took a seat among the white passengers. The driver, under new company regulations, did not attempt to throw him off but simply stopped the car, lit a cigar, and refused to proceed until the Negro moved to "his place." While the governor, the Louisville chief of police, and other prominent citizens looked on from the sidewalks, a large crowd which included an increasingly noisy mob of jeering white teen-agers gathered around the streetcar.

Before long, there were shouts of "Put him out!" "Hit him!" "Kick him!" "Hang him!" Several white youths climbed into the car and began yelling insults in the face of the young Negro rider. He refused to answer—or to move. The youths dragged him from his seat, pulled him off the car, and began to beat him. Only when the Negro started to defend himself did the city police intervene: they arrested him for disturbing the peace and took him to jail.

This time the trial was held in Louisville city court, not the federal court. The magistrate ruled that streetcar companies were not under any obligation to treat Negroes exactly as they treated whites, and that any federal measures purporting to create such obligations would be "clearly invalid" under the constitutions of Kentucky and the United States. The defendant was fined, and the judge delivered a warning to Louisville Negroes that further ride-ins would be punished.

But the ride-in campaign was not halted that easily. In the following days, streetcar after streetcar was entered by Negroes who took seats in the white section. Now the drivers got off the cars entirely. On several occasions, the Negro riders drove the cars themselves, to the sound of cheers from Negro spectators. Then violence erupted. Bands of white youths and men began to throw Negro riders off the cars: windows were broken, cars were overturned, and for a time a general race riot threatened. Moderate Kentucky newspapers and many community leaders deplored the fighting; the Republican candidate for governor denounced the streetcar company's segregation policies and blamed the violence on Democratic encouragement of white extremists.

By this time, newspapers across the country were carrying reports of the conflict, and many editorials denounced the seating regulations. In Louisville, federal marshals and the United States attorney backed the rights of the Negro riders and stated that federal court action would be taken if necessary. There were even rumors that the President might send troops.

Under these threats, the streetcar company capitulated. Soon, all the city transit companies declared that "it was useless to try to resist or evade the enforcement by the United States authorities of the claim of Negroes to ride in the cars." To "avoid serious collisions," the company would thereafter allow all passengers to sit where they chose. Although a few disturbances took place in the following months, and some white intransigents boycotted the streetcars, mixed seating became a common practice. The Kentucky press soon pointed with pride to the spirit of conciliation and harmony which prevailed in travel facilities within the city, calling it a model for good race relations. Never again would Louisville streetcars be segregated.

The event may have a familiar ring, but it should not, for it occurred almost one hundred years ago, in 1871. The streetcars were horse-drawn. The President who considered ordering troops to Louisville was ex-General Grant, not ex-General Eisenhower. The Republican gubernatorial candidate who supported the Negro riders, John Marshall Harlan, was not a post-World War II leader of the G.O.P. but a former slaveholder from one of Kentucky's oldest and most famous political families. And the "new" Negroes who waged this ride-in were not members of the Congress of Racial Equality and the National Association for the Advancement of Colored People, or followers of Dr. Martin Luther King, but former slaves who were fighting for civil rights in their own time, and with widespread success.

And yet these dramatic sit-ins, ride-ins, and walk-ins of the 1870's are almost unknown to the American public today. The standard American histories do not mention them, providing only thumbnail references to "bayonet-enforced" racial contacts during Reconstruction. Most commentators view the Negro's resort to direct action as an invention of the last decade. Clearly, then, it is time that the civil-rights struggle of the 1870's and 1880's was rescued from newspaper files and court archives, not only because it is historically important but also because it has compelling relevance for our own era.

Contrary to common assumptions today, no state in the Union during the 1870's, including those south of the Mason-Dixon line, required separation of whites and Negroes in places of public accommodation. Admission and arrangement policies were up to individual owners. In the North and West, many theatres, hotels, restaurants, and public carriers served Negro patrons without hesitation or discrimination. Some accepted Negroes only in second-class accommodations, such as smoking cars on railroads or balconies in theatres, where they sat among whites who did not have first-class tickets. Other northern and

An 1875 Harper's Weekly cartoon bore the caption, "Shall
We Withdraw Our Troops?"

western establishments, especially the more exclusive ones, refused
Negro patronage entirely.

The situation was similar in the large cities of the southern and
border states. Many establishments admitted Negroes to second-class
facilities. Some gave first-class service to those of privileged social
status—government officials, army officers, newspapermen, and clergymen. On the other hand, many places of public accommodation, particularly in the rural areas and smaller cities of the South, were
closed to Negroes whatever their wealth or status.

From 1865 through the early 1880's, the general trend in the
nation was toward wider acceptance of Negro patronage. The federal
Civil Rights Act of 1866, with its guarantee to Negroes of "equal
benefit of the laws," had set off a flurry of enforcement suits—for
denying berths to Negroes on a Washington-New York train; for refusing to sell theatre tickets to Negroes in Boston; and for barring
Negro women from the waiting rooms and parlor cars of railroads in
Virginia, Illinois, and California. Ratification of the Fourteenth
Amendment in 1868 had spurred more challenges. Three northern
states, and two southern states under Reconstruction regimes, passed
laws making it a crime for owners of public-accommodation businesses
to discriminate. Most state and federal court rulings on these laws
between 1865 and 1880 held in favor of Negro rights, and the rulings
built up a steady pressure on owners to relax racial bars.

Nevertheless, instances of exclusion and segregation continued
throughout the 1870's. To settle the issue once and for all (thereby

Cartoonist Thomas Nast mocked the provision of the Civil Rights Act of 1875 that allowed Negroes to collect $500 from those who barred them from places of public accommodation.

reaping the lasting appreciation of the Negro voters), congressional Republicans led by Senator Charles Sumner pressed for a federal statute making discrimination in public accommodations a crime. Democrats and conservative Republicans warned in the congressional debates that such a law would trespass on the reserved powers of the states and reminded the Sumner supporters that recent Supreme Court decisions had taken a narrow view of federal power under the Civil War amendments.

After a series of legislative compromises, however, Sumner's forces were able to enact the statute; on March 1, 1875, "An Act to Protect all Citizens in their Civil and Legal Rights" went into effect. "It is essential to just government," the preamble stated, that the nation "recognize the equality of all men before the law, and . . . it is the duty of government in its dealings with the people to mete out equal and exact justice to all, of whatever nativity, race, color, or persuasion, religious or political . . ."

Section 1 of the act declared that "All persons within the jurisdiction of the United States shall be entitled to the full and equal enjoyment of the accommodations . . . of inns, public conveyances on land or water, theaters and other places of public amusement; subject only to the conditions and limitations established by law, and applicable alike to citizens of every race or color. . . ." Section 2 provided that any person violating the act could be sued in federal district court for a penalty of $500, could be fined $500 to $1,000, or could be imprisoned from thirty days to one year. (A separate section forbade racial discrimination in the selection of juries.)

Reaction to the law was swift. Two Negro men were admitted to the dress circle of Macauley's Theatre in Louisville and sat through the performance without incident. In Washington, Negroes were served for the first time at the bar of the Willard Hotel, and a Negro broke the color line when he was seated at McVicker's Theatre in Chicago. But in other instances, Negroes were rejected despite "Sumner's law." Several hotels in Chattanooga turned in their licenses, became private boardinghouses, and accepted whites only. Restaurants and barber shops in Richmond turned away Negro customers.

Suits challenging refusals were filed en masse throughout the country. Perhaps a hundred were decided in the federal district courts during the late 1870's and early 1880's. Federal judges in Pennsylvania, Texas, Maryland, and Kentucky, among others, held the law to be constitutional and ruled in favor of Negro complainants. In North Carolina, New Jersey, and California, however, district judges held the law invalid. And when other courts in New York, Tennessee, Missouri, and Kansas put the issue to the federal circuit judges, the judges divided on the question, and the matter was certified to the United States Supreme Court.

But the Supreme Court did not exactly rush to make its ruling. Though two cases testing the 1875 act reached it in 1876 and a third in 1877, the Justices simply held them on their docket. In 1879, the Attorney General filed a brief defending the constitutionality of the law, but still the Court reached no decisions. In 1880, three additional cases were filed, but two years elapsed before the Solicitor General presented a fresh brief supporting the statute. It was not until late in 1883 that the Supreme Court passed upon the 1875 act, in what became famous as the *Civil Rights Cases* ruling. True, the Court was badly behind in its work in this period, but clearly the Justices chose to let the civil-rights cases "ripen" for almost eight years.

When they finally came to grips with the issue, six separate test suits were involved. The most celebrated had arisen in New York City in November of 1879. Edwin Booth, the famous tragedian and brother of John Wilkes Booth, had opened a special Thanksgiving week engagement at the Grand Opera House. After playing *Hamlet*, *Othello*, and *Richelieu* to packed houses, he was scheduled to perform Victor Hugo's *Ruy Blas* at the Saturday matinee on November 22.

One person who had decided to see Booth that Saturday was William R. Davis, Jr., who was later described in the press as a tall, handsome, and well-spoken Negro of twenty-six. He was the business agent of the *Progressive-American*, a Negro weekly published in New York City. At 10 o'clock Saturday morning, Davis' girl friend ("a bright octoroon, almost white," as the press put it), purchased two reserved seats at the box office of the Grand Opera House. At 1:30 P.M., Davis and his lady presented themselves at the theatre, only to be told by the doorkeeper, Samuel Singleton, that "these tickets are no good." If he would step out to the box office, Singleton told Davis, his money would be refunded.

It is unlikely that Davis was surprised by Singleton's action, for this was not the first time he had encountered such difficulties. Shortly after the passage of the 1875 act, Davis had been refused a ticket to the dress circle of Booth's Theatre in New York. He had sworn out a

In this cartoon Leslie's Weekly *praised theatres that flaunted the 1875 law and refused to sell Negroes tickets.*

warrant against the ticket seller, but the failure of his witnesses to appear at the grand jury proceedings had led to a dismissal of the complaint. This earlier episode, as well as Davis' activity as a Negro journalist, made it probable that this appearance at the Opera House in 1879 was a deliberate test of the management's discriminatory policies.

Though Davis walked out of the lobby at Singleton's request, he did not turn in his tickets for a refund. Instead, he summoned a young white boy standing near the theatre, gave him a dollar (plus a dime for his trouble), and had him purchase two more tickets. When Davis and his companion presented these to Singleton, only the lady was allowed to pass. Again Davis was told that his ticket was "no good." When he now refused to move out of the doorway, Singleton called a policeman and asked that Davis be escorted off the theatre property. The officer told Davis that the Messrs. Poole and Donnelly, the managers of the Opera House, did not admit colored persons. "Perhaps the managers do not," Davis retorted, "but the laws of the country [do]."

The following Monday, November 24, Davis filed a criminal complaint; on December 9, this time with witnesses in abundance, Singleton was indicted in what the press described as the first criminal proceeding under the 1875 act to go to trial in New York. When the case opened on January 14, 1880, Singleton's counsel argued that the 1875 law was unconstitutional. "It interferes," he said, "with the right of the State of New York to provide the means under which citizens of the State have the power to control and protect their rights in respect to their private property." The assistant United States attorney replied that such a conception of states' rights had been "exploded and superseded long ago." It was unthinkable, he declared, that "the United States could not extend to one citizen of

New York a right which the State itself gave to others of its citizens—
the right of admission to places of public amusement.''

The presiding judge decided to take the constitutional challenge
under advisement and referred it to the circuit court, for consideration at its February term. This left the decision up to Justice Samuel
Blatchford of the Supreme Court, who was assigned to the circuit court
for New York, and District Judge William Choate. The two judges
reached opposite conclusions and certified the question to the United
States Supreme Court.

Davis' case, under the title of *United States v. Singleton,* reached
the Supreme Court in 1880. Already lodged on the Court's docket
were four similar criminal prosecutions under the act of 1875. *U.S. v.
Stanley* involved the refusal of Murray Stanley in 1875 to serve a
meal at his hotel in Topeka, Kansas, to a Negro, Bird Gee. *U.S. v.
Nichols* presented the refusal in 1876 of Samuel Nichols, owner of
the Nichols House in Jefferson City, Missouri, to accept a Negro
named W. H. R. Agee as a guest. *U.S. v. Ryan* involved the conduct
of Michael Ryan, doorkeeper of Maguire's Theatre in San Francisco,
in denying a Negro named George M. Tyler entry to the dress circle
on January 4, 1876. In *U.S. v. Hamilton,* James Hamilton, a conductor
on the Nashville, Chattanooga, and St. Louis Railroad, had on April
21, 1879, denied a Negro woman with a first-class ticket access to the
ladies' car.

There was a fifth case, with a somewhat different setting. On the
evening of May 22, 1879, Mrs. Sallie J. Robinson, a twenty-eight-year-
old Negro, purchased two first-class tickets at Grand Junction, Tennessee, for a trip to Lynchburg, Virginia, on the Memphis and
Charleston Railroad. Shortly after midnight she and her nephew,
Joseph C. Robinson, described as a young Negro "of light complexion,
light hair, and light blue eyes,'' boarded the train and started into
the parlor car. The conductor, C. W. Reagin, held Mrs. Robinson
back ("bruising her arm and jerking her roughly around,'' she
alleged) and pushed her into the smoker.

A few minutes later, when Joseph informed the conductor that
he was Mrs. Robinson's nephew and was a Negro, the conductor looked
surprised. In that case, he said, they could go into the parlor car at
the next stop. The Robinsons finished the ride in the parlor car but
filed complaints with the railroad about their treatment and then
sued for $500 under the 1875 act. At the trial, Reagin testified that he
had thought Joseph to be a white man with a colored woman, and his
experience was that such associations were "for illicit purposes.''

Counsel for the Robinsons objected to Reagin's testimony, on the
ground that his actions were based on race and constituted no defense. Admitting the constitutionality of the 1875 law for purposes
of the trial, the railroad contended that the action of its conductor
did not fall within the statute. The district judge ruled that the
motive for excluding persons was the decisive issue under the act:
if the jury believed that the conductor had acted because he thought
Mrs. Robinson "a prostitute travelling with her paramour,'' whether

"well or ill-founded" in that assumption, the exclusion was not because of race and the railroad was not liable. The jury found for the railroad, and the Robinsons appealed.

These, with William Davis' suit against the doorkeeper of New York's Grand Opera House, were the six cases to which the Supreme Court finally turned in 1882. The Justices were presented with a learned and eloquent brief for the United States submitted by Solicitor General Samuel F. Phillips, who reviewed the leading cases, described the history of the Civil War amendments to the Constitution, and stressed the importance to the rights of citizens of equal access to public accommodation. Four times since 1865, Phillips noted, civil-rights legislation had been enacted by a Congress filled with men who had fought in the Civil War and had written the war amendments. These men understood that "every rootlet of slavery has an individual vitality, and, to its minutest hair, should be anxiously followed and plucked up. . . ." They also knew that if the federal government allowed Negroes to be denied accommodation "by persons who notably were sensitive registers of local public opinion," then "what upon yesterday was only 'fact' will become 'doctrine' tomorrow."

The Supreme Court Justices who considered Phillips' brief and the six test cases were uncommonly talented, among them being Chief Justice Morrison R. Waite, a man underrated today; Joseph P. Bradley, that Court's most powerful intellect; and Stephen J. Field, a *laissez-faire* interpreter of American constitutional law. John Marshall Harlan, the youngest man on the Court, had already started on the course which was to mark him as the most frequent and passionate dissenter in the Gilded Age.

As a whole, the Court might have appeared to be one which would have looked favorably on the 1875 act. All were Republicans except Justice Field, and he was a Democrat appointed by Abraham Lincoln. All except Justice Harlan, who was the Court's only southerner, had made their careers primarily in the northern and western states. Without exception, all had supported the Northern cause in the war, and none had any hostility toward Negroes as a class.

Yet on the afternoon of October 15, 1883, Justice Bradley announced that the Court found Sections 1 and 2 of the Civil Rights Act of 1875 to be unconstitutional. (This disposed of five of the cases; the sixth, *U.S. v. Hamilton*, was denied review on a procedural point.) There was added irony in the fact that Bradley delivered the majority opinion for eight of the Justices. A one-time Whig, Bradley had struggled for a North-South compromise in the darkening months of 1860–61, then had swung to a strong Unionist position after the firing on Fort Sumter. He had run for Congress on the Lincoln ticket in 1862 and in 1868 headed the New Jersey electors for Grant. When the Thirteenth and Fourteenth Amendments were adopted, he had given them firm support, and his appointment to the Supreme Court by Grant in 1870 had drawn no criticism from friends of the Negro, as had the appointment of John Marshall Harlan seven years later.

Bradley's opinion had a tightly reasoned simplicity. The Thirteenth Amendment forbade slavery and involuntary servitude, he noted, but protection against the restoration of bondage could not be stretched to cover federal regulation of "social" discriminations such as those dealt with in the 1875 statute. As for the Fourteenth Amendment, that was addressed only to deprivations of rights by the *states;* it did not encompass *private* acts of discrimination. Thus there was no source of constitutional authority for "Sumner's law"; it had to be regarded as an unwarranted invasion of an area under state jurisdiction. Even as a matter of policy, Bradley argued, the intention of the war amendments to aid the newly freed Negro had to have some limits. At some point, the Negro must cease to be "the special favorite of the law" and take on "the rank of a mere citizen."

At the Atlanta Opera House on the evening of the Court's decision, the end man of Haverly's Minstrels interrupted the performance to announce the ruling. The entire orchestra and dress circle audience rose and cheered. Negroes sitting in the balcony kept their seats, "stunned," according to one newspaper account. A short time earlier, a Negro denied entrance to the dress circle had filed charges against the Opera House management under the 1875 act. Now his case—their case—was dead.

Of all the nine Justices, only John Marshall Harlan, a Kentuckian and a former slaveholder, announced that he dissented from the

Justice John Marshall Harlan wrote the dissenting opinion on the Civil Rights Cases.

ruling. He promised to give a full opinion soon.

Justice Harlan's progress from a supporter of slavery to a civil-rights dissenter makes a fascinating chronicle. Like Bradley, he had entered politics as a Whig and had tried to find a middle road between secessionist Democrats and antislavery Republicans. Like Bradley, he became a Unionist after the firing on Fort Sumter. But there the parallels ended. Although Harlan entered the Union Army, he was totally opposed to freeing the slaves, and his distaste for Lincoln and the Radicals was complete. Between 1863 and 1868, he led the Conservative party in Kentucky, a third-party movement which supported the war but opposed pro-Negro and civil-rights measures as "flagrant invasions of property rights and local government."

By 1868, however, Harlan had become a Republican. The resounding defeat of the Conservatives in the 1867 state elections convinced him that a third party had no future in Kentucky. His antimonopoly views and his general ideas about economic progress conflicted directly with state Democratic policies, and when the Republicans nominated his former field commander, Ulysses S. Grant, for President, in 1868, Harlan was one of the substantial number of Conservatives who joined the G.O.P.

His views on Negro rights also changed at this time. The wave of vigilante activities against white Republicans and Negroes that swept Kentucky in 1868–70, with whippings and murders by the scores, convinced Harlan that federal guarantees were essential. He watched Negroes in Kentucky moving with dignity and skill toward useful citizenship, and his devout Presbyterianism led him to adopt a "brotherhood-of-man" outlook in keeping with his church's national position. Perhaps he may have been influenced by his wife, Mallie, whose parents were New England abolitionists. As a realistic Republican politician, he was also aware that 60,000 Kentucky Negroes would become voters in 1870.

Thus a "new" John Harlan took the stump as Republican gubernatorial candidate in 1871, the year of the Louisville streetcar ride-ins. He opened his rallies by confessing that he had formerly been anti-Negro. But "I have lived long enough," he said, "to feel that the most perfect despotism that ever existed on this earth was the institution of African slavery." The war amendments were necessary "to place it beyond the power of any State to interfere with . . . the results of the war. . . ." The South should stop agitating the race issue, and should turn to rebuilding itself on progressive lines. When the Democrats laughed at "Harlan the Chameleon" and read quotations from his earlier anti-Negro speeches, Harlan replied: "Let it be said that I am right rather than consistent."

Harlan soon became an influential figure in the Republican party and, when President Rutherford B. Hayes decided to appoint a southern Republican to the Supreme Court in 1877, he was a logical choice. Even then, the Negro issue rose to shake Harlan's life again. His confirmation was held up because of doubts by some senators as to his "real" civil-rights views. Only after Harlan produced his speeches between 1871 and 1877 and party leaders supported his firmness on the question was he approved.

Once on the Supreme Court, Harlan could have swung back to a conservative position on civil rights. Instead, he became one of his generation's most intense and uncompromising defenders of the Negro. Perhaps his was the psychology of the convert who defends his new faith more passionately, even more combatively, than the born believer. Harlan liked to think that he had changed because he knew the South and realized that any relaxation of federal protection of the rights of Negroes would encourage the "white irreconcilables" first to acts of discrimination and then to violence, which would destroy all hope of accommodation between the races.

When Harlan sat down in October of 1883 to write his dissent in the *Civil Rights Cases,* he hoped to set off a cannon of protest. But he simply could not get his thoughts on paper. He worked late into the night, and even rose from half-sleep to write down ideas that he was afraid would elude him in the morning. "It was a trying time for him," his wife observed. "In point of years, he was much the youngest man on the Bench; and standing alone, as he did in regard to a decision which the whole nation was anxiously awaiting, he felt that . . . he must speak not only forcibly but wisely." After weeks of drafting and discarding, Harlan seemed to reach a dead end. The dissent would not "write." It was at this point that Mrs. Harlan contributed a dramatic touch to the history of the *Civil Rights Cases.*

When the Harlans had moved to Washington in 1877, the Justice had acquired from a collector the inkstand which Chief Justice Roger Taney had used in writing all his opinions. Harlan was fond of showing this to guests and remarking that "it was the very inkstand from which the infamous *Dred Scott* opinion was written." Early in the 1880's, however, a niece of Taney's, who was engaged in collecting her uncle's effects, visited the Harlans. When she saw the inkstand she asked Harlan for it, and the Justice agreed. The next morning Mrs. Harlan, noting her husband's reluctance to part with his most prized possession, quietly arranged to have the inkstand "lost." She hid it away, and Harlan was forced to make an embarrassed excuse to Taney's niece.

Now, on a Sunday morning, probably early in November of 1883, after Harlan had spent a sleepless night working on his dissent, Mallie Harlan remembered the inkstand. While the Justice was at church, she retrieved it from its hiding place, filled it with a fresh supply of ink and pen points, and placed it on the blotter of his desk. When her husband returned from church, she told him, with an air of mystery, that he would find something special in his study. Harlan was overjoyed to recover his symbolic antique. Mrs. Harlan's gesture was successful, for as she relates:

> The memory of the historic part that Taney's inkstand had played in the Dred Scott decision, in temporarily tightening the shackles of slavery upon the negro race in those ante-bellum days,

seemed, that morning, to act like magic in clarifying my husband's thoughts in regard to the law . . . intended by Sumner to protect the recently emancipated slaves in the enjoyment of equal 'civil rights.' His pen fairly flew on that day and, with the running start he then got, he soon finished his dissent.

How directly the recollection of Dred Scott pervaded Harlan's dissent is apparent to anyone who reads the opinion. He began by noting that the pre-Civil War Supreme Court had upheld congressional laws forbidding individuals to interfere with recovery of fugitive slaves. To strike down the act of 1875 meant that "the rights of freedom and American citizenship cannot receive from the Nation that efficient protection which heretofore was unhesitatingly accorded to slavery and the rights of masters."

Harlan argued that the Civil Rights Act of 1875 was constitutional on any one of several grounds. The Thirteenth Amendment had already been held to guarantee "universal civil freedom"; Harlan stated that barring Negroes from facilities licensed by the state and under legal obligation to serve all persons without discrimination restored a major disability of slavery days and violated that civil freedom. As for the Fourteenth Amendment, its central purpose had been to extend national citizenship to the Negro, reversing the precedent upheld in the Dred Scott decision; its final section gave Congress power to pass appropriate legislation to enforce that affirmative grant as well as to enforce the section barring any state action which might deny liberty or equality. Now, the Supreme Court was deciding what legislation was appropriate and necessary for those purposes, although that decision properly belonged to Congress.

Even under the "State action" clause of the Fourteenth Amendment, Harlan continued, the 1875 act was constitutional; it was well established that "railroad corporations, keepers of inns and managers of places of public accommodation are agents or instrumentalities of the State." Finally, Harlan attacked the unwillingness of the Court's majority to uphold the public-carrier section of the act under Congress' power to regulate interstate trips. That was exactly what was involved in Mrs. Robinson's case against the Memphis and Charleston Railroad, he reminded his colleagues; it had not been true before that Congress had had to cite the section of the Constitution on which it relied.

In his peroration, Harlan replied to Bradley's comment that Negroes had been made "a special favorite of the law." The war amendments had been passed not to "favor" the Negro, he declared, but to include him as "part of the people for whose welfare and happiness government is ordained."

Today, it is the colored race which is denied, by corporations and individuals wielding public authority, rights fundamental in their freedom and citizenship. At some future time, it may be that some other race will fall under the ban of race discrimination. If the constitutional amendments be enforced, according to the intent with which, as I conceive, they were adopted, there cannot be in this republic, any class of human beings in practical subjection to another class. . . .

The *Civil Rights Cases* ruling did two things. First, it destroyed the delicate balance of federal guarantee, Negro protest, and private enlightenment which was producing a steadily widening area of peacefully integrated public facilities in the North and South during the 1870's and early 1880's. Second, it had an immediate and profound effect on national and state politics as they related to the Negro. By denying Congress power to protect the Negro's rights to equal treatment, the Supreme Court wiped the issue of civil rights from the Republican party's agenda of national responsibility. At the same time, those southern political leaders who saw anti-Negro politics as the most promising avenue to power could now rally the "poor whites" to the banner of segregation.

If the Supreme Court had stopped with the *Civil Rights Cases* of 1883, the situation of Negroes would have been bad but not impossible. Even in the South, there was no immediate imposition of segregation in public facilities. During the late 1880's, Negroes could be found sharing places with whites in many southern restaurants, streetcars, and theatres. But increasingly, Democratic and Populist politicians found the Negro an irresistible target. As Solicitor General Phillips had warned the Supreme Court, what had been tolerated as the "fact" of discrimination was now being translated into "doctrine": between 1887 and 1891, eight southern states passed laws requiring railroads to separate all white and Negro passengers. The Supreme Court upheld these laws in the 1896 case of *Plessy v. Ferguson.* Then in the Berea College case of 1906, it upheld laws forbidding private schools to educate Negro and white children together. Both decisions aroused Harlan's bitter dissent. In the next fifteen or twenty years, the chalk line of Jim Crow was drawn across virtually every area of public contact in the South.

Today, as this line is slowly and painfully being erased, we may do well to reflect on what might have been in the South if the Civil Rights Act of 1875 had been upheld, in whole or in part. Perhaps everything would have been the same. Perhaps forces at work between 1883 and 1940 were too powerful for a Supreme Court to hold in check. Perhaps "Sumner's law" was greatly premature. Yet it is difficult to believe that total, state-enforced segregation was inevitable in the South after the 1880's. If in these decades the Supreme Court had taken the same *laissez-faire* attitude toward race relations as it took toward economic affairs, voluntary integration would have survived as a countertradition to Jim Crow and might have made the transition of the 1950's less painful than it was. At the very least, one cannot help thinking that Harlan was a better sociologist than his colleagues and a better southerner than the "irreconcilables." American constitutional history has a richer ring to it because of the protest that John Marshall Harlan finally put down on paper from Roger Taney's inkwell in 1883.

C. Vann Woodward

Plessy v. Ferguson

The process of eroding the constitutional gains of Negroes begun by the Civil Rights Cases of 1883 was carried a long step forward in 1896 in the case of Plessy v. Ferguson. This decision, which froze school segregation on the nation for more than half a century, roused little notice at the time, despite Justice John Marshall Harlan's famous dissent, in which he reminded the nation that the Constitution was "color-blind."

The story of the case that led to the 1896 decision is told here by Professor C. Vann Woodward of Yale University. Woodward has done more than any other contemporary historian to throw light on the history of the South and of the Negro during the late nineteenth and early twentieth centuries. His Strange Career of Jim Crow called attention to the fact that complete segregation was a relatively late development in America, not a permanent part of southern civilization. His Reunion and Reaction, a history of the Compromise of 1877 ending Reconstruction, and his Origins of the New South, a general history of the period between 1877 and World War I, are standard works.

*I*n the spring of 1885, Charles Dudley Warner, Mark Twain's friend, neighbor, and his onetime collaborator from Hartford, Connecticut, visited the International Exposition held in New Orleans. He was astonished to find that "white and colored people mingled freely, talking and looking at what was of common interest," that Negroes "took their full share of the parade and the honors," and that the two races associated "in unconscious equality of privileges." During his visit he saw "a colored clergyman in his surplice seated in the chancel of the most important white Episcopal church in New Orleans, assisting in the service."

It was a common occurrence in the 1880's for foreign travellers and northern visitors to comment, sometimes with distaste and always with surprise, on the freedom of association between white and colored people in the South. Yankees in particular were unprepared for what they found and sometimes estimated that conditions below the Potomac were better than those above. There was discrimination, to be sure, and Negroes were often excluded from first-class public accommodations— as they were in the North. But that was done on the responsibility of private owners or managers and not by requirement of law. According to the Supreme Court's decision in the Civil Rights Cases of 1883 the federal law gave no protection from such private acts.

Where discrimination existed it was often erratic and inconsistent. On trains the usual practice was to exclude Negroes from first-class or "ladies' " cars but to permit them to mix with whites in second-class or "smoking" cars. In the old seaboard states of the South, however, Negroes were as free to ride first class as whites. In no state was segregation on trains complete, and in none was it enforced by law. The age of Jim Crow was still to come.

The first genuine Jim Crow law requiring railroads to carry Negroes in separate cars or behind partitions was adopted by Florida in 1887. Mississippi followed this example in 1888; Texas in 1889; Louisiana in 1890; Alabama, Arkansas, Georgia, and Tennessee in 1891; and Kentucky in 1892. The Carolinas and Virginia did not fall into line until the last three years of the century.

Negroes watched with despair while the legal foundations for the Jim Crow system were laid and the walls of segregation mounted around them. Their disenchantment with the hopes based on the Civil War amendments and the Reconstruction laws was nearly complete by 1890. The American commitment to equality, solemnly attested by three amendments to the Constitution and by elaborate civil rights acts, was virtually repudiated. The "compromise of 1877" between the Hayes Republicans and the southern conservatives had resulted in the withdrawal of federal troops from the South and the formal end of Reconstruction. What had started then as a retreat had within a decade turned into a rout. Northern radicals and liberals had abandoned the cause: the courts had rendered the Constitution helpless; the Republican party had forsaken the cause it had sponsored. A tide of racism was mounting in the country unopposed.

The colored community of New Orleans, with its strong infusion of

French and other nationalities, was in a strategic position to furnish leadership for the resistance against segregation. Many of these people had culture, education, and some wealth, as well as a heritage of several generations of freedom. Unlike the great majority of Negroes, they were city people with an established professional class and a high degree of literacy. By ancestry as well as by residence they were associated with Latin cultures at variance with Anglo-American ideas of race relations. Their forebears had lived under the Code Noir decreed for Louisiana by Louis XIV, and their city faced out upon Latin America.

When the Jim Crow car bill was introduced in the Louisiana legislature, New Orleans Negroes organized to fight it. Negroes were still voting in large numbers, and there were sixteen colored senators and representatives in the Louisiana General Assembly. On May 24, 1890, that body received "A Protest of the American Citizens' Equal Rights Association of Louisiana Against Class Legislation." An organization of colored people, the association protested that the pending bill was "unconstitutional, unamerican, unjust, dangerous and against sound public policy." It would, declared the protest, "be a free license to the evilly-disposed that they might with impunity insult, humiliate, and otherwise maltreat inoffensive persons, and especially women and children who should happen to have a dark skin."

On July 10, 1890, the Assembly passed the bill, the governor signed it, and it became law. Entitled "An Act to promote the comfort of passengers," the new law required railroads "to provide equal but separate accommodations for the white and colored races." Two members of the Equal Rights Association, L. A. Martinet, editor of the New Orleans *Crusader,* and R. L. Desdunes, placed heavy blame on the sixteen colored members of the Assembly for the passage of the bill. According to Martinet, "they were completely the masters of the situation." They had but to withhold their support for a bill desired by the powerful Louisiana Lottery Company until the Jim Crow bill was killed. "But in an evil moment," he added, "our Representatives turned their ears to listen to the golden siren," and "did so for a 'consideration.'"

Putting aside recriminations, the *Crusader* declared: "The Bill is now a law. The next thing is what are we going to do?" The editor spoke testily of boycotting the railroads, but concluded that "the next thing is . . . to begin to gather funds to test the constitutionality of this law. We'll make a case, a test case, and bring it before the Federal Courts." On September 1, 1891, a group of eighteen men of color formed a "Citizens' Committee to Test the Constitutionality of the Separate Car Law."

Money came in slowly at first, but by October 11, Martinet could write that the committee had already collected $1,500 and that more could be expected "after we have the case well started." Even before the money was collected, Martinet had opened a correspondence about the case with Albion Winegar Tourgée of Mayville, New York, and on October 10 the Citizens' Committee formally elected Tourgée "leading

*In 1832 a minstrel named "Daddy"
Rice introduced "Jim Crow" as a symbol
in a blackface act ("Weel a-bout and turn
a-bout/And . . . jump Jim Crow") based
on the antics of a slave of that name.*

counsel in the case, from beginning to end, with power to choose associates.''

This action called back into the stream of history a name prominent in the annals of Reconstruction. Albion Tourgée was in 1890 probably the most famous surviving carpetbagger. His fame was due not so much to his achievements as a carpetbagger in North Carolina, significant though they were, as to the six novels about his Reconstruction experiences that he had published since 1879. Born in Ohio, of French Huguenot descent, he had served as an officer in the Union Army, and moved to Greensboro, North Carolina, in 1865 to practice law. He soon became a leader of the Radical Republican party, took a prominent part in writing the Radical Constitution of North Carolina, and served as a judge of the superior court for six years with considerable distinction. He brought to the fight against segregation in Louisiana a combination of zeal and ability that the Citizens' Committee of New Orleans would have found it hard to duplicate. They had reason to write him, ''we know we have a friend in you & we know your ability is beyond question.'' He was informed that the committee's decision was made ''spontaneously, warmly, & gratefully.''

Tourgée's first suggestion was that the person chosen for defendant in the test case be ''nearly white,'' but that proposal raised some doubts. ''It would be quite difficult,'' explained Martinet, ''to have a lady *too* nearly white refused admission to a 'white' car.'' He pointed out that ''people of tolerably fair complexion, even if unmistakably colored, enjoy here a large degree of immunity from the accursed prejudice. . . . To make this case would require some tact.'' He would volunteer himself, ''but I am one of those whom a fair complexion favors. I go everywhere, in all public places, though well-known all over the city, & never is anything said to me. On the cars it would be

New Yorker Albion Tourgée—
carpetbagger, novelist, lawyer,
and self-appointed warrior
against racial discrimination.

the same thing. In fact, color prejudice, in this respect does not affect me. But, as I have said, we can try it, with another.''

Railroad officials proved surprisingly co-operative. The first one approached, however, confessed that his road ''did not enforce the law.'' It provided the Jim Crow car and posted the required sign, but told its conductors to molest no one who ignored instructions. Officers of two other roads ''said the law was a bad and mean one; they would like to get rid of it,'' and asked for time to consult counsel. ''They want to help us,'' said Martinet, ''but dread public opinion.'' The extra expense of separate cars was one reason for railroad opposition to the Jim Crow law.

It was finally agreed that a white passenger should object to the presence of a Negro in a ''white'' coach, that the conductor should direct the colored passenger to go to the Jim Crow car, and that he should refuse to go. ''The conductor will be instructed not to use force or molest,'' reported Martinet, ''& *our* white passenger will swear out the affidavit. This will give us our *habeas corpus* case, I hope.'' On the appointed day, February 24, 1892, Daniel F. Desdunes, a young colored man, bought a ticket for Mobile, boarded the Louisville & Nashville Railroad, and took a seat in the white coach.

All went according to plan. Desdunes was committed for trial to the Criminal District Court in New Orleans and released on bail. On March 21, James C. Walker, a local attorney associated with Tourgée in the case, filed a plea protesting that his client was not guilty and attacking the constitutionality of the Jim Crow law. He wrote Tourgée that he intended to go to trial as early as he could.

Between the lawyers there was not entire agreement on procedure. Walker favored the plea that the law was void because it attempted to regulate interstate commerce, over which the Supreme Court held that

Congress had exclusive jurisdiction. Tourgée was doubtful. "What we want," he wrote Walker, "is not a verdict of not guilty, nor a defect in this law but a decision whether such a law can be legally enacted and enforced in any state and we should get everything off the track and out of the way for such a decision." Walker confessed that "it's hard for me to give up my pet hobby that the law is void as a regulation of interstate commerce," and Tourgée admitted that he "may have spoken too lightly of the interstate commerce matter."

The discussion was ended abruptly and the whole approach altered before Desdunes' case came to trial by a decision of the Louisiana Supreme Court handed down on May 25. In this case, which was of entirely independent origin, the court reversed the ruling of a lower court and upheld the Pullman Company's plea that the Jim Crow law was unconstitutional in so far as it applied to interstate passengers.

Desdunes was an interstate passenger holding a ticket to Alabama, but the decision was a rather empty victory. The law still applied to intrastate passengers, and since all states adjacent to Louisiana had by this time adopted similar or identical Jim Crow laws, the exemption of interstate passengers was of no great importance to the Negroes of Louisiana, and it left the principle against which they contended unchallenged. On June 1, Martinet wired Tourgée on behalf of the committee, saying that "Walker wants new case wholly within state limits," and asking Tourgée's opinion. Tourgée wired his agreement.

One week later, on June 7, Homer Adolph Plessy bought a ticket in New Orleans, boarded the East Louisiana Railroad bound for Covington, a destination "wholly within the state limits," and took a seat in the white coach. Since Plessy later described himself as "seven-eighths Caucasian and one-eighth African blood," and swore that "the admixture of colored blood is not discernible," it may be assumed that the railroad had been told of the plan and had agreed to co-operate. When Plessy refused to comply with the conductor's request that he move to the Jim Crow car, he was arrested by Detective Christopher C. Cain "and quietly accompanied the officer." The New Orleans *Times-Democrat* remarked that "It is generally believed that Plessy intends testing the law before the courts."

In due course Homer Plessy's case became *Plessy v. Ferguson*. The latter name belonged to John H. Ferguson, Judge of Section A of the Criminal District Court for the Parish of New Orleans, who overruled the plea of Tourgée and Walker, the defendant's counsel, that the Jim Crow law was null and void because it was in conflict with the Constitution of the United States. Plessy then applied to the State Supreme Court for a writ of prohibition and certiorari and was given a hearing in November, 1892. The court recognized that neither the interstate commerce clause nor the question of equality of accommodations was involved and held that "the sole question" was whether a law requiring "separate but equal accommodations" violated the Fourteenth Amendment. Citing numerous decisions of lower federal courts to the effect that accommodations did not have to be identical to be equal, the court as expected upheld the law.

"We have been at pains to expound this statute," added the court, "because the dissatisfaction felt with it by a portion of the people seems to us so unreasonable that we can account for it only on the ground of some misconception."

Chief Justice Francis Redding Tillou Nicholls, heading the court that handed down this decision in 1892, had signed the Jim Crow act as governor when it was passed in 1890. Previously he had served as the "Redeemer" governor who took over Louisiana from the carpetbaggers in 1877 and inaugurated a brief regime of conservative paternalism. In those days Nicholls had denounced race bigotry, appointed Negroes to office, and attracted many of them to his party. L. A. Martinet wrote Tourgée that Nicholls in those years had been "fair & just to colored men" and had, in fact, "secured a degree of protection to the colored people not enjoyed under Republican Governors." But in November, 1892, the wave of Populist rebellion among the white farmers was reaching its crest in the South, and Judge Nicholls' change of course typified the concessions to racism that conservatives of his class made in their efforts to forestall or divert the rebellion. Nonetheless, at a further hearing Nicholls granted Plessy's petition for a writ of error that permitted him to seek redress before the Supreme Court of the United States.

The brief that Albion Tourgée submitted to the Supreme Court in behalf of Plessy breathed a spirit of equalitarianism that was more in tune with his carpetbagger days than with the prevailing spirit of the mid-nineties. At the very outset, he advanced an argument in behalf of his client that unconsciously illustrated the paradox that had from the start haunted the American attempt to reconcile strong color prejudice with deep equalitarian commitments.

Plessy, he contended, had been deprived of property without due process of law. The "property" in question was the "reputation of being white." It was "the most valuable sort of property, being the master-key that unlocks the golden door of opportunity." Intense race prejudice excluded any man suspected of having Negro blood "from the friendship and companionship of the white man," and therefore from the avenues to wealth, prestige, and opportunity. "Probably most white persons if given the choice," he held, "would prefer death to life in the United States as *colored persons.*"

Since Tourgée had proposed that a person who was "nearly white" be selected for the test case, it may be presumed that he did so with this argument in mind. But this was not a defense of the colored man against discrimination by whites, but a defense of the "nearly" white man against the penalties of color. The argument, whatever its merits, apparently did not impress the Court.

Tourgée went on to develop more relevant points. He emphasized especially the incompatibility of the segregation law with the spirit and intent of the Thirteenth and particularly the Fourteenth amendments. Segregation perpetuated distinctions "of a servile character, coincident with the institution of slavery." He held that "slavery was a caste, a legal condition of subjection to the dominant class, a bondage quite separable from the incident of ownership." He scorned the pretense of impartiality and equal protection advanced in the defense of the "separate but equal" doctrine.

"The object of such a law," he declared, "is simply to debase and distinguish against the inferior race. Its purpose has been properly interpreted by the general designation of 'Jim Crow Car' law. Its object is to separate the Negroes from the whites in public conveyances for the gratification and recognition of the sentiment of white superiority and white supremacy of right and power." He asked the members of the Court to imagine the tables turned and themselves ordered into a Jim Crow car. "What humiliation, what rage would then fill the judicial mind!" he exclaimed.

The clue to the true intent of the Louisiana statute was that it did not apply "to nurses attending the children of the other race." On this clause Tourgée shrewdly observed:

> The exemption of nurses shows that the real evil lies not in the color of the skin but in the relation the colored person sustains to the white. If he is a dependent it may be endured: if he is not, his presence is insufferable. Instead of being intended to promote the *general* comfort and moral well-being, this act is plainly and evidently intended to promote the happiness of one class by asserting its supremacy and the inferiority of another class. Justice is pictured blind and her daughter, the Law, ought at least to be color-blind.

Tourgée then asked the Court to look to the future. Should the separate-car law be upheld, he inquired, "what is to prevent the application of the same principle to other relations?" Was there any limit to such laws? "Why not require all colored people to walk on one side of the street and whites on the other? . . . One side of the street may be just as good as the other. . . . The question is not as to the *equality* of the privileges enjoyed, but *the right of the State to label one citizen as white and another as colored* in the common enjoyment of a public highway."

The Supreme Court did not get around to handing down a decision on *Plessy v. Ferguson* until 1896. In the years that intervened between the passage of the Louisiana segregation law in July, 1890, and the time of the eventual decision on its constitutionality in 1896, the retreat from the commitment to equality had quickened its pace in the South and met with additional acquiescence, encouragement, and approval in the North. Two states had already disfranchised the Negro, and several others, including Louisiana, were planning to take the same course. In 1892 Congress defeated the Lodge Bill, designed to extend federal protection to elections, and in 1894 it wiped from the federal statute books a mass of Reconstruction laws for the protection of equal rights. And then, on September 18, 1895, Booker T. Washington delivered a famous speech embodying the so-called "Atlanta Compromise," which was widely interpreted as an acceptance of subordinate status for the Negro by the foremost leader of the race.

Justice Henry B. Brown
delivered the majority opinion
in Plessy v. Ferguson.

On May 18, 1896, Justice Henry Billings Brown, a resident of Michigan but a native of Massachusetts, delivered the opinion of the Court in the case of *Plessy v. Ferguson.* His views upholding the defendant's case—that the "separate but equal" doctrine was constitutional—were in accord with those of all his brothers, with the possible exception of Justice David Josiah Brewer, who did not participate, and the certain exception of Justice John Marshall Harlan, who vigorously dissented in phrases that often echoed Tourgée's arguments. In approving, to all intents and purposes, the principle of segregation, Justice Brown followed not only the trend of the times, but a host of state judicial precedents, which he cited at length. That there were no federal judicial precedents to the contrary only added to the technical strength of his position. Just as telling, perhaps, was Brown's mention of the action of Congress in establishing segregated schools for the District of Columbia, an action endorsed by Radical Republicans who had supported the Fourteenth Amendment, and sustained in regular congressional appropriations ever since.

Similar laws, wrote Brown, were adopted by "the legislatures of many states, and have been generally, if not uniformly, sustained by the courts." The validity of such segregation laws, he maintained, depended on their "reasonableness." And in determining reasonableness, the legislature "is at liberty to act with reference to the established usages, customs, and traditions of the people, and with a view to the promotion of their comfort, and the preservation of the public peace and good order."

In addition to judicial precedent and accepted practice, Justice Brown ventured into the more uncertain fields of sociology and psychology for support of his opinion. He wrote:

> We consider the underlying fallacy of the plaintiff's argument to consist in the assumption that the enforced separation of the two races stamps the colored race with a badge of inferiority. If this be so, it is not by reason of anything found in the act, but solely because the colored race chooses to put that construction upon it. . . . The argument also assumes that social prejudices may be overcome by legislation, and that equal rights cannot be secured by the negro except by an enforced commingling of the two races. We cannot accept this proposition. . . . Legislation is powerless to eradicate racial instincts, or to abolish distinctions based upon physical differences, and the attempt to do so can only result in accentuating the difficulties of the present situation. If the civil and political rights of both races be equal, one cannot be inferior to the other civilly or politically. If one race be inferior to the other socially, the constitution of the United States cannot put them upon the same plane.

One of the most fascinating paradoxes in American jurisprudence is that the opinion of a native son of Massachusetts, Brown, should have bridged the gap betweeen the radical equalitarian commitment of 1868 and the reactionary repudiation of that commitment in 1896; and that Harlan, a southerner, should have bridged the greater gap between the repudiation of 1896 and the radical rededication to the equalitarian idealism of 1868 in 1954. For the dissenting opinion of Justice Harlan, embodying many of the arguments of Plessy's ex-carpetbagger counsel, foreshadowed the Court's eventual repudiation of the *Plessy v. Ferguson* decision and the doctrine of "separate but equal" more than half a century later.

The elder John Marshall Harlan is correctly described by Robert Cushman as "a Southern gentleman and a slave-holder, and at heart a conservative." A Kentuckian of the Whig persuasion, Harlan had opposed secession and fought in the Union Army, but at the same time he opposed both the emancipation of the slaves and the passage of civil rights laws to protect the rights of the freedmen. Shocked by Ku Klux excesses, he experienced a sudden conversion, renounced his former views, became a Republican in 1868, and was appointed to the Supreme Court by President Hayes in 1877.

After his conversion Harlan became one of the most outspoken champions of Negro rights of his time, and during his thirty-four years on the bench he lifted his voice repeatedly against denial of those rights by the dominant opinion of the Court. His famous dissent in the Civil Rights Cases of 1883 had denounced the "subtle and ingenious verbal criticism" by which "the substance and spirit of the recent amendments of the Constitution have been sacrificed." And in 1896 he was ready to strike another blow for his adopted cause.

Harlan held the Louisiana segregation law in clear conflict with both the Thirteenth and the Fourteenth amendments. The former "not only struck down the institution of slavery," but also "any burdens or disabilities that constitute badges of slavery or servitude,'' and segregation was just such a burden or badge. Moreover, the Fourteenth Amendment ''added greatly to the dignity and glory of American citizenship, and to the security of personal liberty,'' and segregation denied to Negroes the equal protection of both dignity and liberty. ''The arbitrary separation of citizens, on the basis of race, while they are on a public highway,'' he said, ''is a badge of servitude wholly inconsistent with the civil freedom and the equality before the law established by the constitution. It cannot be justified upon any legal grounds.''

Harlan was as scornful as Tourgée had been of the claim that the separate-car law did not discriminate against the Negro. ''Everyone knows,'' he declared, that its purpose was ''to exclude colored people from coaches occupied by or assigned to white persons.'' This was simply a poorly disguised means of asserting the supremacy of one class of citizens over another. The Justice continued:

> But in view of the constitution, in the eye of the law, there is in this country no superior, dominant, ruling class of citizens. There is no caste here. Our constitution is color-blind, and neither knows nor tolerates classes among citizens. In respect of civil rights, all citizens are equal before the law. The humblest is the peer of the most powerful. The law regards man as man, and takes no account of his surroundings, or of his color when his civil rights as guarantied by the supreme law of the land are involved. . . . We boast of the freedom enjoyed by our people above all other peoples. But it is difficult to reconcile that boast with a state of law which, practically, puts the brand of servitude and degradation upon a large class of our fellow citizens,—our equals before the law. The thin disguise of ''equal'' accommodations for passengers in railroad coaches will not mislead any one, nor atone for the wrong this day done.

''The present decision, it may well be apprehended,'' predicted Harlan, ''will not only stimulate aggressions, more or less brutal and irritating, upon the admitted rights of colored citizens, but will encourage the belief that it is possible, by means of state enactments, to defeat the beneficent purposes which the people of the United States had in view when they adopted the recent amendments of the constitution. . . .'' For if the state may so regulate the railroads, ''why may it not so regulate the use of the streets of its cities and towns as to compel white citizens to keep on one side of a street, and black citizens to keep on the other,'' or, for that matter, apply the same regulations to streetcars and other vehicles, or to courtroom, the jury box, the legislative hall, or to any other place of public assembly?

''In my opinion,'' the Kentuckian concluded, ''the judgment this day rendered will, in time, prove to be quite as pernicious as the decision made by this tribunal in the Dred Scott Case.''

But Harlan was without allies on the Court, and the country as a whole received the news of its momentous decision upholding the "separate but equal" doctrine in relative silence and apparent indifference. Thirteen years earlier the Civil Rights Cases had precipitated pages of news reports, hundreds of editorials, indignant rallies, congressional bills, a Senate report, and much general debate. In striking contrast, the *Plessy* decision was accorded only short, inconspicuous news reports and virtually no editorial comment outside the Negro press. A great change had taken place, and the Court evidently now gave voice to the dominant mood of the country. Justice Harlan had spoken for the forgotten convictions of a bygone era.

The racial aggressions he foresaw came in a flood after the decision of 1896. Even Harlan indicated by his opinion of 1899 in *Cummings v. Board of Education* that he saw nothing unconstitutional in segregated public schools. Virginia was the last state in the South to adopt the separate-car law, and she resisted it only until 1900. Up to that year this was the only law of the type adopted by a majority of the southern states. But on January 12, 1900, the editor of the Richmond *Times* was in full accord with the new spirit when he asserted: "It is necessary that this principle be applied in every relation of Southern life. God Almighty drew the color line and it cannot be obliterated. The negro must stay on his side of the line and the white man must stay on his side, and the sooner both races recognize this fact and accept it, the better it will be for both."

With a thoroughness approaching the incredible, the color line *was* drawn and the Jim Crow principle was applied even in those areas that Tourgée and Harlan had suggested a few years before as absurd extremes. In sustaining all these new laws, courts universally and confidently cited *Plessy v. Ferguson* as their authority. They continued to do so for more than half a century.

On April 4, 1950, Justice Robert H. Jackson wrote old friends in Jamestown, New York, of his surprise in running across the name of Albion W. Tourgée, once a resident of the nearby village of Mayville, in connection with segregation decisions then pending before the Supreme Court. "The *Plessy* case arose in Louisiana," he wrote, "and how Tourgée got into it I have not learned. In any event, I have gone to his old brief, filed here, and there is no argument made today that he would not make to the Court. He says, 'Justice is pictured blind and her daughter, the Law, ought at least to be color-blind.' Whether this was original with him, it has been gotten off a number of times since as original wit. Tourgée's brief was filed April 6, 1896 and now, just fifty-four years after, the question is again being argued whether his position will be adopted and what was a defeat for him in '96 be a post-mortem victory."

Plessy v. Ferguson remained the law of the land for fifty-eight years lacking one day, from May 18, 1896, to May 17, 1954, when the Supreme Court at last renounced it in the school segregation cases of *Brown* et al. *v. Board of Education of Topeka*, et al. In that decision could indeed be found, at long last, a vindication, "a post-mortem victory"—not only for the ex-carpetbagger Tourgée, but for the ex-slaveholder Harlan as well.

Walter Lord

Mississippi: The Past That Has Not Died

The situation that southern Negroes and their white supporters had to contend with after the Civil War, a situation that had much to do with the frustration of President Johnson's policies and which helped to produce the Supreme Court decisions in the Civil Rights Cases and in Plessy v. Ferguson, *is described in the following essay by Walter Lord.*

This is a case study—a very useful historical approach that seeks, by examining one part of a subject, to throw light on the whole. The main advantages of the case study method are that it concentrates on a more easily mastered body of materials and permits the use of details and examples that in a broader treatment would have to be sacrificed to avoid excessive length. The disadvantages lie chiefly in the inevitable loss of perspective, and in the not always correct assumption that the case chosen is entirely typical. The effect is like looking at a distant landscape through a telescope or at a piece of tissue under a microscope. Elements that would be lost to the "normal" view are brought sharply into focus, but the image of the total object is lost or distorted.

Lord's essay on Mississippi after the Civil War is a fine example of the intelligent use of the case study. His selection of Mississippi, home of the most intransigent foes of Negro equality but also a region where blacks exercised considerable power during Reconstruction, produces undoubtedly a heightening effect that is somewhat at variance with the whole truth, but it brings out very clearly all the problems of the postwar South and the "solutions" found for them in the late nineteenth century. Mr. Lord is best known for his "you are there" style of history, first developed in his popular book, A Night to Remember, *the story of the sinking of the liner* Titanic. *However, he makes relatively little use of that technique in this essay, thus demonstrating that he is a sound analytical historian as well as a graphic storyteller.*

*S*plinters flew in every direction as the northern troops hacked apart the chairs and tables of Edward McGehee, one of the wealthiest cotton planters in Wilkinson County, Mississippi. It was October 5, 1864, and Colonel E. D. Osband's men were simply acting on the philosophy expressed by General Sherman when he told a group of protesting Mississippians, "It is our duty to destroy, not build up; therefore do not look to us to help you."

Soon the work was done, the house in flames, and Edward McGehee left contemplating his only remaining possession—a gracefully carved grand piano. It was no comfort to Mr. McGehee, once the owner of hundreds of Negro slaves, that these deeds were done by a company of stern, efficient Negro soldiers.

Ruin upon ruin, the destruction continued for six more gruelling months of war. By the end, Mississippi seemed but a forest of chimneys. The whole town of Okolona could be bought for $5,000. There was not a fence left within miles of Corinth, not a clock running in Natchez. The capital, Jackson, was in ashes—the Confederate Hotel as complete a wreck as the cause it honored.

The first visitors from the North were stunned. Approaching old Charles Langworthy's home near Aberdeen, a man from Chicago recalled spending two pleasant weeks there back in 1855. Greeting the owner, the visitor quickly asked after Mr. Langworthy's five boys and two girls.

"Where is John, your oldest son?"

"Killed at Shiloh."

"Where is William?"

"Died of smallpox in the Army."

"And the other boys?"

"All were killed. . . ."

The Langworthy daughters came forward, dripping with mourning. Not only were their brothers gone; both also had lost their husbands in the service.

The incident was all too typical. Mississippi had sent 78,000 into the fight; only 28,000 came back. Whole companies were wiped out— the Vicksburg Cadets marched off 123 strong; only six returned. One legacy of this sacrifice was 10,000 orphans.

Nor were those who returned always able to play their full part. Surgery was not one of the happier aspects of the Civil War. Empty sleeves flapped everywhere. At a town meeting in Aberdeen a visitor noticed that one hundred of the three hundred men present had lost either an arm or a leg. It is not surprising that in the first year after the war Mississippi spent one fifth of its entire revenue for artificial limbs.

Painfully, the people of the state struggled to live again. Nearly everyone was wiped out. The greatest source of wealth—436,000 slaves worth over 218 million dollars—had vanished with Emancipation. The farm animals that meant so much to a rural people had been carried off—one out of every three mules gone. Most of the cotton was confiscated as Confederate property; any that escaped was mercilessly

*D. H. Euyett painted this water color of
the ruins of Jackson, Mississippi, in 1863,
shortly after Sherman took the state's capital.*

taxed by Washington. Land values crashed—on December 13, 1865,
alone, the Vicksburg *Herald* advertised forty-eight plantations for
sale or lease. After five years of war Mississippi tumbled from the
nation's fifth state in per capital wealth to the very bottom of the list.

"My children, I am a ruined man," Thomas Dabney told his
daughters one evening in November, 1866. In happier days Mr. Dabney had endorsed some notes. At the time there seemed little danger—
the risk was good and Dabney was the wealthy owner of Burleigh,
a fabulous plantation near the town of Raymond. But now times had
changed, and the sheriff was downstairs.

Ultimately, Burleigh was auctioned off, and Dabney managed to
buy it back only by consigning his cotton crop for years to come.
Meanwhile, the family had nothing—even the "loyal" Negro servants
had vanished. As the once pampered Dabney girls faced the novel
prospect of housework, it looked like a major victory for General
Sherman's perhaps apocryphal boast that he would force every southern woman to the washtub.

But this time the General had met his match. "He shall never
bring my daughters to the washtub," Dabney thundered. "I'll do
the washing myself!" And he did. Dabney was now seventy years
old, but for the next two years he scrubbed away, grimly satisfied that
here at least he was foiling the hated Yankee.

There were other consolations too, as the people of Mississippi
struggled to recover. There was relief that the war was over—whatever
their original feelings, most Mississippians were heartily sick of
destruction. There was also hope that the state could get back into
the Union rather painlessly; President Andrew Johnson had decided
to carry on Lincoln's lenient plans for restoration. Best of all, there

was the land. Mississippi's towns might lie in ruins, but her matchless asset was the soil itself. If only cotton could get going again . . .

But that was the problem. If the key to prosperity was cotton, the key to cotton had always been slaves—and there weren't any slaves any more. Over 380,000 freedmen aimlessly roamed the state, nearly all of them at loose ends, living where they chose, eating off the federal troops. The former owners had no influence. Most Negroes felt this was what freedom meant—no work. And there were plenty of people around the Union Army camps who advised them not to go back to their old masters. There were even rumors that Washington soon would be dividing up the plantations—forty acres and a mule for everyone.

Actually Washington was never more at cross-purposes. President Johnson suffered from being a states' rights Democrat from Tennessee, and as his prestige waned so did the chances for his lenient program. The Radical Republicans in Congress were winning control over national policy, but beyond a thirst for revenge, they had no clear-cut plans at all. As late as October, 1865, the Radical leader Thaddeus Stevens was asking his friend Charles Sumner if he knew of any good books on how the Russians freed their serfs.

The Negroes themselves could be of very little help in solving their problems. Over ninety-five per cent were illiterate. In the old days it had been illegal to teach the slaves to read or write, and now they were hopelessly ignorant. Few had any idea of citizenship, law, suffrage, or responsibility. Hauled before a court for stealing a bag of corn, one ex-slave happily camping on Jefferson Davis' plantation was asked if he wanted a jury trial.

"What's that?" was all he could say.

The whites felt cornered and helpless. For years they had done as they wanted with these people, and now the tables were turned. They were generally outnumbered, and in the rich cotton areas the margin seemed appalling—Bolivar County was eighty-seven per cent Negro; Issaquena County had 7,000 Negroes, only 600 whites.

But most frightening of all to white Mississippi residents were the Negro troops. When the United States Army's XVI Corps went home in August, 1865, 9,122 of the 10,193 Union soldiers still in the state were Negroes. Their mere presence seemed to invite the most hideous trouble. In Jackson, Major Barnes, commanding the 5th U.S. Colored Infantry, urged the local Negroes to defend their rights even to the "click of the pistol and at the point of the bayonet."

And incidents did happen. William Wilkinson was murdered at Lauderdale Springs by five of his former slaves for selling his plantation—they claimed it was rightfully theirs by Christmas. This sort of bloodshed was rare, but it was enough to set off the whites.

Terror bred fantastic rumors. The Natchez *Courier* warned that the county's Negroes were supposed to rise on New Year's Day. In Yazoo City the date was Christmas. The Brandon *Republican* set no date but reported, "They are evidently preparing something and it behooves us to be on the alert and prepare for the worst." There was nothing to any of these reports, but each rumor hardened the feelings of the whites.

They soon developed a fierce callousness toward the Negro, no matter how harmless he might be. On a quiet Sunday afternoon in Natchez an elderly freedman protested to a small white boy raiding his turnip patch. The boy shot him dead, and that was that. In Vicksburg the *Herald* complained that the town's children were hitting innocent bystanders when using their "nigger shooters."

Nor was it just the specter of Negro supremacy that aroused white Mississippians—Negro equality was just as bad. "God damn your soul, get off this boat!" raged the captain of the Memphis–Vicksburg packet on Christmas morning, 1865. The greeting was directed at a Negro couple who had dared ask for first-class passage. As their luggage was pitched ashore, the captain turned back to his work muttering, "They can't force their damned nigger equality on me."

Even when the principle of equality was acknowledged, the practice must have mystified the beneficiaries. "Take off your hat, you black scoundrel, or I'll cut your throat," a Mississippi state legislator yelled at his former slave; later he explained, "Sam, you've got just the same rights as a white man now, but not a bit better, and if you come into my room again without taking off your hat, I'll shoot you."

The case of Negro suffrage showed that even token equality was too much for whites to stomach. In 1865 President Johnson—already fearing for his generous Reconstruction program—urged William L. Sharkey, a former Mississippi Chief Justice whom the President had appointed as provisional governor, to make some gesture toward Negro enfranchisement. It might allay congressional doubts, for instance, if Mississippi gave the vote to those who could read the Constitution and write their names and who owned at least $250 in property—perhaps five per cent of the Negro population. Governor Sharkey couldn't have been less interested.

But the greatest anathema was Negro education. It was not so much a question of integrated schools; it was a question of any schools at all. At Oxford an angry band drove off the missionary assigned to the local freedmen's school, even though he was a southern man. At Okolona someone fired four shots at Dr. Lacy, the old Episcopal minister who was trying to teach the town's young Negroes.

"If any man from the North comes down here expecting to hold and maintain radical or abolitionist sentiments," warned the *Nation*'s correspondent, "let him expect to be shot down from *behind* the first time he leaves his home." Visitors were shocked by the sheer violence of the state's reaction. Lulled by a carefully cultivated tradition of moonlight and magnolias, they forgot that life in Mississippi had always been closer to the frontier than the Tidewater, indeed had been a true frontier as late as the 1830's.

Harder to explain was the stream of contradictory assurances that soon became so familiar. Negroes? "The southern people are really their best friends," a planter told author John T. Trowbridge in 1865. "We're the only ones that understand them," someone explained to Whitelaw Reid, another visitor. Just give the southerners time, begged the sympathetic editor of *DeBow's Review:* "If let alone to manage affairs in their own way, and with their intimate knowledge of Negro character, everything possible will be done in good time for the social, physical, and political advancement of the race."

There was also an odd element of fantasy in it all—almost as if the war hadn't been lost . . . in fact, as if Mississippi were dealing with Washington as an equal. When Whitelaw Reid doubted that Congress would seat the ex-Confederates who swept Mississippi's first postwar election of 1865, his listeners scoffed at the very thought. Of course they would be seated—"because of the tremendous pressure we can bring to bear." The Natchez *Courier* agreed: "The State of Mississippi still stands in all its grand individuality. Massachusetts has no more right to dictate to us now about our internal laws than she had five years ago—nor has she half the power. . . ."

Occasionally a voice of doubt was raised, but the moderates seemed, in the *Nation's* words, "somewhat bewildered . . . bullied . . . humbugged." Usually they could be quickly silenced. When one Mississippi planter suggested in August, 1865, that the Negroes might be trained to use their rights, his companion shot back the clincher that was also getting familiar: "They'll be wanting to marry your daughters next."

And this was the heart of the matter. To the ordinary white Mississippian, political equality automatically led to social equality, which in turn automatically led to race-mixing. It was inevitable—and unthinkable. To a people brought up to believe that Negroes were genetically inferior—after all, that was why they were slaves—the mere hint of "mongrelization" was appalling. And all the more so in view of the homage paid the white southern woman. It was she who had sacrificed so much, whose purity, in fact, carried on the whole system. She was everything.

Of course there were other factors too. Cotton planters didn't want their field hands getting out of line; the red-neck farmers worried about Negroes taking their bread. Yet these were areas where something might be worked out; but there could be no compromise— not an inch—on anything that might open the door to race-mixing. Emancipation made absolutely no difference. "A monkey with his tail off," explained the Natchez *Courier*, "is a monkey still."

It didn't matter that the position was illogical. Northerners might snigger that if the Negro was so backward, why might he advance so far? Other visitors might wonder about the high percentage of Negroes with white blood—surely race-mixing must have once been all right with somebody. None of this made any difference. So in November, 1865, it was easy for the Jackson *Daily News* to lecture the state's first postwar government: "We must keep the ex-slave in a position of inferiority. We must pass such laws as will make him *feel* his inferiority."

Mississippi's new government understood. Under President Johnson's generous terms the state had freed the slaves but done little else.

A new constitution had been drafted—but it seemed pretty much along prewar lines. A new state legislature had been chosen—but it featured many old leaders. A new governor had been elected—but he was Benjamin G. Humphreys, an outstanding Confederate general who hadn't even been pardoned yet. On November 20, 1865, Governor Humphreys set the tone of things in a message to the legislature: "Under the pressure of federal bayonets, urged on by the misdirected sympathies of the world, the people of Mississippi have abolished the institution of slavery. The Negro is free, whether we like it or not; we must realize that fact now and forever. To be free, however, does not make him a citizen, or entitle him to social or political equality with the white man."

A series of laws, later known as the Black Code, swiftly put the Negro in his place. He was allowed to marry, own property, sue and be sued, even testify if he was a party—but that was all. No Negro could vote, keep firearms, rent a home outside town, ride in a first-class railroad car with whites, or "make insulting gestures." Any unemployed Negro over eighteen was declared a vagrant, fined $50, and turned over to whoever paid up. Any unsupported Negro under eighteen could be apprenticed out. If he tried to run away, "the master or mistress" (the law easily slipped back into ante-bellum language) had the right to pursue and recapture.

Reaction was not long in coming. "We tell the white men of Mississippi," exploded the Chicago *Tribune* on December 1, "that the men of the North will convert the state of Mississippi into a frog pond before they will allow any such laws to disgrace one foot of soil in which the bones of our soldiers sleep and over which the flag of freedom waves."

Northern fury grew as other southern states followed Mississippi's lead with Black Codes of their own. Finally, in 1867 Congress threw out President Johnson's Reconstruction program and launched a far harsher one of its own. The Confederate-dominated state governments were scrapped, and the South was divided into five military districts, each under martial law. Negroes were given the vote, new constitutional conventions held. No state could get back into the Union until Congress approved its new government . . . until it granted Negro suffrage . . . until it ratified the Fourteenth Amendment, guaranteeing the people of every state (among other things) "equal protection of the laws."

Mississippi eventually knuckled under, but only after three more years of rear-guard defiance. By 1870, however, the state was "reconstructed," and by 1873 the local Radical Republicans were riding high. The electorate was fifty-seven per cent Negro—mostly illiterate and easily controlled. The legislature boasted sixty-four Negroes and twenty-four carpetbaggers. The Speaker of the House, the lieutenant governor, the superintendent of education were all Negroes. The new Reconstruction governor himself was an ex-Union officer—General Adelbert Ames, a remote, tactless New Englander who stayed away from Mississippi for protracted periods.

It would later be argued that this state government turned in an impressive performance, and indeed there were many bright spots. The Negro legislators included at least fifteen well-educated, conscientious clergymen. The carpetbaggers were often solid middle westerners who had come not to loot but to farm. The Negro troops had all been withdrawn, and only a token force of federals remained—for instance, 59 at Natchez, 129 at Vicksburg, about 700 men altogether. The state debt never got out of hand. There was little stealing —the only major case involved the carpetbag treasurer of the state hospital in Natchez who took $7,251.81. And all the while important things were being accomplished—war-damaged bridges repaired, northern innovations like free hospitals established, courts expanded to take care of freedmen, and a public-school system launched.

All this was done, but it would take the perspective of a century to appreciate it. At the time the white people of Mississippi felt only bitterness. They didn't care if most of the troops were gone; one blue uniform was too many. They didn't know about worthy projects; they only knew taxes on land had soared 1,300 per cent in five years. They didn't notice that most key officials were honest; in their frayed poverty, they only saw any sign of waste: why, the state contingency fund even paid for Governor Ames' bedpan. And perhaps most important, they knew little about the conscientious work of many Negroes in top-level positions; they only knew their own county, where they were in daily contact, and that was often appalling.

Negro sheriffs, clerks, and magistrates thrashed about in confusion and ignorance. In Warren County the sheriff couldn't write a simple return. In Issaquena County not one member of the board of supervisors—responsible for handling the county's business—could read a contract. There wasn't a justice of the peace in Madison County who could write a summons.

Petty corruption spread everywhere, often induced by light-fingered whites. Hinds County ran up a bigger printing bill in nine months than the whole state paid in 1866–67. The Wilkinson County board of supervisors shelled out $1,500 for three bridges—containing four, eight, and twenty planks respectively. Vicksburg's Republican candidate for mayor staggered under twenty-three indictments. Nor were the dethroned Democrats entirely innocent. An officer in Vicksburg's clean-government group was caught charging the city $500 to move a safe from the river to the courthouse.

Little matter—it was all the same to most of white Mississippi. Reconstruction was to blame, and that meant the Negroes. Free voting and the shadow of federal bayonets might make them invulnerable to ordinary political tactics, but there were other ways. . . .

The shifting seasons merged into one long blur of desperate violence. There was the sunny October morning when Thomas Dabney's daughters heard a hail of shots and watched a Negro's riderless horse race across the Burleigh lawn . . . the starlit winter night in Monroe County when carpetbagger A. P. Huggins knelt on a lonely road as the K.K.K. delivered seventy-five lashes with a stirrup strap . . . the

Entitled Reconstruction, *or "A White Man's Government," this 1868 Currier and Ives cartoon summed up Northern liberals' simplistic view of the Southern dilemma.*

bright March day when the Meridian courthouse erupted in rifle fire and the Radical judge fell dead on his bench. . . .

"Life is not sacred as it is in the North," wrote correspondent Charles Nordhoff:

> Everybody goes armed, and every trifling dispute is ended with the pistol. The respectable people of the State do not discourage the practice of carrying arms as they should, they are astonishingly tolerant of acts which would arouse a Northern community to the utmost, and I believe that to this may be ascribed all that is bad in Mississippi—to an almost total lack of a right opinion; a willingness to see men take the law into their own hands; and, what is still worse, to let them openly defy the laws, without losing, apparently, the respect of the community.

In this atmosphere there was no hope for a man with the "wrong" attitude, whatever his credentials. At Aberdeen the town teacher, Dr. Ebart, had an impeccable southern background, but he favored Negro schools, and that was the end of his job. The pressure was too much. The white Republicans soon melted away. Many crossed over to the Democratic fold; others fled north; only a few stood by the helpless mass of Negroes. The moderates, who might have been a third force, seemed mesmerized by the fury of the blast. "The quiet, sensible and orderly people," mused Charles Nordhoff, "seem to have almost entirely resigned the power and supremacy which belong to them."

This was the picture by 1875, when, with state and local elections scheduled, the Democrats decided that the time had come formally to recapture control. A skillfully conceived strategy—to be known as the Mississippi Plan and later to be copied throughout the South—took care of the two chief obstacles: the Negro majority and federal bayonets.

"We are determined to have an honest election if we have to stuff the ballot box to get it," shouted one Democratic leader, and this was only a small part of the plan. Newspaper notices warned Negroes that they would be thrown off their land if they voted the Republican ticket. Democratic "rifle clubs," usually sporting conspicuous red shirts, drilled endlessly near Negro sections. In Hinds, Lowndes, and other counties, cannon appeared and "salutes" were fired near Republican rallies.

The Negro voters got the message, but the Democrats still faced the danger of federal intervention. The trick here was not to let things go too far, and the Democratic campaign chairman, General J. Z. George, proved a past master at the art of intimidation by indirection. Still, it was a delicate tightrope. The embattled Governor Ames was calling Washington for help, and the slightest slip might bring in the federals. . . .

A crash of rifle fire scattered the 1,200 Negroes swarming around the Republican barbecue at the little town of Clinton on September 4, 1875. Here and there men fell—not all of them black. Two young white hecklers were cut down by return fire as they scurried from the scene. It seemed that Negroes too could feel strongly about elections. Wholesale shooting began, and for days undeclared war raged around Clinton. On September 8 Governor Ames appealed to General Grant for troops to restore peace and supervise the coming elections. The whole future of Mississippi hung in the balance. A nod from the President, and all of General George's strategy would fall apart.

Grant looked the other way. "The whole public are tired out with these annual autumnal outbreaks in the South," the President sighed, "and the great majority are ready now to condemn any interference on the part of the government." Word was passed to Governor Ames through Attorney General Pierrepont to try harder, to exhaust his own resources before calling on Washington for aid.

It was really not Grant's fault. The country was indeed tired of Reconstruction, and the President was but echoing the national mood. Most people had never been for Negro civil rights in the first place. Freedom, yes; but that didn't necessarily mean all the privileges of citizenship. At the end of the war only six northern states let Negroes vote, and in 1867 the District of Columbia rejected Negro suffrage 7,337 to 36. Nor did anyone feel the Fourteenth Amendment had much to do with education. In fact, stalwart Union states like New York, Pennsylvania, and Ohio all had segregated schools. Congress itself set up a segregated school system in Washington only weeks after approving the Fourteenth Amendment.

These feelings were rising to the surface, now that the initial exhilaration of winning the war was over. Other forces were at work too : the implacable Thaddeus Stevens had died . . . anti-Grant liberals were happy to attack everything about the Administration, including Reconstruction . . . northern investors were anxious to resume "normal" relations with the South . . . the nation's eyes were turning to fresh, exciting visions in the Far West.

The new mood showed itself in various ways. Congress had indeed passed the Civil Rights Act of 1875 (protecting the Negro in public places like trains and restaurants), but it was the dying gasp of a lame-duck session. Besides, it was a shaky victory. A school integration provision had been defeated; also a "force bill" giving the measure teeth. Even more significant, the Supreme Court was now nibbling away at the earlier Reconstruction Acts. And in the background came a steady chorus from the press, "Let the South solve its own problems." The President understood and gave the nation its way.

The Silver Cornet Band led the Jackson victory parade to General George's house on election night, November 2, 1875. The returns were rolling in, and huge Democratic majorities were piling up: Morton, 233 to 17 . . . Deasonville, 181 to 0 . . . Yazoo County, 4,052 to 7. In the end the Democrats carried sixty-two of the state's seventy-four counties. In the time-honored fashion of all political leaders everywhere, General George gave full credit to the rank and file "for the redemption of our common mother, Mississippi." Governor Ames was a practical man. Exactly 146 days later, in exchange for the withdrawal by Democrats of a set of impeachment charges, he resigned his office, packed his bags, and left the state forever. In the word of the times, Mississippi had been "redeemed."

To Mississippi's Negroes redemption meant a loss of power but not the trappings. The men now running the state came from the old cotton-planting gentry, who got along well with their former slaves. Some of these leaders, like Lucius Quintus Cincinnatus Lamar, were far more interested in corporation law than in eight-cent cotton, but they still had a tradition of *noblesse oblige* and gave the Negroes considerable leeway—as long as they were "good."

This arrangement was further cemented by a sort of gentlemen's agreement with Washington after the presidential election of 1876. The South accepted Hayes' dubious claims to the Presidency, and in return the Republicans adopted Grant's hands-off attitude as the new administration line. The last troops were withdrawn, and the old Confederacy was left free to work out its own problems. But at the same time it was always understood that the Negroes would retain at least their surface gains. The redemption leaders happily agreed. In fact, the Jackson *Clarion* had accepted the obligation on the very morning after the great 1875 victory. Observing that Negroes had helped make the triumph possible, the paper declared that the state must now "carry out in good faith the pledges of equal and even justice to them and theirs in which they placed their confidence."

So the Negroes continued to vote and often held minor offices. Nor were they barred from most public places. The two races drank at the same bars and ate at the same restaurants, though at separate tables. In Jackson, Angelo's Hall echoed with Negro laughter one week, white the next. And when life was done, both races could rest together in Greenwood Cemetery.

With the Negro's role settled, Mississippi's redemption government launched a massive economy wave. The conservative landowning leaders had been hit hardest by the staggering taxes of Reconstruction, and now they were determined to end all that. State expenditures were slashed from $1,430,000 in 1875 to $518,000 in 1876. Teachers' salaries alone fell from $55.47 a month in 1875 to $29.19 the following year.

In a way it was all justifiable. Mississippi remained wretchedly poor. In 1877 the state's per capita wealth was only $286, compared to a $1,086 average in the northern states. Even as late as 1890 there were only forty-six banks in the state, with combined cash assets of but $635,000. The war had wiped out Mississippi, and there just seemed no way to get going again. In those days the idea of federal recovery aid was unknown—between 1865 and 1875 Washington spent 21 million dollars on public works in Massachusetts and New York, only $185,000 in Mississippi and Arkansas.

Still, whatever the justification, Mississippi paid a high price for her sweeping economies. Letting roads disintegrate meant even more stagnant communities. Appropriating merely $5,392 a year for health meant the end of nearly all services. Spending only $2 a head on schoolchildren (against $20 in Massachusetts) meant mounting illiteracy and a new generation utterly untrained to advance in life.

Nor was cost-cutting a viable solution to the state's problems. Despite all the economies, conditions continued to slide. From the mid-seventies to the early nineties cotton sagged from 11 cents to 5.8 cents a pound. Field hands' pay fell from $15 to $12 a month . . . when there was any cash at all. More often there was the share-cropping system, which saw little money ever change hands. Yet the plantation owners themselves were certainly not getting rich. Under a vicious system of liens, they mortgaged their future crops for months or even years ahead to get the tools and supplies needed for tomorrow.

Everything seemed to conspire against Mississippi. While crop prices fell, the farmer's costs soared. Freight rates rigged in the East increased his shipping charges. Combinations like the jute-bagging trust raised the cost of his supplies. High tariffs added more to his burden. Creditors insisted that he plant only cotton; shackled to a one-crop system, his land quickly eroded. Even nature joined the conspiracy—a flood, freeze, or drought usually came along to spoil the few otherwise good years. Whether holding out in some paint-peeled mansion or hanging on in the squalor of a dog-trot cabin, most Mississippians knew only the bitterest poverty.

The state's landed leaders proved utterly unable to cope with the situation. They came from the lowlands—the cotton belt that had run everything in prewar days. They owed their authority to an odd combination of ante-bellum nostalgia and redemption heroics—certainly not new ideas. They easily took to the laissez-faire views of eastern business—tax concessions, hard money, railroad grabs like the Texas-Pacific. They shied away from new panaceas like government regulation and flexible currency. Their most lustrous figure, L. Q. C. Lamar, shuddered at the Greenback movement's "boundless, bottomless, and brainless schemes."

Such men neither understood nor even liked the up-country farmers who scratched away at the red clay hills to the east. Desperately these red-necks—along with a growing number of poor white tenants all over the state—turned to new and more radical sources of hope: the Farmers' Alliance and later the Populists.

And all the while they smouldered with growing hate—hatred for the Yankee banks and railroads that squeezed them so tightly . . . hatred for the Black Belt leaders who seemed to care so little . . . and, above all, hatred for the Negroes to whose level they were sinking so fast.

Jim Crow laws began to sprout . . . the first in twenty years. In 1888 Mississippi became the first state to have segregated waiting rooms. In 1890 Jackson extended the racial barrier beyond death by establishing a separate cemetery for Negroes. The rules grew ever more strict as the margin narrowed between white and colored living standards. If race was all the whites might have left, that was all the more reason to guard this sacred heritage. Woe to the Negro who flirted with crossing the line.

Lynchings multiplied at a fearful rate—nobody knows how many, for the press handled the incidents as casually as the weather. "Four Negroes were lynched at Grenada last week," remarked the Raymond *Gazette* on July 18, 1885, "also one at Oxford." That was the whole item.

With Mississippi in this mood, it certainly didn't help matters when the big landowners met the red-neck challenge with thousands of Negro votes from the black counties they controlled. A weird political duel, utterly lacking in logic or principle, developed as the eighties wore on. The old conservative leaders represented traditional white supremacy, yet relied on Negro votes to hold their power. The mass of poor whites had much in common with the Negro, yet fought him as a mortal enemy. The remaining Republicans in the state stood for the Negro's freedom, yet deserted him as a hopeless handicap. No wonder the Negro himself soon lost interest. Untrained in politics anyhow, he found Mississippi's brand far too confusing. Usually he just sold his vote to the highest bidder or was thrust aside while someone else cast it for him.

The situation proved too sordid to last. In 1890 a special convention assembled in Jackson to draw up a new state constitution. The solution, most people felt, was to take away the Negro's vote. Even the Black Belt leaders now agreed—the advantage Negro suffrage gave them was outweighed by the cost (usually a dollar a vote) and the ever-haunting possibility that the Negroes might some day decide to go back into politics for themselves. It was, of course, a little odd to keep Negroes from casting votes in order to stop white people from stealing them, but nobody worried too much about that. A far greater problem was how to do it. The Fifteenth Amendment specifically stated that the right to vote should not be abridged on account of color.

Clearly, the trick was to frame a set of qualifications that would technically apply to everybody but actually eliminate the Negro without touching the white. A poll tax alone was not enough—it might discourage more whites than Negroes. Nor would a literacy test do— there were thousands of good white voters who couldn't even write their names. In the end the convention came up with a series of devices which were, in the words of one delegate, "a monument to the resourcefulness of the human mind."

Most important were the new qualifications: all voters had to be able to read any section of the state constitution, or understand it when read to him, or give it a reasonable interpretation. This, of course, dumped the final decision into the lap of the examining registrar . . . who would know exactly what to do.

Reregistration began immediately. In 1885 over 1,600 Negroes had qualified in Panola County; by 1896 the figure stood at 114. The same thing happened everywhere: in Coahoma County only four per cent of its once-eligible Negroes now could vote; in De Soto, only five per cent; in Tunica, two per cent. Loyal Mississippians held their breath— how would the nation react to this giant wink at the Fifteenth Amendment?

They need not have worried. The White House was in friendly hands—first under the conservative Grover Cleveland, later under the benign William McKinley. Congress was no threat either—in 1894 it repealed most of the remaining civil rights laws. The western Populists were bitter at the Negroes for sticking by their old masters. The southern progressives felt that white solidarity would weld all classes more closely together. Eastern liberals recalled the reactionary leaders who had engineered Reconstruction—and found it easy to sympathize with Mississippi. And above all, there was the American mood—a moment of bursting national pride and pious imperialism. As the liberal *Atlantic Monthly* noted with gentle irony: "If the stronger and cleverer race is free to impose its will upon the 'new-caught sullen peoples' on the other side of the globe, why not in South Carolina and Mississippi?"

The Supreme Court added its blessing in 1898. In *Williams v. Mississippi* the justices solemnly declared there was no reason to suppose that the state's new voting qualifications were aimed especially at Negroes. . . .

As the new century dawned, it was clear that the Negro—stripped of his gains, abandoned by the courts, and rejected by the country— was in a highly vulnerable position. And for the Negro in Mississippi —the state which had invented the Black Code in 1865, pioneered the "Mississippi Plan" in 1875, and led the way to disenfranchisement in 1890—the future looked bleak indeed. . . .

Part
Two

IMPACT
OF
INDUSTRIALISM

Robert L. Heilbroner

Andrew Carnegie, Captain of Industry

The driving force behind late nineteenth-century economic growth, social change, and the thousand new developments that heralded the birth of modern America was the rapid expansion of industry. Industrialization made the United States the richest nation in the world and placed some of its citizens among the world's richest men. At one and the same time it fostered the belief that individuals could rise from rags to riches in a generation and the fear that great extremes between the wealthy and the poor would destroy opportunity, even democracy. It lent credence to the idea that Americans were gross materialists, but it also produced a philanthropic outpouring of unprecedented dimensions.

The career of Andrew Carnegie reflects all these tendencies. Carnegie came to America as a poor immigrant boy and became the master of the American steel industry. He was a "robber baron" in the eyes of his critics, an "industrial statesman" in his own eyes and in those of many of his contemporaries. He accumulated material goods on an immense scale but dispensed hundreds of millions of dollars to a variety of worthy causes. He was even an intellectual of sorts, writing books and articles about the character of American society, the industrial system, and the duties and obligations of rich men like himself.

Professor Robert L. Heilbroner, an economist at the New School for Social Research, the author of this essay on Carnegie, has written extensively in the field of economic history and thought. In works such as The Worldly Philosophers, The Great Ascent, *and* The Limits of American Capitalism *he has repeatedly demonstrated that it is possible to write history that is at once popular and scholarly even when dealing with highly technical material.*

*T*oward the end of his long life, at the close of World War I, Andrew Carnegie was already something of a national legend. His meteoric rise, the scandals and successes of his industrial generalship—all this was blurred into nostalgic memory. What was left was a small, rather feeble man with a white beard and pale, penetrating eyes, who could occasionally be seen puttering around his mansion on upper Fifth Avenue, a benevolent old gentleman who still rated an annual birthday interview but was even then a venerable relic of a fast-disappearing era. Carnegie himself looked back on his career with a certain savored incredulity. "How much did you say I had given away, Poynton?" he would inquire of his private secretary; "$324,657,399" was the answer. "Good Heaven!" Carnegie would exclaim. "Where did I ever get all that money?"

Where he *had* got all that money was indeed a legendary story, for even in an age known for its acquisitive triumphs, Carnegie's touch had been an extraordinary one. He had begun, in true Horatio Alger fashion, at the bottom; he had ended, in a manner that put the wildest of Alger's novels to shame, at the very pinnacle of success. At the close of his great deal with J. P. Morgan in 1901, when the Carnegie steel empire was sold to form the core of the new United States Steel Company, the banker had extended his hand and delivered the ultimate encomium of the times: "Mr. Carnegie," he said, "I want to congratulate you on being the richest man in the world."

It was certainly as "the richest man in the world" that Carnegie attracted the attention of his contemporaries. Yet this is hardly why we look back on him with interest today. As an enormous money-maker Carnegie was a flashy, but hardly a profound, hero of the times; and the attitudes of Earnestness and Self-Assurance, so engaging in the young immigrant, become irritating when they are congealed in the millionaire. But what lifts Carnegie's life above the rut of a one-dimensional success story is an aspect of which his contemporaries were relatively unaware.

Going through his papers after his death, Carnegie's executors came across a memorandum that he had written to himself fifty years before, carefully preserved in a little yellow box of keepsakes and mementos. It brings us back to December, 1868, when Carnegie, a young man flushed with the first taste of great success, retired to his suite in the opulent Hotel St. Nicholas in New York, to tot up his profits for the year. It had been a tremendous year and the calculation must have been extremely pleasurable. Yet this is what he wrote as he reflected on the figures:

> Thirty-three and an income of $50,000 per annum! By this time two years I can so arrange all my business as to secure at least $50,000 per annum. Beyond this never earn—make no effort to increase fortune, but spend the surplus each year for benevolent purposes. Cast aside business forever, except for others.
>
> Settle in Oxford and get a thorough education, making the

acquaintance of literary men—this will take three years of active work—pay especial attention to speaking in public. Settle then in London and purchase a controlling interest in some newspaper or live review and give the general management of it attention, taking part in public matters, especially those connected with education and improvement of the poorer classes.

Man must have an idol—the amassing of wealth is one of the worst species of idolatry—no idol more debasing than the worship of money. Whatever I engage in I must push inordinately; therefore should I be careful to choose that life which will be the most elevating in its character. To continue much longer overwhelmed by business cares and with most of my thoughts wholly upon the way to make more money in the shortest time, must degrade me beyond hope of permanent recovery. I will resign business at thirty-five, but during the ensuing two years I wish to spend the afternoons in receiving instruction and in reading systematically.

It is a document which in more ways than one is Carnegie to the very life: brash, incredibly self-confident, chockablock with self-conscious virtue—and more than a little hypocritical. For the program so nobly outlined went largely unrealized. Instead of retiring in two years, Carnegie went on for thirty-three more; even then it was with considerable difficulty that he was persuaded to quit. Far from shunning further money-making, he proceeded to roll up his fortune with an uninhibited drive that led one unfriendly biographer to characterize him as "the greediest little gentleman ever created." Certainly he was one of the most aggressive profit seekers of his time. Typically, when an associate jubilantly cabled: "No. 8 furnace broke all records today," Carnegie coldly replied, "What were the other furnaces doing?"

It is this contrast between his hopes and his performance that makes Carnegie interesting. For when we review his life, what we see is more than the career of another nineteenth-century acquisitor. We see the unequal struggle between a man who loved money—loved making it, having it, spending it—and a man who, at bottom, was ashamed of himself for his acquisitive desires. All during his lifetime, the money-maker seemed to win. But what lifts Carnegie's story out of the ordinary is that the other Carnegie ultimately triumphed. At his death public speculation placed the size of his estate at about five hundred million dollars. In fact it came to $22,881,575. Carnegie *had* become the richest man in the world—but something had also driven him to give away ninety per cent of his wealth.

Actually, his contemporaries knew of Carnegie's inquietude about money. In 1889, before he was world-famous, he had written an article for the *North American Review* entitled "The Gospel of Wealth"—an article that contained the startling phrase: "The man who dies

Andrew Carnegie,
the Steelmaster.

thus rich dies disgraced.'' It was hardly surprising, however, if the
world took these sentiments at a liberal discount: homiletic millionaires who preached the virtues of austerity were no novelty; Carnegie
himself, returning in 1879 from a trip to the miseries of India, had
been able to write with perfect sincerity, ''How very little the millionaire has beyond the peasant, and how very often his additions tend
not to happiness but to misery.''

What the world may well have underestimated, however, was a
concern more deeply rooted than these pieties revealed. For, unlike
so many of his self-made peers, who also rose from poverty, Carnegie
was the product of a *radical* environment. The village of Dunfermline,
Scotland, when he was born there in 1835, was renowned as a center
of revolutionary ferment, and Carnegie's family was itself caught
up in the radical movement of the times. His father was a regular
speaker at the Chartist rallies, which were an almost daily occurrence
in Dunfermline in the 1840's, and his uncle was an impassioned
orator for the rights of the working class to vote and strike. All this
made an indelible impression on Carnegie's childhood.

''I remember as if it were yesterday,'' he wrote seventy years later, "being awakened during the night by a tap at the back window by men who had come to inform my parents that my uncle, Bailie Morrison, had been thrown in jail because he dared to hold a meeting which had been forbidden . . . It is not to be wondered at that, nursed amid such surroundings, I developed into a violent young Republican whose motto was 'death to privilege.' "

From another uncle, George Lauder, Carnegie absorbed a second passion that was also to reveal itself in his later career. This was his love of poetry, first that of the poet Burns, with its overtones of romantic egalitarianism, and then later, of Shakespeare. Immense quantities of both were not only committed to memory, but made into an integral—indeed, sometimes an embarrassingly evident—part of his life: on first visiting the Doge's palace in Venice he thrust a companion in the ducal throne and held him pinioned there while he orated the appropriate speeches from *Othello*. Once, seeing Vanderbilt walking on Fifth Avenue, Carnegie smugly remarked, "I would not exchange his millions for my knowledge of Shakespeare."

But it was more than just a love of poetry that remained with Carnegie. Virtually alone among his fellow acquisitors, he was driven by a genuine respect for the power of thought to seek answers for questions that never even occurred to them. Later, when he "discovered" Herbert Spencer, the English sociologist, Carnegie wrote to him, addressing him as "Master," and it was as "Master" that Spencer remained, even after Carnegie's lavishness had left Spencer very much in his debt.

But Carnegie's early life was shaped by currents more material than intellectual. The grinding process of industrial change had begun slowly but ineluctably to undermine the cottage weaving that was the traditional means of employent in Dunfermline. The Industrial Revolution, in the shape of new steam mills, was forcing out the hand weavers, and one by one the looms which constituted the entire capital of the Carnegie family had to be sold. Carnegie never forgot the shock of his father returning home to tell him, in despair, "Andra, I can get nae mair work."

A family council of war was held, and it was decided that there was only one possible course—they must try their luck in America, to which two sisters of Carnegie's mother, Margaret, had already emigrated. With the aid of a few friends the money for the crossing was scraped together, and at thirteen Andrew found himself transported to the only country in which his career would have been possible.

It hardly got off to an auspicious start, however. The family made their way to Allegheny, Pennsylvania, a raw and bustling town where Carnegie's father again sought work as an independent weaver. But it was as hopeless to compete against the great mills in America as in Scotland, and soon father and son were forced to seek work in the local cotton mills. There Andrew worked from six in the morning until six at night, making $1.20 as a bobbin boy.

After a while his father quit—factory work was impossible for the traditional small enterpriser—and Andrew got a "better" job with a new firm, tending an engine deep in a dungeon cellar and dipping newly made cotton spools in a vat of oil. Even the raise to $3 a week—and desperately conjured visions of Wallace and the Bruce—could not overcome the horrors of that lonely and foul-smelling basement. It was perhaps the only time in Carnegie's life when his self-assurance deserted him: to the end of his days the merest whiff of oil could make him deathly sick.

Yet he was certain, as he wrote home at sixteen, that "anyone could get along in this Country," and the rags-to-riches saga shortly began. The telegraph had just come to Pittsburgh, and one evening over a game of checkers, the manager of the local office informed Andrew's uncle that he was looking for a messenger. Andy got the job and, in true Alger fashion, set out to excel in it. Within a few weeks he had carefully memorized the names and the locations, not only of the main streets in Pittsburgh, but of the main firms, so that he was the quickest of all the messenger boys.

He came early and stayed late, watched the telegraphers at work, and at home at night learned the Morse code. As a result he was soon the head of the growing messenger service, and a skilled telegrapher himself. One day he dazzled the office by taking a message "by ear" instead of by the commonly used tape printer, and since he was then only the third operator in the country able to turn the trick, citizens used to drop into the office to watch Andy take down the words "hot from the wire."

One such citizen who was especially impressed with young Carnegie's determination was Thomas A. Scott, in time to become one of the colorful railway magnates of the West, but then the local superintendent of the Pennsylvania Railroad. Soon thereafter Carnegie became "Scott's Andy"—telegrapher, secretary, and general factotum—at thirty-five dollars a month. In his *Autobiography* Carnegie recalls an instance which enabled him to begin the next stage of his career.

> One morning I reached the office and found that a serious accident on the Eastern Division had delayed the express passenger train westward, and that the passenger train eastward was proceeding with a flagman in advance at every curve. The freight trains in both directions were standing on the sidings. Mr. Scott was not to be found. Finally I could not resist the temptation to plunge in, take the responsibility, give "train orders" and set matters going. "Death or Westminster Abbey" flashed across my mind. I knew it was dismissal, disgrace, perhaps criminal punishment for me if I erred. On the other hand, I could bring in the wearied freight train men who had lain out all night. I knew I could. I knew just what to do, and so I began.

Signing Scott's name to the orders, Carnegie flashed out the necessary instructions to bring order out of the tangle. The trains moved; there were no mishaps. When Scott reached the office Carnegie told him what he had done. Scott said not a word but looked carefully over all that had taken place. After a little he moved away from Carnegie's desk to his own, and that was the end of it. "But I noticed," Carnegie concluded good-humoredly, "that he came in very regularly and in good time for some mornings after that."

It is hardly to be wondered at that Carnegie became Scott's favorite, his "white-haired Scotch devil." Impetuous but not rash, full of enthusiasm and good-natured charm, the small lad with his blunt, open features and his slight Scottish burr was every executive's dream of an assistant. Soon Scott repaid Andy for his services by introducing him to a new and very different kind of opportunity. He gave Carnegie the chance to subscribe to five hundred dollars' worth of Adams Express stock, a company which Scott assured Andy would prosper mightily.

Carnegie had not fifty dollars saved, much less five hundred, but it was a chance he could ill afford to miss. He reported the offer to his mother, and that pillar of the family unhesitatingly mortgaged their home to raise the necessary money. When the first dividend check came in, with its ornate Spencerian flourishes, Carnegie had something like a revelation. "I shall remember that check as long as I live," he subsequently wrote. "It gave me the first penny of revenue from capital—something that I had not worked for with the sweat of my brow. 'Eureka!' I cried, 'Here's the goose that lays the golden eggs.'" He was right; within a few years his investment in the Adams Express Company was paying annual dividends of $1,400.

It was not long thereafter that an even more propitious chance presented itself. Carnegie was riding on the Pennsylvania line one day when he was approached by a "farmer-looking" man carrying a small green bag in his hand. The other introduced himself as T. T. Woodruff and quite frankly said that he wanted a chance to talk with someone connected with the railroad. Whereupon he opened his bag and took out a small model of the first sleeping car.

Carnegie was immediately impressed with its possibilities, and he quickly arranged for Woodruff to meet Scott. When the latter agreed to give the cars a trial, Woodruff in appreciation offered Carnegie a chance to subscribe to a one-eighth interest in the new company. A local banker agreed to lend Andy the few hundred dollars needed for the initial payment—the rest being financed from dividends. Once again Andy had made a shrewd investment: within two years the Woodruff Palace Car Company was paying him a return of more than $5,000 a year.

Investments now began to play an increasingly important role in Carnegie's career. Through his railroad contacts he came to recognize the possibilities in manufacturing the heavy equipment needed by the rapidly expanding lines, and soon he was instrumental in organizing companies to meet these needs. One of them, the Keystone Bridge Company, was the first successful manufacturer of iron railway bridges. Another, the Pittsburgh Locomotive Works, made engines. And most important of all, an interest in a local iron works run by an irascible German named Andrew Kloman brought Carnegie into actual contact with the manufacture of iron itself.

None of these new ventures required any substantial outlay of cash. His interest in the Keystone Bridge Company, for instance, which was to earn him $15,000 in 1868, came to him "in return for services rendered in its promotion"—services which Carnegie, as a young railroad executive, was then in a highly strategic position to deliver. Similarly the interest in the Kloman works reflected no contribution on Carnegie's part except that of being the human catalyst and buffer between some highly excitable participants.

By 1865 his "side" activities had become so important that he decided to leave the Pennsylvania Railroad. He was by then superintendent, Scott having moved up to a vice presidency, but his salary of $2,400 was already vastly overshadowed by his income from various ventures. One purchase alone—the Storey farm in Pennsylvania oil country, which Carnegie and a few associates picked up for $40,000—was eventually to pay the group a million dollars in dividends in *one* year. About this time a friend dropped in on Carnegie and asked him how he was doing. "Oh, I'm rich, I'm rich!" he exclaimed.

He was indeed embarked on the road to riches, and determined, as he later wrote in his *Autobiography*, that "nothing could be allowed to interfere for a moment with my business career." Hence it comes as a surprise to note that it was at this very point that Carnegie retired to his suite to write his curiously introspective and troubled thoughts about the pursuit of wealth. But the momentum of events was to prove far too strong for these moralistic doubts. Moving his headquarters to New York to promote his various interests, he soon found himself swept along by a succession of irresistible opportunities for money-making.

One of these took place quite by chance. Carnegie was trying to sell the Woodruff sleeping car at the same time that a formidable rival named George Pullman was also seeking to land contracts for his sleeping car, and the railroads were naturally taking advantage of the competitive situation. One summer evening in 1869 Carnegie found himself mounting the resplendent marble stairway of the St. Nicholas Hotel side by side with his competitor.

"Good evening, Mr. Pullman," said Carnegie in his ebullient manner. Pullman was barely cordial.

"How strange we should meet here," Carnegie went on, to which the other replied nothing at all.

"Mr. Pullman," said Carnegie, after an embarrassing pause, "don't you think we are making nice fools of ourselves?" At this Pullman evinced a glimmer of interest: "What do you mean?" he inquired. Carnegie quickly pointed out that competition between the two companies was helping no one but the railroads. "Well," said Pullman, "what do you suggest we do?"

"Unite!" said Carnegie. "Let's make a joint proposition to the

Union Pacific, your company and mine. Why not organize a new company to do it?" "What would you call it?" asked Pullman suspiciously. "The Pullman Palace Car Company," said Carnegie and with this shrewd psychological stroke won his point. A new company was formed, and in time Carnegie became its largest stockholder.

Meanwhile, events pushed Carnegie into yet another lucrative field. To finance the proliferating railway systems of America, British capital was badly needed, and with his Scottish ancestry, his verve, and his excellent railroad connections Carnegie was the natural choice for a go-between. His brief case stuffed with bonds and prospectuses, Carnegie became a transatlantic commuter, soon developing intimate relations both with great bankers like Junius Morgan (the father of J. P. Morgan), and with the heads of most of the great American roads. These trips earned him not only large commissions—exceeding on occasion $100,000 for a single turn—but even more important, established connections that were later to be of immense value. He himself later testified candidly on their benefits before a group of respectfully awed senators:

> For instance, I want a great contract for rails. Sidney Dillon of the Union Pacific was a personal friend of mine. Huntington was a friend. Dear Butler Duncan, that called on me the other day, was a friend. Those and other men were presidents of railroads . . . Take Huntington; you know C. P. Huntington. He was hard up very often. He was a great man, but he had a great deal of paper out. I knew his things were good. When he wanted credit I gave it to him. If you help a man that way, what chance has any paid agent going to these men? It was absurd.

But his trips to England brought Carnegie something still more valuable. They gave him steel. It is fair to say that as late as 1872 Carnegie did not see the future that awaited him as the Steel King of the world. The still modest conglomeration of foundries and mills he was gradually assembling in the Allegheny and Monongahela valleys was but one of many business interests, and not one for which he envisioned any extraordinary future. Indeed, to repeated pleas that he lead the way in developing a steel industry for America by substituting steel for iron rails, his reply was succinct: "Pioneering don't pay."

What made him change his mind? The story goes that he was awe-struck by the volcanic, spectacular eruption of a Bessemer converter, which he saw for the first time during a visit to a British mill. It was precisely the sort of display that would have appealed to Carnegie's mind—a wild, demonic, physical process miraculously contained and controlled by the dwarfed figures of the steel men themselves. At any rate, overnight Carnegie became the perfervid prophet of steel. Jumping on the first available steamer, he rushed home with the cry, "The day of iron has passed!" To the conster-

The drama of the Bessemer Process is depicted in Aaron Bohrod's 1948 painting, The Big Blow.

nation of his colleagues, the hitherto reluctant pioneer became an advocate of the most daring technological and business expansion; he joined them enthusiastically in forming Carnegie, McCandless & Company, which was the nucleus of the empire that the next thirty years would bring forth.

The actual process of growth involved every aspect of successful business enterprise of the times: acquisition and merger, pools and commercial piracy, and even, on one occasion, an outright fraud in selling the United States government overpriced and underdone steel armor plate. But it would be as foolish to maintain that the Carnegie empire grew by trickery as to deny that sharp practice had its place. Essentially what lay behind the spectacular expansion were three facts.

The first of these was the sheer economic expansion of the industry in the first days of burgeoning steel use. Everywhere steel replaced iron or found new uses—and not only in railroads but in ships, buildings, bridges, machinery of all sorts. As Henry Frick himself once remarked, if the Carnegie group had not filled the need for steel another would have. But it must be admitted that Carnegie's company did its job superlatively well. In 1885 Great Britain led the world in the production of steel. Fourteen years later her total output was 695,000 tons less than the output of the Carnegie Steel Company alone.

Second was the brilliant assemblage of personal talent with which

Carnegie surrounded himself. Among them, three in particular stood out. One was Captain William Jones, a Homeric figure who lumbered through the glowing fires and clanging machinery of the works like a kind of Paul Bunyan of steel, skilled at handling men, inventive in handling equipment, and enough of a natural artist to produce papers for the British Iron and Steel Institute that earned him a literary as well as a technical reputation. Then there was Henry Frick, himself a self-made millionaire, whose coke empire naturally complemented Carnegie's steelworks. When the two were amalgamated, Frick took over the active management of the whole, and under his forceful hand the annual output of the Carnegie works rose tenfold. Yet another was Charles Schwab, who came out of the tiny monastic town of Loretto, Pennsylvania, to take a job as a stake driver. Six months later he had been promoted by Jones into the assistant managership of the Braddock plant.

These men, and a score like them, constituted the vital energy of the Carnegie works. As Carnegie himself said, "Take away all our money, our great works, ore mines and coke ovens, but leave our organization, and in four years I shall have re-established myself."

But the third factor in the growth of the empire was Carnegie himself. A master salesman and a skilled diplomat of business at its highest levels, Carnegie was also a ruthless driver of his men. He pitted his associates and subordinates in competition with one another until a feverish atmosphere pervaded the whole organization. "You cannot imagine the abounding sense of freedom and relief I experience as soon as I get on board a steamer and sail past Sandy Hook," he once said to Captain Jones. "My God!" replied Jones. "Think of the relief to us!"

But Carnegie could win loyalties as well. All his promising young men were given gratis ownership participations—minuscule fractions of one per cent, which were enough, however, to make them millionaires in their own right. Deeply grateful to Jones, Carnegie once offered him a similar participation. Jones hemmed and hawed and finally refused; he would be unable to work effectively with the men, he said, once he was a partner. Carnegie insisted that his contribution be recognized and asked Jones what he wanted. "Well," said the latter, "you might pay me a hell of a big salary." "We'll do it!" said Carnegie. "From this time forth you shall receive the same salary as the President of the United States." "Ah, Andy, that's the kind of talk," said Captain Bill.

Within three decades, on the flood tide of economic expansion, propelled by brilliant executive work and relentless pressure from Carnegie, the company made immense strides. "Such a magnificent aggregation of industrial power has never before been under the domination of a single man," reported a biographer in 1902, describing the Gargantuan structure of steel and coke and ore and transport. Had the writer known of the profits earned by this aggregation he might have been even more impressed: three and a half million dollars in 1889, seven million in 1897, twenty-one million in 1899, and an immense forty million in 1900. "Where is there such a business!" Carnegie had exulted, and no wonder—the majority share of all these earnings, without hindrance of income tax, went directly into his pockets.

Nevertheless, with enormous success came problems. One of these was the restiveness of certain partners, under the "Iron-Clad" agreement, which prevented any of them from selling their shares to anyone but the company itself—an arrangement which meant, of course, that the far higher valuation of an outside purchaser could not be realized. Particularly chagrined was Frick, when, as the culmination of other disagreements between them, Carnegie sought to buy him out "at the value appearing on the books." Another problem was a looming competitive struggle in the steel industry itself that presaged a period of bitter industrial warfare ahead. And last was Carnegie's own growing desire to "get out."

Already he was spending half of each year abroad, first traveling, and then, after his late marriage, in residence in the great Skibo Castle he built for his wife on Dornoch Firth, Scotland. There he ran his business enterprises with one hand while he courted the literary and creative world with the other, entertaining Kipling and Matthew Arnold, Paderewski and Lloyd George, Woodrow Wilson and Theodore Roosevelt, Gladstone, and of course, Herbert Spencer, the Master. But even his career as "Laird" of Skibo could not remove him from the worries—and triumphs—of his business: a steady flow of cables and correspondence intruded on the "serious" side of life.

It was Schwab who cut the knot. Having risen to the very summit of the Carnegie concern he was invited in December, 1900, to give a speech on the future of the steel industry at the University Club in New York. There, before eighty of the nation's top business leaders he painted a glowing picture of what could be done if a super-company of steel were formed, integrated from top to bottom, self-sufficient with regard to its raw materials, balanced in its array of final products. One of the guests was the imperious J. P. Morgan, and as the speech progressed it was noticed that his concentration grew more and more intense. After dinner Morgan rose and took the young steel man by the elbow and engaged him in private conversation for half an hour while he plied him with rapid and penetrating questions; then a few weeks later he invited him to a private meeting in the great library of his home. They talked from nine o'clock in the evening until dawn. As the sun began to stream in through the library windows, the banker finally rose. "Well," he said to Schwab, "if Andy wants to sell, I'll buy. Go and find his price."

Carnegie at first did not wish to sell. Faced with the actual prospect of a withdrawal from the business he had built into the mightiest single industrial empire in the world, he was frightened and dismayed. He sat silent before Schwab's report, brooding, loath to inquire into details. But soon his enthusiasm returned. No such opportunity was likely to present itself again. In short order a figure of $492,000,000 was agreed on for the entire enterprise, of which Carnegie himself was to receive $300,000,000 in five per cent gold bonds and preferred stock. Carnegie jotted down the terms of the transaction on a slip of paper and told Schwab to bring it to Morgan. The banker glanced only briefly at the paper. "I accept," he said.

After the formalities were in due course completed, Carnegie was in a euphoric mood. "Now, Pierpont, I am the happiest man in the world," he said. Morgan was by no means unhappy himself: his own banking company had made a direct profit of $12,500,000 in the underwriting transaction, and this was but a prelude to a stream of lucrative financings under Morgan's aegis, by which the total capitalization was rapidly raised to $1,400,000,000. A few years later, Morgan and Carnegie found themselves aboard the same steamer en route to Europe. They fell into talk and Carnegie confessed, "I made one mistake, Pierpont, when I sold out to you."

"What was that?" asked the banker.

"I should have asked you for $100,000,000 more than I did."

Morgan grinned. "Well," he said, "you would have got it if you had."

Thus was written *finis* to one stage of Carnegie's career. Now it would be seen to what extent his "radical pronouncements" were serious. For in the *Gospel of Wealth*—the famous article combined with others in book form—Carnegie had proclaimed the duty of the millionaire to administer and distribute his wealth *during his lifetime*. Though he might have "proved" his worth by his fortune, his heirs had shown no such evidence of their fitness. Carnegie bluntly concluded: "By taxing estates heavily at his death, the State marks its condemnation of the selfish millionaire's unworthy life."

Coming from the leading millionaire of the day, these had been startling sentiments. So also were his views on the "labor question" which, if patronizing, were nonetheless humane and advanced for their day. The trouble was, of course, that the sentiments were somewhat difficult to credit. As one commentator of the day remarked, "His vision of what might be done with wealth had beauty and breadth and thus serenely overlooked the means by which wealth had been acquired."

For example, the novelist Hamlin Garland visited the steel towns from which the Carnegie millions came and bore away a description of work that was ugly, brutal, and exhausting: he contrasted the lavish care expended on the plants with the callous disregard of the pigsty homes: "the streets were horrible; the buildings poor; the sidewalks sunken and full of holes . . . Everywhere the yellow mud of the streets lay kneaded into sticky masses through which groups of pale, lean men slouched in faded garments . . ." When the famous Homestead strike erupted in 1892, with its private army of Pinkerton detectives virtually at war with the workers, the Carnegie benevolence seemed revealed as shabby fakery. At Skibo Carnegie stood firmly behind the company's iron determination to break the strike. As a result, public sentiment swung sharply and suddenly against him; the St. Louis *Post-Dispatch* wrote: "Three months ago Andrew Carnegie

The Homestead Strike as it was pictured in a drawing from Harper's Weekly.

was a man to be envied. Today he is an object of mingled pity and contempt. In the estimation of nine-tenths of the thinking people on both sides of the ocean he has . . . confessed himself a moral coward.''

In an important sense the newspaper was right. For though Carnegie continued to fight against ''privilege,'' he saw privilege only in its fading aristocratic vestments and not in the new hierarchies of wealth and power to which he himself belonged. In Skibo Castle he now played the role of the benign autocrat, awakening to the skirling of his private bagpiper and proceeding to breakfast to the sonorous accompaniment of the castle organ.

Meanwhile there had also come fame and honors in which Carnegie wallowed unashamedly. He counted the ''freedoms'' bestowed on him by grateful or hopeful cities and crowed. ''I have fifty-two and Gladstone has only seventeen.'' He entertained the King of England and told him that democracy was better than monarchy, and met the German Kaiser: ''Oh, yes, yes,'' said the latter worthy on being introduced. ''I have read your books. You do not like kings.'' But Mark Twain, on hearing of this, was not fooled. ''He says he is a scorner of kings and emperors and dukes,'' he wrote, ''whereas he is like the rest of the human race: a slight attention from one of these

A New York World *cartoonist labeled Carnegie "The Modern Baron with the Old Methods."*

can make him drunk for a week . . ."

And yet it is not enough to conclude that Carnegie was in fact a smaller man than he conceived himself. For this judgment overlooks one immense and irrefutable fact. He did, in the end, abide by his self-imposed duty. He did give nearly all of his gigantic fortune away.

As one would suspect, the quality of the philanthropy reflected the man himself. There was, for example, a huge and sentimentally administered private pension fund to which access was to be had on the most trivial as well as the most worthy grounds: if it included a number of writers, statesmen, scientists, it also made room for two maiden ladies with whom Carnegie had once danced as a young man, a boyhood acquaintance who had once held Carnegie's books while he ran a race, a merchant to whom he had once delivered a telegram and who had subsequently fallen on hard times. And then, as one would expect, there was a benevolent autocracy in the administration of the larger philanthropies as well. "Now everybody vote Aye," was the way Carnegie typically determined the policies of the philanthropic "foundations" he established.

Yet if these flaws bore the stamp of one side of Carnegie's personality, there was also the other side—the side that, however crudely, asked important questions and however piously, concerned itself with great ideals. Of this the range and purpose of the main philanthropies gave unimpeachable testimony. There were the famous libraries—three thousand of them costing nearly sixty million dollars; there were the Carnegie institutes in Pittsburgh and Washington, Carnegie Hall in New York, the Hague Peace Palace, the Carnegie Endowment for International Peace, and the precedent-making Carnegie Corporation of New York, with its original enormous endowment of $125,-000,000. In his instructions to the trustees of this first great modern foundation, couched in the simplified spelling of which he was an ardent advocate, we see Carnegie at his very best:

> Conditions on erth [*sic*] inevitably change; hence, no wise man will bind Trustees forever to certain paths, causes, or institutions. I disclaim any intention of doing so . . . My chief happiness, as I write these lines lies in the thot [*sic*] that, even after I pass away, the welth [*sic*] that came to me to administer as a sacred trust for the good of my fellow men is to continue to benefit humanity . . .

If these sentiments move us—if Carnegie himself in retrospect moves us at last to grudging respect—it is not because his was the triumph of a saint or a philosopher. It is because it was the much more difficult triumph of a very human and fallible man struggling to retain his convictions in an age, and in the face of a career, which subjected them to impossible temptations. Carnegie is something of America writ large; his is the story of the Horatio Alger hero *after* he has made his million dollars. In the failures of Andrew Carnegie we see many of the failures of America itself. In his curious triumph, we see what we hope is our own steadfast core of integrity.

David Boroff

The Diaspora in America: A Study of Jewish Immigration

Since all Americans are themselves at least the descendants of immigrants, it is perhaps not surprising that "native born" citizens have often displayed a kind of love-hate attitude toward newcomers. They recognize in these newcomers their own successes and failures, their pride in what they have accomplished and their shame at what they have forgotten or rejected in their heritage. This ambivalence has been exacerbated by the very real conflicts that immigration has caused. On the one hand, the immigrant has always been a national asset—his labor and intelligence add to the productivity and wealth of society; his culture enriches and diversifies American civilization. On the other hand, the immigrant has represented competition, strangeness, unsettling change. Most immigrants have been poor, many upon arrival have been ill adjusted to American values and habits. Social and economic problems have frequently resulted, especially when large numbers have flooded into the country in relatively short periods of time. This last point explains why the late nineteenth and early twentieth centuries produced the movement to restrict immigration, for the influx was greater then than at any other time.

In this essay the late David Boroff of New York University discusses the impact of Jewish immigrants on the United States and the impact of the nation on these immigrants. He focuses chiefly on the period after 1880, when Jewish immigration was heaviest. His account provides a vivid picture of the life of these people, and helps explain both why they, as well as other immigrants, were sometimes disliked and why they were themselves at times ambivalent in their reactions to America.

*I*t started with a tiny trickle and ended in a roaring flood. The first to come were just twenty-three Jews from Brazil who landed in New Amsterdam in 1654, in flight from a country no longer hospitable to them. They were, in origin, Spanish and Portuguese Jews (many with grandiloquent Iberian names) whose families had been wandering for a century and a half. New Amsterdam provided a chilly reception. Governor Peter Stuyvesant at first asked them to leave, but kinder hearts in the Dutch West India Company granted them the right to stay, "provided the poor among them . . . be supported by their own nation." By the end of the century, there were perhaps one hundred Jews; by the middle of the eighteenth century, there were about three hundred in New York, and smaller communities in Newport, Philadelphia, and Charleston.

Because of their literacy, zeal, and overseas connections, colonial Jews prospered as merchants, though there were artisans and laborers among them. The Jewish community was tightly knit, but there was a serious shortage of trained religious functionaries. There wasn't a single American rabbi, for example, until the nineteenth century. Jews were well regarded, particularly in New England. Puritan culture leaned heavily on the Old Testament, and Harvard students learned Hebrew; indeed, during the American Revolution, the suggestion was advanced that Hebrew replace English as the official language of the new country. The absence of an established national religion made it possible for Judaism to be regarded as merely another religion in a pluralistic society. The early days of the new republic were thus a happy time for Jews. Prosperous and productive, they were admitted to American communal life with few restrictions. It is little wonder that a Jewish spokesman asked rhetorically in 1820: "On what spot in this habitable Globe does an Israelite enjoy more blessings, more privileges?"

The second wave of immigration during the nineteenth century is often described as German, but that is misleading. Actually, there were many East European Jews among the immigrants who came in the half century before 1870. However, the German influence was strong, and there was a powerful undercurrent of Western enlightenment at work. These Jews came because economic depression and the Industrial Revolution had made their lot as artisans and small merchants intolerable. For some there was also the threatening backwash of the failure of the Revolution of 1848. Moreover, in Germany at this time Jews were largely disfranchised and discriminated against. During this period, between 200,000 and 400,000 Jews emigrated to this country, and the Jewish population had risen to about half a million by 1870.

This was the colorful era of the peddler and his pack. Peddling was an easy way to get started—it required little capital—and it often rewarded enterprise and daring. Jewish peddlers fanned out through the young country into farmland and mining camp, frontier and Indian territory. The more successful peddlers ultimately settled in one place as storekeepers. (Some proud businesses—including that of Senator Goldwater's family—made their start this way.) Feeling somewhat alienated from the older, settled Jews, who had a reputation for declining piety, the new immigrants organized their own synagogues and community facilities, such as cemeteries and hospitals. In general, these immigrants were amiably received by native Americans, who, unsophisticated about differences that were crucial to the immigrants themselves, regarded all Central Europeans as "Germans."

Essentially, the emigration route was the same between 1820 and 1870 as it would be in the post-1880 exodus. The travellers stayed in emigration inns while awaiting their ship, and since they had all their resources with them, they were in danger of being robbed. The journey itself was hazardous and, in the days of the sailing vessels when a good wind was indispensable, almost interminable. Nor were the appointments very comfortable even for the relatively well to do. A German Jew who made the journey in 1856 reported that his cabin, little more than six feet by six feet, housed six passengers in triple-decker bunks. When a storm raged, the passengers had to retire to their cabins lest they be washed off the deck by waves. "Deprived of air," he wrote, "it soon became unbearable in the cabins in which six sea-sick persons breathed." On this particular journey, sea water began to trickle into the cabins, and the planks had to be retarred.

Still, the emigration experience was a good deal easier than it would be later. For one thing, the immigrants were better educated and better acquainted with modern political and social attitudes than the oppressed and bewildered East European multitudes who came after 1880. Fewer in number, they were treated courteously by ships' captains. (On a journey in 1839, described by David Mayer, the ship's captain turned over his own cabin to the Jewish passengers for their prayers and regularly visited those Jews who were ill.) Moreover, there was still the bloom of adventure about the overseas voyage. Ships left Europe amid the booming of cannon, while on shore ladies enthusiastically waved their handkerchiefs. On the way over, there was a holiday atmosphere despite the hazards, and there was great jubilation when land was sighted.

There were, however, rude shocks when the voyagers arrived in this country. The anguish of Castle Garden and Ellis Island was well in the future when immigration first began to swell. But New York seemed inhospitable, its pace frantic, the outlook not entirely hopeful. Isaac M. Wise, a distinguished rabbi who made the journey in 1846, was appalled. "The whole city appeared to me like a large shop," he wrote, "where everyone buys or sells, cheats or is cheated. I had never before seen a city so bare of all art and of every trace of good taste; likewise I had never witnessed anywhere such rushing, hurrying, chasing, running . . . Everything seemed so pitifully small and paltry; and I had had so exalted an idea of the land of freedom." Moreover, he no sooner landed in New York than he was abused by a German drayman whose services he had declined. "Aha! thought I," he later wrote, "you have left home and kindred in order to get away from the disgusting Judaeophobia and here the first German greeting that sounds in your ears is hep! hep!'' (The expletive was a Central European equivalent of ''Kike.'') Another German Jew who worked as a clothing salesman was affronted by the way customers were to be ''lured'' into buying (''I did not think this occupation corresponded in any way to my views of a merchant's dignity'').

After 1880, Jewish immigration into the United States was in flood tide. And the source was principally East Europe, where by 1880 three quarters of the world's 7.7 million Jews were living. In all, over two million Jews came to these shores in little more than three decades—about one third of Europe's Jewry. Some of them came, as their predecessors had come, because of shrinking economic opportunities. In Russia and in the Austro-Hungarian empire, the growth of large-scale agriculture squeezed out Jewish middlemen as it destroyed the independent peasantry, while in the cities the development of manufacturing reduced the need for Jewish artisans. Vast numbers of Jews became petty tradesmen or even *luftmenschen* (men without visible means of support who drifted from one thing to another). In Galicia, around 1900, there was a Jewish trader for

Her decks jammed with hopeful immigrants, the S.S. Patricia *arrives at Ellis Island in 1906.*

every ten peasants, and the average value of his stock came to only twenty dollars.

Savage discrimination and pogroms also incited Jews to emigrate. The Barefoot Brigades—bands of marauding Russian peasants— brought devastation and bloodshed to Jewish towns and cities. On a higher social level, there was the "cold pogrom," a government policy calculated to destroy Jewish life. The official hope was that one third of Russia's Jews would die out, one third would emigrate, and one third would be converted to the Orthodox Church. Crushing restrictions were imposed. Jews were required to live within the Pale of Settlement in western Russia, they could not Russify their names, and they were subjected to rigorous quotas for schooling and professional training. Nor could general studies be included in the curriculum of Jewish religious schools. It was a life of poverty and fear.

Nevertheless, the *shtetl*, the typical small Jewish town, was a triumph of endurance and spiritual integrity. It was a place where degradation and squalor could not wipe out dignity, where learning flourished in the face of hopelessness, and where a tough, sardonic humor provided catharsis for the tribulations of an existence that was barely endurable. The abrasions and humiliations of everyday life were healed by a rich heritage of custom and ceremony. And there was always Sabbath—"The Bride of the Sabbath," as the Jews called the day of rest—to bring repose and exaltation to a life always sorely tried.

To be sure, even this world showed signs of disintegration. Secular learning, long resisted by East European Jews and officially denied to them, began to make inroads. Piety gave way to revolutionary fervor, and Jews began to play a heroic role in Czarist Russia's bloody history of insurrection and suppression.

This was the bleak, airless milieu from which the emigrants came. A typical expression of the Jewish attitude toward emigration from Russia—both its hopefulness and the absence of remorse—was provided by Dr. George Price, who had come to this country in one of the waves of East European emigration:

> Should this Jewish emigrant regret his leave-taking of his native land which fails to appreciate him? No! A thousand times no! He must not regret fleeing the clutches of the bloodthirsty crocodile. Sympathy for this country? How ironical it sounds! Am I not despised? Am I not urged to leave? Do I not hear the word *Zhid* constantly? . . . Be thou cursed forever my wicked homeland, because you remind me of the Inquisition . . . May you rue the day when you exiled the people who worked for your welfare.

After 1880, going to America—no other country really lured— became the great drama of redemption for the masses of East European Jews. (For some, of course, Palestine had that role even in the late nineteenth century, but these were an undaunted Zionist cadre prepared to endure the severest hardships.) The assassination of Czar

Alexander II in 1881, and the subsequent pogrom, marked the beginning of the new influx. By the end of the century, 700,000 Jews had arrived, about one quarter of them totally illiterate, almost all of them impoverished. Throughout East Europe, Jews talked longingly about America as the "goldene medinah" (the golden province), and biblical imagery—"the land of milk and honey"—came easily to their lips. Those who could write were kept busy composing letters to distant kin—or even to husbands—in America. (Much of the time, the husband went first, and by abstemious living saved enough to fetch wife and children from the old country.) Children played at "emigrating games," and for the entire *shtetl* it was an exciting moment when the mail-carrier announced how many letters had arrived from America.

German steamship companies assiduously advertised the glories of the new land and provided a one-price rate from *shtetl* to New York. Emigration inns were established in Brody (in the Ukraine) and in the port cities of Bremen and Hamburg, where emigrants would gather for the trip. There were rumors that groups of prosperous German Jews would underwrite their migration to America; and in fact such people often did help their co-religionists when they were stranded without funds in the port cities of Germany. Within Russia itself, the government after 1880 more or less acquiesced in the emigration of Jews, and connived in the vast business of "stealing the border" (smuggling emigrants across). After 1892, emigration was legal—except for those of draft age—but large numbers left with forged papers, because that proved to be far easier than getting tangled in the red tape of the Czarist bureaucracy. Forged documents, to be sure, were expensive—they cost twenty-five rubles, for many Jews the equivalent of five weeks' wages. Nor was the departure from home entirely a happy event. There were the uncertainties of the new life, the fear that in America "one became a gentile." Given the Jewish aptitude for lugubriousness, a family's departure was often like a funeral, lachrymose and anguished, with the neighbors carting off the furniture that would no longer be needed.

For people who had rarely ventured beyond the boundaries of their own village, going to America was an epic adventure. They travelled with pitifully little money; the average immigrant arrived in New York with only about twenty dollars. With their domestic impedimenta—bedding, brass candlesticks, samovars—they would proceed to the port cities by rail, cart, and even on foot. At the emigration inns, they had to wait their turn. Thousands milled around, entreating officials for departure cards. There were scenes of near chaos—mothers shrieking, children crying; battered wicker trunks, bedding, utensils in wild disarray. At Hamburg, arriving emigrants were put in the "unclean" section of the *Auswandererhallen* until examined by physicians who decided whether their clothing and baggage had to be disinfected. After examination, Jews could not leave the center; other emigrants could.

The ocean voyage provided little respite. (Some elected to sail by way of Liverpool at a reduction of nine dollars from the usual rate of thirty-four dollars.) Immigrants long remembered the "smell of ship," a distillation of many putrescences. Those who went in steerage slept on mattresses filled with straw and kept their clothes on to keep warm. The berth itself was generally six feet long, two feet wide, and two and a half feet high, and it had to accommodate the passenger's luggage. Food was another problem. Many Orthodox Jews subsisted on herring, black bread, and tea which they brought because they did not trust the dietary purity of the ship's food. Some ships actually maintained a separate galley for kosher food, which was coveted by non-Jewish passengers because it was allegedly better.

Unsophisticated about travel and faced by genuine dangers, Jewish emigrants found the overseas trip a long and terrifying experience. But when land was finally sighted, the passengers often began to cheer and shout. "I looked up at the sky," an immigrant wrote years later. "It seemed much bluer and the sun much brighter than in the old country. It reminded me on [sic] the Garden of Eden."

Unhappily, the friendly reception that most immigrants envisioned in the new land rarely materialized. Castle Garden in the Battery, at the foot of Manhattan—and later Ellis Island in New York Harbor —proved to be almost as traumatic as the journey itself. "Castle Garden," an immigrant wrote, "is a large building, a Gehenna, through which all Jewish arrivals must pass to be cleansed before they are considered worthy of breathing freely the air of the land of the almighty dollar. . . . If in Brody, thousands crowded about, here tens of thousands thronged about; if there they were starving, here they were dying; if there they were crushed, here they were simply beaten."

One must make allowances for the impassioned hyperbole of the suffering immigrant, but there is little doubt that the immigration officials were harassed, overworked, and often unsympathetic. Authorized to pass on the admissibility of the newcomers, immigration officers struck terror into their hearts by asking questions designed to reveal their literacy and social attitudes. "How much is six times six?" an inspector asked a woman in the grip of nervousness, then casually asked the next man, "Have you ever been in jail?"

There were, of course, representatives of Jewish defense groups present, especially from the Hebrew Immigrant Aid Society. But by this time, the immigrants, out of patience and exhausted, tended to view them balefully. The Jewish officials tended to be highhanded, and the temporary barracks which they administered on Ward's Island for those not yet settled became notorious. Discontent culminated in a riot over food; one day the director—called The Father— had to swim ashore for his life, and the police were hastily summoned.

Most immigrants went directly from Castle Garden or Ellis Island to the teeming streets of Manhattan, where they sought relatives or *landsleit* (fellow townsmen) who had gone before them. Easy marks for hucksters and swindlers, they were overcharged by draymen for carrying their paltry possessions, engaged as strikebreakers, or hired at shamelessly low wages.

*Immigrant women and children at Ellis Island
eating their first American meal (1906).*

"Greenhorn" or "greener" was their common name. A term of
vilification, the source of a thousand cruel jokes, it was their shame and
their destiny. On top of everything else, the immigrants had to abide
the contempt of their co-religionists who had preceded them to America
by forty or fifty years. By the time the heavy East European immigration set in, German Jews had achieved high mercantile status and an
uneasy integration into American society. They did not want to be
reminded of their kinship with these uncouth and impoverished Jews
who were regarded vaguely as a kind of Oriental influx. There was a
good deal of sentiment against "aiding such paupers to emigrate to
these shores." One charitable organization declared: "Organized immigration from Russia, Roumania, and other semi-barbarous countries
is a mistake and has proved to be a failure. It is no relief to the Jews
of Russia, Poland, etc., and it jeopardizes the well-being of the American Jews."

A genuine uptown-downtown split soon developed, with condescen-
sion on one side and resentment on the other. The German Jews
objected as bitterly to the rigid, old-world Orthodoxy of the immigrants
as they did to their new involvement in trade unions. They were fearful, too, of the competition they would offer in the needle trades.
(Indeed, the East Europeans ultimately forced the uptown Jews out
of the industry.) On the other side of the barricades, Russian Jews
complained that at the hands of their uptown brethren, "every man is
questioned like a criminal, is looked down upon . . . just as if he were
standing before a Russian official." Nevertheless, many German Jews

responded to the call of conscience by providing funds for needy immigrants and setting up preparatory schools for immigrant children for whom no room was yet available in the hopelessly overcrowded public schools.

Many comfortably settled German Jews saw dispersion as the answer to the problem. Efforts were made to divert immigrants to small towns in other parts of the country, but these were largely ineffective. There were also some gallant adventures with farming in such remote places as South Dakota, Oregon, and Louisiana. Though the Jewish pioneers were brave and idealistic, drought, disease, and ineptitude conspired against them. (In Oregon, for example, they tried to raise corn in cattle country, while in Louisiana they found themselves in malarial terrain.) Only chicken farming in New Jersey proved to be successful to any great degree. Farm jobs for Jews were available, but as one immigrant said: "I have no desire to be a farm hand to an ignorant Yankee at the end of the world. I would rather work here at half the price in a factory; for then I would at least be able to spend my free evenings with my friends."

It was in New York, then, that the bulk of the immigrants settled —in the swarming, tumultuous Lower East Side—with smaller concentrations in Boston, Philadelphia, and Chicago. Far less adaptable than the German Jews who were now lording it over them, disoriented and frightened, the East European immigrants constituted a vast and exploited proletariat. According to a survey in 1890, sixty per cent of all immigrant Jews worked in the needle trades. This industry had gone through a process of decentralization in which contractors carried out the bulk of production, receiving merely the cut goods from the manufacturer. Contracting establishments were everywhere in the Lower East Side, including the contractors' homes, where pressers warmed their irons on the very stove on which the boss's wife was preparing supper. The contractors also gave out "section" work to families and *landsleit* who would struggle to meet the quotas at home. The bondage of the sewing machine was therefore extended into the tenements, with entire families enslaved by the machine's voracious demands. The Hester Street "pig market," where one could buy anything, became the labor exchange; there tailors, operators, finishers, basters, and pressers would congregate on Saturday in the hope of being hired by contractors.

Life in the sweatshops of the Lower East Side was hard, but it made immigrants employable from the start, and a weekly wage of five dollars—the equivalent of ten rubles—looked good in immigrant eyes. Moreover, they were among their own kin and kind, and the sweatshops, noisome as they were, were still the scene of lively political and even literary discussions. (In some cigar-making shops, in fact, the bosses hired "readers" to keep the minds of the workers occupied with classic and Yiddish literature as they performed their repetitive chores.) East European Jews, near the end of the century, made up a large part of the skilled labor force in New York, ranking first in twenty-six out of forty-seven trades, and serving, for example, as

The immigrants' new home: a crowded, noisy, but friendly street on New York's Lower East Side.

bakers, building-trade workers, painters, furriers, jewellers, and tinsmiths.

Almost one quarter of all the immigrants tried their hands as tradesmen—largely as peddlers or as pushcart vendors in the madhouse bazaar of the Lower East Side. For some it was an apprenticeship in low-toned commerce that would lead to more elegant careers. For others it was merely a martyrdom that enabled them to subsist. It was a modest enough investment—five dollars for a license, one dollar for a basket, and four dollars for wares. They stocked up on pins and needles, shoe laces, polish, and handkerchiefs, learned some basic expressions ("You wanna buy somethin'?"), and were on their hapless way.

It was the professions, of course, that exerted the keenest attraction to Jews, with their reverence for learning. For most of them it was too late; they had to reconcile themselves to more humble callings. But it was not too late for their children, and between 1897 and 1907, the number of Jewish physicians in Manhattan rose from 450 to 1,000. Of all the professions it was medicine that excited the greatest veneration. (Some of this veneration spilled over into pharmacy, and "druggists'' were highly respected figures who were called upon to prescribe for minor—and even major—ills, and to serve as scribes for the letters that the immigrants were unable to read and write themselves.) There were Jewish lawyers on the Lower East Side and by 1901 over 140 Jewish policemen, recruited in part by Theodore Roosevelt, who, as police commissioner, had issued a call for ''the Maccabee or fighting Jewish type.''

The Lower East Side was the American counterpart of the ghetto for Jewish immigrants, as well as their glittering capital. At its peak, around 1910, it packed over 350,000 people into a comparatively small area—roughly from Canal Street to Fourteenth Street—with as many as 523 people per acre, so that Arnold Bennett was moved to remark that ''the architecture seemed to sweat humanity at every window and door.'' The most densely populated part of the city, it held one sixth of Manhattan's population and most of New York's office buildings and factories. ''Uptowners'' used to delight in visiting it (as a later generation would visit Harlem) to taste its exotic flavor. But the great mass of Jews lived there because the living was cheap, and there was a vital Jewish community that gave solace to the lonely and comfort to the pious.

A single man could find lodgings of a sort, including coffee morning and night, for three dollars a month. For a family, rent was about ten dollars a month, milk was four cents a quart, kosher meat twelve cents a pound, bread two cents a pound, herring a penny or two. A kitchen table could be bought for a dollar, chairs at thirty-five cents each. One managed, but the life was oppressive. Most families lived in the notorious ''dumbbell'' flats of old-law tenements (built prior to 1901). Congested, often dirty and unsanitary, these tenements were six or seven stories high and had four apartments on each floor. Only one room in each three or four room apartment received direct air and sunlight, and the families on each floor shared a toilet in the hall.

Many families not only used their flats as workshops but also took in boarders to make ends meet. Jacob Riis tells of a two-room apartment on Allen Street which housed parents, six children, and six boarders. ''Two daughters sewed clothes at home. The elevator railway passed by the window. The cantor rehearses, a train passes, the shoemaker bangs, ten brats run around like goats, the wife putters. . . . At night we all try to get some sleep in the stifling, roach-infested two rooms.'' In the summer, the tenants spilled out into fire escapes and rooftops, which were converted into bedrooms.

Nevertheless, life on the Lower East Side had surprising vitality. Despite the highest population density in the city, the Tenth Ward had one of the lowest death rates. In part, this was because of the strenuous personal cleanliness of Jews, dictated by their religion. Though only eight per cent of the East European Jews had baths, bathhouses and steam rooms on the Lower East Side did a booming business. There was, of course, a heavy incidence of tuberculosis—''the white plague.'' Those who were afflicted could be heard crying out, *''Luft! Gib mir luft!''* (''Air! Give me air!''). It was, in fact, this terror of "consumption" that impelled some East Side Jews to become farmers in the Catskills at the turn of the century, thus forerunning the gaudy career of the Catskill Borscht Belt resort hotels. The same fear impelled Jews on the Lower East Side to move to Washington Heights and the Bronx, where the altitude was higher, the air presumably purer.

Alcoholism, a prime affliction of most immigrant groups, was almost unknown among Jews. They drank ritualistically on holidays but almost never to excess. They were, instead, addicted to seltzer or soda water—Harry Golden's "2¢ plain"—which they viewed as "the worker's champagne." The suicide rate was relatively low, though higher than in the *shtetl*, and there was always a shudder of sympathy when the Yiddish press announced that someone had *genumen di ges* (taken gas).

The Lower East Side was from the start the scene of considerable crime. But its inhabitants became concerned when the crime rate among the young people seemed to rise steeply around 1910. There was a good deal of prostitution. The dancing academies, which achieved popularity early in this century, became recruiting centers for prostitutes. In 1908–9, of 581 foreign women arrested for prostitution, 225 were Jewish. There was the notorious Max Hochstim Association, which actively recruited girls, while the New York Independent Benevolent Association—an organization of pimps—provided sick benefits, burial privileges, bail, and protection money for prostitutes.

A New York sweatshop, photographed about 1910.

The membership was even summoned to funerals with a two-dollar fine imposed on those who did not attend. Prostitution was so taken for granted that Canal Street had stores on one side featuring sacerdotal articles, while brothels were housed on the other.

Family life on the Lower East Side was cohesive and warm, though there was an edge of shrillness and hysteria to it. Marriages were not always happy, but if wives were viewed as an affliction, children were regarded as a blessing. The kitchen was the center of the household, and food was almost always being served to either family or visitors. No matter how poor they were, Jewish families ate well—even to excess—and mothers considered their children woefully underweight unless they were well cushioned with fat.

It was a life with few conventional graces. Handkerchiefs were barely known, and the Yiddish newspapers had to propagandize for their use. Old men smelled of snuff, and in spite of bathing, children often had lice in their hair and were sent home from school by the visiting nurse for a kerosene bath. Bedbugs were considered an inevitability, and pajamas were viewed as an upper-class affectation. Parents quarrelled bitterly—with passionate and resourceful invective —in the presence of their children. Telephones were virtually unknown, and a telegram surely meant disaster from afar.

The zeal of the immigrants on behalf of their children was no less than awe-inspiring. Parents yearned for lofty careers for their offspring, with medicine at the pinnacle. In better-off homes, there was always a piano (''solid mahogany''), and parents often spent their precious reserves to arrange a ''concert'' for their precocious youngsters, followed by a ball in one of the Lower East Side's many halls.

To be sure, the children inspired a full measure of anxiety in their parents. ''Amerikane kinder'' was the rueful plaint of the elders, who could not fathom the baffling new ways of the young. Parents were nervous about their daughters' chastity, and younger brothers—often six or seven years old—would be dispatched as chaperones when the girls met their boy friends. There was uneasiness about Jewish street gangs and the growing problem of delinquency. The old folks were vexed by the new tides of secularism and political radicalism that were weaning their children from traditional pieties. But most of all, they feared that their sons would not achieve the success that would redeem their own efforts, humiliations, and failures in the harsh new land. Pressure on their children was relentless. But on the whole the children did well, astonishingly well. ''The ease and rapidity with which they learn,'' Jacob Riis wrote, ''is equalled only by their good behavior and close attention while in school. There is no whispering and no rioting at these desks.'' Samuel Chotzinoff, the music critic, tells a story which reveals the attitude of the Jewish schoolboy. When an altercation threatened between Chotzinoff and a classmate, his antagonist's reaction was to challenge him to spell ''combustible.''

The Lower East Side was a striking demonstration that financial want does not necessarily mean cultural poverty. The immigrant Jews were nearly always poor and often illiterate, but they were not culturally deprived. In fact, between 1890 and World War I, the Jewish community provides a remarkable chapter in American cultural history. Liberated from the constrictions of European captivity, immigrant Jews experienced a great surge of intellectual vitality. Yiddish, the Hebrew-German dialect which some people had casually dismissed as a barbarous "jargon," became the vehicle of this cultural renascence. Between 1885 and 1914, over 150 publications of all kinds made their appearance. But the new Yiddish journalism reached its apogee with the *Jewish Daily Forward* under the long editorial reign of Abraham Cahan. The *Forword* was humanitarian, pro-labor, and socialistic. But it was also an instrument for acclimatizing immigrants in the new environment. It provided practical hints on how to deal with the new world, letters from the troubled (*Bintel Brief*), and even, at one time, a primer on baseball ("explained to non-sports"). The *Forward* also published and fostered an enormous amount of literature in Yiddish—both original works by writers of considerable talent, and translations of classic writers.

In this cultural ferment, immigrants studied English in dozens of night schools and ransacked the resources of the Aguilar Free Library on East Broadway. "When I had [a] book in my hand," an immigrant wrote, "I pressed it to my heart and wanted to kiss it." The Educational Alliance, also on East Broadway, had a rich program designed to make immigrant Jews more American and their sons more Jewish. And there were scores of settlement houses, debating clubs, ethical societies, and literary circles which attracted the young. In fact, courtships were carried on in a rarefied atmosphere full of lofty talk about art, politics, and philosophy. And though there was much venturesome palaver about sexual freedom, actual behavior tended to be quite strait-laced.

But the most popular cultural institution was the café or coffee house, which served as the Jewish saloon. There were about 250 of them, each with its own following. Here the litterateurs sat for hours over steaming glasses of tea; revolutionaries and Bohemians gathered to make their pronouncements or raise money for causes; actors and playwrights came to hold court. For immigrant Jews, talk was the breath of life itself. The passion for music and theatre knew no bounds. When Beethoven's Ninth Symphony was performed one summer night in 1915, mounted police had to be summoned to keep order outside Lewisohn Stadium, so heavy was the press of crowds eager for the twenty-five-cent stone seats. Theatre (in Yiddish) was to the Jewish immigrants what Shakespeare and Marlowe had been to the groundlings in Elizabethan England. Tickets were cheap—twenty-five cents to one dollar—and theatregoing was universal. It was a raucous, robust, and communal experience. Mothers brought their babies (except in some of the "swellest" theatres, which forbade it), and peddlers hawked their wares between the acts. There were theatre parties for trade unions and *landsmanschaften* (societies of fellow townsmen), and the audience milled around and renewed old friendships or argued the merits of the play. The stage curtain had bold advertisements of stores or blown-up portraits of stars.

There was an intense cult of personality in the Yiddish theatre and a system of claques not unlike that which exists in grand opera today. The undisputed monarch was Boris Thomashefsky, and a theatre program of his day offered this panegyric:

Thomashefsky! Artist great!
No praise is good enough for you!
Of all the stars you remain the king
You seek no tricks, no false quibbles;
One sees truth itself playing.
Your appearance is godly to us
Every movement is full of grace
Pleasing is your every gesture
Sugar sweet your every turn
You remain the king of the stage
Everything falls to your feet.

Many of the plays were sentimental trash—heroic "operas" on historical themes, "greenhorn" melodramas full of cruel abandonments and tearful reunions, romantic musicals, and even topical dramas dealing with such immediate events as the Homestead Strike, the Johnstown Flood, and the Kishinev Pogrom of 1903. Adaptability and a talent for facile plagiarism were the essence of the playwright's art in those days, and "Professor" Moses Horwitz wrote 167 plays, most of them adaptations of old operas and melodramas. The plays were so predictable that an actor once admitted he didn't even have to learn his lines; he merely had to have a sense of the general situation and then adapt lines from other plays.

There was, of course, a serious Yiddish drama, introduced principally by Jacob Gordin, who adapted classical and modernist drama to the Yiddish stage. Jewish intellectuals were jubilant at this development. But the process of acculturation had its amusing and grotesque aspects. Shakespeare was a great favorite but *"verbessert and vergrossert"* (improved and enlarged). There was the Jewish *King Lear* in which Cordelia becomes Goldele. (The theme of filial ingratitude was a "natural" on the Lower East Side, where parents constantly made heroic sacrifices.) *Hamlet* was also given a Jewish coloration, the prince becoming a rabbinical student who returns from the seminary to discover treachery at home. And *A Doll's House* by Ibsen was transformed into *Minna,* in which a sensitive and intelligent young woman, married to an ignorant laborer, falls in love with her boarder and ultimately commits suicide.

Related to the Jewish love of theatre was the immigrant's adoration of the cantor, a profession which evoked as much flamboyance and egotistical preening as acting did. (In fact, actors would sometimes grow beards before the high holydays and find jobs as cantors.) Synagogues vied with each other for celebrated cantors, sometimes as a way of getting out of debt, since tickets were sold for the high-holyday services.

The Lower East Side was a vibrant community, full of color and gusto, in which the Jewish immigrant felt marvelously at home, safe from the terrors of the alien city. But it was a setting too for fierce conflict and enervating strain. There were three major influences at work, each pulling in a separate direction: Jewish Orthodoxy, assimilationism, and the new socialist gospel. The immigrants were Orthodox, but their children tended to break away. *Cheders* (Hebrew schools) were everywhere, in basements and stores and tenements, and the old custom of giving a child a taste of honey when he was beginning to learn to read—as symbolic of the sweetness of study—persisted. But the young, eager to be accepted into American society, despised the old ways and their ''greenhorn'' teachers. Fathers began to view their sons as ''freethinkers,'' a term that was anathema to them. Observance of the Law declined, and the Saturday Sabbath was ignored by many Jews. A virulent antireligious tendency developed among many ''enlightened'' Jews, who would hold profane balls on the most sacred evening of the year—Yom Kippur—at which they would dance and eat nonkosher food. (Yom Kippur is a fast day.) And the trade-union movement also generated uneasiness among the pious elders of the Lower East Side. ''Do you want us to bow down to your archaic God?'' a radical newspaper asked. ''Each era has its new Torah. Ours is one of freedom and justice.''

But for many immigrants the basic discontent was with their American experience itself. The golden province turned out to be a place of tenements and sweatshops. A familiar cry was *''a klug af Columbus!''* (''a curse on Columbus'') or, ''Who ever asked him, Columbus, to discover America?'' Ellis Island was called *Trernindzl* (Island of Tears), and Abraham Cahan, in his initial reaction to the horrors of immigration, thundered: ''Be cursed, immigration! Cursed by those conditions which have brought you into being. How many souls have you broken, how many courageous and mighty souls have you shattered.'' The fact remains that most Jewish immigrants, in the long run, made a happy adjustment to their new land.

After 1910, the Lower East Side went into a decline. Its strange glory was over. New areas of Jewish settlement opened up in Brooklyn, the Bronx, and in upper Manhattan. By the mid-twenties, less than ten per cent of New York's Jews lived on the Lower East Side, although it still remained the heartland to which one returned to shop, to see Yiddish theatre, and to renew old ties. By 1924 Jewish immigration into the United States was severely reduced by new immigration laws, and the saga of mass immigration was done. But the intensities of the Jewish immigrant experience had already made an indelible mark on American culture and history that would endure for many years.

William V. Shannon

The Age
of the Bosses

The rapid industrialization of the United States after the Civil War, which produced great tycoons like Andrew Carnegie and encouraged millions of work-hungry Europeans to migrate, changed the shape of society in a variety of ways. One of the most obvious and important of these was industrialization's effect on where and how people lived. Huge industrial concerns brought together masses of workers in one place; commercial and service enterprises sprang up alongside the factories; in short, great cities rapidly developed and America was on its way to becoming an urban nation.

The advantages of urbanization were great—new wealth, better educational opportunities, a wide range of amusements; soon a more refined and complex culture emerged. But great problems also appeared—crowded, unhealthy living conditions, crime and vice, and countless others. Not the least of these was the problem of how to govern these gigantic agglomerations. More government was essential to run a city, yet the nation had lived for the better part of a century by the motto: "that government is best which governs least." New kinds of government were necessary—building and sanitary codes, social services, a system of representation suited to a mass but atomized society—for which no precedents existed.

It was this situation, as William V. Shannon explains below, that produced the big-city political machines and the bosses who ran them. Shannon shows that the bosses served a function; they filled a gap in the political system created by the changes resulting from swift industrialization and urban growth. Eventually better machinery than the "machine" was devised to perform that function, although the proper government of cities still eludes us today. As an editor of the New York Times, Mr. Shannon brings to this subject a thorough knowledge of modern urban politics and, as the author of The American Irish, an equally solid understanding of the old boss system.

*T*he big cities and the political bosses grew up together in America. Bossism, with all its color and corruption and human drama, was a natural, perhaps even a necessary accompaniment to the rapid development of cities. The new urban communities did not grow slowly and according to plan; on the contrary, huge conglomerations of people from all over the world and from widely varying backgrounds came together suddenly, and in an unplanned, unorganized fashion fumbled their way toward communal relationships and a common identity. The political bosses emerged to cope with this chaotic change and growth. Acting out of greed, a ruthless will for mastery, and an imperfect understanding of what they were about, the bosses imposed upon these conglomerations called cities a certain feudal order and direction.

By 1890 virtually every sizable city had a political boss or was in the process of developing one. By 1950, sixty years later, almost every urban political machine was in an advanced state of obsolescence and its boss in trouble. The reason is not hard to find. Some of the cities kept growing and all of them kept changing, but the bosses, natural products of a specific era, could not grow or change beyond a certain point. The cities became essentially different, and as they did, the old-style organizations, like all organisms which cannot adapt, began to die. The dates vary from city to city. The system began earlier and died sooner in New York. Here or there, an old-timer made one last comeback. In Chicago, the organization and its boss still survive. But exceptions aside, the late nineteenth century saw the beginning, and the middle twentieth, the end, of the Age of the Bosses. What follows is a brief history of how it began, flourished, and passed away.

Soft-spoken Irish farmers from County Mayo and bearded Jews from Poland, country boys from Ohio and sturdy peasants from Calabria, gangling Swedes from near the Arctic Circle and Chinese from Canton, laconic Yankees from Vermont villages and Negro freedmen putting distance between themselves and the old plantation—all these and many other varieties of human beings from every national and religious and cultural tradition poured into America's cities in the decades after the Civil War.

Rome and Alexandria in the ancient world had probably been as polyglot, but in modern times the diversity of American cities was unique. Everywhere in the Western world, cities were growing rapidly in the late nineteenth century; but the Germans from the countryside who migrated to Hamburg and Berlin, the English who moved to Birmingham and London, and the French who flocked to Paris stayed among fellow nationals. They might be mocked as country bumpkins and their clothes might be unfashionable, but everyone they met spoke the same language as themselves, observed the same religious and secular holidays, ate the same kind of food, voted—if they had the franchise at all—in the same elections, and shared the same sentiments and expectations. To move from farm or village to a big

Two of the most memorable and politically long-lived of the bosses were Jersey City's Frank Hague (left) and Boston's James M. Curley (right).

European city was an adventure, but one still remained within the reassuring circle of the known and the familiar.

In American cities, however, the newcomers had nothing in common with one another except their poverty and their hopes. They were truly "the up-rooted." The foreign-born, unless they came from the British Isles, could not speak the language of their new homeland. The food, the customs, the holidays, the politics, were alien. Native Americans migrating to the cities from the countryside experienced their own kind of cultural shock: they found themselves competing not with other Americans but with recently arrived foreigners, so that despite their native birth they, too, felt displaced, strangers in their own country.

It was natural for members of each group to come together to try to find human warmth and protection in Little Italy or Cork Hill or Chinatown or Harlem. These feelings of clannish solidarity were one basis of strength for the political bosses. A man will more readily give his vote to a candidate because he is a neighbor from the old country or has some easily identifiable relationship, if only a similar name or the same religion, than because of agreement on some impersonal issue. Voters can take vicarious satisfaction from his success: "One of our boys is making good."

With so many different races and nationalities living together, however, mutual antagonisms were present, and the opportunity for hostility to flare into open violence was never far away. Ambitious, unscrupulous politicians could have exploited these antagonisms for their own political advantage, but the bosses and the political organizations which they developed did not function that way. If a man could vote and would "vote right," he was accepted, and that was the end of the matter. What lasting profit was there in attacking his religion or deriding his background?

Tammany early set the pattern of cultivating every bloc and faction and making an appeal as broad-based as possible. Of one precinct captain on the Lower East Side it was said: "He eats corned beef and kosher meat with equal nonchalance, and it's all the same to him whether he takes off his hat in the church or pulls it down over his ears in the synagogue."

Bosses elsewhere instinctively followed the same practice. George B. Cox, the turn-of-the-century Republican boss of Cincinnati, pasted together a coalition of Germans, Negroes, and old families like the Tafts and the Longworths. James M. Curley, who was mayor of Boston on and off for thirty-six years and was its closest approximation to a political boss, ran as well in the Lithuanian neighborhood of South Boston and the Italian section of East Boston as he did in the working-class Irish wards. In his last term in City Hall, he conferred minor patronage on the growing Negro community and joined the N.A.A.C.P.

The bosses organized neighborhoods, smoothed out antagonisms, arranged ethnically balanced tickets, and distributed patronage in accordance with voting strength as part of their effort to win and hold power. They blurred divisive issues and buried racial and religious hostility with blarney and buncombe. They were not aware that they were actually performing a mediating, pacifying function. They did not realize that by trying to please as many people as possible they were helping to hold raw new cities together, providing for inexperienced citizens a common meeting ground in politics and an experience in working together that would not have been available if the cities had been governed by apolitical bureaucracies. Bossism was usually corrupt and was decidedly inefficient, but in the 1960's, when antipoverty planners try to stimulate "community action organizations" to break through the apathy and disorganization of the slums, we can appreciate that the old-style machines had their usefulness.

When William Marcy Tweed, the first and most famous of the big-city bosses, died in jail in 1878, several hundred workingmen showed up for his funeral. The *Nation* wrote the following week:

> Let us remember that he fell without loss of reputation among the bulk of his supporters. The bulk of the poorer voters of this city today revere his memory, and look on him as the victim of rich men's malice; as, in short, a friend of the needy who applied the public funds, with as little waste as was possible under the circumstances, to the purposes to which they ought to be applied—and that is to the making of work for the working man. The odium heaped on him in the pulpits last Sunday does not exist in the lower stratum of New York society.

This split in attitude toward political bosses between the impoverished many and the prosperous middle classes lingers today and still colors historical writing. To respectable people, the boss was an exotic, even grotesque figure. They found it hard to understand why anyone would vote for him or what the sources of his popularity were. To the urban poor, those sources were self-evident. The boss ran a kind of ramshackle welfare state. He helped the unemployed find jobs, interceded in court for boys in trouble, wrote letters home to the old country for the illiterate; he provided free coal and baskets of food to tide a widow over an emergency, and organized parades, excursions to the beach, and other forms of free entertainment. Some bosses, such as Frank Hague in Jersey City and Curley in Boston, were energetic patrons of their respective city hospitals, spending public funds lavishly on new construction, providing maternity and children's clinics, and arranging medical care for the indigent. In an era when social security, Blue Cross, unemployment compensation, and other public and private arrangements to cushion life's shocks did not exist, these benefactions from a political boss were important.

In every city, the boss had his base in the poorer, older, shabbier section of town. Historians have dubbed this section the "walking city" because it developed in the eighteenth and early nineteenth centuries, when houses and businesses were jumbled together, usually near the waterfront, and businessmen and laborers alike had to live within walking distance of their work. As transportation improved, people were able to live farther and farther from their place of work. Population dispersed in rough concentric circles: the financially most successful lived in the outer ring, where land was plentiful and the air was clean; the middle classes lived in intermediate neighborhoods;

and the poorest and the latest arrivals from Europe crowded into the now-rundown neighborhoods in the center, where rents were lowest. Politics in most cities reflected a struggle between the old, boss-run wards downtown and the more prosperous neighborhoods farther out, which did not need a boss's services and which championed reform. The more skilled workingmen and the white-collar workers who lived in the intermediate neighborhoods generally held the balance of power between the machine and the reformers. A skillful boss could hold enough of these swing voters on the basis of ethnic loyalty or shared support of a particular issue. At times, he might work out alliances with business leaders who found that an understanding with a boss was literally more businesslike than dependence upon the vagaries of reform.

But always it was the poorest and most insecure who provided the boss with the base of his political power. Their only strength, as Professor Richard C. Wade of the University of Chicago has observed, was in their numbers.

These numbers were in most cases a curse; housing never caught up with demand, the job market was always flooded, the breadwinner had too many mouths to feed. Yet in politics such a liability could be turned into an asset. If the residents could be mobilized, their combined strength would be able to do what none could do alone. Soon the "boss" and the "machine" arose to organize this potential. The boss system was simply the political expression of inner city life.

At a time when many newcomers to the city were seeking unskilled work, and when many families had a precarious economic footing, the ability to dispense jobs was crucial to the bosses. First, there were jobs to be filled on the city payroll. Just as vital, and far more numerous, were jobs on municipal construction projects. When the machine controlled a city, public funds were always being spent for more schools, hospitals, libraries, courthouses, and orphanages. The growing cities had to have more sewer lines, gas lines, and waterworks, more paved streets and trolley tracks. Even if these utilities were privately owned, the managers needed the goodwill of city hall and were responsive to suggestions about whom to hire.

The payrolls of these public works projects were often padded, but to those seeking a job, it was better to be on a padded payroll than on no payroll. By contrast, the municipal reformers usually cut back on public spending, stopped projects to investigate for graft, and pruned payrolls. Middle- and upper-income taxpayers welcomed these reforms, but they were distinctly unpopular in working-class wards.

Another issue that strengthened the bosses was the regulation of the sale of liquor. Most women in the nineteenth century did not drink, and with their backing, the movement to ban entirely the manufacture and sale of liquor grew steadily stronger. It had its greatest support among Protestants with a rural or small-town background.

To them the cities, with their saloons, dance halls, cheap theatres, and red-light districts, were becoming latter-day versions of Sodom and Gomorrah.

Many of the European immigrants in the cities, however, had entirely different values. Quite respectable Germans took their wives to beer gardens on Sundays. In the eyes of the Irish, keeping a "public house" was an honorable occupation. Some Irish women drank beer and saw no harm in going to the saloon or sending an older child for a bucketful—"rushing the growler," they called it. Poles, Czechs, Italians, and others also failed to share the rage of the Prohibitionists against saloons. Unable to entertain in their cramped tenements, they liked to congregate in neighborhood bars.

The machine also appealed successfully on the liquor issue to many middle-class ethnic voters who had no need of the machine's economic assistance. Thus, in New York in 1897, Tammany scored a sweeping victory over an incumbent reform administration that had tried to enforce a state law permitting only hotels to sell liquor on Sundays. As one of the city's three police commissioners, Theodore Roosevelt became famous prowling the tougher neighborhoods on the hunt for saloon violations, but on the vaudeville stage the singers were giving forth with the hit song, "I Want What I Want When I Want It!" As a character in Alfred Henry Lewis' novel *The Boss* explained it, the reformers had made a serious mistake: "They got between the people and its beer!"

In 1902, Lincoln Steffens, the muckraker who made a name for himself writing about political bossism, visited St. Louis to interview Joseph W. Folk, a crusading district attorney. "It is good businessmen that are corrupting our bad politicians," Folk told him. "It is good business that causes bad government in St. Louis." Thirty-five years later, Boss Tom Pendergast was running the entire state of Missouri on that same reciprocal relationship.

Although many factory owners could be indifferent to politics, other businessmen were dependent upon the goodwill and the efficiency of the municipal government. The railroads that wanted to build their freight terminals and extend their lines into the cities, the contractors who erected the office buildings, the banks that held mortgages on the land and loaned money for the construction, the utility and transit companies, and the department stores were all in need of licenses, franchises, rights of way, or favorable rulings from city inspectors and agencies. These were the businesses that made the big pay-offs to political bosses in cash, blocks of stock, or tips on land about to be developed.

In another sense, profound, impersonal, and not corrupt, the business community needed the boss. Because the Industrial Revolution hit this country when it was still thinly populated and most of its cities were overgrown towns, American cities expanded with astonishing speed. For example, in the single decade from 1880 to 1890, Chicago's population more than doubled, from a half million to over a million. Minneapolis and St. Paul tripled in size. New York City increased from a million to a million and a half; Detroit, Milwaukee, Columbus, and Cleveland grew by sixty to eighty per cent.

Municipal governments, however, were unprepared for this astonishing growth. Planning and budgeting were unknown arts. City charters had restrictive provisions envisaged for much smaller, simpler communities. The mayor and the important commissioners were usually amateurs serving a term or two as a civic duty. Authority was dispersed among numerous boards and special agencies. A typical city would have a board of police commissioners, a board of health, a board of tax assessors, a water board, and many others. The ostensible governing body was a city council or board of aldermen which might have thirty, fifty, or even a hundred members. Under these circumstances, it was difficult to get a prompt decision, harder still to coordinate decisions taken by different bodies acting on different premises, and easy for delays and anomalies to develop.

In theory, the cities could have met their need for increased services by municipal socialism, but the conventional wisdom condemned that as too radical, although here and there a city did experiment with publicly owned utilities. In theory also, the cities could have financed public buildings and huge projects such as water and sewer systems by frankly raising taxes or floating bonds. But both taxes and debt were no more popular then than they are now. Moreover, the laissez-faire doctrine which holds that "that government is best which governs least" was enshrined orthodoxy in America from the 1870's down to the 1930's.

As men clung to such orthodox philosophies, the structures of government became obsolete; they strained to meet unexpected demands as a swelling number of citizens in every class clamored for more services. In this climate the bosses emerged. They had no scruples about taking shortcuts through old procedures or manipulating independent boards and agencies in ways that the original city fathers had never intended. They had no inhibiting commitment to any theory of limited government. They were willing to spend, tax, and build— and to take the opprobrium along with the graft. Sometimes, like Hague in Jersey City, Curley in Boston, and Big Bill Thompson in Chicago, they got themselves elected mayor and openly assumed responsibility. More often, like Pendergast in Kansas City, Cox in Cincinnati, the leaders of Tammany, and the successive Republican bosses of Philadelphia, they held minor offices or none, stayed out of the limelight, and ran city government through their iron control of the party organization. In ruling Memphis for forty years, Ed Crump followed one pattern and then the other. Impeached on a technicality after being elected three times as mayor, Crump retreated to the back rooms and became even more powerful as the city's political boss.

What manner of men became political bosses? They were men of little education and no social background, often of immigrant parentage. A college-educated boss like Edward Flynn of The Bronx was a rarity. Bosses often began as saloonkeepers, because the saloon was a natural meeting place in poorer neighborhoods in the days before

Prohibition. They were physically strong and no strangers to violence. Seventy-five years ago, most men made their living with brawn rather than brain, and a man who expected to be a leader of men had to be tough as well as shrewd. Open violence used to be common at polling places on Election Day, and gangs of repeaters roamed from one precinct to another. Although the typical boss made his way up through that roughneck system, the logic of his career led him to suppress violence. Bloody heads make bad publicity, and it is hard for any political organization to maintain a monopoly on violence. Bosses grew to prefer quieter, more lawful, less dangerous methods of control. Ballot-box stuffing and overt intimidation never disappeared entirely, but gradually they receded to weapons of last resort.

Political bosses varied in their idiosyncrasies and styles. A few, like Curley, became polished orators; others, like the legendary Charles Murphy of Tammany Hall, never made speeches. They were temperate, businesslike types; among them a drunk was as rare as a Phi Beta Kappa. If they had a generic failing it was for horses and gambling. Essentially they were hardheaded men of executive temper and genuine organizing talents; many, in other circumstances and with more education, might have become successful businessmen.

They have disappeared now, most of them. Education has produced a more sophisticated electorate; it has also encouraged potential bosses to turn away from politics toward more secure, prestigious, and profitable careers. A young man who had the energy, persistence, and skill in 1899 to become a successful political boss would in 1969 go to college and end up in an executive suite.

The urban population has also changed. The great flood of bewildered foreigners has dwindled to a trickle. In place of the European immigrants of the past, today's cities receive an influx of Negroes from the rural South, Puerto Ricans, Mexicans, and the white poor from Appalachia. As they overcome the language barrier and widen their experience, the Puerto Ricans are making themselves felt in urban politics. New York City, where they are most heavily concentrated, may have a Puerto Rican mayor in the not too distant future.

But the other groups are too isolated from the rest of the community to put together a winning political coalition of have-nots. The Mexicans and the ex-hillbillies from Appalachia are isolated by their unique cultural backgrounds, the Negroes by the giant fact of their race. Inasmuch as they make up a quarter to a third of the population in many cities, are a cohesive group, and still have a high proportion of poor who have to look to government for direct help, the Negroes might have produced several bosses and functioning political machines had they been of white European ancestry. But until Negroes attain a clear numerical majority, they find it difficult to take political power in any city because various white factions are reluctant to coalesce with them.

Regardless of the race or background of the voters, however, there are factors which work against the old-style machines. Civil service

In this contemporary cartoon Michael Ramus has pictured Mayor Daley of Chicago as "The Last Leaf" on the blasted tree of old-style urban bossism.

regulations make it harder to create a job or pad a payroll. Federal income taxes and federal accounting requirements make it more difficult to hide the rewards of graft. Television, public relations, and polling have created a whole new set of political techniques and undermined the personal ties and neighborhood loyalties on which the old organizations depended.

The new political style has brought an increase in municipal government efficiency and probably some decline in political corruption and misrule. But the politics of the television age puts a premium on hypocrisy. Candor has gone out the window with the spoils system. There is still a lot of self-seeking in politics and always will be. But gone are the days of Tammany's Boss Richard Croker, who when asked by an investigating committee if he was "working for his own pocket," shot back: "All the time—same as you." Today's politicians are so busy tending their images that they have become incapable of even a mildly derogatory remark such as Jim Curley's: "The term 'codfish aristocracy' is a reflection on the fish."

Curley entitled his memoirs *I'd Do It Again*. But the rough-and-tumble days when two-fisted, rough-tongued politicians came roaring out of the slums to take charge of America's young cities are not to come again.

Robert L. Beisner

Two Early Critics
of Industrial
America

Critics, as creators have always been quick to point out, are
seldom truly objective in their judgments; they tend to impose their
own prejudices on the work they presume to evaluate. This has been
as true of social critics as of persons who review books or theatrical
productions. Robert L. Beisner's essay on E. L. Godkin and Charles
Eliot Norton, two sharp critics of post-Civil War American society,
proves beyond question that these men were fundamentally subjective
in their attitudes. They disliked the changes that industrialization
was bringing to America and, viewing their world with jaundiced
eyes, exaggerated and distorted the evils they complained about.
Furthermore, they sought to reverse irreversible trends, to turn back
the clock of history. Since we know—actually they knew it too—
that this was impossible, we tend either to scorn or laugh at critics
like Godkin and Norton, to dismiss them as crabbed, selfish reaction-
aries. Yet their criticism was not necessarily inaccurate because it
was self-serving. And, as Beisner shows, it had a constructive as well
as a destructive side; dislike of what was happening to American
society did not destroy their commitment to that society.

Professor Beisner, who is an associate professor of history at The
American University, is a specialist in late nineteenth-century social
and intellectual history. His book Twelve Against Empire: The Anti-
Imperialists, 1898–1900 won the Allan Nevins prize of the Society of
American Historians.

*I*t used to be said in Cambridge, Massachusetts, that all of the dogs in the town wailed mournfully whenever E. L. Godkin and Charles Eliot Norton got together to swap their pessimistic views on the state of the nation. In the summer of 1897 Norton wrote Godkin that he had recently been forced to put his paper aside one evening ''because with each note or article the gloom deepened till it grew darker than it used to be even in my study when after an evening of talk you declared that it was enough to make Rome howl.'' For more than thirty years Godkin and Norton sustained and fed each other's pessimism, sorely disappointed as they both were with developments in post-Civil War America. They believed that American morality had declined precipitately since the early days of the republic. They lamented the lack of good men in politics and the domination of the public service by men of coarse and corrupt nature. They watched with jaundiced eyes as millions of immigrants poured into their country. They took in the ''General Grant'' architecture, read the new literature, deplored the new wealth, saw successful businessmen gain entrance to their private clubs, faced America's plunge into imperialism and the glaring headlines of the yellow press—and declared it an age of vulgarity and a nation of ''chromo-civilization.''

There have always been such men, convinced in the core of their being that what had been in their youth a world of gold had lately turned to dross. In the era of industrialism and mass democracy these Jeremiahs have more often than not come from the ranks of the old landed, learned, or professional elites most in danger of being superseded or ignored by a democratic and acquisitive society. The quicker the rate of change and the fresher the memory of better times, the greater the likelihood that these gentle Brahmins would deplore the life around them. The rapidly changing America which emerged from the Civil War provoked just such an outcry of genteel despair—a dismay eloquently expressed by E. L. Godkin and Charles Eliot Norton. Both men placed the blame for their unhappiness on precisely those features of American civilization which were most highly valued by the majority of their countrymen: material prosperity and democratic government.

Edwin Lawrence Godkin was born in Moyne, County Wicklow, Ireland, on October 2, 1831. His father was a Presbyterian clergyman who became a political journalist after being ejected from the pulpit for his advocacy of home rule for Ireland. Young Edwin, too, went into journalism after making an indifferent record at Queen's College, Belfast. Already the youthful author of a history of Hungary, Godkin left for the Crimea in 1853 as a war correspondent for the London *Daily News*. Upon his return two years later he resolved to emigrate to the United States. In November of 1856 he reached America, where for nearly a decade (except for a short period spent in Ireland and Europe) he occupied himself with law studies and writing letters on American affairs for the London *Daily News*. His early friends included a number of important eastern Republicans, and in 1865, when they decided to found a journal that would reflect their political and

The critics: Editor Edwin Lawrence Godkin (left) and Professor Charles Eliot Norton (right).

economic views, they established the weekly *Nation* and selected to edit it the thirty-four-year-old Godkin. One of the prime backers of the enterprise and a close friend of the new editor was Charles Eliot Norton.

Godkin's sharp and authoritative editorials quickly made the *Nation* a habit for thousands of readers (one would be hard put to recognize it in the *Nation* that is published today); later on, his work performed the same service for the daily New York *Evening Post* (equally unrecognizable in the modern *Post*), whose editor he became in 1881 while retaining his position on the *Nation*. The critical tone of the *Nation* made it seem to some a "weekly judgment day," and neither it nor the *Evening Post* attracted a large circulation. Both, however, exercised wide influence. College students adopted Godkin's opinions for their own the way later generations of students would parrot H. L. Mencken and Walter Lippmann. And other newspapermen paid close attention to Godkin's editorials. Once when New York's Democratic Governor David B. Hill was under attack by the *Evening Post* he remarked: "I don't care anything about the handful of Mugwumps who read it in New York [City]. The trouble with the damned sheet is that every editor in New York State reads it."

Yet Godkin had formidable critics. The most vehement among them was Theodore Roosevelt, who called Godkin almost every disagreeable epithet that came to his fertile mind. To him Godkin was an unpatriotic man, "a malignant and dishonest liar" who suffered from

"a species of moral myopia, complicated with intellectual strabismus."
Lincoln Steffens, who worked for a short time with Godkin, thought
that his editorials were "clever, forceful, [and] ripping" but also
"personal and not very thoughtful." The Boston banker and philan-
thropist Henry L. Higginson believed that as Godkin's career unfolded,
his words became "so twisted and stained by great conceit, arrogance,
evil temper, that they lost their fairness, their perspicacity, their
virtue and therefore their value."

Charles Eliot Norton had those qualities of gentleness and con-
templativeness that his friend Godkin lacked. He too was the son of
a clergyman, Andrews Norton, a prominent Unitarian divine. Born in
Cambridge, Massachusetts, in 1827, Norton spent his youth in the
scholarly surroundings of a home frequented by such distinguished
visitors as Francis Parkman, George Bancroft, George Ticknor, and
Henry Wadsworth Longfellow. While still a youth he developed a
great passion for rare books and art objects, thus demonstrating an
early and serious interest in the field to which he was unable to devote
his full attention until he was nearly fifty. He made Phi Beta Kappa
at Harvard, and after his graduation in 1846 spent a decade in
business. The next twenty years were passed in studying, living in
Europe, writing and editing books, supervising Union propaganda
activities during the Civil War, and working both as editor and con-
tributor for the cream of American journals—the *Atlantic Monthly,
North American Review,* and the *Nation.* Finally, in 1875, he was

appointed Harvard's first professor of fine arts, a post which he retained until he retired in 1897.

As a scholar, Norton was an acknowledged master of medieval studies and a respected translator of Dante. He wrote an important volume entitled *Historical Studies of Church-Building in the Middle Ages* as well as studies of Dante, Donne, Ruskin, Gray, Michelangelo, Holbein, and Turner. In addition, he edited the letters of James Russell Lowell, the Thomas Carlyle-Ralph Waldo Emerson correspondence, the Carlyle-Goethe correspondence, and the letters he had received from John Ruskin. As a teacher, Norton's aim was to advance aesthetic values and inculcate high standards of taste. Art was not to be studied merely for its own sake. Norton believed that man had reached his greatest moral and intellectual heights in ancient Greece and medieval Italy, and he thought that this superiority could be seen in the artistic achievements of those epochs. It was his habit in class to illustrate this relationship between art and morality with frequent deprecating references to the barrenness of American art and the moral and intellectual inferiority of American life.

The story is told that Norton once began a lecture on the idea of the "gentleman" by remarking airily: "None of you, probably, has ever seen a gentleman." It was inevitable that a teacher with such a rarefied taste for the antique would become the subject of parodies and the source of much campus amusement. One story has it, for instance, that an undergraduate emerged after three meetings of Norton's Fine Arts 3 course with his total notes reading:

(1) Greece.

(2) Bully for Greece.

(3) There are no flies on Greece.

Norton's general aesthetic sensibilities and his displeasure with the design of many new buildings at Harvard were parodied in a tale to the effect that he had died and was about to enter heaven when he suddenly drew back, shaded his eyes and exclaimed: "Oh! Oh! Oh! So overdone! So garish! So Renaissance!" Despite the numerous campus jokes made at his expense, Norton's encouragement of the fine arts and his efforts to direct public attention to the advancing deterioration of America's landscape and cities made him an important figure in post-Civil War America—a friend of art museums, conservation projects, parks, and schools. In the opinion of Van Wyck Brooks, "no one aroused the country more to a sense of its general ugliness and a will to create a beautiful civilization."

In politics Godkin and Norton were mugwumps—independents who refused to commit themselves to the fortunes of any particular party. Both feared that American politics had rejected the country's "good men," and hoped for a breakup of the old party organizations. As early as 1859 Godkin had complained that the "nominating conventions toss men like Clay and Webster aside, and fish out from amongst the obscurities Pierces and Buchanans as likely to prove more pliable instruments in factious hands." The political machines, he charged, put up such bad men to run for office that good men were

A Harvard student drew this caricature of Professor of Fine Arts Norton in 1901.

no longer tempted to enter public affairs.

For Godkin and Norton the decline in political morality was but one aspect of a more serious decline in the quality of American life. Each felt that the United States had once enjoyed a Golden Age of reason, simplicity, and high morality. But the push toward an industrial way of life was transforming the social and physical landscape of their once-Arcadian America, and wherever they looked they now saw deterioration and decadence. Godkin deplored the "moral anarchy" of modern business methods and despised those who employed them. He fought the admission of businessmen to the Century Club of New York, complaining that most of them "rarely open a book" and "know no more, read no more, and have no more to say than the bricklayer and the plumber." For his part, Norton was particularly concerned with the aesthetic changes and the unfortunate transformation in the tone of society. The country he had known had vanished under a wave of vulgarity. The "barren" art and literature of the late nineteenth century depressed him:

> Nowhere in the civilized world are the practical concerns of life more engrossing; nowhere are the conditions of life more prosaic; nowhere is the poetic spirit less evident, and the love of beauty less diffused. The concern for beauty, as the highest end of work, and as the noblest expression of life, hardly exists among us, and forms no part of our character as a nation.

Norton told a friend in 1873 that America had lost its original bright promise and was "not a pleasing child." Only Harvard, Yale, the *Nation,* and the *North American Review* stood firm as "solid

barriers against the invasion of modern barbarism & vulgarity." The
other landmarks and manners of an earlier and better day were dis-
appearing before his very eyes. Even Cambridge was slipping away;
Norton felt himself a stranger in his birthplace. The few houses that
remained from his childhood were occupied by "new people." Norton
could find only "half a dozen men or women" who could converse
on those general subjects once familiar to all people of education—
"My fair neighbor asks, 'What are Pericles?'" Thus Norton, condemned to live in an age of industrialization and specialization, sighed
under his burden of nostalgia. One of his students—young Josephine
Peabody, who heard him lecture at Radcliffe in 1895, wrote:

> Professor Norton lectured in Italian 4 this afternoon. The dear
> old man looks so mildy happy and benignant while he regrets
> everything in the age and the country—so contented, while he
> gently tells us it were better for us had we never been born in
> this degenerate and unlovely age.

What had brought America to its present condition? Godkin
found in the very heart of the American Experiment—in its commitment to political democracy and social equality—the cause of what
he deemed to be its failure. These noble ideals simply did not work in
practice. The triumph of popular rule had come to mean only that
politicians catered to the lowest level of understanding. The ideal of
equality, which in theory referred to an "equality of burdens," had
in actuality degenerated into a contempt for the excellent and superior,
a "disregard for special fitness." Could anything but disaster be
expected from the masses whom this egalitarian democracy had thrown
to the top? Godkin wrote in 1870:

> Their rush into the forum and into the temples and palaces and
> libraries is not an agreeable sight to witness, and it would be
> foolish to expect that under their ruthless touch many gifts and
> graces will not be obscured, many arts will not be lost, many a
> great ideal, at whose shrine the best men and women of three
> generations have found courage and inspiration, will not vanish
> from the earth . . .

Along with equality and democracy both Godkin and Norton
believed that the third agent of destruction was prosperity. Norton
had long maintained that there was a causal connection between
great wealth and the dissolution of national character. The decline of
Greece had been set off by the "increase of private luxury [and]
selfishness" and the rise of "unrestrained individuality." Surely it
was vanity to believe that America could be spared the disastrous
effects of excessive material wealth. As early as 1853 Norton had
warned that the long and uninterrupted history of prosperity enjoyed
by the United States was beginning to take its toll in a declining
national character. After the Civil War the blight grew worse and
spread beyond the frontiers and across the ocean. Money-getting was
proving the ruin of literature and was blunting the intelligence of

the people; even in Europe materialism was leaving its imprint. A foolish optimism was in the air. From Florence in 1869 Norton wrote:

> Italy in losing tyrants, in becoming constitutional, in taking to trade, is doing what she can to spoil her charm. The railroad whistle just behind the church of Santa Maria Novella, or just beyond the Campo Santo at Pisa, sounds precisely as it sounds on the Back Bay or at the Fitchburg Station,—and it and the common school are Americanizing the land to a surprising degree. Happy country! Fortunate people! Before long they may hope for their Greeleys, their Beechers, and their Fisks.

Norton did not deny that democracy could "work," but as he said following the election of 1884, it appeared to work "ignobly, ignorantly, brutally." Or it could work as it had begun to in Europe, bringing about "the destruction of old shrines, the disregard of beauty, the decline in personal distinction, the falling off in manners." What was clear was that democracy did not work as Norton had hoped it would. In his view democracy was supposed to mean that everyone in society would be public-spirited. But it had turned out in practice to mean that everyone was involved in the selfish pursuit of private interests. Rather than heightening the individual's awareness of his civic responsibilities, universal suffrage had furnished "a distinct source of moral corruption." Rather than increasing the wisdom of all citizens, democracy had diminished the regard for intelligent counsel and produced a general "rejection of authority." The sense of license and the smug complacency that had been created by democracy and prosperity had made "extravagant self-confidence" and willful conduct the hallmarks of the American people. Writing in 1896, Norton declared: "It seems to me not unlikely that for a considerable time to come there will be an increase of lawlessness and of public folly."

Godkin was savage in his dislike for the many immigrants who were so rapidly being incorporated into the American political system. Their votes gave power to the corrupt urban bosses who exploited them. One could see on every hand, Godkin exclaimed, the "ignorant" foreign voter "eating away the political structure, like a white ant, with a group of natives standing over him and encouraging him." In 1891 he proposed that all immigrants be shut out unless they could read and write the English language. This would mean, he admitted, that all but a few immigrants would perforce come from the British Isles, "but why not, if the restriction be really undertaken in the interest of American civilization? We are under no obligation to see that all races and nations enjoy an equal chance of getting here." Godkin called it natural law "that the more intelligent and thoughtful of the race shall inherit the earth and have the best time, and that all others shall find life on the whole dull and unprofitable."

Godkin did not pretend to have answers to the problems of the age that he and Norton castigated. The structure of American life seemed too corrupt to save, too rotten to shore up with marginal improvements, and he eventually determined to return to England rather than witness its expected collapse. Norton had no answers either, but his pessimism was relieved by a limited belief in the worth of ameliorative action, and his distrust of acquisitiveness and democracy was mitigated by his interest in the unprecedented material and educational achievements of America's lower classes.

As an active participant in the social and political processes, Norton established a night school for the poor in 1846; he promoted better housing for the underprivileged; he was in the forefront of the campaign for female suffrage and education (with the hope that women would raise the ideals and tone of American society); and, in the interest of preserving at least the landscape of America, he fought hard and effectively to save both the Adirondacks and Niagara Falls from exploitation and desecration. In an effort to exert direct influence upon public opinion, Norton founded the Ashfield "academy dinners," held each summer from 1879 to 1903 in Ashfield, Massachusetts. On these occasions civil-service reform, tariff reduction, Negro education, and anti-imperialism, as well as many other mugwump interests, were discussed by William Dean Howells, George Washington Cable, William James, James Russell Lowell, Booker T. Washington, and many others, including Norton himself.

Norton was consoled and reassured by the knowledge that, in his country, the economic and educational level of the lower classes had been elevated to the highest point in history. When William Dean Howells inquired of him, "Well, after all, if you could change, would you rather have been an Englishman than an American?" Norton unhesitatingly replied: "No, if I could choose I would rather have been American."

But, at best, progress came at a maddeningly slow pace, and Norton succeeded only intermittently in maintaining his optimism. In 1871 he bitterly predicted that the creation of a really sound republic would take as long as the evolution from monkey to man. In 1884 he described himself as an "absolute" pessimist—a man who had learned not to hope for any good in the world and who thus lived a life free of expectations and complaints:

> Your out-and-out pessimist is cheerful, even though nature herself plays false, and uses loaded dice against him in the game. Darwinism has helped us a good deal. You expect less of men when you look at them not as a little lower than the angels, but as a little higher than the anthropoid apes.

By the mid-1890's E. L. Godkin and Charles Eliot Norton had lived for a third of a century believing that their country was in a steady decline, that its onetime promise had been largely submerged by a rising tide of corruption, immorality, tastelessness, and stupidity. Thus it was more than coincidental that, at this time, the thoughts of each man turned to the fall of Rome. In 1895 Godkin wrote Norton:

> You see I am not sanguine about the future of democracy. I think we shall have a long period of decline like that which

followed the fall of the Roman Empire, and then a recrudescence
under some other form of society.

A year later Norton wrote an English friend:

> It is hard to have the whole background of life grow darker as
> one grows old. I can understand the feeling of a Roman as he
> saw the Empire breaking down, and civilization dying out. It
> will take much longer than we once hoped, for the world to
> reorganize itself upon a democratic basis, and for a new and
> desirable social order to come into existence.

But—with the faith that never completely left him—he added: "If
we set our hope far enough forward we need not lose it."

By 1895 Godkin and Norton had come to sound increasingly like
men who were close to abandoning all hope for their country. From
the *Nation* and from Harvard they watched the ailing American
Experiment falter and fail. It was the Spanish-American War and the
expansionism that accompanied it that administered the *coup de
grâce*. Godkin and Norton were angry and saddened but not surprised,
for they had expected all along that something of the sort would
happen. The times had long been out of joint, and imperialism was
but another blow—albeit the heaviest—against the America they had
known. Only one question remained for them: was the blow fatal?

For thirty years Godkin had been an opponent of expansionism,
hammering away against every annexation scheme that dared to raise
its head. Three months before the outbreak of the Spanish-American
War, when the Senate was considering the annexation of Hawaii,
Godkin had summarized his objections to a policy of territorial annexation in a *Nation* editorial:

> The sudden departure from our traditions; the absence from
> our system of any machinery for governing dependencies; the
> admission of alien, inferior, and mongrel races to our national-
> ity; the opening of fresh fields to carpetbaggers, speculators,
> and corruptionists; the un-Americanism of governing a large
> body of people against their will, and by persons not responsible
> to them; the entrance on a policy of conquest and annexation
> while our own continent was still unreclaimed, our population
> unassimilated, and many of our most serious political problems
> still unsolved; and finally the danger of the endorsement of a
> gross fraud for the first time by a Christian nation.

At the close of the war in August, 1898, Godkin remained firmly
opposed to all annexation schemes, and throughout the rest of that year
and all of the next he repeatedly emphasized the difficulties the United
States would face if it became an imperialist power. He believed that
the establishment of a colonial administration would necessitate a
drastic overhaul of the American government, "a complete change in
our destiny, political, military, and naval." If the United States annexed the Philippines and had to defend them from the covetousness

of other powers, it would be necessary to arm to the teeth with naval and military forces capable of being "instantly" mobilized and dispatched to any danger spot on the globe. And we would need a "permanent" colonial service:

> It will not do to vote money and build ships, simply, and drill armies and sailors. If we are going to annex and rule over countries the population of which differs from us in race, religion, language, in history and every variety of antecedent, and who will probably hate us and treat our rule as a "yoke," we shall have to get administrators ready, as well as guns and ships. We shall have to do what the other conquering and colonizing nations do, what England does, what Russia and Germany do.

In his anger Godkin railed at the expansionists for their betrayal of American principles. In the Philippines, he charged, McKinley, "drunk with glory and flattery," had substituted "keen effective slaughter for Spanish old-fashioned, clumsy slaughter." When eager missionaries began planning new translations of the Bible in the various tongues of the Filipinos, the *Nation* derisively commented that they should read: "Mow down the natives like grass and say unto them, the Syndicate has arrived." But there was no longer much heart in Godkin's protest, for he had concluded that the fight was virtually lost. In late 1898 and early 1899 he gave way to utter despair, publicly declaring that "the old American republic is in a bad way." In private letters he poured out his full sorrow:

> I am, heart and soul, an American of the *vielle roche*. American ideals were the intellectual food of my youth, and to see America converted into a senseless, Old World conqueror, embitters my age. [May, 1899]

> I came here fifty years ago with high and fond ideals about America. . . . They are now all shattered, and I have apparently to look elsewhere to keep even moderate hopes about the human race alive. [Late 1899]

> I have suffered from seeing the America of my youthful dreams vanish from my sight, and the commencement on this continent of the old story. . . . [November 13, 1899]

Godkin suffered a stroke in February of 1900. Fifteen months later he left his adopted country and returned to England. Occasionally the bitter humor of former days would return to him, as when he wrote James Bryce: "Do come over soon, and we'll lie under a tree at Dublin while you abuse Great Britain and I abuse the United States." He died in Devon on May 21, 1902, and was buried in the Hazelbeach churchyard, Northampton, to rest forever in England. In America, the country he had abandoned, the *Nation* published a fitting epitaph:

He grew old in an age he condemned
Felt the dissolving throes
Of a Social order he loved,
And, like Theban seer,
    Died in his enemies' day.

Charles Eliot Norton, like Godkin, interpreted the Spanish-American War and its aftermath as final proof that his early hopes for a special American destiny had been in vain. Amid the popular enthusiasm aroused by early American victories in Cuba and at Manila Bay, he advised students not to enlist (familiar note!) and declared before an audience in Cambridge that the United States had rashly:

> hurried into war, and . . . she who more than any other land was pledged to peace and goodwill on earth, unsheathes her sword, compels a weak and unwilling nation to a fight, rejecting without due consideration her earnest and repeated offers to meet every legitimate demand of the United States. It is a bitter disappointment to the lover of his country; it is a turning-back from the path of civilization to that of barbarism.

Godkin and Norton were among those nineteenth-century idealists who had hoped, like the Puritans of the seventeenth century, that America would be a city set on a hill—a state and civilization that would attract the admiration of and serve as an example to the world. Despite disappointments, these two remarkable men, schooled in the genteel tradition, were never able to resist the lingering hope that America might yet be saved, and they flattered themselves that men such as they might yet create in the distant future a superior civilization in America. In 1902—with Americans in control of Cuba, Puerto Rico, and the Philippines—Norton counselled his friends not to give up:

> While all the congregation of the children of Israel are wandering in the wilderness of Sin . . . we, the little remnant of the house of Judah that has escaped, must comfort one another as best we may. . . . we are defeated for the time; but the war is not ended, and we are enlisted for the war.

Richard Hofstadter

The Myth
of the
Happy Yeoman

The following essay, like Oliver La Farge's essay on the American Indian in Volume I, is a study in the differences between reality and men's view of reality. Usually the historian seeks only for the reality and discards the myths that surround it in the records of the past. But in some contexts the myths themselves are vitally important; if the subject is men's views, these views become the reality in question, and thus the proper subject of historical analysis.

The concept of the yeoman farmer had, as Professor Richard Hofstadter of Columbia University demonstrates, a solid basis in fact in early America. Farming was for many a way of life, not primarily a way of making a living. But national growth and development changed this steadily, and after the rapid expansion of industrialization the true yeoman practically disappeared. Why the myth persisted is the subject of Hofstadter's inquiry. The tale is part of the larger story of the impact of the industrial revolution on American thought, a subject which Hofstadter develops at greater length in his Pulitzer Prize history, The Age of Reform.

The United States was born in the country and has moved to the city. From the beginning its political values as well as ideas were of necessity shaped by country life. The early American politician, the country editor, who wished to address himself to the common man, had to draw upon a rhetoric that would touch the tillers of the soil; and even the spokesman of city people knew that his audience had been in very large part reared upon the farm.

But what the articulate people who talked and wrote about farmers and farming—the preachers, poets, philosophers, writers, and statesmen—liked about American farming was not, in every respect, what the typical working farmer liked. For the articulate people were drawn irresistibly to the noncommercial, non-pecuniary, self-sufficient aspect of American farm life. To them it was an ideal.

Writers like Thomas Jefferson and Hector St. John de Crèvecœur admired the yeoman farmer not for his capacity to exploit opportunities and make money but for his honest industry, his independence, his frank spirit of equality, his ability to produce and enjoy a simple abundance. The farmer himself, in most cases, was in fact inspired to make money, and such self-sufficiency as he actually had was usually forced upon him by a lack of transportation or markets, or by the necessity to save cash to expand his operations.

For while early American society was an agrarian society, it was fast becoming more commercial, and commercial goals made their way among its agricultural classes almost as rapidly as elsewhere. The more commercial this society became, however, the more reason it found to cling in imagination to the noncommercial agrarian values. The more farming as a self-sufficient way of life was abandoned for farming as a business, the more merit men found in what was being left behind. And the more rapidly the farmers' sons moved into the towns, the more nostalgic the whole culture became about its rural past. Throughout the nineteenth and even in the twentieth century, the American was taught that rural life and farming as a vocation were something sacred.

This sentimental attachment to the rural way of life is a kind of homage that Americans have paid to the fancied innocence of their origins. To call it a "myth" is not to imply that the idea is simply false. Rather the "myth" so effectively embodies men's values that it profoundly influences their way of perceiving reality and hence their behavior.

Like any complex of ideas, the agrarian myth cannot be defined in a phrase, but its component themes form a clear pattern. Its hero was the yeoman farmer, its central conception the notion that he is the ideal man and the ideal citizen. Unstinted praise of the special virtues of the farmer and the special values of rural life was coupled with the assertion that agriculture, as a calling uniquely productive and uniquely important to society, had a special right to the concern and protection of government. The yeoman, who owned a small farm and worked it with the aid of his family, was the incarnation of the simple, honest, independent, healthy, happy human being. Because he lived in close communion with beneficent nature, his life was believed to have a wholesomeness and integrity impossible for the depraved populations of cities.

His well-being was not merely physical, it was moral: it was not merely personal, it was the central source of civic virtue; it was not merely secular but religious, for God had made the land and called man to cultivate it. Since the yeoman was believed to be both happy and honest, and since he had a secure propertied stake in society in the form of his own land, he was held to be the best and most reliable sort of citizen. To this conviction Jefferson appealed when he wrote: "The small land holders are the most precious part of a state."

In origin the agrarian myth was not a popular but a literary idea, a preoccupation of the upper classes, of those who enjoyed a classical education, read pastoral poetry, experimented with breeding stock, and owned plantations or country estates. It was clearly formulated and almost universally accepted in America during the last half of the eighteenth century. As it took shape both in Europe and America, its promulgators drew heavily upon the authority and the rhetoric of classical writers—Hesiod, Xenophon, Cato, Cicero, Virgil, Horace, and others—whose works were the staples of a good education. A learned agricultural gentry, coming into conflict with the industrial classes, welcomed the moral strength that a rich classical ancestry brought to the praise of husbandry.

Chiefly through English experience, and from English and classical writers, the agrarian myth came to America, where, like so many other cultural importations, it eventually took on altogether new dimensions in its new setting. So appealing were the symbols of the myth that even an arch-opponent of the agrarian interest like Alexander Hamilton found it politic to concede in his *Report on Manufactures* that "the cultivation of the earth, as the primary and most certain source of national supply . . . has intrinsically a strong claim to pre-eminence over every other kind of industry." And Benjamin Franklin, urban cosmopolite though he was, once said that agriculture was "the only *honest way*" for a nation to acquire wealth, "wherein man receives a real increase of the seed thrown into the ground, a kind of continuous miracle, wrought by the hand of God in his favour, as a reward for his innocent life and virtuous industry."

Among the intellectual classes in the eighteenth century the agrarian myth had virtually universal appeal. Some writers used it to give simple, direct, and emotional expression to their feelings about life and nature; others linked agrarianism with a formal philosophy of natural rights. The application of the natural rights philosophy to land tenure became especially popular in America. Since the time of Locke it had been a standard argument that the land is the common stock of society to which every man has a right—what Jefferson called "the fundamental right to labour the earth"; that since the occupancy and use of land are the true criteria of valid ownership, labor expended in cultivating the earth confers title to it; that since govern-

According to this 1869 engraving from The Prairie Farmer, *each occupation has its uses, but the farmer alone foots all the bills.*

ment was created to protect property, the property of working land-holders has a special claim to be fostered and protected by the state.

At first the agrarian myth was a notion of the educated classes, but by the early nineteenth century it had become a mass creed, a part of the country's political folklore and its nationalist ideology. The roots of this change may be found as far back as the American

Revolution, which, appearing to many Americans as the victory of a band of embattled farmers over an empire, seemed to confirm the moral and civic superiority of the yeoman, made the farmer a symbol of the new nation, and wove the agrarian myth into his patriotic sentiments and idealism.

Still more important, the myth played a role in the first party battles under the Constitution. The Jeffersonians appealed again and again to the moral primacy of the yeoman farmer in their attacks on the Federalists. The family farm and American democracy became indissolubly connected in Jeffersonian thought, and by 1840 even the more conservative party, the Whigs, took over the rhetorical appeal to the common man, and elected a President in good part on the strength of the fiction that he lived in a log cabin.

The Jeffersonians, moreover, made the agrarian myth the basis of a strategy of continental development. Many of them expected that the great empty inland regions would guarantee the preponderance of the yeoman—and therefore the dominance of Jeffersonianism and the health of the state—for an unlimited future. The opening of the trans-Allegheny region, its protection from slavery, and the purchase of the Louisiana Territory were the first great steps in a continental strategy designed to establish an internal empire of small farms. Much later the Homestead Act was meant to carry to its completion the process of continental settlement by small homeowners. The failure of the Homestead Act "to enact by statute the fee-simple empire" was one of the original sources of Populist grievances, and one of the central points at which the agrarian myth was overrun by the commercial realities.

Above all, however, the myth was powerful because the United States in the first half of the nineteenth century consisted predominantly of literate and politically enfranchised farmers. Offering what seemed harmless flattery to this numerically dominant class, the myth suggested a standard vocabulary to rural editors and politicians. Although farmers may not have been much impressed by what was said about the merits of a noncommercial way of life, they could only enjoy learning about their special virtues and their unique services to the nation. Moreover, the editors and politicians who so flattered them need not in most cases have been insincere. More often than not they too were likely to have begun life in little villages or on farms, and what they had to say stirred in their own breasts, as it did in the breasts of a great many townspeople, nostalgia for their early years and perhaps relieved some residual feelings of guilt at having deserted parental homes and childhood attachments. They also had the satisfaction in the early days of knowing that in so far as it was based upon the life of the largely self-sufficient yeoman the agrarian myth was a depiction of reality as well as the assertion of an ideal.

Oddly enough, the agrarian myth came to be believed more widely and tenaciously as it became more fictional. At first it was propagated with a kind of genial candor, and only later did it acquire overtones of insincerity. There survives from the Jackson era a painting that shows Governor Joseph Ritner of Pennsylvania standing by a primitive plow at the end of a furrow. There is no pretense that the Governor has actually been plowing—he wears broadcloth pants and a silk vest, and his tall black beaver hat has been carefully laid in the grass beside him—but the picture is meant as a reminder of both his rustic origin and his present high station in life. By contrast, Calvin Coolidge posed almost a century later for a series of photographs that represented him as haying in Vermont. In one of them the President sits on the edge of a hay rig in a white shirt, collar detached, wearing highly polished black shoes and a fresh pair of overalls; in the background stands his Pierce Arrow, a secret service man on the running board, plainly waiting to hurry the President away from his bogus rural labors. That the second picture is so much more pretentious and disingenuous than the first is a measure of the increasing hollowness of the myth as it became more and more remote from the realities of agriculture.

Throughout the nineteenth century hundreds upon hundreds of thousands of farm-born youths sought their careers in the towns and cities. Particularly after 1840, which marked the beginning of a long cycle of heavy country-to-city migration, farm children repudiated their parents' way of life and took off for the cities where, in agrarian theory if not in fact, they were sure to succumb to vice and poverty.

When a correspondent of the *Prairie Farmer* in 1849 made the mistake of praising the luxuries, the "polished society," and the economic opportunities of the city, he was rebuked for overlooking the fact that city life "*crushes, enslaves,* and *ruins so many thousands of our young men* who are insensibly made the victims of *dissipation,* of *reckless speculation,* and of *ultimate crime.*" Such warnings, of course, were futile. "Thousands of young men," wrote the New York agriculturist Jesse Buel, "who annually forsake the plough, and the honest profession of their fathers, if not to win the fair, at least form an opinion, too often confirmed by mistaken parents, that agriculture is not the road to wealth, to honor, nor to happiness. And such will continue to be the case, until our agriculturists become qualified to assume that rank in society to which the importance of their calling, and their numbers, entitle them, and which intelligence and self-respect can alone give them."

Rank in society! That was close to the heart of the matter, for the farmer was beginning to realize acutely not merely that the best of the world's goods were to be had in the cities and that the urban middle and upper classes had much more of them than he did but also that he was losing in status and respect as compared with them. He became aware that the official respect paid to the farmer masked a certain disdain felt by many city people. "There has . . . a certain class of individuals grown up in our land," complained a farm writer in 1835, "who treat the cultivators of the soil as an inferior caste . . . whose utmost abilities are confined to the merit of being able to discuss a boiled potato and a rasher of bacon." The city was symbolized as the home of loan sharks, dandies, fops, and aristocrats with European ideas who despised farmers as hayseeds.

The growth of the urban market intensified this antagonism. In areas like colonial New England, where an intimate connection had existed between the small town and the adjacent countryside, where a community of interests and even of occupations cut across the town line, the rural-urban hostility had not developed so sharply as in the newer areas where the township plan was never instituted and where isolated farmsteads were more common. As settlement moved west, as urban markets grew, as self-sufficient farmers became rarer, as farmers pushed into commercial production for the cities they feared and distrusted, they quite correctly thought of themselves as a vocational and economic group rather than as members of a neighborhood. In the Populist era the city was totally alien territory to many farmers, and the primacy of agriculture as a source of wealth was reasserted with much bitterness. "The great cities rest upon our broad and fertile prairies," declared Bryan in his "Cross of Gold" speech. "Burn down your cities and leave our farms, and your cities will spring up again as if by magic; but destroy our farms, and the grass will grow in the streets of every city in the country." Out of the beliefs nourished by the agrarian myth there had arisen the notion that the city was a parasitical growth on the country. Bryan spoke for a people raised for generations on the idea that the farmer was a very special creature, blessed by God, and that in a country consisting largely of farmers the voice of the farmer was the voice of democracy and of virtue itself.

The agrarian myth encouraged farmers to believe that they were not themselves an organic part of the whole order of business enterprise and speculation that flourished in the city, partaking of its character and sharing in its risks, but rather the innocent pastoral victims of a conspiracy hatched in the distance. The notion of an innocent and victimized populace colors the whole history of agrarian controversy.

For the farmer it was bewildering, and irritating too, to think of the great contrast between the verbal deference paid him by almost everyone and the real economic position in which he found himself. Improving his economic position was always possible, though this was often done too little and too late; but it was not within anyone's power to stem the decline in the rural values and pieties, the gradual rejection of the moral commitments that had been expressed in the early exaltations of agrarianism.

It was the fate of the farmer himself to contribute to this decline. Like almost all good Americans he had innocently sought progress from the very beginning, and thus hastened the decline of many of his own values. Elsewhere the rural classes had usually looked to the past, had been bearers of tradition and upholders of stability. The American farmer looked to the future alone, and the story of the American land became a study in futures.

In the very hours of its birth as a nation Crèvecœur had congratulated America for having, in effect, no feudal past and no industrial present, for having no royal, aristocratic, ecclesiastical, or monarchial power, and no manufacturing class, and had rapturously concluded: "We are the most perfect society now existing in the world." Here was the irony from which the farmer suffered above all others: the United States was the only country in the world that began with perfection and aspired to progress.

To what extent was the agrarian myth actually false? During the colonial period, and even well down into the nineteenth century, there were in fact large numbers of farmers who were very much like the yeomen idealized in the myth. They were independent and self-sufficient, and they bequeathed to their children a strong love of crafts-manlike improvisation and a firm tradition of household industry. These yeomen were all too often yeomen by force of circumstance. They could not become commercial farmers because they were too far from the rivers or the towns, because the roads were too poor for bulky traffic, because the domestic market for agricultural produce was too small and the overseas markets were out of reach. At the beginning of the nineteenth century, when the American population was still living largely in the forests and most of it was east of the Appalachians, the yeoman farmer did exist in large numbers, living much as the theorists of the agrarian myth portrayed him.

But when the yeoman practiced the self-sufficient economy that was expected of him, he usually did so not because he wanted to stay out of the market but because he wanted to get into it. "My farm," said a farmer of Jefferson's time, "gave me and my family a good living on the produce of it; and left me, one year with another, one hundred and fifty dollars, for I have never spent more than ten dollars a year, which was for salt, nails, and the like. Nothing to wear, eat, or drink was purchased, as my farm provided all. With this saving, I put money to interest, bought cattle, fatted and sold them, and made great profit." Great profit! Here was the significance of self-sufficiency for the characteristic family farmer. Commercialism had already begun to enter the American Arcadia.

For, whatever the spokesman of the agrarian myth might have told him, the farmer almost anywhere in early America knew that all around him there were examples of commercial success in agriculture—the tobacco, rice, and indigo, and later the cotton planters of the South, the grain, meat, and cattle exporters of the middle states.

The farmer knew that without cash he could never rise above the hardships and squalor of pioneering and log-cabin life. So the savings from his self-sufficiency went into improvements—into the purchase of more land, of herds and flocks, of better tools; they went into the building of barns and silos and better dwellings. Self-sufficiency, in short, was adopted for a time in order that it would eventually be unnecessary.

Between 1815 and 1860 the character of American agriculture was transformed. The rise of native industry created a home market for agriculture, while demands arose abroad for American cotton and foodstuffs, and a great network of turnpikes, canals, and railroads helped link the planter and the advancing western farmer to the new markets. As the farmer moved out of the forests onto the flat, rich prairies, he found possibilities for machinery that did not exist in the forest. Before long he was cultivating the prairies with horse-drawn mechanical reapers, steel plows, wheat and corn drills, and threshers.

The farmer was still a hardworking man, and he still owned his own land in the old tradition. But no longer did he grow or manufacture almost everything he needed. He concentrated on the cash crop, bought more and more of his supplies from the country store. To take full advantage of the possibilities of mechanization, he engrossed as much land as he could and borrowed money for his land and machinery. The shift from self-sufficient to commercial farming varied in time throughout the West and cannot be dated with precision, but it was complete in Ohio by about 1830 and twenty years later in Indiana, Illinois, and Michigan. All through the great Northwest, farmers whose fathers might have lived in isolation and self-sufficiency were surrounded by jobbers, banks, stores, middlemen, horses, and machinery.

This transformation affected not only what the farmer did but how he felt. The ideals of the agrarian myth were competing in his breast, and gradually losing ground, to another, even stronger ideal, the notion of opportunity, of career, of the self-made man. Agrarian sentiment sanctified labor in the soil and the simple life; but the prevailing Calvinist atmosphere of rural life implied that virtue was rewarded with success and material goods. Even farm boys were taught to strive for achievement in one form or another, and when this did not take them away from the farms altogether, it impelled them to follow farming not as a way of life but as a *career*—that is, as a way of achieving substantial success.

The sheer abundance of the land—that very internal empire that had been expected to insure the predominance of the yeoman in American life for centuries—gave the *coup de grâce* to the yeomanlike way of life. For it made of the farmer a speculator. Cheap land invited extensive and careless cultivation. Rising land values in areas of new settlement tempted early liquidation and frequent moves. Frequent and sensational rises in land values bred a boom psychology in the American farmer and caused him to rely for his margin of profit more on the appreciation in the value of his land than on the sale of crops. It took a strong man to resist the temptation to ride skyward on lands that might easily triple or quadruple their value in one decade and then double in the next.

What developed in America, then, was an agricultural society whose real attachment was not, like the yeoman's, to the land but to land values. The characteristic product of American rural society, as it developed on the prairies and the plains, was not a yeoman or a villager, but a harassed little country businessman who worked very hard, moved all too often, gambled with his land, and made his way alone.

While the farmer had long since ceased to act like a yeoman, he

was somewhat slower in ceasing to think like one. He became a businessman in fact long before he began to regard himself in this light. As the
nineteenth century drew to a close, however, various things were
changing him. He was becoming increasingly an employer of labor,
and though he still worked with his hands, he began to look with suspicion upon the working classes of the cities, especially those organized in trade unions, as he had once done upon the urban fops and
aristocrats. Moreover, when good times returned after the Populist
revolt of the 1890's, businessmen and bankers and the agricultural
colleges began to woo the farmer, to make efforts to persuade him
to take the businesslike view of himself that was warranted by the
nature of his farm operations. "The object of farming," declared a
writer in the *Cornell Countryman* in 1904, "is not primarily to make
a living, but it is to make money. To this end it is to be conducted on
the same business basis as any other producing industry."

The final change, which came only with a succession of changes in
the twentieth century, wiped out the last traces of the yeoman of old,
as the coming first of good roads and rural free delivery, and mail
order catalogues, then the telephone, the automobile, and the tractor,
and at length radio, movies, and television largely eliminated the
difference between urban and rural experience in so many important
areas of life. The city luxuries, once so derided by farmers, are now
what they aspire to give to their wives and daughters.

In 1860 a farm journal satirized the imagined refinements and
affectations of a city girl in the following picture:

> Slowly she rises from her couch. . . . Languidly she gains
> her feet, and oh! what vision of human perfection appears
> before us: Skinny, bony, sickly, hipless, thighless, formless,
> hairless, teethless. What a radiant belle! . . . The ceremony of
> enrobing commences. In goes the dentist's naturalization efforts;
> next the witching curls are fashioned to her "classically molded
> head." Then the womanly proportions are properly adjusted;
> hoops, bustles, and so forth, follow in succession, then a pro-
> fuse quantity of whitewash, together with a "permanent rose
> tint" is applied to a sallow complexion; and lastly the "killing"
> wrapper is arranged on her systematical and matchless form.

But compare this with these beauty hints for farmers' wives from
the *Idaho Farmer*, April, 1935:

> Hands should be soft enough to flatter the most delicate
> of the new fabrics. They must be carefully manicured, with
> none of the hot, brilliant shades of nail polish. The lighter
> and more delicate tones are in keeping with the spirit of fresh-
> ness. Keep the tint of your fingertips friendly to the red of your
> lips, and check both your powder and your rouge to see that they
> best suit the tone of your skin in the bold light of summer.

Nothing can tell us with greater finality of the passing of the
yeoman ideal than these light and delicate tones of nail polish.

Unemployed white and Negro workers parade in New York City in 1909 to protest discriminatory hiring practices.

Part
Three

AGE
OF
REFORM

Thurman Arnold

Economic Reform and the Sherman Antitrust Act

The growth of industry in the United States produced not only more manufactured goods but bigger manufacturing establishments, and these large organizations tended to combine with one another into huge complexes called trusts. This development roused profound anxieties in the minds of many persons. The fear of monopoly, which these trusts created, was only the surface manifestation of these anxieties; more basic was the fear that these enormous enterprises presaged the appearance of sharp cleavages between rich and poor and the development of a rigid social structure. Thus, it was thought that the trusts might undermine democracy itself. The Sherman Antitrust Act of 1890 was one result of the public distaste for these large organizations.

The Sherman act did not check the trend toward large-scale manufacturing, but over a period of time bigness itself proved less dangerous than late nineteenth-century citizens had feared. Democracy has survived despite U.S. Steel and General Motors, although there have been (and still are) those who see such giants as a threat to American institutions. Nevertheless, the Sherman act has remained on the statute books, and it has served a useful if changing function as the character of American industry has evolved. The author of this essay, Thurman Arnold, headed the federal government's antitrust division from 1938 to 1943. He has written, among other works, The Folklore of Capitalism *and* Democracy and Free Enterprise.

*E*ver since the Civil War ended there has been a continuous conflict between two opposing ideals in American economic thinking. The first of them states that business management, if relieved from the rigors of cutthroat competition, will be fair and benevolent. The age of competition is over, the theory continues, and great corporations with the power to dominate prices benefit the economy. In the field of big business, this philosophy justifies giant mergers. In the field of small business, it leads to the passage of fair trade laws and similar forms of legalized price fixing.

J. P. Morgan is the traditional hero of this philosophy. He organized United States Steel, our first billion-dollar enterprise, to make investments secure, and to eliminate cutthroat competition in steel. Andrew Carnegie, who was doing pretty well as an aggressive competitor, was paid twice what he thought his business was worth to go along. Morgan made the steel business safer for the investor but tough on the consumer, and it has been so ever since.

The opposing economic ideal says that industrial progress can best be obtained in a free market, where prices are fixed by competition and where success depends on efficiency rather than market control. Under this theory it becomes the government's function not to control or regulate but only to maintain freedom in the market place by prosecuting combinations whenever they become large enough to fix prices. Henry Ford represents this ideal. By producing cars at cut prices on a nationwide scale, he helped wreck many of the existing automobile companies. But he also revolutionized the industry.

This second ideal is also represented by a remarkable piece of legislation called the Sherman Antitrust Act, passed by Congress on July 2, 1890, which states that "Every contract, combination in the form of trust or otherwise, or conspiracy, in restraint of trade or commerce among the several States, or with foreign nations, is hereby declared to be illegal." The act goes on to authorize the federal government to proceed against trusts which violate the act, and empowers federal circuit courts with jurisdiction over such violations.

If I may be permitted to say so, as one who has had some experience with enforcing it, this law is historically unique. Prior to the Second World War, no other nation had any legislation like it. It is different from any other criminal statute because it makes it a crime to violate a vaguely stated economic policy—and a policy, what is more, on which public attitudes often change. The average American citizen— and, indeed, the average court which administers the Sherman act— would like to believe simultaneously in both of the conflicting economic ideals described above. For that reason, the Supreme Court swings back and forth in Sherman act cases, in more important ones splitting five to four. The history of the Sherman act is the history of the conflicts and compromises between these two economic ideals.

But the dominant ideal in our American economic thinking has been the ideal of the Sherman act. The business pressures against its actual enforcement are great, but support of the *principle* of the act is so unanimous that no one ever suggests its repeal. Big business, labor, farmers—each economic group wants the Sherman act strictly enforced, against everyone but itself.

In meeting these pressures the Sherman act has shown extraordinary elasticity. It may bend at times, but it always bounces back. Thus it is like a constitutional provision rather than an ordinary statute, and its history tells much about our national attempt to create an economy that will be at the same time both disciplined and free.

How was this ideal born in the first place? The most improbable feature of the Sherman act is that this apparently anti-big business measure was introduced by a senator who was a high-tariff advocate and an extreme conservative, and was passed with only one dissenting vote by a big-business Republican Congress.

The initial pressure for it came from agriculture, which since the Civil War had been reduced to a fairly steady depression. Railroad monopolies were charging farmers all the traffic would bear, and sometimes a little more. Rates were rigged to favor big railroad customers and ruin small ones. As farm income fell, prices that farmers had to pay rose steadily. Monopolies kept them high. If the pressure from the agricultural states was strong, so was the rebellion against other aspects of the dog-eat-dog business ethics of the times. The necessity of some restraint on such practices came at last to be recognized even by business itself.

Big business during the latter half of the nineteenth century had come to regard competition as an unmitigated evil which could be alleviated only by combination. At first the combinations took the form of "pools" or agreements—regional rather than national—to restrain trade, to control prices, to restrict output and divide markets. But businessmen soon learned that agreements between members of an industry were too weak. Only the surrender of business independence by the units could make domination of the market certain.

Pools gave way to trusts, the first of which, established by Standard Oil in 1879, became a model for subsequent business combinations. Each party to the trust surrendered his stock-voting power to trustees, receiving trust certificates in return. Thus the nine trustees of the Standard Oil Trust, without the investment of a dollar, obtained absolute power over the nation's oil industry. The pattern set by Standard Oil was so widely followed that the name "trust" became a byword for any large industrial combination even after the trust device had been abandoned.

Prior to the Sherman act the federal government had no power to prevent predatory business activities. Therefore, the states themselves began an ineffective attack on the trusts in state courts. In 1887 Louisiana prosecuted the Cotton Oil Trust. In 1889 California prosecuted the Sugar Trust; in 1890 Nebraska prosecuted the Whiskey Trust. The attorney general of Ohio sought to repeal the charter of the Standard Oil Company of Ohio.

In 1892 the supreme court of Ohio ordered the local oil company to sever its connections with the Standard Oil Trust. The order was never effectively enforced. But these state attacks on it made the device

In 1888 Senator John Sherman introduced the resolution that two years later became the Sherman Antitrust Act.

so risky that corporate organizations looked for some other form of combination that could not be prosecuted under state law. New Jersey provided the model, by amending its incorporation statute to permit one corporation to own the stock of another. From then on it was easy.

Corporations A, B, and C would give 51 per cent of their stock to holding company X. Holding company X would in turn give 51 per cent of its stock to holding company Y. Thus holding company Y, with only about 25 per cent interest in the operating companies, controlled them completely. Y would transfer enough stock to Z, at which point Z needed only 12½ per cent to control the industry. And so on until fantastic pyramids were built up. No state could attack these pyramids because they were legal in the state of incorporation. Only Congress could interfere with this process.

In July, 1888, John Sherman, senator from Ohio, introduced the resolution that led to the passage of the Sherman act. He had been Secretary of the Treasury under President Hayes and was known as an expert in finance and taxation. He was big business-minded and an ardent advocate of high tariffs. In this important respect, he was opposed to the very interests that were demanding antimonopoly legislation. In the farm belt the tariff was called the mother of monopoly. Sherman could have no part in such radical doctrine. His resolution reconciled that contradiction very neatly. It asked the Finance Committee to report on a bill that would

> tend to preserve freedom of trade and production, the natural competition of increasing production, the lowering of prices by such competition, and the full benefit designed by and hitherto conferred by the policy of the government to protect and encourage American industries by levying duties on imported goods.

In other words, Sherman contended that the increased production by local industry protected by tariffs would more than offset the increased prices due to the tariffs, if domestic competition was free and unrestrained.

The Sherman act as it reads today was passed in the Senate 52 yeas to 1 nay, and signed by President Harrison on July 2, 1890. No votes were cast against it in the House.

The act is unexampled in economic legislation. In effect it says: "We want competition in the United States and we will leave it to the federal judiciary to determine, case by case, just what action constitutes a restraint on competition." That this law could be passed by a conservative Republican Congress whose most influential leaders were closely associated with big business is remarkable in the extreme. Many writers have argued that the act was a hypocritical piece of legislation, designed as a political sop to the farm belt, and that no one expected it to be of any consequence. For example, Senator Nelson W. Aldrich, who was known as J. P. Morgan's floor broker in the Senate, voted for it.

Such facts are sometimes cited to support the view that the original passage of the bill was only an attempt to placate western senators in exchange for votes on higher tariffs. But this interpretation has been completely refuted by Hans B. Thorelli in his recent book, *The Federal Antitrust Policy,* the most complete and objective analysis of the history of American monopoly policy. Thorelli concludes that a majority of congressmen were sincere and that the Sherman act represented for men of both parties the symbol and the image of what they sincerely desired the American economy to become.

By that I do not mean that the Republican supporters of the act would have welcomed the breakup of great American combinations into smaller units. At the same time, they would have instinctively rejected the system of domestic and international cartels that had been growing up in Germany and spreading to France from 1870 on, which would surely have become the American pattern if the Sherman act had not been passed.

The Sherman act fitted in with the American economic and legal philosophy that was religiously held in 1890 and which is still our dominant philosophy today. In 1890 Americans distrusted any form of governmental regulation. It was the tradition of the American common law that the relation between business and government should be based on some broad common-law principle which would acquire definite meaning only through a series of court decisions. The Sherman act followed that tradition. Our faith in the common law was such that Congress believed that the courts could give a better and more practical meaning to the principles of the act than Congress could possibly do by further definition or regulation.

The Sherman act was definitely on the shelf during the administrations of Presidents Harrison, Cleveland, and McKinley. Cleveland's attorney general not only instituted no proceedings but dropped the prosecution of the notorious Cash Register Trust, even though he had won a victory in the lower court. Under Cleveland the principal impact of the Sherman act was against labor in breaking the Pullman strike. McKinley was equally indifferent to the Sherman act. During his four and one half years only three suits were brought.

The first Sherman act decision by the Supreme Court was in the case of United States *v.* E. C. Knight & Co. It amounted to a virtual repeal of the act. The Supreme Court held that the Sugar Trust, in acquiring a monopoly over sugar manufacturing, affected interstate commerce only indirectly and, therefore, did not violate the act. As Justice John Marshall Harlan pointed out in his dissent: "While the opinion of the Court in this case does not declare the Act of 1890 to be unconstitutional, it defeats the main object for which it was passed." The Knight case thus emasculated the Sherman act. As a result of that decision the government became powerless to prevent the formation of a monopoly through the device of a holding company.

Yet within the short space of eight years, through the daring and ingenuity of Theodore Roosevelt, the Sherman act was transformed again from a meaningless and ineffective formula into a sharp weapon. Theodore Roosevelt was one of the few politicians of his time who had seriously studied the antitrust problem. He had his first experience with monopoly power as a New York State assemblyman during the investigation of Jay Gould. He campaigned for re-election on the antimonopoly issue in 1882. In 1899, as governor, he wrote: "I have been in a great quandary over trusts. I do not know what attitude to take. I do not intend to play a demagogue. On the other hand, I do intend, so far as in me lies, to see that the rich man is held to the same accountability as the poor man, and when the rich man is rich enough *to buy unscrupulous advice from very able lawyers, this is not always easy.*" (Italics added.)

It was the empire-building ambition of J. P. Morgan that gave Theodore Roosevelt his chance. During the last year of the McKinley Administration the Northern Securities Company had been formed as a compromise between E. H. Harriman and Morgan in their fight to control the Northern Pacific Railroad. The holding company device was used to combine under one management two of the nation's largest competing railroads, the Northern Pacific and the Great Northern. Had the scheme succeeded, it could have led to the domination of all American railroads by this group. It could have created a pattern for the cartelization of all American industry.

Roosevelt, as one of the first acts of his Administration, determined to attack this respected citadel of corporate power. This enterprise was very different from that of using the act to attack mere dishonesty in business, and Roosevelt must have realized that the legal odds were very much against him. A careful lawyer would have advised him that the Knight case exempted J. P. Morgan's ambitious plans. The decision in the Knight case stood for the principle that the acquisition of monopoly control was immune from attack because, though it affected prices "indirectly," it was not a conspiracy to fix them "directly."

The issue as Roosevelt saw it went far beyond the merger of the two railroads involved in Northern Securities. The issue was nothing less than effective national sovereignty. The federal government had been relegated to such minor roles as distributing the mail and collecting tariff duties. Big business was the real sovereign in infinitely

Joseph Keppler, the founder of Puck,
*captioned this 1904 cartoon of Teddy
Roosevelt fighting the merger- and
monopoly-minded titans of American business, "Jack and the Wall Street Giants."*

more important areas. In the Northern Securities case, Theodore Roosevelt was to obtain for the federal government a magna carta limiting the power of the business princes.

Roosevelt gambled that the Supreme Court, with new faces in it since the Knight case, would repudiate or at least alter that decision. He directed Attorney General Philander C. Knox to draw up a case against the Northern Securities Company. It was to be a head-on attack on the philosophy of the Knight case decision. Fully aware of the tremendous pressures that would be exerted against him, he directed Knox to prepare the prosecution in complete secrecy. Not even his close friend and adviser, Elihu Root, the Secretary of War, was told.

When Knox finally released to the press his intention to prosecute Northern Securities, there was consternation and panic in the financial world. Root, a Wall Street lawyer, was dismayed and resentful. Morgan and his like-minded friend, Senator Chauncey Depew of New York, descended upon the White House like the emissaries of some independent sovereignty whose rights were being invaded. But by that time the prosecution was a *fait accompli*.

On this case all of Roosevelt's antitrust program depended. It came before the Supreme Court in March, 1904. By that time, Roosevelt had appointed Oliver Wendell Holmes to the Court, believing that Holmes's reputation as a liberal was an indication that he would vote against the tremendous extension of monopoly power. In this hope he was to be bitterly disappointed. Had Holmes been able to win over to his side Justice David Brewer, as he thought he had, the legitimacy of monopoly would have been established, perhaps for all time, in this country as it was in Europe.

The Court was bitterly divided, five to four. The majority held that the Sherman act was intended to prevent giant combinations formed under any device and that such exercise of congressional power over industry was not unconstitutional.

Holmes, who wrote one of the two principal dissents, made the statement, believed by many at that time, that the Sherman act was not intended to prevent combinations in restraint of trade. He said: "It was the ferocious extreme of competition with others, not the cessation of competition among the partners, that was the evil feared."

Justice Holmes had faith in the benevolence and efficiency of the rich. He believed that the Constitution should protect them in their efforts to create industrial empires. But the ideal of a dynamic competitive economy and government-maintained freedom of industrial opportunity, I believe, was beyond him. He would have approved of the system of domestic and international cartels that dominated industry and caused it to stagnate in Europe before World War II.

Roosevelt, though a rich man himself, was one of the few men of his time to realize the destiny of America as a land of economic freedom. He had the ability to infuse the public with his point of view. Senator Sherman initiated the antitrust act, but it was Teddy Roosevelt who gave it vigor and meaning, made the policy of the Sherman act an economic religion and its violation an economic sin, and, finally, made it emotionally impossible for American business to co-operate in the European cartel system.

To appraise the effect of the Sherman act on American business institutions correctly we must view it apart from particular prosecutions, or particular periods of enforcement or nonenforcement. Theodore Roosevelt's achievement was to enshrine the ideal of the act as part of our national folklore. And its influence has continued in a far more potent way than perhaps any other statute on the books. The image of the Sherman act has not prevented tremendous concentrations of economic power, but it has prevented such concentrations from obtaining legitimate status.

Only once since its passage has the principle of the act been repudiated. That was in production codes of the National Recovery Administration during Franklin D. Roosevelt's New Deal. They were designed to raise prices and restrict production, after the European model. The theory was that this would protect investments and rescue business from insolvency.

But the competitive tradition represented by the Sherman act was too strong for the NRA. The Sherman act over the years, even when it was unenforced, had built up an abiding faith that the elimination of competition in business was morally and economically wrong. Then the Supreme Court threw out the NRA, and Franklin Roosevelt turned back to the antitrust laws as a major instrument of economic policy, and placed me in charge of their enforcement.

When I took office, years of disuse of the Sherman act, culminating in its repudiation by NRA, had made violation of the antitrust laws common, almost respectable. I will never forget the amazement of the Wisconsin Alumni Research Foundation, an organization whose profits were used to support the University of Wisconsin, when the Justice Department charged it with using a vitamin patent to raise prices and restrict manufacture of important food products. It never occurred to the high-minded management of this foundation that it was doing anything wrong. The indictment was considered an attack on education itself.

Thurman Arnold, former head of the Antitrust Division of the Justice Department, testifying before the Senate Banking Committee in 1949.

I believed that my principal function was to convince American businessmen that the Sherman act represented something more than a pious platitude; second, that its enforcement was an important economic policy. But there was very little support among economists for the latter notion.

As indictments of respectable people began to pour out from the Justice Department in unprecedented numbers, cries of outrage could be heard from coast to coast. I will never forget the pain and astonishment caused when criminal charges were brought against the American Medical Association, which had established a pretty effective boycott on all forms of group health plans. I was pictured as a wild man whose sanity was in considerable doubt. One major newspaper referred to me as "an idiot in a powder mill." Letters of protest poured into the White House. Adverse publicity reached its peak when the Associated Press was charged with violation of the Sherman act for refusing to sell its news service to any new newspaper that would be competing with one of its member publications. Editorials appeared from coast to coast accusing the department of destroying freedom of the press.

Yet the enforcement program of the Antitrust Division on a nationwide scale between 1938 and the outbreak of World War II survived all such attacks. This was because American businessmen did not want to repudiate the principle of the Sherman act, however much they disliked particular prosecutions. It showed that the Henry Ford tradition was still dominant.

It is difficult now to appraise the economic effect of the revival of the Sherman act at that time. Opinions differ, and my own is, of course, biased. But this at least can be said: American business learned that the Sherman act was something more than a false front to our business structure. The public gained an idea of the purpose of the act, the act itself gained renewed vitality, and American business approved this revival.

There are two principal evils of concentrated economic power in a democracy. The first is the power of concentrated industry to charge administered prices rather than prices based on competitive demand. A second is the tendency of such empires to swallow up local businesses and drain away local capital. Prior to the Depression this condition had advanced so far that our concentrated industrial groups had helped destroy their own markets by siphoning off the dollars that could have been a source of local purchasing power.

It is idle to say that periodic enforcement of the antitrust laws has solved these problems, but the laws themselves have given us an image of what our economy should be. In a cartel economy no one could question the legitimacy of the recent rises in steel—or any other—prices. In an antitrust-minded economy it seems a legitimate and natural thing for a congressional committee to call the companies to account. . . .

John A. Garraty

Robert M. La Follette: The Promise Unfulfilled

The leading figures of the Progressive Era have suffered considerably at the hands of historians in recent years. Their insensitivity to the fate of Negroes becomes ever more apparent as scholars study their attitudes toward racial minorities. Their middle-class orientation stands out in contrast to their radical rhetoric. Their inconsistent record on such questions as immigration and labor legislation, as well as their widespread support of imperialistic ventures, appears less than liberal from a contemporary point of view. Indeed, one historian, Gabriel Kolko, has titled his study of the Progressive Era The Triumph of Conservatism.

The following essay criticizes the Progressives from a different perspective and is in part an attempt to cast certain doubts on the character and motivation of all American reformers. The subject examined here, Robert M. La Follette, was one of the most vigorous and effective of the Progressives; he has often been seen as the beau idéal of the type. Yet as I have tried to show, his personal inadequacies raise serious questions about his liberalism, as well as about his judgment.

*O*ne day in July, 1904, Lincoln Steffens, the famous muckraking reporter of *McClure's Magazine,* appeared unannounced in Milwaukee, Wisconsin, hot on the trail of a big story. Steffens had won a well-deserved reputation as an exposer of what he called *The Shame of the Cities;* now he was studying corrupt state politics, and the Wisconsin "machine" of Governor Robert M. La Follette was next on his list. He arrived in Milwaukee convinced that despite a lot of fancy talk about "reform," La Follette was a "demagogue . . . a charlatan and a crook."

Steffens' first informant was a prominent banker. When asked for evidence of the Governor's corruption, the banker could not contain himself. La Follette was a "crooked hypocrite" and a "socialist-anarchist"; he was ruining Wisconsin. But the banker was too angry to present a reasoned indictment. Next Steffens turned to a local railroad lawyer. Though this man had better control of his temper, his detailed analysis of La Follette was studded with words like "fanatic," "boss," and "actor."

Presently, Steffens moved on to Madison to confront the Governor directly. He was met at the Capitol by a man approaching fifty, short and stocky but so brimming with vitality and enthusiasm that he appeared taller than he actually was. He had a shock of brown hair sparingly flecked with gray and a thick bull neck. His lips were sensitive, his eyes calm, his forehead noble. His strong chin and square, muscular jaw reflected a person who habitually set his teeth hard in the face of opposition. Somehow he projected an image which combined kindliness with strength, immense energy with serenity of spirit. The Governor literally ran to greet Steffens, assuming that any reformer would come as a friend. He insisted upon bringing him home to dinner, where Mrs. La Follette and the children offered a warm welcome, also taking it for granted that Steffens was on their side. But the journalist, still unconvinced, did not respond to these advances. Instead he arranged to interview La Follette at length about his whole career.

Thus it was that Lincoln Steffens learned the story of one of the most remarkable personalities of modern times, a man who, finding the state of Wisconsin a satrapy controlled by a handful of lumber barons and hack politicians, changed it into a great laboratory for democratic reform, the home of the "Wisconsin Idea." That he would also help to wreck the whole Republican party and deliver it for a long generation into the hands of its own right wing neither Steffens nor La Follette himself could possibly have known in 1904.

It was a fascinating tale that the Governor related to Steffens. Born in a log cabin at Primrose, Wisconsin, in 1855, he was accustomed to farm life and in later years prided himself on his ability with scythe and plow. He had also developed a wide assortment of other skills; for example, he was a first-class carpenter and an expert barber. As his wife, Belle, explained, Bob seemed to pick up special skills "without anybody's knowing when or how." He also had a strong intellectual bent, and had worked his way through the University of Wisconsin. As a student, he did well; also, he was so remarkably successful in campus theatricals that he seriously considered making the stage his career. But his primary ambition was to be a "statesman," and after graduation he went on to law school and then entered politics.

From the start he was a rebel. In 1880, after being admitted to the bar, he declared himself a candidate for the Republican nomination for district attorney in his home county. The local party boss, Postmaster E. W. Keyes, had other plans. He took La Follette aside and in a firm but kindly way told him that another man had already been decided upon for the job. The young lawyer had neither money nor influence, but the fighter in him was instantly roused. "I intend to go on with this canvass," he told Keyes, "and I intend to be elected district attorney. . . ." He intensified his campaign at once. "I traveled by day and by night," he later recalled. "I stayed at farm-houses, I interviewed every voter in the county whom I could reach." These tactics paid off. The boss could not control his own convention, and La Follette was nominated. In the election, although the angry Keyes supported a Democrat, La Follette carried the district.

This victory established the pattern of his career. Always within the framework of the Republican party (he became a warm admirer of William McKinley), he made his way independently and against the opposition of the Wisconsin Republican machine. Diligent campaigning at the grass roots and a reputation for honesty, courage, and faithful service to his constituents enabled him repeatedly to defy the local powers. He exposed the chairman of the party's state committee, who had been robbed while dead drunk in a Madison hotel room and had later sought to hush the case up. When various politicos tried to have minor legal cases quashed for influential friends, he refused to go along. Later, when U.S. Senator Philetus Sawyer, the powerful lumber king, offered him a "retainer" in a case where Sawyer stood to lose over $150,000, La Follette indignantly announced that the Senator had tried to bribe him.

La Follette was elected to Congress in 1884, after another battle with the Republican machine. In Washington he was a model legislator, attending sessions faithfully, caring for the needs of his constituents, and diligently seeking to master the complications of public issues upon which he felt himself inadequately informed. When he was placed on the unimportant Committee on Indian Affairs, for example, he swallowed his disappointment, bought a small library of secondhand books on Indians, and soon became an expert on the subject. One is reminded of the youthful Bryan (for a time his colleague in the House) laboring to master tariff and monetary problems.

Although by no means a radical at this period, La Follette made a name for himself as an uncompromising foe of "pork-barrel" legislation and of business interests like lumber companies and railroads seeking fat land grants and other special favors from Congress. But after three terms he was defeated in the Democratic tidal wave of 1890 and forced to resume his law practice back home.

He then began a ten-year struggle to gain control of the Wisconsin

Robert Marion La Follette,
a photographic portrait, 1922.

Republican party. He spoke everywhere in the state and wrote countless letters—1,200 in a single campaign on behalf of his friend Nils P.
Haugen. He conducted a "county fair crusade" to win the support of
the rural people. Frustrated by the bosses in his efforts to win the
gubernatorial nomination, he made the direct primary one of his chief
demands, attracting national attention with a brilliant oration on
"The Menace of the Political Machine," at the University of Chicago
in 1897. Finally, in 1900, he could no longer be denied. He won the
nomination for governor and was easily elected.

Still, for a time, the bosses managed to frustrate his program of
reform. A primary bill was smothered in the state senate, and a scheme
of his to increase railroad taxes failed in the lower house. Re-elected
in 1902, La Follette was able to force through the primary bill (subject
to popular ratification at the next election) and to obtain some revision
of the railroad tax structure. His broad plan for a powerful railroad
commission was defeated, however, despite a tremendous 181-page
special message by the Governor explaining why the commission was
needed. In 1904, sensing that their day would soon be over if La Follette were not stopped, the conservatives made a supreme effort to

defeat his bid for a third term. It was at this critical point that Steffens came to Wisconsin.

Steffens was a cynic. Long experience had led him to believe that all politicians were interested primarily in power and position. "Reform" was the cry of the demagogue; Steffens personally preferred the forthright scoundrel to the hypocrite posing as a friend of "good government." But his conversations with La Follette convinced him of the Governor's honesty and good intentions. His story, published in the October *McClure's,* no doubt contributed to La Follette's re-election the following month, a victory that enabled the Governor eventually to carry out his entire program. But Steffens' help was really of minor importance: by 1904, years of struggle had made "Fighting Bob" a master politician and a brilliant public leader in his own right.

Under La Follette Wisconsin became, in the words of Russel B. Nye, "the proving ground" of twentieth-century Progressivism. "The Wisconsin Idea" became famous. Actually the "Idea" was more a practical program than a theory, but whether as theory or as example, it had a remarkable impact on other states and in time on the federal government. It made the political machinery more directly responsive to the popular will. Besides the direct primary law, Wisconsin by 1914 had a corrupt practices act and laws restricting lobbying and excessive campaign expenditures. Furthermore, much was done in the way of social legislation: pure-food, child-labor, and workingmen's-compensation laws were passed, and the educational system was greatly

The genuine effectiveness of La Follette's reform politics was the subject of this cartoon by John T. McCutcheon; from the Chicago Tribune, *1911.*

improved. New regulatory commissions were set up to protect the public against economic exploitation by "the interests." Finally, the tax structure was overhauled, and the burden of paying for these reforms distributed more equitably. A tax commission, headed by the able Nils Haugen, was established, and state income and inheritance taxes were added to the heavier levies on corporations. Small wonder that the party bosses—and even many unbossed conservative Republicans—did not go along quietly.

Not all of these programs originated in Wisconsin; indeed, some of the basic Progressive ideas, such as the initiative and referendum, were not enacted there. What really made "the Wisconsin Idea" so influential was the comprehensiveness and practicality of the program and the effective way it was administered. For this La Follette deserves most of the credit, even though much of what was done came after he left the governorship for service in the U.S. Senate.

It was in this great forum that Robert Marion La Follette was to make his mark upon America; there he would serve, through one of the country's most exciting periods, until his death. To understand this later career, in prospect so promising, in the end a promise unfulfilled, it is necessary to examine the formidable strengths—and important weaknesses—he brought with him on his return to Washington.

To begin with, he was an exceptionally fine public speaker. While only a small child he was in demand at picnics and other rural social gatherings where formal recitations were in order; at college he won an interstate oratorical contest. As a political speaker, his only fault was longwindedness: he could go on for hours at a stretch, and usually did. His performances, often staged beneath a blazing summer sun, drew heavily on his stamina; he reported upon occasion becoming so giddy from the heat that he almost lost the thread of his argument, and he suffered so from blistered feet that he finally bought himself some cool white canvas shoes. His wife, worried by the strain of such ordeals, gave him an alarm watch and made him promise to set it for two hours after he began speaking. Yet he seldom allowed the tinkling alarm to stop him. "I talked too long & beg your forgiveness," he wrote her after a speech in San Francisco. "My audience held on till 12 o'clock and would *not let* me stop!" He might talk endlessly, but always to a purpose; his speeches were solid with statistics, concrete illustrations, vivid arguments. He was militant, determined, a crusader, a doughty champion, a tribune, a standard bearer.

And if he spoke too long, his audiences were seldom bored. "After Bob began," his wife once wrote, "it seemed to me no one moved until he had finished." And an observer who heard him at the 1897 Winnebago County Fair said: "The speech made a profound and lasting impression on me. . . . I was a Democrat and always before that time I had gone away from a Republican meeting more a Democrat than ever. But here was a man who spoke to me as a citizen, not as a partisan."

Another important La Follette asset was his superb political skill. While in the House of Representatives he had had a form printed with blank spaces for recording the names of "active Republicans" and "fair-minded Democrats." These he sent to key supporters all over Wisconsin, and thus built up a large mailing list of influential voters whom he kept supplied with copies of his speeches and other political matter. And no congressman was more assiduous in attending to the needs of his constituents or in squiring visitors around Washington.

La Follette had in fact developed a mastery of every technique for influencing public opinion. In each campaign he concentrated on no more than one or two issues, hammering at them relentlessly, riveting the attention of the voters upon them. He could take advantage of defeat, occasionally even deliberately cultivating it in order to develop a campaign issue. As governor, in 1903 he had pushed a bill establishing a powerful commission to regulate Wisconsin's railroads. When, as he had expected, the legislature rejected this bill, he took the question to the people in the 1904 campaign.

And he was capable of dramatizing a controversial question. In 1898 he had caused a furor by announcing that a railroad had allowed Governor Edward Schofield to ship a cow halfway across the state without cost. It was a trivial matter, and Schofield's action was perfectly legal, but it pointed up La Follette's crusade against special favors to public officials. "Schofield's cow became famous," La Follette recalled in his *Autobiography*, "her picture appeared in the newspapers, and she came to be known in every home in the state." The next year a law outlawing such favors was passed.

But the greatest source of the new senator's strength lay in his intimate understanding of the desires, needs, and prejudices of the Wisconsin farmers. Like Bryan, he was a product of the agricultural unrest that had engulfed the Middle West after the Civil War. He was convinced that "big business" was an evil force in society, exploiting the farmer at every turn. At eighteen he had been profoundly impressed by a local orator who denounced "vast corporate combinations" and "the accumulation of individual wealth . . . greater than it ever has been since the downfall of the Roman Empire." He took up this cry himself, and half a century later he was still tilting at big corporations like U.S. Steel and "wealth [that] will not and cannot be made to bear its full share of taxation." Throughout his political life he would assail Wall Street, lobbyists, and the other standard spectres that haunted the rural imagination. Late in his Senate career he would denounce the Four-Power Pact of the Washington Arms Conference as a conspiracy of international bankers bent on protecting their investments. One may smile at his obvious prejudice, but his pronouncements were taken as gospel by many in Wisconsin and throughout the Middle West.

This rapport with the ordinary citizens of his region developed in La Follette an abiding faith in democracy, a belief that the average man could judge rightly on public issues. Of course this faith was characteristic of nearly all Progressives—men as dissimilar as Bryan, Wilson, and George Perkins shared it—but La Follette possessed it completely and acted upon it consistently. "Bob was always conscious of this native power of the plain people to grasp thought,'' his wife has recorded. ''It never occurred to him to speak 'down' to his audiences or to consider any theme beyond their reach.'' Or, one might add, to wonder whether popular majorities could not be wrong, whether in installing prohibition or electing a Huey Long.

He was an energetic campaigner. To take only one example: in the 1900 gubernatorial contest he covered 6,433 miles in three weeks, making 61 speeches to a total of some 200,000 people. He believed that if he could reach the voters they would see that he was right and sweep him to victory. His espousal of the direct primary reflected his wish to take nominations away from the politicians and give them to the people.

Genuine though it was, La Follette's faith in the intelligence and good sense of farmers was neither mystical nor unrealistic. He knew that government was a complicated science and a delicate art; its effective administration called for special skills and technical knowledge that the average man did not possess. The easy Jacksonian confidence that any ordinary citizen could handle most government positions—the belief that led Bryan to pack the State Department with ''deserving Democrats''—did not enchant ''Fighting Bob.'' Instead he employed many experts, drawing especially upon the faculty of the University of Wisconsin, where, after 1903, his classmate Charles R. Van Hise was president. ''The University exists for the state,'' La Follette said. Soon he was drafting economists and political scientists as advisers and civil servants.

"Fighting Bob" campaigning in 1900 for the governorship of Wisconsin. He won handily.

This reliance on experts and intellectuals marked La Follette as something more than a rural spellbinder. So did his emphasis on regulatory commissions to control railroads, other public utilities, and insurance companies. Here again, his faith in the people was tempered with realism : the personnel of such commissions were to be appointed rather than elected, for the best railroad commissioner, La Follette knew, might not be a good campaigner.

All these qualities had helped La Follette rise to power in Wisconsin, and his success in his home state not only took him to the Senate chamber, but made him the idol of early twentieth-century reformers. Still, success tended to obscure certain rather unfortunate aspects of his personality, certain disturbing elements in his thinking. He spoke frequently (and he was sincere enough) about his principles, but in the last analysis he cared more for ends than for means. He was too much the zealot, considering himself an infallible judge of right and wrong. This conviction served him effectively in battle, but in the long run it led many people to mistrust his judgment and resent his power.

As governor, for example, he made effective—even ruthless—use of patronage. He demanded absolute obedience from his henchmen, and rewarded their faithfulness with appointments to public office. The Wisconsin game wardens became notorious for their political activities. Instead of tracking down poachers, one editor complained, they devoted their energies to "strolling around . . . hunting for men who will vote for La Follette." Furthermore, if his speeches were effective and filled with facts, they were also often oversimplified and sometimes distorted the information he was presenting to the electorate. In his powerful attacks on the "interests," he never tried to understand the motives, methods, or accomplishments of the "villains" he assaulted. His was the hard-handed farmer's unreasoning suspicion of men who won wealth by manipulating symbols.

When La Follette talked of trusting "the people," he had, as we have seen, important if unspoken reservations. His dislike of the big cities with their teeming millions scarcely differed from that of his rural constituents. In this and other ways, without realizing what he was doing, he sometimes undermined the very precepts of democracy he was sworn to defend. He could even, upon occasion, be as much the representative of a special-interest group as any other politician. As a congressman, for example, he had assailed the meat packers as one of the evil interests ; but he argued for a federal tax on oleomargarine that benefited only the dairy interests so powerful in Wisconsin.

Like many crusaders, La Follette tended to discount the possibility that others could disagree with him and still be sincere. He was wont to override even friendly critics; like Woodrow Wilson (whom he resembled in many ways) he left a trail of shattered friendships wherever he went. "I can no more compromise . . . than I could by wishing it add twenty years to my life," he once said. He took everything too seriously; he was too intent and too intense.

It is very revealing that he was prone to imagine all sorts of plots and conspiracies against him. In the governor's mansion in Wisconsin he often claimed to hear mysterious knocks on the door, and the door-bell sometimes rang in an inexplicable manner. Although a careful watch was kept, no one was ever caught thus harassing him. In later life he actually claimed that someone had tried to kill him by poisoning a glass of milk he was drinking while filibustering in Congress against a banking bill. "Bob ran constant risk of violence," his adoring wife firmly believed. But no actual attack was ever made on him. Consider-ing his reputation for integrity and courage, it is remarkable how many people supposedly tried to bribe or threaten him. Could his enemies really have been so foolish? In his controversy with Philetus Sawyer, for example, Sawyer hotly denied that he had tried to buy La Follette's support by offering him a retainer. Probably La Follette's ingrained suspicions sometimes made him interpret in the worst possible light the efforts of practical politicians to reach agreement.

These, then, were the strengths and weaknesses, the great-hearted instincts and the narrowing limitations, which Senator La Follette brought with him to Washington. At home, where a solid majority shared his prejudices, he had been able to bend the Republican organ-ization to his will. In the United States Senate conditions were very different, and he was less successful—but no less determined. In 1906, when he took his seat, the sands of the national arena were compara-tively smooth. Theodore Roosevelt, midway in his second term, had instituted changes the significance of which people were only beginning to understand. By reviving the Sherman Antitrust Act and by moving toward stricter regulation of railroads, the protection of natural re-sources, a pure-food-and-drug act, and other reforms, Roosevelt had encouraged Republican liberals. At the same time he had roused con-servatives to the defense of the old order typified by McKinley and Mark Hanna. Soon controversial questions like the protective tariff and the control of monopoly were to divide the liberals themselves into warring factions. Both La Follette and George Perkins, for example, considered themselves Republicans and Progressives, yet La Follette was for breaking up the trusts and lowering the tariff, while Perkins—who would be one of T. R.'s major backers in the Bull Moose revolt of 1912—wanted to keep the tariff high and regulate, rather than dis-member, the trusts.

In this explosive situation, La Follette was determined (as always) to remain a Republican. But he was also (again as always) unwilling to grant quarter to fellow Republicans whose views he disliked. He would no more deal with Senator Nelson Aldrich and other G.O.P. conserva-tives in Washington than with Boss Keyes or Philetus Sawyer back in Wisconsin. As a result, no man had more to do with the disruption of the party than he.

In the Senate he was a maverick from the start. Tradition dictated that new senators should not take part in debates during their first year. La Follette refused to conform; on April 19, 1906, a month after taking his seat, he rose to speak on an important railroad bill. Many senators indignantly left the floor. La Follette took no notice until he had finished the first part of his speech. Then he turned coolly to the presiding officer and said:

> I cannot be wholly indifferent to the fact that Senators by their absence at this time indicate their want of interest in what I have to say upon this subject. The public is interested. Unless this important question is rightly settled seats now temporarily vacant may be permanently vacated by those who have the right to occupy them at this time.

It was no idle threat. As soon as Congress adjourned, La Follette took to the stump. In state after state he described how his bills had been sidetracked in the Senate. Everywhere he "read the roll calls" to show how local senators had voted on these proposals.

Actions like these were hardly calculated to endear the freshman to the Senate as a whole. Nevertheless, by 1909 La Follette was the leader of a small group of liberal senators who were beginning to call themselves Progressives. He also organized a magazine, *La Follette's Weekly,* in which he regularly flayed the conservatives of both parties. In the Senate he led the fight against the Republican-sponsored Payne-Aldrich tariff, and broke with Taft when the President supported it. He even accused Taft of trying to ruin him politically. He organized a National Progressive Republican League—the accent fell on the word "Progressive"—which endorsed a comprehensive reform program, including national primaries and the direct election of senators.

No one can doubt La Follette's sincerity as a reformer, but at least part of his militancy was the result of ambition. He wanted to be President and had set his sights on 1912. Taft stood in his way, and to win the Republican nomination (a third-party nomination would have had little practical value) La Follette had to make a final break with him. But the ideological split thus fostered affected others as well as himself. Theodore Roosevelt, the most distinctive political personality of the era, was also a Progressive. No liberal movement in the Republican party could succeed without his support. Yet what would his place in such a movement be?

La Follette considered Roosevelt a lukewarm reformer at best. In 1907 he had written: "[Roosevelt] will always say a lot of good things and half do a good many things—But it all ends rather disappointingly." He later wrote that T. R. disliked "the plodding investigation necessary to a solution of great economic questions," although he confessed that the former President was superb at "arousing the public conscience." When Roosevelt refused to join La Follette's League, the Senator was probably more pleased than disappointed. In any case, the League proceeded to make its main business the nomination of La Follette for the Presidency.

In the battle between Taft and La Follette, Roosevelt hoped to remain neutral. He saw little chance for either to win the election, and hoped to reassert command of the party after the expected defeat. But events soon threw him into the anti-Taft camp.

As soon as Roosevelt swung over to the Progressives, many of La Follette's most enthusiastic supporters prepared to switch their alle-

THE ONLY ADEQUATE REWARD.

In March of 1917 the New York World printed this cartoon by Rollin Kirby taking La Follette severely to task for his outspoken opposition to American entry into World War I.

giance to the attractive ex-President, for he seemed far more popular in the nation at large. Fear of being abandoned had much to do with La Follette's unfortunate performance in a speech before a group of magazine publishers on February 2, 1912. Tired, ill, worried, and frustrated, he lost control of himself and delivered an intemperate, confused, and repetitious harangue that caused even friendly observers to question his mental and emotional stability. Although a short rest completely restored him, many of his former backers seized the opportunity to flock to Roosevelt.

La Follette reacted characteristically: he refused to quit the race. After the Republicans had nominated Taft, and Roosevelt had organized what La Follette called the "Roosevelt-Perkins-Steel-Trust-Party," he would support neither group. Nor would he come out for the Democratic candidate, Woodrow Wilson, at least not officially. He gave Wilson indirect aid in the columns of *La Follette's Weekly* but himself cast a blank ballot in November.

During the Wilson administration La Follette was still nominally a Republican, but he pursued no fixed course. He was the only member of his party to vote for the new low Democratic tariff, and later he supported the administration's Railway Labor Act. But the Federal Reserve Act, which he might have been expected to embrace, he opposed on the ground that it gave bankers too much control over the currency. His greatest contribution in this period was the La Follette Seamen's Act—designed to protect the rights of merchant sailors and increase the safety of passengers at sea—which he pushed through Congress

*The aging warrior speaks on
radio in 1924 as presidential
candidate of the League for
Progressive Political Action.*

after a long fight in 1915.

He broke with Wilson over the question of American entry into the First World War. Europe's troubles were none of our own, he said; the war was the work of international bankers and profiteers. Thereafter, terrible abuse was his lot; even the faculty of his beloved alma mater turned almost unanimously against him, and an effort was made to expel him from the Senate.

But La Follette would not change his course. He opposed conscription, objected to the Espionage Act, attacked profiteering even where it did not exist. After the defeat of the Central Powers, La Follette was conspicuous in the Senate fight against the League of Nations. But he also fought consistently against all efforts to restrict civil liberties, and he urged that war costs be met by taxation rather than by borrowing.

The reaction against Wilsonian internationalism that followed the war restored La Follette's popularity. In 1922 he was re-elected to the Senate by a huge majority. But he was no more at home in the Republican party in the twenties than he had been in the time of Taft. He could not stomach Harding and Coolidge, who seemed too obviously allied to the "interests." In 1920 he had refused to head a ·Farmer-Labor party but by 1922 he was willing to consider running independently for the Presidency in order to "drive special privilege out of the control of the government." In 1924, with Burton K. Wheeler as his running mate, he polled nearly five million votes, although he carried only Wisconsin. Though nearly seventy, he was undaunted, and ready to continue the battle. "We have just begun to fight," he said. But a few months later, on June 18, 1925, he suffered a heart attack and died.

La Follette was certainly more "progressive" than most of the well-known politicians of his era. He fought for labor as well as for depressed farmers and businessmen, supported basic civil liberties as well as narrow political reforms. His lifelong dedication to public service and the principles of democracy entitles him to a high place in the liberal pantheon.

But his grave personal weaknesses limited his effectiveness. Despite his really remarkable talents and many virtues, there were, as we have seen, important flaws in his personality. He was headstrong, ruthless, suspicious, sometimes intellectually confused if not dishonest; and these qualities, perhaps even more than the consistent opposition of the "interests," were responsible for his repeated failure to achieve the Presidency. And if, as age came upon him, he never developed Bryan's bland, ignorant self-assurance, he remained, like most zealots, annoyingly certain that God and justice were always on his side.

Yet withal, Robert La Follette was indeed the *beau idéal* of the reformer, and hence liberals are conscious of an element of sadness, even of resentment, as they contemplate his career. For they expect more of their leaders than of ordinary men, so that their "human" failings, more tolerable in lesser men, prove preternaturally disillusioning. In the first decades of the century, Progressive leaders asked much of the voters, who, responding, flocked by the millions to the standard of Reform. But Bryan ended by insulting their intelligence, Perkins by refusing to let them help run their own party, La Follette by insisting that his was the one way to Heaven. Theodore Roosevelt spent his last years assailing pacifists and internationalists instead of fighting for the Square Deal. Even Woodrow Wilson, the greatest idealist of them all, sacrificed principle to expediency at Versailles and then arrogantly dug in his heels and refused to compromise at all when it came to seeking Senate approval of the League of Nations. The Progressive movement collapsed suddenly, but little wonder: its failure, essentially, was the failure of its leaders to measure up to their own ideals.

Anne Firor Scott

Jane Addams:
Urban
Crusader

As the reputations of Progressive political leaders have declined, those of some of the social reformers of the era have risen. This is particularly true of social workers like Jane Addams and other founders of the settlement-house movement, who in modern eyes seem to have had a more profound grasp of the true character of the problems of their age and to have worked more effectively and with greater dedication in trying to solve those problems than did any of the politicians.

These social workers were quite different from those of today—they were more personally involved and far less professionally oriented. Many were also, it is true, somewhat patronizing in their approach to those they sought to help and took a rather romantic and thus un-realistic view of the potentialities both of the poor and of their own capacity to help the poor. This essay by Professor Anne Firor Scott of Duke University makes clear, however, that Jane Addams of Chicago's Hull-House was neither patronizing nor a romantic. Mrs. Scott, who is engaged in writing a biography of Jane Addams, is also an authority on American urban history and the history of the South.

*I*f Alderman Johnny Powers of Chicago's teeming nineteenth ward had only been prescient, he might have foreseen trouble when two young ladies not very long out of a female seminary in Rockford, Illinois, moved into a dilapidated old house on Halsted Street in September, 1889, and announced themselves "at home" to the neighbors. The ladies, however, were not very noisy about it, and it is doubtful if Powers was aware of their existence. The nineteenth ward was well supplied with people already—growing numbers of Italians, Poles, Russians, Irish, and other immigrants—and two more would hardly be noticed.

Johnny Powers was the prototype of the ward boss who was coming to be an increasingly decisive figure on the American political scene. In the first place, he was Irish. In the second, he was, in the parlance of the time, a "boodler": his vote and influence in the Chicago Common Council were far from being beyond price. As chairman of the council's finance committee and boss of the Cook County Democratic party he occupied a strategic position. Those who understood the inner workings of Chicago politics thought that Powers had some hand in nearly every corrupt ordinance passed by the council during his years in office. In a single year, 1895, he was to help to sell six important city franchises. When the mayor vetoed Powers' measures, a silent but significant two-thirds vote appeared to override the veto.

Ray Stannard Baker, who chanced to observe Powers in the late nineties, recorded that he was shrewd and silent, letting other men make the speeches and bring upon their heads the abuse of the public. Powers was a short, stocky man, Baker said, "with a flaring gray pompadour, a smooth-shaven face [sic], rather heavy features, and a restless eye." One observer remarked that "the shadow of sympathetic gloom is always about him. He never jokes; he has forgotten how to smile . . ." Starting life as a grocery clerk, Powers had run for the city council in 1888 and joined the boodle ring headed by Alderman Billy Whalen. When Whalen died in an accident two years later, Powers moved swiftly to establish himself as successor. A few weeks before his death Whalen had collected some thirty thousand dollars— derived from the sale of a city franchise—to be divided among the party faithful. Powers alone knew that the money was in a safe in Whalen's saloon, so he promptly offered a high price for the furnishings of the saloon, retrieved the money, and divided it among the gang—at one stroke establishing himself as a shrewd operator and as one who would play the racket fairly.

From this point on he was the acknowledged head of the gang. Charles Yerkes, the Chicago traction tycoon, found in Powers an ideal tool for the purchase of city franchises. On his aldermanic salary of three dollars a week, Powers managed to acquire two large saloons of his own, a gambling establishment, a fine house, and a conspicuous collection of diamonds. When he was indicted along with two other corrupt aldermen for running a slot machine and keeping a "common gambling house," Powers was unperturbed. The three appeared before a police judge, paid each other's bonds, and that was the end of that.

Proof of their guilt was positive, but convictions were never obtained.

On the same day the Municipal Voters League published a report for the voters on the records of the members of the city council. John Powers was described as "recognized leader of the worst element in the council . . . [who] has voted uniformly for bad ordinances." The League report went on to say that he had always opposed securing any return to the city for valuable franchises, and proceeded to document the charge in detail.

To his constituents in the nineteenth ward, most of whom were getting their first initiation into American politics, Powers turned a different face. To them, he was first and last a friend. When there were celebrations, he always showed up: if the celebration happened to be a bazaar, he bought freely, murmuring piously that it would all go to the poor. In times of tragedy he was literally Johnny on the spot. If the family was too poor to provide the necessary carriage for a respectable funeral, it appeared at the doorstep—courtesy of Johnny Powers and charged to his standing account with the local undertaker. If the need was not so drastic, Powers made his presence felt with an imposing bouquet or wreath. "He has," said the Chicago *Times-Herald,* "bowed with aldermanic grief at thousands of biers."

Christmas meant literally tons of turkeys, geese, and ducks—each one handed out personally by a member of the Powers family, with good wishes and no questions asked. Johnny provided more fundamental aid, too, when a breadwinner was out of work. At one time he is said to have boasted that 2,600 men from his ward (about one third of

The antagonists: Jane Addams (left) in London in 1888 just prior to taking on Johnny Powers, Democratic ward boss, seen here (right) in a photograph taken about 1910.

the registered voters) were working in one way or another for the city of Chicago. This did not take into account those for whom the grateful holders of traction franchises had found a place. When election day rolled around, the returns reflected the appreciation of job-holders and their relatives.

The two young ladies on Halsted Street, Jane Addams and Ellen Starr, were prototypes too, but of a very different kind of figure: they were the pioneers of the social settlement, the original "social workers." They opposed everything Johnny Powers stood for.

Jane Addams' own background could hardly have been more different from that of John Powers. The treasured daughter of a well-to-do small-town businessman from Illinois, she had been raised in an atmosphere of sturdy Christian principles.

From an early age she had been an introspective child concerned with justifying her existence. Once in a childhood nightmare she had dreamed of being the only remaining person in a world desolated by some disaster, facing the responsibility for rediscovering the principle of the wheel! At Rockford she shared with some of her classmates a determination to live to "high purpose," and decided that she would become a doctor in order to "help the poor."

After graduation she went to the Woman's Medical College of Philadelphia, but her health failed and she embarked on the grand tour of Europe customary among the wealthy. During a subsequent trip to Europe in 1888, in the unlikely setting of a Spanish bull ring, an idea that had long been growing in her mind suddenly crystallized: she would rent a house "in a part of the city where many primitive and actual needs are found, in which young women who had been given over too exclusively to study, might restore a balance of activity along traditional lines and learn something of life from life itself . . ." So the American settlement-house idea was born. She and Ellen Starr, a former classmate at the Rockford seminary who had been with her in Europe, went back to Chicago to find a house among the victims of the nineteenth century's fast-growing industrial society.

The young women—Jane was twenty-nine and Ellen thirty in 1889 —had no blueprint to guide them when they decided to take up residence in Mr. Hull's decayed mansion and begin helping "the neighbors" to help themselves. No school of social work had trained them for this enterprise: Latin and Greek, art, music, and "moral philosophy" at the seminary constituted their academic preparation. Toynbee Hall in England—the world's first settlement house, founded in 1884 by Samuel A. Barnett—had inspired them. Having found the Hull house at the corner of Polk and Halsted—in what was by common consent one of Chicago's worst wards—they leased it, moved in, and began doing what came naturally.

Miss Starr, who had taught in an exclusive girls' preparatory school, inaugurated a reading party for young Italian women with George Eliot's *Romola* as the first book. Miss Addams, becoming aware of the desperate problem of working mothers, began at once to organize a kindergarten. They tried Russian parties for the Russian neighbors, organized boys' clubs for the gangs on the street, and offered to bathe all babies. The neighbors were baffled, but impressed. Very soon children and grownups of all sorts and conditions were finding their way to Hull-House—to read Shakespeare or to ask for a volunteer midwife; to learn sewing or discuss socialism; to study art or to fill an empty stomach. There were few formalities and no red tape, and the young ladies found themselves every day called upon to deal with some of the multitude of personal tragedies against which the conditions of life in the nineteenth ward offered so thin a cushion.

Before long, other young people feeling twinges of social conscience and seeking a tangible way to make their convictions count in the world of the 1890's came to live at Hull-House. These "residents," as they were called, became increasingly interested in the personal histories of the endless stream of neighbors who came to the House each week. They began to find out about the little children sewing all day long in the "sweated" garment trade, and about others who worked long hours in a candy factory. They began to ask why there were three thousand more children in the ward than there were seats in its schoolrooms, and why the death rate was higher there than in almost any other part of Chicago. They worried about youngsters whose only playground was a garbage-spattered alley that threatened the whole population with disease. (Once they traced a typhoid epidemic to its source and found the sewer line merging with the water line.) In the early days Hull-House offered bathtubs and showers, which proved so popular a form of hospitality that the residents became relentless

Chicago's old Hull mansion, refurbished and renamed Hull-House, about 1910.

lobbyists for municipal baths.

Hull-House was not the only American settlement house—indeed, Jane Addams liked to emphasize the validity of the idea by pointing out that it had developed simultaneously in several different places. But Hull-House set the pace, and in an astonishingly short time its founder began to acquire a national reputation. As early as 1893 Jane Addams wrote to a friend: "I find I am considered the grandmother of social settlements." She was being asked to speak to gatherings of learned gentlemen, sociologists and philosophers, on such subjects as "The Subjective Necessity for Social Settlements." When the Columbian Exposition attracted thousands of visitors to Chicago in 1893, Hull-House became—along with the lake front and the stockyards— one of the things a guest was advised not to miss. By the mid-nineties, distinguished Europeans were turning up regularly to visit the House and examine its workings. W. T. Stead, editor of the English *Review of Reviews,* spent much time there while he gathered material for his sensational book, *If Christ Came to Chicago.* By that time two thousand people a week were coming to Hull-House to participate in some of its multifarious activities, which ranged from philosophy classes to the Nineteenth Ward Improvement Association.

Neither her growing reputation nor the increasing demand for speeches and articles, however, distracted Jane Addams from what was to be for forty years the main focus of a many-sided life: Hull-House and the nineteenth ward. Much of her early writing was an attempt to portray the real inner lives of America's proliferating immigrants, and much of her early activity, an effort to give them a voice to speak out against injustice.

The Hull-House residents were becoming pioneers in many ways, not least in the techniques of social research. In the *Hull-House Maps and Papers,* published in 1895, they prepared some of the first careful studies of life in an urban slum, examining the details of the "home-work" system of garment making and describing tumble-down houses, overtaxed schools, rising crime rates, and other sociological problems. The book remains today an indispensable source for the social historian of Chicago in the nineties.

Jane Addams' own interest in these matters was far from academic. Her concern for the uncollected garbage led her to apply for—and receive—an appointment as garbage inspector. She rose at six every morning and in a horse-drawn buggy followed the infuriated garbage contractor on his appointed rounds, making sure that every receptacle was emptied. Such badgering incensed Alderman Powers, in whose hierarchy of values cleanliness, though next to godliness, was a good bit below patronage—and he looked upon garbage inspection as a job for one of his henchmen. By now John Powers was becoming aware of his new neighbors; they were increasingly inquisitive about things close to Johnny Powers' source of power. By implication they were raising a troublesome question: Was Johnny Powers really "taking care of the poor"?

For a while, as one resident noted, the inhabitants of the House were "passive though interested observers of their representative, declining his offers of help and co-operation, refusing politely to distribute his Christmas turkeys, but feeling too keenly the smallness of their numbers to work against him." They were learning, though, and the time for passivity would end.

In company with many other American cities, Chicago after 1895 was taking a critical look at its political life and at the close connections that had grown up between politics and big business during the explosive era of industrial expansion following the Civil War. "The sovereign people may govern Chicago in theory," Stead wrote; "as a matter of fact King Boodle is monarch of all he surveys. His domination is practically undisputed."

The Municipal Voters League, a reform organization that included many of Jane Addams' close friends, was founded in 1896 in an effort to clean up the Common Council, of whose sixty-eight aldermen fifty-eight were estimated to be corrupt. The League aimed to replace as many of the fifty-eight as possible with honest men. But it was not easy: in 1896, as part of this campaign, a member of the Hull-House Men's Club ran for the second aldermanic position in the ward and against all expectations was elected. Too late, his idealistic backers found that their hero had his price: Johnny Powers promptly bought him out.

Jane Addams was chagrined but undiscouraged. By the time Powers came up for re-election in 1898, she had had time to observe him more closely and plan her attack. Her opening gun was a speech—delivered,

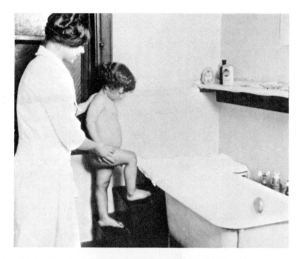

Children were Hull-House's
first concern. Infants were
bathed (right) and moppets put
into nursery school (below).

Older boys (right) took shop
lessons to prepare them to
become successful artisans.

improbably enough, to the Society for Ethical Culture—with the ponderous and apparently harmless title, "Some Ethical Survivals in Municipal Corruption." But appearances were deceptive: once under way, she took the hide off Powers and was scarcely easier on his opponents among the so-called "better elements."

She began by pointing out that for the immigrants, who were getting their first initiation in self-government, ethics was largely a matter of example: the officeholder was apt to set the standard and exercise a permanent influence upon their views. An engaging politician whose standards were low and "impressed by the cynical stamp of the corporations" could debauch the political ideals of ignorant men and women, with consequences that might, she felt, take years to erase.

Ethical issues were further complicated, she said, by habits of thought brought to the New World from the Old. Many Italians and Germans had left their respective fatherlands to escape military service; the Polish and Russian Jews, to escape government persecution. In all these cases, the government had been cast in the role of oppressor. The Irish, in particular, had been conditioned by years of resentment over English rule to regard any successful effort to feed at the public crib as entirely legitimate, because it represented getting the better of their bitterest enemies.

On the other hand, Miss Addams continued, there was nothing the immigrants admired more than simple goodness. They were accustomed to helping each other out in times of trouble, sharing from their own meager store with neighbors who were even more destitute. When Alderman Powers performed on a large scale the same good deeds which they themselves were able to do only on a small scale, was it any wonder that they admired him?

Given this admiration, and their Old World resentments toward government, the immigrants' developing standards of political morality suffered when Powers made it clear that he could "fix" courts or find jobs for his friends on the city payroll. It cheapened their image of American politics when they began to suspect that the source of their benefactor's largess might be a corrupt bargain with a traction tycoon, or with others who wanted something from the city of Chicago and were willing to pay for it.

Hull-House residents, Miss Addams said, very early found evidence of the influence of the boss's standards. When the news spread around the neighborhood that the House was a source of help in time of trouble, more and more neighbors came to appeal for aid when a boy was sent to jail or reform school, and it was impossible to explain to them why Hull-House, so ready to help in other ways, was not willing to get around the law as the Alderman did.

Removing Alderman Powers from office, Jane Addams told the sober gentlemen of the Society for Ethical Culture, would be no simple task. It would require a fundamental change in the ethical standards of the community, as well as the development of a deeper insight on the part of the reformers. These latter, she pointed out, with all their zeal for well-ordered, honest politics, were not eager to undertake the responsibilities of self-government 365 days a year. They were quite willing to come into the nineteenth ward at election time to exhort the citizenry, but were they willing to make a real effort to achieve personal relationships of the kind that stood Johnny Powers in such good stead?

On this last point, Hull-House itself had some experience. As Florence Kelley—a Hull-House resident who was to become a pioneer in the Illinois social reform movement—subsequently wrote:

> The question is often asked whether all that the House undertakes could not be accomplished without the wear and tear of living on the spot. The answer, that it could not, grows more assured as time goes on. You must suffer from the dirty streets, the universal ugliness, the lack of oxygen in the air you daily breathe, the endless struggle with soot and dust and insufficient water supply, the hanging from a strap of the overcrowded street car at the end of your day's work; you must send your children to the nearest wretchedly crowded school, and see them suffer the consequences, if you are to speak as one having authority and not as the scribes . . .

By 1898, after nine years of working with their neighbors, the Hull-House residents were ready to pit their influence against that of Powers. Jane Addams' philosophical address to the Ethical Culture society was followed by others in which she explained more concretely the relationships between Yerkes, Chicago's traction czar, and the city council, relationships in which Johnny Powers played a key role. With several important deals in the making, 1898 would be a bad year for Yerkes to lose his key man in the seats of power.

The election was scheduled for April. The reformers—led by Hull-House and supported by independent Democrats, the Cook County Republicans, and the Municipal Voters League—put up a candidate of their own, Simeon Armstrong, to oppose Powers, and undertook to organize and underwrite Armstrong's campaign. By the end of January, the usually imperturbable Powers suddenly began paying attention to his political fences. The newspapers noted with some surprise that it was the first time he had felt it necessary to lift a finger more than two weeks in advance of election day.

His first move was an attack on Amanda Johnson, a Hull-House resident who had succeeded Miss Addams as garbage inspector. A graduate of the University of Wisconsin and described by the papers as blond, blue-eyed, and beautiful, she had taken the civil service examination and duly qualified for the position. Alderman Powers announced to the world that Miss Johnson, shielded by her civil service status, was telling his constituents not to vote for him. The Chicago *Record* dropped a crocodile tear at the sad picture of the martyred alderman:

> General sympathy should go out to Mr. Powers in this, his

latest affliction. Heretofore he has been persecuted often by people opposed to bad franchise ordinances. He has been hounded by the upholders of civil service reform. He has suffered the shafts of criticism directed at his career by disinterested citizens. A grand jury has been cruel to him. Invidious comments have been made in his hearing as to the ethical impropriety of gambling institutions. . . . It is even believed that Miss Johnson in her relentless cruelty may go so far as to insinuate that Mr. Powers' electioneering methods are no better than those attributed to her—that, indeed, when he has votes to win, the distinctions of the civil service law do not deter him from going after those votes in many ways.

Powers' next move was to attempt a redistricting that would cut off the eastern, or Italian, end of his ward, which he took to be most seriously under Hull-House influence. It was reported that he also felt this area had been a "large source of expense to him through the necessity of assisting the poor that are crowded into that district." "These people," the Chicago *Record* reported, "formerly tied to him by his charities are said to be turning toward Hull-House and will vote solidly against him next spring."

Neither of Powers' first efforts was notably successful. A few days after his attack on Miss Johnson the *Tribune* reported:

Trouble sizzled and boiled for Alderman John Powers in his own bailiwick last night. The Nineteenth Ward Independent club raked over the Alderman's sins . . . and . . . much indignation was occasioned by Alderman Powers' opposition to Miss Amanda Johnson. One Irish speaker says Johnny is a disgrace to the Irish race now that he has descended to fighting "poor working girls."

Meantime, Powers' colleagues on the council redistricting committee had no intention of saving his skin at the expense of their own, and stood solidly against his gerrymandering effort. Now the shaken boss began to show signs of losing his temper. He told reporters that if Miss Addams didn't like the nineteenth ward she should move out. Later, still more infuriated, he announced that Hull-House should be driven out. "A year from now there will be no such institution," he said flatly, adding that the women at Hull-House were obviously jealous of his charities. The *Record* published a cartoon showing Powers pushing vainly against the wall of a very substantial house.

The news of the campaign soon spread beyond the bounds of Chicago. The New York *Tribune* commented that Powers

wouldn't mind Miss Addams saying all those things about him if he didn't begin to fear that she may succeed in making some of his well-meaning but misled constituents believe them. She is a very practical person, and has behind her a large volunteer staff of other practical persons who do not confine their efforts to "gassin' in the parlors," but are going about to prove to the plain people of the nineteenth ward that a corrupt and dishonest man does not necessarily become a saint by giving a moiety of his ill-gotten gains to the poor.

By March the campaign was waxing warm, and Powers resorted to an attempt to stir up the Catholic clergy against Miss Addams and the reform candidate. One of the Hull-House residents, a deputy factory inspector and a Catholic herself, went directly to the priests to find out why they were supporting Powers. When she reported, Jane Addams wrote to a friend:

> As nearly as I can make out, the opposition comes from the Jesuits, headed by Father Lambert, and the parish priests are not in it, and do not like it. Mary talked for a long time to Father Lambert and is sure it is jealousy of Hull-House and money obligations to Powers, that he does not believe the charges himself. She cried when she came back.

In another letter written about the same time, Miss Addams said that Powers had given a thousand dollars to the Jesuit "temperance cadets," who had returned the favor with a fine procession supporting Powers' candidacy. "There was a picture of your humble servant on a transparency and others such as 'No petticoat government for us . . .' We all went out on the corner to see it, Mr. Hinsdale carefully shielding me from the public view."

By now the battle between Hull-House and Johnny Powers was sharing headlines in Chicago newspapers with the blowing up of the *Maine* in Havana's harbor and the approach of the war with Spain. "Throughout the nineteenth ward," said the *Tribune*, "the one absorbing topic of conversation wherever men are gathered is the fight being made against Alderman Powers." It was rumored that Powers had offered a year's free rent to one of the opposition leaders if he would move out of the ward before election day, and the Hull-House group let it be known that the Alderman was spending money freely in the ward, giving his lieutenants far more cash to spread around than was his custom. "Where does the money come from?" Jane Addams asked, and answered her own question: "From Mr. Yerkes." Powers was stung, and challenged her to prove that he had ever received one dollar from any corporation.

"Driven to desperation," said the *Tribune*, "Ald. Powers has at last called to his aid the wives and daughters of his political allies." Determined to fight fire with fire, he dropped his opposition to "petticoat politicians" and gave his blessing to a Ladies Auxiliary which was instructed to counteract the work of the women of Hull-House. An enterprising reporter discovered that few of the ladies had ever seen Miss Addams or been to Hull-House, but all were obediently repeating the charge that she had "blackened and maligned the whole ward" by saying that its people were ignorant, criminal, and poor.

As the campaign became more intense, Jane Addams received numbers of violent letters, nearly all of them anonymous, from Powers' partisans, as well as various communications from lodginghouse keepers quoting prices for votes they were ready to deliver! When the Hull-House residents discovered evidence of ties between banking, ecclesiastical, and journalistic interests, with Powers at the center, they proceeded to publicize all they knew. This brought upon their heads a violent attack by the Chicago *Chronicle,* the organ of the Democratic ring.

Suddenly a number of nineteenth-ward businessmen who had signed petitions for the reform candidate came out for Powers. They were poor and in debt; Powers gave the word to a landlord here, a coal dealer there, and they were beaten. The small peddlers and fruit dealers were subjected to similar pressure, for each needed a license to ply his trade, and the mere hint of a revocation was enough to create another Powers man.

When Alderman John M. Harlan, one of the stalwarts of the Municipal Voters League, came into the ward to speak, Powers supplied a few toughs to stir up a riot. Fortunately Harlan was a sturdy character, and offered so forcefully to take on all comers in fisticuffs that no volunteers appeared. Allowed to proceed, he posed some embarrassing questions: Why did nineteenth-ward residents have to pay ten-cent trolley fares when most of the city paid five? Why, when Powers was head of the city council's free-spending committee on street paving, were the streets of the ward in execrable condition? Why were the public schools so crowded, and why had Powers suppressed a petition, circulated by Hull-House, to build more of them?

Freely admitting Powers' reputation for charity, Harlan made the interesting suggestion that the councilman's motives be put to the test: Would he be so generous as a private citizen? "Let us retire him to private life and see."

Powers was pictured by the papers as being nearly apoplectic at this attack from Miss Addams' friend. He announced that he would not be responsible for Harlan's safety if he returned to the nineteenth ward. (Since no one had asked him to assume any such responsibility, this was presumed to be an open threat.) Harlan returned at once, telling a crowd well-laced with Powers supporters that he would "rather die in my tracks than acknowledge the right of John Powers to say who should and who should not talk in this ward." Summoning up the memory of Garibaldi, he urged the Italians to live up to their tradition of freedom and not allow their votes to be "delivered."

In a quieter vein, Miss Addams too spoke at a public meeting of Italians, where, it was reported, she received profound and respectful attention. "Show that you do not intend to be governed by a boss," she told them. "It is important not only for yourselves but for your children. These things must be made plain to them."

As the campaign progressed, the reformers began to feel they had a real chance of defeating Powers. Jane Addams was persuaded to go in search of funds with which to carry out the grand finale. "I sallied forth today and got $100," she wrote, and "will have to keep it up all week; charming prospect, isn't it?" But on about the twentieth of

March she began to have serious hopes, too, and redoubled her efforts.

As election day, April 6, approached, the Chicago *Tribune* and the Chicago *Record* covered the campaign daily, freely predicting a victory for the reformers. Alas for all predictions. When election day came, Powers' assets, which Jane Addams had so cogently analyzed in that faraway speech to the Society for Ethical Culture, paid off handsomely. It was a rough day in the nineteenth ward, with ten saloons open, one man arrested for drawing a gun, and everything, as Miss Addams wrote despondently when the count began to come in, "as bad as bad can be." Too many election judges were under Powers' thumb. The reform candidate was roundly defeated. Hull-House went to court to challenge the conduct of the election, but in the halls of justice Powers also had friends. It was no use.

Even in victory, however, Powers was a bit shaken. Hull-House had forced him, for the first time, to put out a great effort for re-election. It was obviously *not* going to move out of the nineteenth ward; indeed, if the past was any portent, its influence with his constituents would increase.

Powers decided to follow an ancient maxim, "If you can't lick 'em, join 'em." Early in the 1900 aldermanic campaign, several Chicago papers carried a straight news story to the effect that Hull-House and Johnny Powers had signed a truce, and quoted various paternally benevolent statements on the Alderman's part. In the *Chronicle*, for example, he was reported to have said: "I am not an Indian when it comes to hate . . . let bygones be bygones." A day or two later another rash of stories detailed a number of favors the Alderman was supposed to have done for Hull-House.

Jane Addams was furious, and after considerable deliberation she decided to reply. It was one of the few times in her long public career when she bothered to answer anything the newspapers said about her. She knew that with his eye on the campaign, the master politician was trying to give the appearance of having taken his most vigorous enemy into camp. She had been observing him too long not to realize what he was up to, and she could not possibly let him get away with it.

On February 20, 1900, a vigorous letter from Miss Addams appeared in nearly all the Chicago papers, reaffirming the attitude of Hull-House toward Mr. Powers. "It is needless to state," she concluded, "that the protest of Hull-House against a man who continually disregards the most fundamental rights of his constituents must be permanent."

Permanent protest, yes, but as a practical matter there was no use waging another opposition campaign. Powers held too many of the cards. When all was said and done, he had proved too tough a nut to crack, though Hull-House could—and did—continue to harass him. An observer of the Municipal Voters League, celebrating its success in the *Outlook* in June, 1902, described the vast improvement in the Common Council, but was forced to admit that a few wards were "well-nigh hopeless." He cited three: those of "Blind Billy" Kent, "Bathhouse John" Coughlin, and Johnny Powers.

From a larger standpoint, however, the battle between "Saint Jane" (as the neighbors called Jane Addams when she was not around) and the Ward Boss was not without significance. It was one of numerous similar battles that would characterize the progressive era the country over, and many of them the reformers would win. Because of her firsthand experience, because she lived *with* the immigrants instead of coming into their neighborhood occasionally to tell them what to do, Jane Addams was perhaps the first of the urban reformers to grasp the real pattern of bossism, its logic, the functions it performed, and the reason it was so hard to dislodge. Years later political scientists, beginning to analyze the pattern, would add almost nothing to her speech of 1898. If copies of *The Last Hurrah* have reached the Elysian fields, Jane Addams has spent an amused evening seeing her ideas developed so well in fictional form.

The campaign of 1898 throws considerable light on Jane Addams' intensely practical approach to politics, and upon a little-known aspect of the settlement-house movement. If anyone had told her and Ellen Starr in 1889 that the logic of what they were trying to do would inevitably force them into politics, they would have hooted. But in due time politics, in many forms, became central to Hull-House activity. For Jane Addams herself, the campaign against Powers was the first in a long series of political forays, all essentially based on the same desire—to see that government met the needs of the "other half."

The regulation of child labor, for example, was one political issue in which Hull-House residents became involved because of their knowledge of the lives of the neighbors. The first juvenile court in Chicago was set up as a result of their efforts; it was a direct response to the anxious mothers who could not understand why Hull-House would not help get their boys out of jail. The first factory inspection law in Illinois was also credited to Hull-House, and Florence Kelley became the first inspector. Another Hull-House resident—Dr. Alice Hamilton— pioneered in the field of industrial medicine. Because of their intimate acquaintance with the human cost of industrialization, settlement workers became vigorous advocates of promoting social justice through law.

It was a long jump but not an illogical one from the campaign against Powers to the stage of the Chicago Coliseum in August, 1912, when Jane Addams arose to second the nomination of Teddy Roosevelt by the Progressive party on a platform of social welfare. More remarkable than the ovation—larger than that given to any other seconder—was the fact that the huge audience seemed to listen carefully to what she had to say.

Some newspapers grandly estimated her value to T.R. at a million votes. "Like the report of Mark Twain's death," she commented, "the report is greatly exaggerated." But she campaigned vigorously, in the face of criticism that this was not a proper role for a woman, and when the Bull Moose cause failed, she did not believe it had been a waste of time. It had brought about, she wrote Roosevelt, more discussion of social reform than she had dared to hope for in her lifetime.

Alderman Powers was still in office—as were many like him—but the sources of his power were being attacked at the roots.

When the 1916 campaign came around, Democrats and Republicans alike made bids for Jane Addams' support. The outbreak of war in Europe had turned her attention, however, in a different direction. As early as 1907, in a book called *Newer Ideals of Peace,* she had begun to elaborate William James's notion of a "moral equivalent of war," and had suggested that the experience of polyglot immigrant populations in learning to live together might be laying the foundations for a true international order. Like her ideals of social justice, those that she conceived on international peace had their beginning in the nineteenth ward.

To her, as to so many idealistic progressives, world war came as a profound shock. Her response was a vigorous effort to bring together American women and women from all the European countries to urge upon their governments a negotiated peace. In Europe, where she went in 1915 for a meeting of the Women's International Peace Conference, she visited prime ministers; at the end of that year she planned to sail on Henry Ford's peace ship, but illness forced her to withdraw at the last moment. At home she appealed to President Wilson. Unshaken in her pacifism, she stood firmly against the war, even after the United States entered it.

Her popularity seemed to melt overnight. Many women's clubs and social workers, who owed so much to her vision, deserted her. An Illinois judge who thought it dangerous for her to speak in wartime was widely supported in the press. For most of 1917 and 1918 she was isolated as never before or again. But she did not waver.

When the war ended she began at once to work for means to prevent another. Through the twenties she was constantly active in searching for ways in which women could cut across national lines in their work for peace. In 1931, in her seventy-first year, she received the Nobel Peace Prize—the second American to be so recognized. She died, full of honors, in 1935.

As for Johnny Powers, he had lived to a ripe old age and died in 1930, remaining alderman almost to the end, still fighting reform mayors, still protesting that he and Miss Addams were really friends, after all. From whichever department of the hereafter he ended up in, he must have looked down—or up—in amazement at the final achievements of his old enemy, who had been so little troubled by his insistence that there should be "no petticoats in politics."

Gerald H. Carson

Consumer Protection: The Pure Food and Drugs Act

If early twentieth-century reform is seen as the attempt to solve problems resulting from industrialization and urbanization, then the relative paucity of significant federal legislation that the Progressive Era produced becomes easy to explain: most of the problems appeared to the people of those days to require local, or at most, state action. Except for regulating railroads and large corporations engaged in interstate commerce, there seemed to be little that the national government could do about contemporary evils. The career of Jane Addams, for example, illustrates this point. In her political battles with Boss Powers and her broader concerns with the needs of Chicago slum dwellers, it was to the state and the city (and to local voters) that she turned for assistance or support.

One national reform that was accomplished during this period, however, was the passage of the Pure Food and Drugs Act of 1906. The story of this reform and of its leading advocate and technician, Dr. Harvey W. Wiley, is told here by Gerald Carson, a former advertising executive who has won a richly deserved reputation as a social historian. Mr. Carson's books include The Old Country Store, *which won the Dunning Prize of the American Historical Association, and* The Social History of Bourbon.

*O*n a hot humid July morning in 1902, a burly 200-pound scientist and connoisseur of good food and drink sat hunched over his desk in a red brick building in Washington, D.C., and he planned deliberately to feed twelve healthy young men a diet containing borax. Dr. Harvey W. Wiley, chief chemist of the Department of Agriculture, had in mind a double objective: first, to determine the effects upon human beings of certain chemicals then commonly used to preserve processed foods; and, more broadly, to educate the public in the need for a federal "pure food" law. Food preparation was becoming industrialized and subject to more complicated processing; products were traveling longer distances, passing through many hands. Manufacturers, facing a novel situation, turned to dubious additives to make their products appear more appetizing or to preserve them. Borax compounds, the first object of Dr. Wiley's investigations, were used to make old butter seem like new.

Volunteers for the experiment were recruited from the Department of Agriculture. They pledged themselves to obey the rules. A small kitchen and dining room were fitted out in the basement of the Bureau of Chemistry offices with the assistant surgeon-general in attendance to see to it that the subjects of the experiment did not get too much borax, and Dr. Wiley to see that they got enough. A bright reporter, George Rothwell Brown, of the Washington *Post,* gave the volunteers an enduring handle, "the poison squad"; and before long the public began referring to Wiley, affectionately or otherwise according to the point of view, as "Old Borax."

Six of Dr. Wiley's co-operators at the hygienic table got a normal ration plus measured doses of tasteless, odorless, invisible boracic acid. The other six also enjoyed a wholesome diet, with equally tasteless, odorless, invisible borate of soda added to their menu. The resulting chemical and physiological data was quite technical. But the meaning was clear. The effects of borax included nausea and loss of appetite, symptoms resembling those of influenza and overburdened kidneys. The feeding experiments continued over a five-year period. After the borax initiation, which made a popular sensation, the squad subsequently breakfasted, lunched, and dined on dishes containing salicylates sulfurous acid and sulfites, benzoates, formaldehyde, sulfate of copper, and saltpeter. Seldom has a scientific experiment stirred the public imagination as did Dr. Wiley's novel procedures in, as he said, "trying it on the dog."

"My poison squad laboratory," said Dr. Wiley, "became the most highly advertised boarding-house in the world."

A popular versifier wrote a poem about it, the "Song of the Pizen Squad." Lew Dockstader introduced a topical song into his minstrel show. The chorus closed with the prediction:

Next week he'll give them mothballs à la Newburgh or else
    plain:
O they may get over it but they'll never look the same!

The New York *Sun* sourly handed Wiley the title of "chief janitor

Dr. Harvey W. Wiley (center rear) and his youthful "poison squad" in 1903.

and policeman of the people's insides," an expression of one line of attack which the opposition was to take—invasion of personal liberty.

The movement to protect the health and pocketbook of the consumer was directed no less at "the patent medicine evil" than it was at the chaotic situation in the food manufacturing field. The "cures" for cancer, tuberculosis, "female weakness," the dangerous fat reducers and "Indian" cough remedies were a bonanza for their proprietors, and many an advertising wizard who knew little enough of drugs or materia medica came to live in a jigsaw mansion and drive a spanking pair of bays because he was a skillful manipulator of hypochondria and mass psychology. Slashing exposés in the popular magazines told of babies' soothing syrups containing morphine and opium, of people who became narcotic addicts, of the use of tonics that depended upon alcohol to make the patient feel frisky.

"Gullible America," said Samuel Hopkins Adams in an angry but thoroughly documented series of articles, "will spend this year [1905] some seventy-five millions of dollars" in order to "swallow huge quantities of alcohol . . . narcotics . . . dangerous heart depressants . . . insidious liver stimulants."

The nostrum vendors at first looked upon the Food and Drugs Act as a joke. In time the manufacturers of Pink Pills for Pale People learned the hard way that they were living dangerously when they ignored the precept, "Thou shalt not lie on the label."

As public interest rose in "the food question," powerful groups took their places in the line of battle to contest the pure food and drug bills which appeared, and died, in Congress with monotonous regularity. On the one side were aligned consumer groups—the General

Federation of Women's Clubs, the National Consumers' League, the Patrons of Husbandry, and the labor unions. With them stood food chemists who had had experience in state control work, the American Medical Association, important periodicals *(Collier's Weekly,* Bok's *Ladies' Home Journal, World's Work, The Independent, Cosmopolitan),* President Theodore Roosevelt, and Dr. Wiley.

In opposition were the food manufacturers and manufacturers of articles used in the adulteration of foods and drugs such as cottonseed oil, the proprietary medicine industry, the distillers, canners, *Leslie's Weekly* (to which Dr. Wiley was anathema), newspaper publishers opposed for business reasons, Chicago meat packers, and powerful lobbyists holed up at the Willard and the Raleigh Hotel; also an obdurate Senate, responsive to pressures from big business. Wiley, as the leading personality in the fight for a food bill, achieved the uncommon distinction of acquiring almost as many enemies as did President Roosevelt himself.

When the average member of Congress, newspaper publisher, or pickle manufacturer smelled socialism and deplored the effects of the proposed legislation upon business, he was only responding normally to two powerful stimuli: self-interest and the nostalgic memory of his lost youth. Most mature Americans of the 1880–1900 period were born on farms or in rural areas and knew the conditions of life of a scattered population. The close-knit farm family was the dominant economic unit. It raised, processed, cured, and stored what it ate, and there is abundant evidence that it ate more and better food than the common man of Europe had ever dreamed of tasting. There was no problem of inspection or of deceptive labels. No "Short-weight Jim" invaded the home kitchen or smokehouse. If the preparation was unsanitary, it was no one else's business. What wasn't raised locally was obtained by barter. There were adequate forces of control over that simple transaction—face-to-face bargaining, community of interest, fear of what the neighbors would say.

As to drugs and medicines, grandma could consult the "family doctor" book and compound her home remedies from roots, herbs, and barks gathered along the edge of forest, meadow, and stream: catnip for colic, mullein leaf for asthma, the dandelion for dyspepsia, and so on through the list of simples, essences, flowers, tinctures, and infusions, whose chief merit was that they did not interfere with the tendency of the living cell to recover.

When Americans were called to the cities by the factory whistle, a dramatic change took place in their food supply. No longer was there personal contact between the producer and consumer, nor could the buyer be wary even if he would. For how could a city man candle every egg, test the milk, inquire into the handling of his meat supply, analyze the canned foods which he consumed in increasing quantities?

Since foodstuffs had to stand up in their long transit from the plant to the home, it is not surprising that unhealthy practices developed. During the "embalmed beef" scandal, for example, there was a debate as to whether a little boric acid in fresh beef was after all only an excusable extension of the ancient and accepted use of saltpeter in corning beef. Analytical chemistry was called upon increasingly to make cheap foods into expensive ones, to disguise and simulate, to arrest the processes of nature. The food manufacturers raided the pharmacopœia. But the salicylic acid that was approved in the treatment of gout or rheumatism was received with mounting indignation on the dining room table where it proved to be a depressant of the processes of metabolism. It was objectionable on another ground too—that it led to carelessness in the selection, cleansing, and processing of foodstuffs.

It is difficult to picture today the vast extent of adulteration at the beginning of this century. More than half the food samples studied in the Indiana state laboratory were sophisticated. Whole grain flour was "cut" with bran and corn meal. The food commissioner of North Dakota declared that his state alone consumed ten times as much "Vermont maple syrup" as Vermont produced. The *Grocer's Companion and Merchant's Hand-Book* (Boston, 1883), warned the food retailer, in his own interest, of the various tricks used to alter coffee and tea, bread and flour, butter and lard, mustard, spices, pepper, pickles, preserved fruits, sauces, potted meats, cocoa, vinegar, and candies. A New York sugar firm was proud to make the point in its advertising of the 1880's that its sugar contained "neither glucose, muriate of tin, muriatic acid, nor any other foreign, deleterious or fraudulent substance whatever." The canned peas looked garden-fresh after treatment with $CuSO_4$ by methods known as "copper-greening." The pork and beans contained formaldehyde, the catsup benzoic acid. As a capstone of inspired fakery, one manufacturer of flavored glucose (sold as pure honey) carefully placed a dead bee in every bottle to give verisimilitude.

The little man of 1900 found himself in a big, big world, filled with butterine and mapleine.

This is not to suggest that the pioneer food manufacturer was as rascally as his contemporaries, the swamp doctor and the lightning rod peddler. What was occurring was less a collapse of human probity than an unexpected testing of human nature in a new context. Someone has said that all morality is based upon the assumption that somebody might be watching. In the milieu of late nineteenth-century business, nobody seemed to be watching. Thus the food crusade became necessary as a means of redressing the balance in the market which had turned so cruelly against the ordinary American and, indeed, against the honest manufacturer.

The ensuing controversy was symptomatic of the passing—painful, nostalgic to many, including no doubt many a big business senator—of the old, simple life of village and farm which was doomed by the expanding national life. It was, one feels, not solely in defense of the hake (sold as genuine codfish with boric acid as a preservative) that Senator George Frisbie Hoar of Massachusetts rose in the Senate to exalt "the exquisite flavor of the codfish, salted, made into balls, and eaten on a Sunday morning by a person whose

ATHLOPHOROS.

FOR RHEUMATISM AND NEURALGIA

"NO MORE RHEUMATISM FOR ME"

The Pure Food and Drugs Act, which demanded accurate labeling, meant the end of flamboyant, misleading advertising for such products as "Athlophoros" and other nostrums.

theology is sound, and who believes in the five points of Calvinism.''

The friends of food reform needed all the courage and public discussion they could muster. Since 1879, when the first federal bill was proposed, 190 measures to protect the consumer had been introduced in Congress, of which 49 had some kind of a subsequent history, and 141 were never heard of again. Meanwhile the states did what they could. About half of them had passed pure food laws by 1895. But there was no uniformity in their regulations. Foods legal in one state might be banned in another. Some of the laws were so loosely drawn that it was quite conceivable that Beechnut Bacon might be seized by the inspectors because no beechnuts were involved in its curing. Was Grape-Nuts misbranded because the great Battle Creek ''brain food'' had only a fanciful connection with either grapes or nuts? One bill actually proposed a numerical count of the contents of a package—the grains of salt, the cherries in a jar of preserves. What if Mr. Kellogg had to count every corn flake which went into his millions of packages?

Conflicts and foolish regulations could be ironed out over a period of time. The fatal flaw was that individual states had no power to get at the real problem: interstate traffic in the ''patented'' bitters, cancer cures, and strawberry jellies made out of dyed glucose, citric acid, and timothy seed.

The act which Wiley drew up was first introduced in 1902. It was successfully sidetracked in one legislative branch or the other for four years. The provisions were simple. In essence, it was a labeling act.

''Tell the truth on the label,'' Dr. Wiley said, ''and let the consumer judge for himself.''

Some of the legislators who opposed the act were states' rights Democrats, concerned about constitutional interpretation, who in the end fortunately saw the wisdom of sacrificing principle for expediency. Others were Old Guard Republicans who were special custodians of the *status quo* and highly sensitive to the sentiments of the business community: men like Senators Aldrich of Rhode Island (wholesale groceries), Kean of New Jersey (preserving and canning), Platt of Connecticut (home of the great Kickapoo Indian remedies), Hale and Frye of Maine, along whose rock-bound coast the familiar Maine herring became "imported French sardines," packaged in boxes with French labels.

The tactic in the Senate was one of unobtrusive obstruction and lip service to the idea of regulation. Open opposition was never much of a factor. "The 'right' to use deceptive labels," observed *The Nation*, "is not one for which impassioned oratory can be readily invoked." When a serious try was made to pass a general pure food law in 1902-3, Senator Lodge was able to direct the attention of the Senate to legislation more urgently needed, such as a Philippine tariff bill. In the last session of the 59th Congress (1904-5) the food bill was considered less pressing than a proposal to award naval commissions to a couple of young men who had been expelled from the Academy for hazing but still wanted very much to become officers in the United States Navy.

President Roosevelt finally decided to push the issue. "Mr. Dooley" offered a version of how it happened. "Tiddy," he said, was reading Upton Sinclair's novel, *The Jungle*, a grisly sociological tract on "Packingtown." "Tiddy was toying with a light breakfast an' idly turnin' over th' pages iv th' new book with both hands. Suddenly he rose fr'm th' table, an' cryin': 'I'm pizened,' begun throwin' sausages out iv th' window. Th' ninth wan sthruck Sinitor Biv'ridge on th' head an' made him a blond. It bounced off, exploded, an' blew a leg off a secret-service agent, an' th' scatthred fragmints desthroyed a handsome row iv ol' oak-trees. Sinitor Biv'ridge rushed in, thinkin' that th' Prisidint was bein' assassynated be his devoted followers in th' Sinit, an' discovered Tiddy engaged in a hand-to-hand conflict with a potted ham. Th' Sinitor fr'm Injyanny, with a few well-directed wurruds, put out th' fuse an' rendered th' missile harmless. Since thin th' Prisidint, like th' rest iv us, has become a viggytaryan. . . ." At any rate, in his annual message to Congress, December 5, 1905, Roosevelt recommended in the interest of the consumer and the legitimate manufacturer "that a law be enacted to regulate interstate commerce in misbranded and adulterated foods, drinks and drugs," and the bill was re-introduced in the Senate by Senator Weldon B. Heyburn of Idaho. Pressure from the American Medical Association, the graphic exposé of revolting conditions in the Chicago packing houses, and Roosevelt's skillful use of the report of an official commission which investigated the stockyards, finally forced a favorable vote in the Senate and then the House on the Pure Food and Drugs Bill. The meat inspection problem was, actually, a different matter. But an angry public was in no mood to make fine distinctions. Meat, processed foods, and fake medicines all tapped the family pocketbook, all went into the human stomach, and all smelled to high heaven in the spring of 1906. Roosevelt signed the bill into law on June 30, 1906.

The enforcement of the law was placed in the hands of Dr. Wiley. According to the Doctor, it was after the bill became law that the real fight began. Most food and drug manufacturers and dealers adjusted their operations to the new law, and found themselves in a better position because of it, with curtailment of the activities of fly-by-night competition and re-establishment of the consumers' confidence in goods of known quality. But there were die-hards like the sugar and molasses refiners, the fruit driers, whisky rectifiers, and purveyors of wahoo bitters, Peruna and Indian Doctor wonder drugs.

The administration of the Food and Drugs Act involved the Bureau of Chemistry in thousands of court proceedings, *United States* v. *Two Barrels of Desiccated Eggs, United States* v. *One Hundred Barrels of Vinegar*; and one merciful judge noted that Section 6 extended the protection of the act to our four-footed friends. Pure food inspectors had seized 620 cases of spoiled canned cat food. When the case of the smelly tuna fish turned up in the western district court of the state of Washington, the judge cited man's experience with cats throughout recorded time: "Who will not feed cats must feed mice and rats." He confirmed the seizure and directed an order of condemnation.

The law was subsequently strengthened both by legal interpretations and by legislative action, as experience developed needs not met by the original act. Government technicians worked with private industry in the solution of specific problems such as refrigeration and the handling of food. When Dr. Wiley retired from public service in 1912, a revolution had occurred in food processing in only six years' time. Yet the food industry had hardly begun to grow.

"The conditions created by the passage of the act," said Clarence Francis, former president and chairman of the board of General Foods Corporation, "invited responsible business men to put real money into the food business."

The next 25 years saw the decline of the barrel as a food container and its replacement by the consumer unit package; the setting of official standards for the composition of basic food products; and the banning of quack therapeutic mechanical devices such as the electric belt, whose galvanic properties were once presented so vividly to the "Lost Manhood" market. We still have with us in some measure the "horse beef" butcher and the "butterlegger." Tap water remains a tempting means of "extending" many foods. But there is no question about the general integrity of our food supply, the contribution to the national well-being of the original food law, as amended, and the readiness of today's food industry leaders to accept what is now called the Food, Drug, and Cosmetic Act as a proper blueprint of their obligation to the nation's consumers.

Battleships of the Great White Fleet en route to Japan lie at anchor in San Francisco harbor in this 1908 photograph.

*Part
Four*

*AMERICA
IN WORLD
AFFAIRS: 1898-1945*

William E. Leuchtenburg

The Needless
War with
Spain

Seldom have events so pregnant with future significance occurred in an atmosphere so devoid of an understanding of their significance as in 1898 when the United States went to war with Spain. It is perhaps not quite accurate to say that the United States emerged from that war as a world power. In retrospect the nation was a world power well before the war began. But the war made Americans aware that the United States was a world power, and from that awareness flowed American imperialism, American participation in World War I, and much that followed.

As William E. Leuchtenburg explains in this essay, there was no shortage of "aggressive, expansionist, jingoistic" feeling in America during the early 1890's. But the conflict with Spain derived chiefly from the desire of Americans to help the beleaguered Cubans win their independence from Spain. Americans wanted the war (which could well have been avoided) but they had little understanding of what the results of that war would be.

Mr. Leuchtenburg, professor of history at Columbia University, is the author of Franklin D. Roosevelt and the New Deal, 1932–1940, which won a Francis Parkman Prize, awarded each year to the book in American history that best combines sound scholarship and literary distinction. This essay also combines these two qualities.

*T*he United States in the 1890's became more aggressive, expansionistic, and jingoistic than it had been since the 1850's. In less than five years, we came to the brink of war with Italy, Chile, and Great Britain over three minor incidents in which no American national interest of major importance was involved. In each of these incidents, our secretary of state was highly aggressive, and the American people applauded. During these years, we completely overhauled our decrepit Navy, building fine new warships like the *Maine*. The martial virtues of Napoleon, the imperial doctrines of Rudyard Kipling, and the naval theories of Captain Alfred T. Mahan all enjoyed a considerable vogue.

There was an apparently insatiable hunger for foreign conquest. Senator Shelby M. Cullom declared in 1895: "It is time that some one woke up and realized the necessity of annexing some property. We want all this northern hemisphere, and when we begin to reach out to secure these advantages we will begin to have a nation and our lawmakers will rise above the grade of politicians and become true statesmen." When, in 1895, the United States almost became involved in a war with Great Britain over the Venezuelan boundary, Theodore Roosevelt noted: "The antics of the bankers, brokers and anglo-maniacs generally are humiliating to a degree. . . . Personally I rather hope the fight will come soon. The clamor of the peace faction has convinced me that this country needs a war." The Washington *Post* concluded: "The taste of Empire is in the mouth of the people. . . ."

In the early nineteenth century, under the leadership of men like Simon Bolivar, Spain's colonies in the New World had launched a series of successful revolutions; of the great Spanish empire that Cortes and Pizarro had built, the island of Cuba, "the Ever Faithful Isle," was the only important Spanish possession to stay loyal to the Crown. Spain exploited the economy of the island mercilessly, forcing Cubans to buy Spanish goods at prices far above the world market, and Madrid sent to Cuba as colonial officials younger sons who had no interest in the island other than making a quick killing and returning to Spain. High taxes to support Spanish officialdom crippled the island; arbitrary arrests and arbitrary trials made a mockery of justice; and every attempt at public education was stifled.

The island of Cuba had been in a state of political turbulence for years when in 1894 the American Wilson-Gorman Tariff placed duties on Cuban sugar which, coupled with a world-wide depression, brought ruin to the economy of the island. The terrible hardship of the winter was the signal for revolution; on February 24, 1895, under the leadership of a junta in New York City headed by José Martí, rebels once more took the field against Spain. At first, the American people were too absorbed with the Venezuelan crisis to pay much attention to another revolt in Cuba. Then, in September, 1895, came the event which changed the course of the Cuban rebellion: William Randolph Hearst, a young man of 32 who had been operating the San Francisco *Examiner* in a sensational fashion, purchased the New York *Morning Journal*, and immediately locked horns with Joseph Pulitzer and the

World in a circulation war that was to make newspaper history.

Hearst capitalized on the fact that the American people had only the most romantic notions of the nature of the Cuban conflict. The rebels under General Máximo Gómez, a tough Santo Domingan guerrilla fighter, embarked on a program of burning the cane fields in the hope not only of depriving the government of revenue but also of so disrupting the life of the island that the government would be forced to submit. Although there were some noble spirits in the group, much of the rebellion had an unsavory odor; one of the main financial supports for the uprising came from American property owners who feared that their sugar fields would be burned unless protection money was paid.

While Gómez was putting Cuba to the torch, American newsmen were filing reports describing the war in terms of nonexistent pitched battles between the liberty-loving Cubans and the cruel Spaniards. The war was presented, in short, as a Byronic conflict between the forces of freedom and the forces of tyranny, and the American people ate it up. When Hearst bought the *Journal* in late 1895, it had a circulation of 30,000; by 1897 it had bounded to over 400,000 daily, and during the Spanish-American War it was to go well over a million.

The sensational newspapers had influence, yet they represented no more than a minority of the press of the country; and in the South and the Middle West, where anti-Spanish feeling became most intense, the representative newspaper was much more conservative. Certainly the yellow press played a tremendous part in whipping up sentiment for intervention in Cuba, but these feelings could not be carried into action unless American political leaders of both parties were willing to assume the terrible responsibility of war.

By the beginning of 1896 the rebels had achieved such success in their guerrilla tactics that Madrid decided on firmer steps and sent General Don Valeriano Weyler y Nicolau to Cuba. When Weyler arrived in February, he found the sugar industry severely disrupted and the military at a loss to meet the rebel tactic of setting fire to the cane fields. Weyler declared martial law and announced that men guilty of incendiarism would be dealt with summarily; he was promptly dubbed "The Butcher" by American newspapermen.

By late 1896 Weyler still had not succeeded in crushing the insurrection, and his measures became more severe. On October 21 he issued his famous *reconcentrado* order, directing the "reconcentration" of the people of Pinar del Río in the garrison towns, and forbidding the export of supplies from the towns to the countryside. Reasoning that he could never suppress the rebellion so long as the rebels could draw secret assistance from people in the fields, Weyler moved the people from the estates into the towns and stripped the countryside of supplies to starve out the rebellion. Since many of the people had already fled to the towns, the *reconcentrado* policy was not as drastic as it appeared; yet the suffering produced by the policy was undeniable. Lacking proper hygienic care, thousands of Cubans, especially women and children, died like flies.

This pro-McKinley cartoon, from Puck's April 13, 1898, *issue, applauded the President's efforts to restrain war hysteria; but two days earlier McKinley had reversed his pacifistic policy.*

When William McKinley entered the White House in 1897, he had no intention of joining the War Hawks. "If I can only go out of office . . . with the knowledge that I have done what lay in my power to avert this terrible calamity," McKinley told Grover Cleveland on the eve of his inauguration, "I shall be the happiest man in the world." McKinley came to power as the "advance agent of prosperity," and business interests were almost unanimous in opposing any agitation of the Cuban question that might lead to war. Contrary to the assumptions of Leninist historians, it was Wall Street which, first and last, resisted a war which was to bring America its overseas empire.

The country had been gripped since 1893 by the deepest industrial depression in its history, a depression that was to persist until the beginning of 1897. Each time it appeared recovery might be on its way, a national crisis had cut it off: first the Venezuelan boundary war scare of December, 1895, then the bitter free silver campaign of 1896. What business groups feared more than anything else was a new crisis. As Julius Pratt writes: "To this fair prospect of a great business revival the threat of war was like a specter at the feast."

McKinley was not a strong President, and he had no intention of being one. Of all the political figures of his day, he was the man most responsive to the popular will. It was his great virtue and, his critics declared, his great weakness. Uncle Joe Cannon once remarked: "McKinley keeps his ear to the ground so close that he gets it full of grasshoppers much of the time." If McKinley was not one of our greatest Presidents, he was certainly the most representative and the most responsive. Anyone who knew the man knew that, although he was strongly opposed to war, he would not hold out against war if the popular demand for war became unmistakable. "Let the voice of the people rule"—this was McKinley's credo, and he meant it.

The threat to peace came from a new quarter, from the South and West, the strongholds of Democracy and free silver. Many Bryanite leaders were convinced that a war would create such a strain on the currency system that the opposition to free silver would collapse. Moreover, with the opposition to war strongest in Wall Street, they found it easy to believe that Administration policy was the product of a conspiracy of bankers who would deny silver to the American people, who would deny liberty to the people of Cuba, who were concerned only with the morality of the countinghouse. Moreover, Bryan was the spokesman for rural Protestantism, which was already speaking in terms of a righteous war against Spain to free the Cubans from bondage. These were forces too powerful for McKinley to ignore. McKinley desired peace, but he was above all, a Republican partisan, and he had no intention of handing the Democrats in 1900 the campaign cry of Free Cuba and Free Silver.

While McKinley attempted to search out a policy that would preserve peace without bringing disaster to the Republican party, the yellow press made his job all the more difficult by whipping up popular anger against Spain. On February 12 the *Journal* published a dispatch from Richard Harding Davis, reporting that as the American steamship *Olivette* was about to leave Havana Harbor for the United States, it was boarded by Spanish police officers who searched three young Cuban women, one of whom was suspected of carrying messages from the rebels. The *Journal* ran the story under the headline, "Does Our Flag Protect Women?" with a vivid drawing by Frederic Remington across one half a page showing Spanish plainclothes men searching a wholly nude woman. War, declared the *Journal,* "is a dreadful thing, but there are things more dreadful than even war, and one of them is dishonor." It shocked the country, and Congressman Amos Cummings immediately resolved to launch a congressional inquiry into the *Olivette* outrage. Before any steps could be taken, the true story was revealed. The *World* produced one of the young women who indignantly protested the *Journal's* version of the incident. Pressured by the *World*, the *Journal* was forced to print a letter from Davis explaining that his article had not said that male policemen had searched the women and that, in fact, the search had been conducted quite properly by a police matron with no men present.

The *Olivette* incident was manufactured by Hearst, but by the spring of 1897 the American press had a new horror to report which was all too true. Famine was stalking the island. Cuba had been in a serious economic state when the rebellion broke out in 1895; two years of war would, under any circumstances, have been disastrous, but the deliberate policies pursued both by the insurgents and by the government forces made the situation desperate. It was a simple matter for Hearst and Pulitzer reporters to pin the full responsibility on Weyler.

By the middle of July, McKinley had formulated a policy which he set down in a letter of instructions to our new American minister

Frederic Remington's rendition of the Olivette *incident was actually the work of Hearst, who had Remington exaggerate the supposed impropriety.*

to Spain, General Stewart L. Woodford. The letter emphasized the need of bringing the Cuban war to an end and said that this could be done to the mutual advantage of both Spain and the Cubans by granting some kind of autonomy to Cuba. If Spain did not make an offer to the rebels and if the "measures of unparalleled severity" were not ended, the United States threatened to intervene.

On August 8 an Italian anarchist assassinated the Spanish premier; and when Woodford reached Madrid in September, a new government was about to take over headed by Señor Sagasta and the Liberals, who had repeatedly denounced the "barbarity" of the previous government's policy in Cuba. Sagasta immediately removed General Weyler, and the prospects for an agreement between the United States and Spain took a decided turn for the better.

While Woodford was carrying on skillful diplomatic negotiations for peace in Madrid, the Hearst press was creating a new sensation in this country with the Cisneros affair. Evangelina Cisneros was a young Cuban woman who had been arrested and imprisoned in the Rocojidas in Havana, guilty, according to the American press, of no other crime than protecting her virtue from an unscrupulous Spanish colonel, an aide to Butcher Weyler. The Rocojidas, Hearst's reporter told American readers, was a cage where the innocent beauty was herded with women criminals of every type, subject to the taunts and vile invitations of men who gathered outside.

When it was reported that Señorita Cisneros, whose father was a rebel leader, was to be sent for a long term to a Spanish penal colony in Africa or in the Canaries, the *Journal* launched one of the most fabulous campaigns in newspaper history. "Enlist the women of America!" was the Hearst war cry, and the women of America proved willing recruits. Mrs. Julia Ward Howe signed an appeal to Pope Leo XIII, and Mrs. Jefferson Davis, the widow of the president of the Confederacy, appealed to the queen regent of Spain to "give Evangelina Cisneros to the women of America to save her from a fate worse than death." When the *Journal* prepared a petition on behalf of Señorita Cisneros, it obtained the names of Mrs. Nancy McKinley, the mother of the President, and Mrs. John Sherman, the wife of the secretary of state, as well as such other prominent ladies as Julia Dent Grant and Mrs. Mark Hanna.

It was a startling coup for Mr. Hearst, but he had not yet even begun to display his ingenuity. On October 10, 1897, the *Journal* erupted across its front page with the banner headline: "An American Newspaper Accomplishes at a Single Stroke What the Best Efforts of Diplomacy Failed Utterly to Bring About in Many Months." Hearst had sent Karl Decker, one of his most reliable correspondents, to Havana in late August with orders to rescue the Cuban Girl Martyr "at any hazard"; and Decker had climbed to the roof of a house near the prison, broken the bar of a window of the jail, lifted Evangelina out, and, after hiding her for a few days in Havana, smuggled her onto an American steamer. Decker, signing his dispatch to the *Journal* "Charles Duval," wrote: "I have broken the bars of Rocojidas and have set free the beautiful captive of monster Weyler. Weyler could blind the Queen to the real character of Evangelina, but he could not build a jail that would hold against *Journal* enterprise when properly set to work." The Cuban Girl Martyr was met at the pier by a great throng, led up Broadway in a triumphal procession, taken to a reception at Delmonico's where 120,000 people milled about the streets surrounding the restaurant, and hailed at a monster reception in Madison Square Garden. The Bishop of London cabled his congratulations to the *Journal*, while Governor Stephens of Missouri proposed that the *Journal* send down 500 of its reporters to free the entire island.

On October 23 Sagasta announced a "total change of immense scope" in Spanish policy in Cuba. He promised to grant local autonomy to the Cubans immediately, reserving justice, the armed forces, and foreign relations to Spain. On November 13 Weyler's successor, Captain-General Blanco, issued a decree modifying considerably the *reconcentrado* policy, and on November 25 the queen regent signed the edicts creating an autonomous government for the island. In essence, Madrid had acceded to the American demands.

While Woodford was conducting negotiations with a conciliatory Liberal government in Madrid and while there was still hope for peace, the fatal incident occurred which made war virtually inevitable. On January 12, 1898, a riot broke out in Havana, and Spanish officers attacked newspaper offices. The nature of the riot is still not clear; it was over in an hour, and it had no anti-American aspects. If the United States now sent a naval vessel to Havana, it might be buying trouble with Spain. Yet if a riot did break out and Americans were killed, the Administration would be stoned for not having a ship there to protect them. For several days McKinley wavered; then he ordered the *Maine* to Havana, but with the explanation that this was a courtesy visit demonstrating that so nonsensical were the rumors of danger to American citizens that our ships could again resume their visits to the island.

As the *Maine* lay at anchor in Havana Harbor, the rebels, with a perfect sense of timing, released a new propaganda bombshell. In December, 1897, in a private letter, Señor Enrique Dupuy de Lôme, the Spanish minister at Washington, had set down his opinions of President McKinley's annual message to Congress: "Besides the ingrained and inevitable bluntness (*grosería*) with which it repeated all that the press and public opinion in Spain have said about Weyler," De Lôme wrote, "it once more shows what McKinley is, weak and a bidder for the admiration of the crowd, besides being a would-be politician (*politicastro*) who tries to leave a door open behind himself while keeping on good terms with the jingoes of his party." De Lôme added: "It would be very advantageous to take up, even if only for effect, the question of commercial relations, and to have a man of some prominence sent here in order that I may make use of him to carry on a propaganda among the Senators and others in opposition to the junta."

De Lôme had, to be sure, written all this in a private letter (which was stolen by an insurgent spy in the Havana post office), not in his official capacity, and his characterization of McKinley was not wholly without merit, but it was a blunder of the highest magnitude. Not only had De Lôme attacked the President, but he had gone on to suggest that the negotiations then going on over a commercial treaty were not being conducted in good faith. Throughout the letter ran precisely the tone which Hearst had been arguing expressed the Spanish temper —a cold, arrogant contempt for democratic institutions. The State Department immediately cabled Woodford to demand the recall of the Spanish minister, but Madrid had the good fortune of being able to tell Woodford that De Lôme, informed of the disaster the night before, had already resigned.

A week after the publication of the De Lôme indiscretion, at 9:40 on the night of February 15, 1898, came the terrible blow which ended all real hope for peace. In the harbor of Havana, the *Maine* was blown up by an explosion of unknown origin. In an instant, the ship was filled with the sounds of shrieking men and rushing water. The blast occurred in the forward part of the ship where, a half hour before, most of the men had turned in for the night; they were killed in their hammocks. Of the 350 officers and men on board, 260 were killed. By morning the proud *Maine* had sunk into the mud of Havana Harbor.

"Public opinion should be suspended until further report," Captain Sigsbee cabled to Washington, but even Sigsbee could not down his suspicions. The *Maine* had gone to a Spanish possession on a courtesy call, and the *Maine* now lay at the bottom of Havana Harbor. What could it mean but war? "I would give anything if President McKinley would order the fleet to Havana tomorrow," wrote Theodore Roosevelt. "The *Maine* was sunk by an act of dirty treachery on the part of the Spaniards." Volunteers lined up for war service, even though there was no one to enlist them; in New York 500 sharpshooting Westchester businessmen volunteered as a unit for the colors. The *Journal* reported: "The Whole Country Thrills With War Fever."

On February 15, 1898, the battleship Maine
exploded; with it went any chance for peace.

The cause of the explosion of the *Maine* has never been finally established. That Spain deliberately decided to blow up the *Maine* is inconceivable, although it is possible that it might have been the work of unauthorized Spanish extremists. The one group which had everything to gain from such an episode was the rebels; yet it seems unlikely that either they or Spanish hotheads could have carried out such an act and remained undetected. The most likely explanation is that it was caused by an explosion of internal origin; yet the evidence for this is not conclusive. In any event, this was the explanation that the Navy in 1898 was least willing to consider since it would reflect seriously on the care with which the Navy was operating the *Maine.*

The move toward war seemed relentless. On March 9 Congress unanimously voted $50,000,000 for war preparations. Yet the days went by and there was no war, in part because important sectors of American opinion viewed Hearst's stories of the atrocious conditions on the island with profound skepticism. Senator Redfield Proctor of Vermont decided to launch his own investigation into conditions on the island. On March 17, after a tour of Cuba, Proctor made one of the most influential speeches in the history of the United States Senate.

Proctor, who Roosevelt reported was "very ardent for the war," had not generally been regarded as a jingo, and no man in the Senate commanded greater respect for personal integrity. Proctor declared that he had gone to Cuba skeptical of reports of suffering there, and he had come back convinced. "Torn from their homes, with foul earth, foul air, foul water, and foul food or none, what wonder that one-half have died and that one-quarter of the living are so diseased that they can not be saved?" Proctor asked. "Little children are still walking about with arms and chest terribly emaciated, eyes swollen, and abdomen bloated to three times the natural size. . . . I was told by one of our consuls that they have been found dead about the markets in the morning, where they had crawled, hoping to get some stray bits of food from the early hucksters."

The question of peace or war now lay with McKinley. The Spaniards, Woodford had conceded, had gone about as far as they could go; but with the *Maine* in the mud of Havana Harbor, with the country, following Proctor's speech, crying for war, how much longer could McKinley hold out? The jingoes were treating his attempt to preserve peace with outright contempt; McKinley, Roosevelt told his friends, "has no more backbone than a chocolate éclair."

"We will have this war for the freedom of Cuba," Roosevelt shouted at a Gridiron Dinner on March 26, shaking his fist at Senator Hanna, "in spite of the timidity of the commercial interests." Nor was McKinley permitted to forget the political consequences. The Chicago *Times-Herald* warned: "Intervention in Cuba, peacefully if we can, forcibly if we must, is immediately inevitable. Our own internal political conditions will not permit its postponement. . . . Let President McKinley hesitate to rise to the just expectations of the American people, and who can doubt that 'war for Cuban liberty' will be the crown of thorns the free silver Democrats and Populists will adopt at the elections this fall?"

On March 28 the President released the report of the naval court of inquiry on the *Maine* disaster. "In the opinion of the court the *Maine* was destroyed by the explosion of a submarine mine, which caused the partial explosion of two or more of the forward magazines," the report concluded. Although no one was singled out for blame, the conclusion was inescapable that if Spain had not willfully done it, Spain had failed to provide proper protection to a friendly vessel on a courtesy visit in its waters. Overnight a slogan with the ring of a child's street chant caught the fancy of the country:

> *Remember the Maine!*
> *To hell with Spain!*

"I have no more doubt than that I am now standing in the Senate of the United States," declared Henry Cabot Lodge, "that that ship was blown up by a government mine, fired by, or with the connivance of, Spanish officials."

Desiring peace yet afraid of its consequences, McKinley embarked on a policy of attempting to gain the fruits of war without fighting. On March 29 Woodford demanded that Spain agree to an immediate armistice, revoke the reconcentration order, and co-operate with the United States to provide relief; Spain was given 48 hours to reply.

On March 31 Spain replied that it had finally revoked the reconcentration orders in the western provinces; that it had made available a credit of three million pesetas to resettle the natives; that it was willing to submit the *Maine* controversy to arbitration; and that it would grant a truce if the insurgents would ask for it. In short, Spain would yield everything we demanded, except that it would not concede defeat; the appeal for a truce would have to come from the rebels. Since the rebels would not make such an appeal, since they were confident of ultimate American intervention, the situation was hopeless; yet Spain had come a long way. Woodford cabled to Washington: "The ministry have gone as far as they dare go to-day. . . . No Spanish ministry would have dared to do one month ago what this ministry has proposed to-day."

For a week the Spaniards attempted to cling to their last shreds of dignity. On Saturday, April 9, Madrid surrendered. Driven to the wall by the American demands, the Spanish foreign minister informed Woodford that the government had decided to grant an armistice in Cuba immediately. Gratified at achieving the final concession, Woodford cabled McKinley: "I hope that nothing will now be done to humiliate Spain, as I am satisfied that the present Government is going, and is loyally ready to go, as fast and as far as it can."

It was too late. McKinley had decided on war. Spain had conceded everything, but Spain had waited too long. Up until the very last moment, Spanish officials had feared that if they yielded to American demands in Cuba, it might mean the overturn of the dynasty, and they preferred even a disastrous war to that. Proud but helpless in the face of American might, many Spanish officials appeared to prefer the dignity of being driven from the island in a heroic defensive war to meek surrender to an American ultimatum. In the end they surrendered and promised reforms. But they had promised reforms before—after the Ten Years' War which ended in 1878—and they had not kept these promises. Throughout the nineteenth century, constitutions had been made and remade, but nothing had changed. Even in the last hours of negotiations with the American minister, they had told Woodford that the President had asked the Pope to intervene, when the President had done nothing of the sort. Even if their intentions were of the best, could they carry them out? Spain had had three full years to end the war in Cuba and, with vastly superior numbers of troops, had not been able to do it. And the insurgents would accept nothing from Madrid, not even peace.

On Monday, April 11, McKinley sent his message to Congress, declaring that "the forcible intervention of the United States as a neutral to stop the war, according to the large dictates of humanity and following many historical precedents" was "justifiable on rational grounds." The fact that Spain had met everything we had asked was buried in two paragraphs of a long plea for war. It took Congress a full week to act. On Monday night, April 18, while the resolution shuttled back and forth between the two chambers and the conference room, congressmen sang "The Battle Hymn of the Republic" and

"Dixie" and shook the chamber with the refrain of "Hang General Weyler to a Sour Apple Tree." At three o'clock the next morning the two houses reached an agreement—the United States recognized the independence of Cuba, asserted that we would not acquire Cuba for ourselves, and issued an ultimatum to Spain to withdraw within three days. On April 20 President McKinley signed the resolution. War had come at last. But not quite. Although hostilities had begun, not until four days later did Congress declare war. When it did declare war, it dated it from McKinley's action in establishing a blockade four days before. To the very end, we protested our peaceful intentions as we stumbled headlong into war.

We entered a war in which no vital American interest was involved, and without any concept of its consequences. Although McKinley declared that to enter such a war for high purposes, and then annex territory, would be "criminal aggression," we acquired as a result of the war the Philippines and other parts of an overseas empire we had not intended to get and had no idea how to defend. Although we roundly attacked Spain for not recognizing the rebel government, we, in our turn, refused to recognize the rebels. Although we were shocked by Weyler's policies in Cuba, we were soon in the unhappy position of using savage methods to put down a rebel uprising in the Philippines, employing violence in a measure that easily matched what Weyler had done.

It would be easy to condemn McKinley for not holding out against war, but McKinley showed considerable courage in bucking the tide. McKinley's personal sympathy for the Cubans was sincere; only after his death was it revealed that he had contributed $5,000 anonymously for Cuban relief. It would be even easier to blame it all on Hearst; yet no newspaper can arouse a people that is not willing to be aroused. At root lay the American gullibility about foreign affairs, with the penchant for viewing politics in terms of a simple morality play; equally important were the contempt of the American people for Spain as a cruel but weak Latin nation and the desire for war and expansion which permeated the decade. The American people were not led into war; they got the war they wanted. "I think," observed Senator J. C. Spooner, "possibly the President could have worked out the business without war, but the current was too strong, the demagogues too numerous, the fall elections too near."

Harold A. Larrabee

The Enemies
of Empire

When the war with Spain ended, the United States found itself in control of Spain's Pacific and Caribbean colonies; what to do with them was the first problem the new proprietor had to confront. The controversy that developed over this issue in America was relatively brief—by 1900 it appeared to have been settled in favor of those who wanted to create an American empire. However, the basic issues raised in this debate have never been settled; the history of American foreign policy in the twentieth century is full of the repercussions and elaborations of the arguments of 1898–1900. To what extent, if any, should questions of national interest and honor take precedence over those of morality and the national interests of other peoples? What is "national honor"? Is colonialism always evil, no matter how administered or for what end?

Professor Harold A. Larrabee of Union College and author of Decision at the Chesapeake *describes below the argument as it first developed between imperialists and anti-imperialists after the Spanish-American War. He takes a strong anti-imperialist position, and few today would disagree. That he is probably too favorable in his estimate of the anti-imperialists of that day—many of them, for example, opposed annexing colonies because they disliked bringing nonwhites under the American flag—detracts little from the value of his essay as a graphic re-creation of the mood of the times. Larrabee provides fascinating glimpses into the minds of the anti-imperialists, the defenders of expansionism, and those many sincere but somewhat befuddled citizens who, like President McKinley, had great trouble deciding between these two positions.*

*W*e know, to the hour and minute, when this country reached the point of no return on its way to becoming a world power. It was at exactly 5:39 A.M., Manila time, on Sunday, May 1, 1898, when Commodore George Dewey, U.S.N., commanding the Asiatic Squadron of four small cruisers and two gunboats, coolly turned from his position on the bridge of his flagship *Olympia,* and said to its captain in words that were to echo across distant America: "You may fire when you are ready, Gridley." The command loosed salvos of shells that swiftly crushed the decrepit fleet of the Spanish Admiral Montojo (two cruisers and seven small gunboats of an antiquated type), which had been huddling under the defenses of Manila. The battle was, in the words of the English historian Herbert W. Wilson, "a military execution rather than a real contest."

Its effects on American foreign policy, however, were incalculable, and the end is not yet. Hawaii was swiftly annexed as a territory on July 7, 1898; and by the ratification of the Treaty of Paris ending the war on February 6, 1899, we found ourselves the sovereign rulers of all the Spanish colonial possessions in the Philippines, there to remain for the next forty-seven years. The Pacific Ocean was thenceforth to be regarded as "an American lake." What we now often forget, however, is how many Americans were in those early days opposed to the idea of an American Empire. Sixty years ago imperialism, then defined as the raising of the flag by force over noncontiguous territory, and called by its friends "expansionism," was the burning issue of the day. It was bitterly contested, largely on abstract moral grounds as a gross betrayal of American principles, by a small but tenacious band of New England reformers.

The hard core of the anti-imperialist movement, both at the start and at the finish, was composed of conservative Boston lawyers and bankers, many of them lineal descendants of the Pilgrims. They soon gathered about them a remarkable nationwide galaxy of literary lights, college presidents, leaders of industry and labor, editors, and politicians, constituting what has been called "the first great national propaganda organization of the twentieth century." Their achievements were greater in the vigorous expression of their views than in practical politics. Yet they lost one of their major battles in the Senate by only one vote; for a time they threatened to endanger McKinley's re-election in 1900; and there can be no doubt that their tireless needling of the American conscience about colonialism, which continued until 1920, hastened the eventual independence of the Philippines.

Crusades being somewhat out of fashion nowadays, it may be difficult to recover the fervor of these heirs of Wendell Phillips and Charles Sumner as they denounced the extension of American rule by force in the Philippines, not because of what it might do to the Filipinos, but because of what they were convinced it was bound to do to American democratic ideals. They saw in the American seizure and retention of the Islands "the infamy of the doctrine that a people may be governed without their consent." At least some of the Filipinos, under Emilio Aguinaldo, were not "consenting" to their "pacification" by our

In Rufus Zogbaum's canvas, Commodore George Dewey directs the American victory at the Battle of Manila Bay from the bridge of the Olympia.

troops. A spineless administration in Washington, too much influenced by a group of jingoes in high places and by the yellow press, had liberated the Islanders from Spain only to try to enslave them again. This was rank apostasy from our professed principles in the Declaration of Independence and the Gettysburg Address. Could it be that Aguinaldo was fighting for *our* principles, while we had succumbed to the evil colonial policy of defeated Spain?

The expansionists' reply to this plea for democracy was the twin slogan: duty and destiny. It was, they said, the moral and religious duty of a civilized nation to accept the white man's burden, imposed upon us, in this instance, by our own idealistic crusade to free the Spanish possessions from centuries of misrule. As a moral aristocrat among nations, blessed with so many special advantages, America must, as a matter of *noblesse oblige,* undertake a self-sacrificing mission of political education in a world of backward peoples. In the words of the archexpansionist Theodore Roosevelt: "Peace cannot be had until the civilized nations have expanded in some shape over the barbarous nations." And besides, such expansion was inevitable. What John Hay called "cosmic tendency" and others invoked as Manifest Destiny (now enlarged to a global scale) was irresistibly impelling the onward march of the white men who spoke what Sir Cecil Spring-Rice called "God's language." Richard Croker, the boss of Tammany, remarked that "My idea of anti-imperialism is opposition to the fashion of shooting everybody who doesn't speak English."

What intensified and prolonged the conflict was the fact that both sides professed to want liberty for the Filipinos: the anti-imperialists believed that for us, as democrats, to deny them *immediate* liberty was to stultify our own ideals; while the expansionists maintained that the hopelessly backward Islanders were to be granted *eventual* liberty after a sufficient but indefinite period of Yankee tutelage. On both sides, then, there was an appeal to conscience by sincere but profoundly ignorant American patriots who found themselves enmeshed in the toils and tangles of historical circumstances, including domestic party politics. Since a moral issue was involved, the other side was not only wrong, but wicked, and words like "blood lust" and "murderer" were hurled at the imperialists, while the antis were denounced as "cowards" and "traitors." Nothing stirs the American people so deeply as a controversy in which both parties claim to be morally right: witness the battles over slavery, woman suffrage, and prohibition. In our day, "imperialism" has become a term battered almost beyond recognition in the cold war. But the central issue of 1898–1902—what constitutes the consent of the governed, and who is qualified to give it—has never been more alive than today, as one former colonial possession after another struggles toward a precariously independent nationhood.

"You have a wolf by the ears in the Philippines. You cannot let go of him with either dignity or safety, and he will not be easy to tame," said an anonymous American diplomat to one of our peace commissioners who was leaving for Paris in the fall of 1898. Even some of the expansionists themselves deplored our grip on the wolf in the first place, but were nevertheless extremely reluctant to let go. This was at once the strength and the weakness of the anti-imperialists' case. The imperialists had to admit, in the words of one of their leaders, Ambassador Whitelaw Reid, that "it was perfectly true that the American people did not wish for more territory, and never dreamed of distant colonies." Yet the grip on the wolf was an accomplished fact, and the practical difficulty of letting go with dignity and safety was the fatal flaw in the position into which the anti-imperialists found themselves maneuvered.

The clinching argument of the imperialists was "where once the flag goes up, it must never come down." The crucial decisions that sent Dewey to Manila in the first place, and ordered troops to his support as early as May 4, even before the news of his victory had reached Washington, were the work of a small elite group in the Republican administration who had managed to convert a pliable President. In 1897, McKinley had told Carl Schurz, "Ah, you may be sure there will be no jingo nonsense under my administration." But there was some truth in the popular conundrum: "Why is McKinley's mind like an unmade bed? Answer: Because it has to be made up for him every time he wants to use it." Theodore Roosevelt's friend Henry Adams spoke of his "alarm and horror of seeing poor weak McKinley, in gaiety . . . plunge into an inevitable war to conquer the Philippines contrary to every profession or so-called principle of our lives and history."

The ringleaders in the open conspiracy to move into the Orient via Hawaii and an isthmian canal, without ever consulting the American people, were two ardent disciples of Captain Alfred Thayer Mahan, U.S.N., the author of *The Influence of Sea Power Upon History, 1660–1783*, namely—Senator Henry Cabot Lodge of Massachusetts and the young and aggressive Assistant Secretary of the Navy, Theodore Roosevelt. It is one of the ironies of history that Captain Mahan himself was an anti-imperialist until the year 1885, and for precisely the reason most often advanced against his later followers: empire "would destroy free government." By 1890, however, a study of British sea power had converted him to the belief that the United States could take "a larger part in external affairs without risk to their institutions and with benefit to the world at large." Theodore Roosevelt, then a civil service commissioner, devoured Mahan's book, and reviewed it with enthusiasm in the *Atlantic Monthly,* later proclaiming Mahan "the only great naval expert who also possessed in international matters the mind of a statesman of the first rank."

Mahan's advice to Roosevelt in May, 1897, was: "Do nothing unrighteous; but take the [Hawaiian] islands first, and solve afterwards." The Roosevelt of 1898, described by William James as "still mentally in the *Sturm und Drang* period of early adolescence," needed little urging. He had been frustrated by President Cleveland's blocking of the annexation of Hawaii, but with the advent of a Republican administration his hopes were high. He was, however, soon indignant over the hesitancy of President McKinley, who, he said, "has no more backbone than a chocolate éclair." Behind McKinley stirred the powerful boss Mark Hanna, senator from Ohio, who flatly opposed the coming Spanish war at a Gridiron dinner on March 26, 1898, less than three weeks before it was declared. Introduced by the toastmaster at the same dinner as "At least one man connected with this administration who is not afraid to fight," Theodore Roosevelt, by that time in the Navy Department, declared: "We will have this war for the freedom of Cuba, Senator Hanna, in spite of the timidity of commercial interests." As William James put it, "Roosevelt gushes over war as the ideal condition of human society, for the manly strenuousness which it involves, and treats peace as a condition of blubberlike and swollen ignobility, fit only for huckstering weaklings, dwelling in gray twilight and heedless of the higher life. . . . One foe is as good as another, for aught he tells us."

Roosevelt's superior, Secretary John D. Long, seems to have had few inklings of what was to come, and "every time his back was turned," says David S. Barry, "Roosevelt would issue some kind of order in the line of military preparedness. . . ." On February 25, 1898, Long went home early, and as Acting Secretary of the Navy for a few hours, Roosevelt proceeded to send his momentous cable to Dewey in Hong Kong specifying "offensive operations in the Philipine [*sic*] islands." Next morning Long found that "in his precipitate way," his assistant had "come very near causing more of an explosion than happened to the *Maine* . . . He has gone at things like a bull in a china shop." Roosevelt was never again left in charge of the Navy Department for even part of a day, but his order to Dewey was not rescinded.

In this cartoon from Frank Leslie's *Official* History of the Spanish-American War, *captioned "Better rags with honor than patches with dishonor," Uncle Sam peers angrily over his shoulder at patches showing the* Maine *exploding and Spanish soldiers blowing off the heads of members of the* Virginius' *crew.*

Long seems to have thought he was dealing merely with a young subordinate who was unduly impetuous, rather than with the representative of a coterie with an elaborate imperialist philosophy and the determination to do something about it. Roosevelt was showing what a man of daring with a plan, influential associates, amenable superiors, and a little brief authority could do in the making of American foreign policy.

That the American people were unprepared for the new possessions supposedly "flung into their arms by Dewey's guns" is a gross understatement of the facts. McKinley freely confessed that, before consulting a globe, he could not have told "within two thousand miles" where the Philippines were. Incredible as it may seem to us, Dewey's staff did not include a public relations officer, and the presence of two newspapermen on board the revenue cutter *McCulloch* was a pure accident.

The public's state of bewilderment, after the first delirious celebrations of Dewey's bloodless victory had subsided, was best expressed by Finley Peter Dunne, editor of the Chicago *Journal*, whose Mr. Dooley conversed with his friend Mr. Hennessy "On the Philippines."

"I know what I'd do if I was Mack," said Mr. Hennessy, "I'd hist a flag over th' Ph'lipeens, an' I'd take in th' whole lot iv thim."

"An' yet," said Mr. Dooley, " 'tis not more thin two months since ye larned whether they were islands or canned goods . . . If yer son Packy was to ask ye where th' Ph'lipeens is, cud ye give him anny good idea whether they was in Rooshia or jus' west iv th' thracks?"

"Mebbe I cudden't," said Mr. Hennessy, haughtily, "but I'm f'r taking thim in, annyhow."

Not everyone in the country, however, went along with the bulk of the press and the expansionist-led administration. One month and one day after Dewey's triumph, the first recorded protest was made against "the insane and wicked ambition which is driving this country to ruin . . . and a slavery worse for Massachusetts, at least, than that of the Negro." It came in the form, classically correct for a proper Bostonian, of a letter to the editor of the *Evening Transcript* of June 2, 1898, entitled "A Cry for Help." It was written by Gamaliel Bradford, father of the well-known biographer. He was a seventh-generation descendant of Governor William Bradford of Plymouth, a retired banker, a Republican mugwump (he had deserted Blaine for Cleveland in 1884), and the author of several thousand letters to the newspapers in behalf of various reforms. His offer to join with any others who would help him in securing Boston's traditional Cradle of Liberty, Faneuil Hall, resulted in the first public meeting "to protest against the adoption of a so-called imperial policy by the United States."

Bradford was soon joined by another Pilgrim descendant, Erving Winslow, who was to prove the most undiscourageable of all the anti-imperialists, and by the able Boston lawyer Moorfield Storey, who was to become the acknowledged long-time champion of the movement. Presiding at the June 15 meeting that he had convened, Bradford took good care to say that its purpose was not to oppose "the vigorous prosecution of the war," but rather to check "the rush of reckless and unbridled ambition for dominion" evident in "a certain faction in Congress," which might turn "a war of liberation into a war of conquest." Storey laid down what was to be the most enduring plank in the anti-imperialist platform when he declared: "When Rome began her career of conquest, the Roman Republic began to decline . . . Let us once govern any considerable body of men without their consent, and it is a question of time how soon this republic shares the fate of Rome." The *Evening Transcript* spoke of the meeting as "a solemn warning against surrendering to the madness of the hour"; but Lodge depicted it to Roosevelt (en route to Cuba with his Rough Riders) as "a very comic incident."

The strange mixture of popular war hysteria, whipped up for their own purposes by Joseph Pulitzer of the *World* and William Randolph Hearst of the *Journal,* and the as-yet-unshaken confidence of many intellectuals in the pacific intentions of McKinley was vividly portrayed and analyzed by the philosopher William James in a letter written to his French friend François Pillon, just before James left his house in Cambridge to attend the Faneuil Hall meeting:

A curious episode of history, showing how a nation's ideals can be changed in the twinkling of an eye, by a succession of outward events partly accidental. It is quite possible that, without the explosion of the *Maine,* we should still be at peace . . . The actual declaration of war by Congress, however, was a case of *psychologie des foules,* a genuine hysteric stampede at the last moment . . . Our Executive has behaved very well. The European nations of the Continent cannot believe that our pretense of humanity, and our disclaiming of all ideas of conquest, is sincere. It has been *absolutely* sincere! The self-conscious feeling of our people has been entirely based in a sense of philanthropic duty . . . But here comes in the psychologic factor: once the excitement of action gets loose, the taxes levied, the victories achieved, etc., the old human instincts will get into play with all their old strength, and the ambition and sense of mastery which our nation has will set up new demands. We shall never take Cuba . . . But Porto Rico, and even the Philippines, are not so sure. We had supposed ourselves (with all our crudity and barbarity in certain ways) a better nation morally than the rest, safe at home, and without the old savage ambition, destined to exert great international influence by throwing in our "moral weight," etc. Dreams! Human Nature is everywhere the same, and at the least temptation all the old military passions rise, and sweep everything before them . . . It all shows by what short steps progress is made . . .

It soon became evident that William James had not overestimated the immense task facing the small band of anti-imperialists: no less than the complete reversal of public opinion in the face of easy victories, promised spoils, and a flag-waving press. For one thing, during the summer of 1898, history was being made at a furious pace. Whether one accepts the John Hay version, "a splendid little war," or "a jolly war," or the London *Saturday Review*'s estimate, "never a more shabby war," it was decidedly a short one. In less than four months it was all over but the disposition of "the waifs of the world deposited on our doorsteps." At a foreign policy conference at Saratoga Springs, New York, on August 18, 1898, just five days after the armistice, Carl Schurz, who had embarked upon a one-man crusade to impress McKinley, delivered a vigorous anti-imperialist address in which, ironically, he used against Senator Lodge and his fellow expansionists "the very principles which Lodge was to exalt so extravagantly twenty years later in the fight against the Covenant of the League of Nations." A delegation from the Sarotoga conference, with Samuel Gompers as one of its members, waited upon McKinley but was received only with suave hospitality.

To the public in the fall of 1898 the President offered the image of a sorely tried pacifist in doubt about the propriety of retaining the Philippines, even speculating that "if old Dewey had just sailed away after he had smashed the Spanish fleet, what a lot of trouble he would have saved us." But his every action was in line with what Lodge called "our large policy" of complete possession. McKinley packed the peace commission virtually four-to-one in favor of expansionism (three of them senators who would later have to vote on their own work), and gave them ever more sweeping instructions about what was to be demanded of the Spaniards, even though his Cabinet was divided on the issue. How he arrived at his final decision to tell the peace commission to demand "the whole archipelago or none" was told by the President himself on November 21, 1899, to a committee representing the General Missionary Committee of the Methodist Episcopal Church, then in session in Washington. Surely it is one of the most amazing descriptions of the workings of a Chief Executive's conscience in the field of foreign policy that has ever been recorded.

The delegation was about to leave the White House, when McKinley turned to them, and said earnestly:

> Hold a moment longer! Not quite yet, gentlemen! Before you go I would like to say just a word about the Philippine business. I have been criticized a good deal about the Philippines, but don't deserve it. The truth is I didn't want the Philippines, and when they came to us, as a gift from the gods, I did not know what to do with them. . . . I sought counsel from all sides—Democrats as well as Republicans—but got little help. I thought first we would take only Manila; then Luzon; then other islands, perhaps, also. I walked the floor of the White House night after night until midnight; and I am not ashamed to tell you, gentlemen, that I went down on my knees and prayed Almighty God for light and guidance more than one night. And one night late it came to me this way—I don't know how it was, but it came: (1) That we could not give them back to Spain—that would be cowardly and dishonorable; (2) that we could not turn them over to France or Germany—our commercial rivals in the Orient—that would be bad business and discreditable; (3) that we could not leave them to themselves—they were unfit for self-government—and they would soon have anarchy and misrule over there worse than Spain's was; and (4) that there was nothing left for us to do but take them all, and to educate the Filipinos, and uplift and civilize and Christianize them, and by God's grace do the very best we could by them, as our fellow men for whom Christ also died. And then I went to bed, and went to sleep, and slept soundly, and the next morning I sent for the chief engineer of the War Department (our map-maker), and I told him to put the Philippines on the map of the United States [pointing to a large map on the wall of his office], and there they are, and there they will stay while I am President!

The anti-imperialists' first battle, for the mind of the President as the chief architect of the nation's foreign policy, was thus lost to higher authority before it had hardly begun. But the country might still be persuaded to reject McKinley's Philippine policy. On November 19,

1898, in the Boston office of Edward Atkinson, retired textile manufacturer—later to become notorious because of the Postmaster General's
closing of the mails to his publications—the Anti-Imperialist League
was organized. Its object was: "to oppose, by every legitimate means,
the acquisition of the Philippine Islands, or of any colonies away
from our shores, by the United States."

The only thing more remarkable than the high quality of the
League's adherents was their extreme diversity. As its perpetual secretary, Erving Winslow, remarked: "We must in our organization
stand shoulder to shoulder: Republican, Democrat, Socialist, Populist,
Gold-Man, Silver-Man, and Mugwump, for the one momentous, vital,
paramount issue, Anti-Imperialism and the preservation of the Republic." Such advice, however, was not always easy to follow, since
the anti-imperialist leader in the Senate, George F. Hoar, regular
Republican, had once called the Mugwumps "the vilest set of political
assassins that ever disgraced this or any other country."

Besides every shade in the country's political spectrum, the
League's ever-lengthening list of vice presidents, many of whom lent
only their names to the movement, included every variety of American
reformer: municipal, civil service, social welfare, single-taxer, free-
trader, pacifist, and prohibitionist. Education furnished a long list of
college presidents: Eliot, Jordan, Rogers, Alderman, Stanley Hall,
Schurman, King, and Faunce, with such distinguished teachers as
Charles Eliot Norton, George Herbert Palmer, William Graham
Sumner, Felix Adler, William James, John Dewey, and Franklin H.
Giddings. From industry and finance came the extremely active donor
Andrew Carnegie, and Richard T. Crane and George Foster Peabody.
The contribution of "interest" groups (beet sugar and tobacco),
which wanted no Philippine competition, was remarkably small.

At the peak of the League's activities in 1899, it claimed thirty
thousand members and "half a million contributors" in branches
located in a dozen large cities from Boston to Portland, Oregon. One
of its conferences, in Chicago on October 17–18, 1899, attracted ten
thousand delegates; and by 1900 the League claimed to have distributed
four hundred thousand pieces of literature. This spreading of its
work enhanced its prestige, no doubt, but it proved to be a handicap
in exerting political influence. For what leader could be found who
could win and keep the confidence of quite so many kinds of followers?

The first political battle fought by the anti-imperialists was the
one in which they came the closest to victory: the heated conflict over
the ratification of the treaty of peace with Spain in January and February, 1899. The only controversial section in the document was the
article providing for the cession of the whole Philippine archipelago
to the United States. As Peace Commissioner Whitelaw Reid put it:
he and his associates were accused of "overdoing the business, looking after the interests of the country too thoroughly . . ." Since a
two-thirds vote was required for ratification in a Senate composed of
forty-six Republicans, thirty-four Democrats, and ten members of
minor parties, it was evident that a substantial number of Democratic

senators would have to be won over.

Fresh from his discharge from the Army, William Jennings Bryan announced in an interview at Savannah, Georgia, on December 13, 1898, that although he was firmly anti-imperialist, he believed that the treaty should be ratified and the issue of imperialism settled by resolution at a later date. The less politically minded anti-imperialists (Carnegie, Schurz, and Storey) regarded this as a sacrifice of principle in order to secure a campaign issue to go along with free silver (which they detested) in the election of 1900. Ten Democratic senators helped to ratify the treaty by only one vote more than the necessary two thirds, and although two or three of them may have been swayed by the outbreak of fighting, two days earlier, between Filipino and Amercian soldiers, Bryan has generally been credited with influencing the key votes. Many senators were undoubtedly influenced by Lodge's argument that failure to ratify would be a repudiation of McKinley and a continuation of the war. If there could have been a clear-cut decision regarding the retention of the Philippines, ''the imperialists,'' says the diplomatic historian Thomas A. Bailey, ''would almost certainly have failed to obtain a two-thirds majority.'' A few days later the Bacon amendment, pledging ultimate independence to the Filipinos, resulted in a tie vote, decided in the negative by the vote of Vice President Garret A. Hobart.

Despite this setback, the movement grew, rather than declined, as the 1900 election approached, although Bryan had created an amount of distrust in the minds of the ''true'' anti-imperialists, which led to talk of a third-party ticket designed to split the McKinley vote. Bryan agreed to make anti-imperialism ''the paramount issue'' of his campaign, and was finally endorsed by the League's Liberty Congress in Indianapolis in August, 1900. But many of the anti-imperialists refused to stomach Bryan's continued insistence upon free silver, and either voted for McKinley or held aloof from both candidates. Bryan secured fewer votes in 1900 than in 1896, and his defeat ''marked the end of anti-imperialism as an important factor in American politics.''

Political failure did not prevent literary success for the cause, although most of the blows struck by the pen came too late to turn the tide of public opinion. The one man whose emotional response to imperialism became enduring literature was the poet William Vaughn Moody. He risked his position as teacher of English at the University of Chicago by publishing several anti-imperialist poems in the *Atlantic Monthly*. In contrast to its noble sacrifices in the Civil War, Moody saw his country engaged in ''ignoble battle,'' but protested:

We have not sold our loftiest heritage
The proud republic hath not stooped to cheat and scramble in the
*   market place of war . . .*
That so our hand with better ease
May wield the driver's whip and grasp the jailer's keys.

Warning the country's leaders to ''tempt not our weakness, our cupidity,'' the poet declares that ''save we let the island men go free,''

In this 1899 cartoon from Puck, E. L. Godkin, William Jennings Bryan, and other anti-imperialists are pictured defiling the favorable image which imperial adventures had won for the United States.

our soldiers will have died in vain. In a shorter poem entitled "On a Soldier Fallen in the Philippines," (*Atlantic Monthly*, February, 1901), Moody makes use of the poignant contradiction between the honor due to the fallen and the dishonor of his cause:

Toll! Let him never guess
What work we set him to . . .
Let him never dream that his bullet's scream went wide of its island
*   mark,*
Home to the heart of his darling land where she stumbled and sinned
*   in the dark.*

Moody's language was mild and temperate compared with that of his fellow Chicagoan, the novelist Henry Blake Fuller, who became convinced that McKinley's policies were not only ignorant and stupid but actually vicious. Fuller addressed the President:

Thou sweating chattel slave to swine!
Who dost befoul the holy shrine
Of liberty with murder! . . .

A much saner poetic approach was that of Ernest Crosby, president of the New York branch of the movement, whose Whitmanesque lines ran:

There is only one possession worth the capturing, and that is the
  hearts of men;
And these hearts can never be won by a nation of slaves.
Be free, and all mankind will flock to your standard.

Mark Twain was one literary figure who was won over from the opposition, in part by the urging of his friend William Dean Howells. "I left these shores at Vancouver [on his way to Vienna]," he wrote, "a red-hot imperialist. I wanted the American eagle to go screaming into the Pacific. It seemed tiresome and tame for it to content itself with the Rockies. Why not spread its wings over the Philippines, I asked myself? And I thought it would be a real good thing to do." But gradually Twain began to see the Philippines in a different light, for early in 1900 he wrote to Joseph Twichell: "Apparently we are not proposing to set the Filipinos free and give their islands to them . . . If these things are so, the war out there has no interest for me." From the day of Twain's triumphant return to this country in October, 1900, he joined forces with Howells in a steady barrage of articles, interviews, petitions, and pamphlets in behalf of anti-imperialism. The League made extensive use on cards of his "salutation-speech from the Nineteenth Century to the Twentieth," in which he said:

> I bring you the stately matron named Christendom, returning bedraggled, besmirched, and dishonored from pirate-raids in Kiao-Chou, Manchuria, South Africa, & the Philippines, with her soul full of meanness, her pocket full of boodle and her mouth full of pious hypocrisies. Give her soap and a towel, but hide the looking glass.

At a welcoming dinner for the young English war correspondent Winston Spencer Churchill in the Waldorf-Astoria Hotel on December 13, 1900, Mark Twain introduced the half-English, half-American speaker with these words: "I think that England sinned when she got herself into a war in South Africa which she could have avoided, just as we have sinned in getting into a similar war in the Philippines . . . yes, we are kin. And now that we are also kin in sin, there is nothing more to be desired. The harmony is complete, the blend is perfect—like Mr. Churchill himself, whom I now have the honor to present to you."

One of the most effective presentations of the case for anti-imperialism was made by the peppery Yale sociologist William Graham Sumner under the striking title, "The Conquest of the United States by Spain," but it was buried in the *Yale Law Journal* for January, 1899. Logic in terms of political theory, however, proved a poor match for the logic of events. Professor Richard Hofstadter has acutely observed that the Spanish-American War was fought because the American people wanted "not so much the freedom of Cuba as a *war for the freedom of Cuba.*" Once war was under way, in the opinion of the late Vice President Charles G. Dawes, who was a close McKinley associate, "the retention of the Philippines was inevitable. . . . No man, or no party, could have prevented it.'' Yet in the sober judgment of Samuel Flagg Bemis, ''looking back on those years of adolescent irresponsibility, we can now see the acquisition of the Philippines, the climax of American expansion, as a great national aberration.''

But it was in vain that the anti-imperialists of that era cited the words of Abraham Lincoln : ''No man is good enough to govern another without that other's consent.'' The missing premise in the arguments of both sides was the lack of adequate knowledge of the Filipinos and their capacity for solving their immediate political problems. The anti-imperialists saw them as ready and able to govern themselves democratically; the imperialists were just as convinced that they were mostly untutored barbarians. Neither side had enough facts, and as a result both substituted passion for logic.

The anti-imperialists saw the whole problem as a simple matter of political morality, which could never be settled until settled ''right.'' By their indefatigable agitating they administered such a shock to sensitive American consciences that the burden of guilt could not be lifted. In time it came to be assumed that the pledge of Philippine independence defeated by a single vote in 1899 had, morally speaking, been given.

What the imperialists, notably Theodore Roosevelt, could never grasp was the Filipinos' yearning for *self*-government. Both sides entertained illusions : the imperialists saw a mirage of untold wealth in trade with the Orient, which did not materialize; the anti-imperialists foresaw ''tyranny at home'' as the sure result of ''tyranny abroad.'' The latter were also incorrect in their belief that their opponents would never ''let go'' of the archipelago, although it was not until 1935 that the Commonwealth was established, with complete independence promised in 1946. The promise was kept, and the Philippines became ''the first colony ever to be surrendered voluntarily.''

The annual reports of the Anti-Imperialist League, which continued until its nineteenth and last meeting in 1917, make melancholy reading as the necrology lengthened and the budgets shrank. Treasurer Greene declared doggedly : ''Anti-Imperialists are not quitters''; but when Erving Winslow died in 1923, Moorfield Storey wrote: ''Almost everybody who belonged to the League is dead, and the young men do not take up the work. I am still its representative, but I have no followers.''

One of the striking characteristics of the League in its heyday was the lack of contact between its zealous leaders in America and the Filipinos in whose behalf they were enduring a steady rain of epithets: little Americans, seditionists, cowards, and traitors. But the Filipinos had subtle ways of showing their appreciation. Long before they were allowed the privilege of self-government, they named the square directly in front of the Malacañang Palace in Manila, the official residence of the American Governor General, *La Liga Anti-Imperialistica.*

Thomas A. Bailey

Woodrow Wilson and the League of Nations

Woodrow Wilson was surely one of the most paradoxical figures in American history. He was both a great idealist and a shrewd practical politician; a man capable of enormous achievements yet physically delicate; one who concealed hot emotional fires beneath an icy exterior; a brilliant public orator but a man who could seldom persuade or inspire other individuals in private confrontations.

In this essay Thomas A. Bailey, professor emeritus of history at Stanford University, analyzes the role played by Wilson's complex personality in the great tragedy that closed his brilliant career—the defeat of his plan to enroll the United States in the League of Nations. That Wilson's personal qualities had a great deal to do with the Senate's rejection of the League goes without saying. However, as Bailey makes clear, forces far larger than those exerted by any man were also involved. Thus his discussion serves as a case study of the interaction of great men with their times. It is one of Bailey's strengths as a historian that he is able to describe the difficult and tangled events of 1918–20 briefly and simply without doing violence to truth and to carry the narrative of events along swiftly and smoothly at the same time that he is focusing the attention of the reader on the personal qualities of Wilson and the other principal actors in the drama.

Among Professor Bailey's many books are Woodrow Wilson and the Lost Peace, Woodrow Wilson and the Great Betrayal, Presidential Greatness, *and two popular textbooks,* A Diplomatic History of the American People, *and* The American Pageant.

The story of America's rejection of the League of Nations revolves largely around the personality and character of Thomas Woodrow Wilson, the twenty-eighth President of the United States. Born in Virginia and reared in Yankee-gutted Georgia and the Carolinas, Wilson early developed a burning hatred of war and a passionate attachment to the Confederate-embraced principle of self-determination for minority peoples. From the writings of Thomas Jefferson he derived much of his democratic idealism and his invincible faith in the judgment of the masses, if properly informed. From his stiff-backed Scotch-Presbyterian forebears, he inherited a high degree of inflexibility; from his father, a dedicated Presbyterian minister, he learned a stern moral code that would tolerate no compromise with wrong, as defined by Woodrow Wilson.

As a leading academician who had first failed at law, he betrayed a contempt for "money-grubbing" lawyers, many of whom sat in the Senate, and an arrogance toward lesser intellects, including those of the "pygmy-minded" senators. As a devout Christian keenly aware of the wickedness of this world, he emerged as a fighting reformer, whether as president of Princeton, governor of New Jersey, or President of the United States.

As a war leader, Wilson was superb. Holding aloft the torch of idealism in one hand and the flaming sword of righteousness in the other, he aroused the masses to a holy crusade. We would fight a war to end wars; we would make the world safe for democracy. The phrase was not a mockery then. The American people, with an amazing display of self-sacrifice, supported the war effort unswervingly.

The noblest expression of Wilson's idealism was his Fourteen Points address to Congress in January, 1918. It compressed his war aims into punchy, placard-like paragraphs, expressly designed for propaganda purposes. It appealed tremendously to oppressed peoples everywhere by promising such goals as the end of secret treaties, freedom of the seas, the removal of economic barriers, a reduction of arms burdens, a fair adjustment of colonial claims, and self-determination for oppressed minorities. In Poland university men would meet on the streets of Warsaw, clasp hands, and soulfully utter one word, "Wilson." In remote regions of Italy peasants burned candles before poster portraits of the mighty new prophet arisen in the West.

The fourteenth and capstone point was a league of nations, designed to avert future wars. The basic idea was not original with Wilson; numerous thinkers, including Frenchmen and Britons, had been working on the concept long before he embraced it. Even Henry Cabot Lodge, the Republican senator from Massachusetts, had already spoken publicly in favor of *a* league of nations. But the more he heard about the Wilsonian League of Nations, the more critical of it he became.

A knowledge of the Wilson-Lodge feud is basic to an understanding of the tragedy that unfolded. Tall, slender, aristocratically bewhiskered, Dr. Henry Cabot Lodge (Ph.D., Harvard), had published a number of books and had been known as the scholar in politics before the appearance of Dr. Woodrow Wilson (Ph.D., Johns Hopkins). The Presbyterian professor had gone further in both scholarship and politics than the Boston Brahmin, whose mind was once described as resembling the soil of his native New England: "naturally barren but highly cultivated." Wilson and Lodge, two icy men, developed a mutual antipathy, which soon turned into freezing hatred.

The German armies, reeling under the blows of the Allies, were ready to give in by November, 1918. The formal armistice terms stipulated that Germany was to be guaranteed a peace based on the Fourteen Points, with two reservations concerning freedom of the seas and reparations.

Meanwhile the American people had keyed themselves up to the long-awaited march on Berlin; eager voices clamored to hang the Kaiser. Thus the sudden end of the shooting left inflamed patriots with a sense of frustration and letdown that boded ill for Wilson's policies. The red-faced Theodore Roosevelt, Lodge's intimate of long standing, cried that peace should be dictated by the chatter of machine guns and not the clicking of typewriters.

Wilson now towered at the dizzy pinnacle of his popularity and power. He had emerged as the moral arbiter of the world and the hope of all peoples for a better tomorrow. But regrettably his wartime sureness of touch began to desert him, and he made a series of costly fumbles. He was so preoccupied with reordering the world, someone has said, that he reminded one of the baseball player who knocks the ball into the bleachers and then forgets to touch home plate.

First came his brutally direct appeal for a Democratic Congress in October, 1918. The voters trooped to the polls the next month and, by a narrow margin, returned a Republican Congress. Wilson had not only goaded his partisan foes to fresh outbursts of fury, but he had unnecessarily staked his prestige on the outcome—and lost. When the Allied leaders met at the Paris peace table, he was the only one not entitled to be there, at least on the European basis of a parliamentary majority.

Wilson next announced that he was sailing for France, presumably to use his still enormous prestige to fashion an enduring peace. At this time no President had ever gone abroad, and Republicans condemned the decision as evidence of a dangerous Messiah complex—of a desire, as former President Taft put it, "to hog the whole show."

The naming of the remaining five men to the peace delegation caused partisans further anguish. Only one, Henry White, was a Republican, and he was a minor figure at that. The Republicans, now the majority party, complained that they had been good enough to die on the battlefield; they ought to have at least an equal voice at the peace table. Nor were any United States senators included, even though they would have a final whack at the treaty. Wilson did not have much respect for the "bungalow-minded" senators, and if he took one, the logical choice would be Henry Cabot Lodge. There were already enough feuds brewing at Paris without taking one along.

Doubtless some of the Big Business Republicans were out to "get" the President who had been responsible for the hated reformist legis-

Woodrow Wilson acknowledging a cheering crowd at the Waldorf-Astoria in New York.

lation of 1913–14. If he managed to put over the League of Nations, his prestige would soar to new heights. He might even arrange—unspeakable thought!—to be elected again and again and again. Much of the partisan smog that finally suffocated the League would have been cleared away if Wilson had publicly declared, as he was urged to do, that in no circumstances would he run again. But he spurned such counsel, partly because he was actually receptive to the idea of a third term.

The American President, hysterically hailed by European crowds as "Voovro Veelson," came to the Paris peace table in January, 1919, to meet with Lloyd George of Britain, Clemenceau of France, and Orlando of Italy. To his dismay, he soon discovered that they were far more interested in imperialism than in idealism. When they sought to carve up the territorial booty without regard for the colonials, contrary to the Fourteen Points, the stern-jawed Presbyterian moralist interposed a ringing veto. The end result was the mandate system—a compromise between idealism and imperialism that turned out to be more imperialistic than idealistic.

Wilson's overriding concern was the League of Nations. He feared that if he did not get it completed and embedded in the treaty, the imperialistic powers might sidetrack it. Working at an incredible pace after hours, Wilson headed the commission that drafted the League Covenant in ten meetings and some thirty hours. He then persuaded the conference not only to approve the hastily constructed Covenant but to incorporate it bodily in the peace treaty. In support of his adopted brain child he spoke so movingly on one occasion that even the hard-boiled reporters forgot to take notes.

Wilson now had to return hurriedly to the United States to sign bills and take care of other pressing business. Shortly after his arrival the mounting Republican opposition in the Senate flared up angrily. On March 4, 1919, 39 senators or senators-elect—more than enough to defeat the treaty—published a round robin to the effect that they would not approve the League in its existing form. This meant that Wilson had to return to Paris, hat in hand, and there weaken his position by having to seek modifications.

Stung to the quick, he struck back at his senatorial foes in an indiscreet speech in New York just before his departure. He boasted that when he brought the treaty back from Paris, the League Covenant would not only be tied in but so thoroughly tied in that it could not be cut out without killing the entire pact. The Senate, he assumed, would not dare to kill the treaty of peace outright.

At Paris the battle was now joined in deadly earnest. Clemenceau, the French realist, had little use for Wilson, the American idealist. "God gave us the ten commandments and we broke them," he reportedly sneered. "Wilson gave us the Fourteen Points—we shall see." Clemenceau's most disruptive demand was for the German Rhineland; but Wilson, the champion of self-determination, would never consent to handing several million Germans over to the tender mercies of the French. After a furious struggle, during which Wilson was stricken with influenza, Clemenceau was finally persuaded to yield the Rhineland and other demands in return for a security treaty. Under it, Britain and America agreed to come to the aid of France in the event of another unprovoked aggression. The United States Senate shortsightedly pigeonholed the pact, and France was left with neither the Rhineland nor security.

Two other deadlocks almost broke up the conference. Italy claimed the Adriatic port of Fiume, an area inhabited chiefly by Yugoslavs. In his battle for self-determination, Wilson dramatically appealed over the head of the Italian delegation to the Italian people, whereupon the delegates went home in a huff to receive popular endorsement. The final adjustment was a hollow victory for self-determination.

The politely bowing Japanese now stepped forward to press their economic claims to China's Shantung, which they had captured from the Germans early in the war. But to submit 30,000,000 Chinese to the influence of the Japanese would be another glaring violation of self-determination. The Japanese threatened to bolt the conference, as the Italians had already done, with consequent jeopardy to the League. In the end, Wilson reluctantly consented to a compromise that left the Japanese temporarily in possession of Shantung.

The Treaty of Versailles, as finally signed in June, 1919, included only about four of the original Fourteen Points. The Germans, with considerable justification, gave vent to loud cries of betrayal. But the iron hand of circumstance had forced Wilson to compromise away many of his points in order to salvage his fourteenth point, the League of Nations, which he hoped would iron out the injustices that had crept into the treaty. He was like the mother who throws her younger children to the pursuing wolves in order to save her sturdy first-born son.

Bitter opposition to the completed treaty had already begun to form in America. Tens of thousands of homesick and disillusioned soldiers were pouring home, determined to let Europe "stew in its own juice." The wartime idealism, inevitably doomed to slump, was now plunging to alarming depths. The beloved Allies had apparently turned out to be greedy imperialists. The war to make the world safe for democracy had obviously fallen dismally short of the goal. And at the end of the war to end wars there were about twenty conflicts of varying intensity being waged all over the globe.

The critics increased their clamor. Various foreign groups, including the Irish-Americans and the Italian-Americans, were complaining that the interests of the old country had been neglected. Professional liberals, for example the editors of the *New Republic,* were denouncing the treaty as too harsh. The illiberals, far more numerous, were denouncing it as not harsh enough. The Britain-haters, like the buzz-saw Senator James Reed of Missouri and the acid-penned William R. Hearst, were proclaiming that England had emerged with undue influence. Such ultra-nationalists as the isolationist Senator William E. Borah of Idaho were insisting that the flag of no superstate should be hoisted above the glorious Stars and Stripes.

When the treaty came back from Paris, with the League firmly riveted in, Senator Lodge despaired of stopping it.

"What are you going to do? It's hopeless," he complained to Borah. "All the newspapers in my state are for it." The best that he could hope for was to add a few reservations. The Republicans had been given little opportunity to help write the treaty in Paris; they now felt that they were entitled to do a little rewriting in Washington.

Lodge deliberately adopted the technique of delay. As chairman of the powerful Senate Committee on Foreign Relations, he consumed

Henry Cabot Lodge in 1909.

A cartoon by Bronstrup in the San Francisco Chronicle *captioned, "They Won't Dovetail" summed up the attitude of many opponents of the League.*

two weeks by reading aloud the entire pact of 264 pages, even though it had already been printed. He then held time-consuming public hearings, during which persons with unpronounceable foreign names aired their grievances against the pact.

Lodge finally adopted the strategy of tacking reservations onto the treaty, and he was able to achieve his goal because of the peculiar composition of the Senate. There were 49 Republicans and 47 Democrats. The Republicans consisted of about twenty "strong reservationists" like Lodge, about twelve "mild reservationists" like future Secretary of State Kellogg, and about a dozen "irreconcilables." This last group was headed by Senator Borah and the no less isolationist Senator Hiram Johnson of California, a fiery spellbinder.

The Lodge reservations finally broke the back of the treaty. They were all added by a simple majority vote, even though the entire pact would have to be approved by a two-thirds vote. The dozen or so Republican mild reservationists were not happy over the strong Lodge reservations, and if Wilson had deferred sufficiently to these men, he might have persuaded them to vote with the Democrats. Had they done so, the Lodge reservations could have all been voted down, and a milder version, perhaps acceptable to Wilson, could have been substituted.

As the hot summer of 1919 wore on, Wilson became increasingly impatient with the deadlock in the Senate. Finally he decided to take his case to the country, as he had so often done in response to his ingrained "appeal habit." He had never been robust, and his friends urged him not to risk breaking himself down in a strenuous barnstorming campaign. But Wilson, having made up his mind, was unyielding. He had sent American boys into battle in a war to end wars; why should he not risk his life in a battle for a League to end wars?

Wilson's spectacular tour met with limited enthusiasm in the

Middle West, the home of several million German-Americans. After him, like baying bloodhounds, trailed Senators Borah and Johnson, sometimes speaking in the same halls a day or so later, to the accompaniment of cries of "Impeach him, impeach him!" But on the Pacific Coast and in the Rocky Mountain area the enthusiasm for Wilson and the League was overwhelming. The high point—and the breaking point—of the trip came at Pueblo, Colorado, where Wilson, with tears streaming down his cheeks, pleaded for his beloved League of Nations.

That night Wilson's weary body rebelled. He was whisked back to Washington, where he suffered a stroke that paralyzed the left side of his body. For weeks he lay in bed, a desperately sick man. The Democrats, who had no first-rate leader in the Senate, were left rudderless. With the wisdom of hindsight, we may say that Wilson might better have stayed in Washington, providing the necessary leadership and compromising with the opposition, insofar as compromise was possible. A good deal of compromise had already gone into the treaty, and a little more might have saved it.

Senator Lodge, cold and decisive, was now in the driver's seat. His Fourteen Reservations, a sardonic parallel to Wilson's Fourteen Points, had been whipped into shape. Most of them now seem either irrelevant, inconsequential, or unnecessary; some of them merely reaffirmed principles and policies, including the Monroe Doctrine, already guaranteed by the treaty or by the Constitution.

But Wilson, who hated the sound of Lodge's name, would have no part of the Lodge reservations. They would, he insisted, emasculate the entire treaty. Yet the curious fact is that he had privately worked out his own set of reservations with the Democratic leader in the Senate, Gilbert M. Hitchcock, and these differed only in slight degree from those of Senator Lodge.

As the hour approached for the crucial vote in the Senate, it appeared that public opinion had veered a little. Although confused by the angry debate, it still favored the treaty—but with some safeguarding reservations. A stubborn Wilson was unwilling to accept this disheartening fact, or perhaps he was not made aware of it. Mrs. Wilson, backed by the President's personal physician, Dr. Cary Grayson, kept vigil at his bedside to warn the few visitors that disagreeable news might shock the invalid into a relapse.

In this highly unfavorable atmosphere, Senator Hitchcock had two conferences with Wilson on the eve of the Senate voting. He suggested compromise on a certain point, but Wilson shot back, "Let Lodge compromise!" Hitchcock conceded that the Senator would have to give ground but suggested that the White House might also hold out the olive branch. "Let Lodge hold out the olive branch," came the stern reply. On this inflexible note, and with Mrs. Wilson's anxiety mounting, the interview ended.

The Senate was ready for final action on November 19, 1919. At the critical moment Wilson sent a fateful letter to the Democratic minority in the Senate, urging them to vote down the treaty with the hated Lodge reservations so that a true ratification could be achieved. The Democrats, with more than the necessary one-third veto, heeded the voice of their crippled leader and rejected the treaty with reservations. The Republicans, with more than the necessary one-third veto, rejected the treaty without reservations.

The country was shocked by this exhibition of legislative paralysis. About four fifths of the senators professed to favor the treaty in some form, yet they were unable to agree on anything. An aroused public opinion forced the Senate to reconsider, and Lodge secretly entered into negotiations with the Democrats in an effort to work out acceptable reservations. He was making promising progress when Senator Borah got wind of his maneuvers through an anonymous telephone call. The leading irreconcilables hastily summoned a council of war, hauled Lodge before them, and bluntly accused him of treachery. Deeply disturbed, the Massachusetts Senator said: "Well, I suppose I'll have to resign as majority leader."

"No, by God!" burst out Borah. "You won't have a chance to resign! On Monday, I'll move for the election of a new majority leader and give the reasons for my action." Faced with an upheaval within his party such as had insured Wilson's election in 1912, Lodge agreed to drop his backstage negotiations.

The second-chance vote in the Senate came on March 19, 1920. Wilson again directed his loyal Democratic following to reject the treaty, disfigured as it was by the hateful Lodge reservations. But by this time there was no other form in which the pact could possibly be ratified. Twenty-one realistic Democrats turned their backs on Wilson and voted Yea; 23 loyal Democrats, mostly from the rockribbed South, joined with the irreconcilables to do the bidding of the White House. The treaty, though commanding a simple majority this time of 49 Yeas to 35 Nays, failed of the necessary two-thirds vote.

Wilson, struggling desperately against the Lodge reservation trap, had already summoned the nation in "solemn referendum" to give him a vote in favor of the League in the forthcoming presidential election of 1920. His hope was that he could then get the treaty approved without reservations. But this course was plainly futile. Even if all the anti-League senators up for re-election in 1920 had been replaced by the pro-League senators, Wilson would still have lacked the necessary two-thirds majority for an unreserved treaty.

The American people were never given a chance to express their views directly on the League of Nations. All they could do was vote either for the weak Democratic candidate, Cox, who stood for the League, and the stuffed-shirt Republican candidate, Harding, who wobbled all over the map of the League arguments. If the electorate had been given an opportunity to express itself, a powerful majority probably would have favored the world organization, with at least some reservations. But wearied of Wilsonism, idealism, and self-denial, and confused by the wordy fight over the treaty, the voters rose up and swept Harding into the White House. The winner had been more anti-League than pro-League, and his prodigious plurality of 7,000,000 votes condemned the League to death in America.

What caused this costly failure of American statesmanship?

Wilson's physical collapse intensified his native stubbornness. A judicious compromise here and there no doubt would have secured Senate approval of the treaty, though of course with modifications. Wilson believed that in any event the Allies would reject the Lodge reservations. The probabilities are that the Allies would have worked out some kind of acceptance, so dire was their need of America's economic support, but Wilson never gave them a chance to act.

Senator Lodge was also inflexible, but prior to the second rejection he was evidently trying to get the treaty through—on his own terms. As majority leader of the Republicans, his primary task was to avoid another fatal split in his party. Wilson's primary task was to get the pact approved. From a purely political point of view, the Republicans had little to gain by engineering ratification of a Democratic treaty.

The two-thirds rule in the Senate, often singled out as the culprit, is of little relevance. Wilson almost certainly would have pigeonholed the treaty if it had passed with the Lodge reservations appended.

Wilson's insistence that the League be wedded to the treaty actually contributed to the final defeat of both. Either would have had a better chance if it had not been burdened by the enemies of the other. The United Nations, one should note, was set up in 1945 independently of any peace treaty.

Finally, American public opinion in 1919-20 was not yet ready for the onerous new world responsibilities that had suddenly been forced upon it. The isolationist tradition was still potent, and it was fortified by postwar disillusionment. If the sovereign voters had spoken out for the League with one voice, they almost certainly would have had their way. A treaty without reservations, or with a few reservations acceptable to Wilson, doubtless would have slipped through the Senate. But the American people were one war short of accepting leadership in a world organization for peace.

By 1919, when this Bronstrup cartoon appeared, Wilson was sinking rapidly in a whirlpool of adverse public opinion.

Colonel T. N. Dupuy

[handwritten annotations:]
Kimmel — Pac, fleet in HA
Short — army in HA

Pearl Harbor:
Who Blundered?

The Japanese attack on Pearl Harbor, aptly characterized in this essay by the military historian Colonel Trevor N. Dupuy as "the worst disaster in the military annals of the United States," was an event so implausible, so shocking, and so enormous in its results that it has been studied exhaustively—by politicians, by military men, by plain citizens, and of course, by historians. "What happened" was never difficult to determine; why it happened—who was responsible for the unpreparedness of the American forces in Hawaii—is a question that has excited the bitterest of controversies.

Colonel Dupuy's effort to untangle the events of late November and early December, 1941, takes an unusual but interesting and effective form. Superficially his essay appears almost a chronicle. He describes day by day from November 25 to December 7 what was going on in Washington, in Hawaii, and in the western Pacific, where the Japanese attack force was steaming toward its destination. The dramatic force of this approach is considerable, but alone it would not produce a sound history of the affair. To it Dupuy adds both a prologue, setting the stage and introducing the main characters in the tragedy, and a conclusion, in which he weighs and balances the evidence and offers his own explanation of what went wrong.

*P*recisely at 7:55 A.M. on Sunday, December 7, 1941, a most devastating Japanese aerial attack struck the island of Oahu, Territory of Hawaii. When it was all over, the battleships of our Pacific Fleet, moored by pairs in their Pearl Harbor base, had received a mortal blow. Our army air strength in Hawaii—the Japanese found its planes ranged neatly wing to wing on airfield ramps—was a tangled mass of smoking wreckage.

The worst disaster in the military annals of the United States had ushered us into World War II. As in most wars, the political and diplomatic background was so complex and confused as to defy definitive analysis—though this has not prevented historians and others from making the attempt. But as to the disaster itself, the military record is clear.

A well-planned and brilliantly executed surprise attack by Japanese carrier-based aircraft was launched against the major American bastion in the Pacific. The United States government, its senior military leaders, and its commanders in Hawaii had had sufficient information to be adequately warned that an attack was possible, and had had time to be prepared to thwart or to blunt the blow. The information was largely ignored; the preparations were utterly inadequate.

Someone had blundered. Who? And how?

At the moment of the attack four professional military men filled posts of vital importance. In Washington, General George C. Marshall, Chief of Staff, was responsible for the entire United States Army and all of its installations. In a nearby office sat his Navy counterpart, Admiral Harold R. Stark, Chief of Naval Operations. On the Hawaiian island of Oahu, Lieutenant General Walter C. Short commanded the Hawaiian Department, the Army's most vital overseas outpost. Commanding the United States Pacific Fleet was Rear Admiral Husband E. Kimmel; his headquarters was also on Oahu, overlooking the great Navy base at Pearl Harbor.

Marshall, product of the Virginia Military Institute, had a well-deserved reputation for brilliant staff work under Pershing in France in World War I. Later he had taken a prominent part in developing the Army's Infantry School at Fort Benning, Georgia. Short, a graduate of the University of Illinois, had entered the Army from civilian life in 1901. Early in 1941 he had been chosen by Marshall to command the Hawaiian Department.

Both Stark and Kimmel had graduated from the United States Naval Academy at Annapolis—Stark in 1903, Kimmel a year later. Both had risen to their high positions in the Navy following exemplary command and staff service at sea and on shore. Close personal friends, both were highly respected by their naval colleagues.

The thinking and attitudes of these four men were shaped by two decades of unanimous opinion among American soldiers and sailors that someday Japan would clash with the United States in a struggle for predominance in the vast Pacific Ocean. All accepted without question the basic elements of U.S. doctrine for the defense of the Pacific in such a war.

The political smoke screen for Japan's surprise attack was provided by both parliamentary speeches in Tokyo and diplomatic moves in Washington. On November 17, 1941, Prime Minister Tojo (right) delivered a warlike harangue to the Japanese legislature.

The doctrine was that the United States Navy—and in particular its Pacific Fleet—was the essential element to American success in a Pacific war. Immobilization or destruction of that fleet would be the greatest damage Japan could inflict on the United States. Upon the Army lay the responsibility for furthering the offensive powers of the fleet by protecting its great Pearl Harbor base; by safeguarding the Panama Canal, the Navy's life line from the Atlantic to the Pacific; and by defending the advanced Philippine delaying position, which in military opinion was likely to be Japan's initial target.

Since 1939 the top military authorities of the nation, including President Franklin D. Roosevelt, had understood the almost inexorable logic of events that pointed to our eventual involvement either in the conflict which Hitler had begun in Europe or that in Asia between Japan and China—or both. And under Roosevelt's skillful guidance the nation, albeit grudgingly, was very slowly building up its military strength.

As 1941 rolled along, it became apparent, even to the man in the street, that the most pressing danger lay in the Far East. Our diplomatic relations with Japan were worsening; by November they appeared to be almost at the breaking point. The long-continued diplomatic bickering between the two nations on a variety of subjects had resulted in the arrival in Washington of a special envoy, Saburo Kurusu, who—with Ambassador Kichisaburo Nomura—had on November 20 presented the State Department with a document that was practically an ultimatum.

Japan would acquiesce to our government's demands that she withdraw from Indochina only upon "establishment of an equitable peace in the Pacific area" and, further, upon "supply to Japan [by the U.S. of] a required quantity of oil."

In 1940, our cipher experts had cracked the Japanese secret codes —a cryptoanalytical procedure known in the War Department as "Magic." Hence our government knew that the envoys had received instructions to press for American acceptance of this "final proposal" by November 25. The ambassadors had been warned that for reasons "beyond your ability to guess" this was essential, but that if the "signing can be completed by the 29th" the Imperial Japanese government would wait. "After that things are automatically going to happen."

It was also known through Magic radio intercepts that a large proportion of Japanese military strength—land, sea, and air—was concentrating in the Indochina and South China Sea areas. No evidence of aircraft carriers had been found, however, either in those areas or in the Japanese mandated islands. Intelligence agencies, monitoring Japanese radio traffic, considered it probable that the carriers were still in their home waters, but they were not certain.

On this basis Marshall, Stark, and their respective staffs concluded that the Japanese were preparing to strike in Southeast Asia; this threat, of course, included the Philippine Commonwealth. Accordingly our Army and Navy commanders in the Philippines and at Guam had been specifically warned. The commanders in Hawaii, Panama, Alaska, and on the West Coast were kept informed of important developments.

This was the situation as Marshall and Stark saw it early on November 25. From that time on events succeeded one another with increasing rapidity, both in Washington and in Hawaii. This is how they unfolded:

Washington, Tuesday, November 25

Marshall and Stark attended a "War Council" meeting with the President, Secretary of State Cordell Hull, Secretary of War Henry L. Stimson, and Secretary of the Navy Frank Knox. Were the Japanese bluffing? Hull thought not; rejection of their terms would mean war. "These fellows mean to fight," he told the group. "You [Marshall and Stark] will have to be prepared."

Adequate preparation could not be guaranteed by either service chief. The great draft army was still only a partly disciplined mass. The Navy, better prepared for an immediate fight, was still far from ready for an extended period of combat. Marshall urged diplomatic delay. If the State Department could hold war off for even three months, the time gained would be precious, especially in the Philippines, where Douglas MacArthur's newly raised Commonwealth Army was only partly organized and equipped.

Perhaps the State Department's formula—*modus vivendi* they called it—which had been sent by cable to our British, Chinese, Australian, and Dutch allies for comment—would gain the needed time. This was a proposal for a three-month truce in Sino-Japanese hostilities, during which the United States, in return for Japan's withdrawal from southern Indochina, would make limited economic concessions to her.

It was evident to all concerned that otherwise hostilities were almost certain to break out within a few days. The President, noting Japan's proclivity for attacking without a declaration of war, impressed on all concerned that if war came, it must result from an initial blow by Japan. How, then, asked Roosevelt, could the United States permit this without too much danger to itself?*

That evening Stark wrote a lengthy warning to Kimmel in Hawaii, informing him that neither the President nor the Secretary of State "would be surprised over a Japanese surprise attack," adding that while "an attack upon the Philippines would be the most embarrassing thing that could happen to us . . . I still rather look for an advance into Thailand, Indochina, Burma Road areas as the most likely." Marshall reviewed the incoming and outgoing messages to overseas commanders, and busied himself with the almost numberless duties of his most important task: preparing our Army for combat.

Honolulu, Tuesday, November 25

Kimmel and Short had more than a passing interest in the status

---

* The claim has been advanced—notably by Rear Admiral Robert A. Theobald in *The Final Secret of Pearl Harbor* (Devin-Adair, 1954)—that President Roosevelt abetted the Japanese surprise "by causing the Hawaiian Commanders to be denied invaluable information from decoded Japanese dispatches concerning the rapid approach of the war and the strong probability that the attack would be directed at Pearl Harbor." He did so, according to now-retired Admiral Kimmel in a recent interview with United Press International, to "induce the Japanese to attack Pearl Harbor and thus permit him to honor his secret commitments to Great Britain and the Netherlands with the full support of the American people."

The report of the Army Pearl Harbor Board, submitted to the Secretary of War on October 20, 1944, apportioned a share of the blame for the surprise to the War and Navy Departments and their top military officers in Washington. Even so, the service inquiries concluded that General Short and Admiral Kimmel had sufficient information to realize that war was imminent and had no excuse for inadequate security measures. They were not court-martialed, despite their requests, largely for political reasons. In this they were grievously wronged, for they had a right to be heard in their own defense. On the other hand, although I am not an apologist for the late President Roosevelt, it is simply ridiculous to suggest that he, who loved the Navy perhaps more than did any of our Presidents, would deliberately offer the Pacific Fleet as a sacrifice to entice Japan into war, and that this scheme was abetted by other responsible military men and statesmen. So many people would have known of such a nefarious plot that it would in fact have been impossible to muffle it.—T.N.D.

On November 17 in Washington Japanese ambassadors Kichisaburo Nomura and Saburo Kurusu (with cane), accompanied by Secretary of State Hull, arrive at the White House for talks with Roosevelt.

of our negotiations with Japan. Admiral Kimmel had been kept informed of the increasingly strained relations by frequent frank and newsy letters from Admiral Stark. One of these, dated November 7, had said in part: "Things seem to be moving steadily towards a crisis in the Pacific. . . . A month may see, literally, most anything . . . It doesn't look good."

Admiral Kimmel undoubtedly was thinking of that letter when he reread the official radio message which he had received the day before, November 24:

> Chances of favorable outcomes of negotiations with Japan very doubtful . . . A surprise aggressive movement in any direction including attack on Philippines or Guam is a possibility. Chief of Staff has seen this dispatch, concurs and requests action addressees to inform senior Army officers their areas. Utmost secrecy necessary in order not to complicate an already tense situation or precipitate Japanese action.

Admiral Kimmel promptly sent a copy of the message to General Short. He had standing instructions to show such messages to the

Army commander: the most critical messages from Washington were usually sent over Navy channels because the Army code was considered to be less secure. The Admiral saw no need for further action. After receiving a warning message on October 16 he had taken some measures for a partial alert and reported those promptly to Stark, who replied: "OK on the disposition which you made."

Admiral Kimmel and General Short had a cordial personal relationship, despite subsequent widespread but unfounded allegations to the contrary. They had frequently discussed, officially and personally, the possibility of a surprise Japanese attack and the measures to be taken to prepare for it and to thwart it if it should come. These plans had been approved in Washington. The Navy was responsible for long-range reconnaissance up to 700 miles, while the Army, with its land-based aircraft, was responsible for inshore reconnaissance for a distance up to twenty miles from shore. The Army's new radar would provide additional reconnaissance and air-warning service for a distance of up to 130 miles from Oahu. Periodically the commanders held joint maneuvers to test the plans and the readiness of their forces to carry them out.

They commanded large forces which might soon be called upon to fight, and it was essential that they maintain an intensive training schedule to assure the highest possible standard of combat efficiency. This was a formidable task, since many of their officers and men were inexperienced and untrained, having only recently been brought into our rapidly expanding armed forces. At the same time, as outpost commanders, both Short and Kimmel were well aware of their responsibilities for assuring the security of the fleet and of the island of Oahu.

Moreover, each commander assumed the other knew his business; each assumed the other's command was running on a full-time status. Each felt—as shown by later testimony—that to probe into the other's shop would be an unpardonable and resented intrusion. As a result, the liaison essential to any sort of joint or concerted operation—the daily constant and intimate exchange of details of command operations between Army and Navy staffs—was almost nonexistent. Each commander, then, was working in a partial vacuum.

On the single island of Oahu were concentrated most of the 42,857 troops that comprised the units of General Short's department. Carrying out the intensive training schedule was the bulk of two infantry divisions, less one regiment scattered in detachments on the other islands of the group. Also on Oahu were most of the antiaircraft and coast defense units of the Coast Artillery Command, and more than 250 aircraft of the Army's Hawaiian air force. Some of these aircraft, aloft on routine training exercises, were being tracked by the inexperienced crews of six Army mobile radar units newly installed at different points on the island.

There was comparable activity at the great Pearl Harbor Navy Yard, on the southern coast of the island, close by the bustling metropolis of Honolulu. Quite a few vessels of the U.S. Pacific Fleet were in port.

Here Kimmel, the fleet's commander in chief, had his headquarters, from which he and his staff closely supervised the intense training programs of their ships in Hawaiian waters. The fleet comprised eight battleships, two aircraft carriers (with a total of 180 planes), sixteen cruisers, forty-five destroyers, twelve submarines, and slightly more than 300 land-based aircraft. In addition another battleship, an aircraft carrier, four cruisers, and various smaller vessels were temporarily absent, many being in mainland yards for repairs.

The Navy Yard itself was the principal installation of the Fourteenth Naval District; both base and the district were commanded by Rear Admiral Claude C. Bloch, who was a direct subordinate of Kimmel both as base commander and as a Pacific Fleet staff officer—a setup which bred no little confusion and which was not helped by the fact that Bloch was Kimmel's senior in the service, though not in command. Kimmel properly held Bloch responsible for the functioning and local security of all the land-based installations of the fleet in Hawaii, while he himself devoted his principal attention to the readiness of the fleet to function offensively at sea. He considered Bloch to be Short's naval counterpart, so far as local protection of the fleet in Hawaii was concerned. Formal co-ordination of Army and Navy activities in Hawaii and nearby Pacific areas, however, was done at conferences—fairly frequent—between Kimmel and Short.

[*On November 25 (Washington date line), Vice Admiral Chuichi Nagumo's First Air Fleet—six aircraft carriers and 414 combat planes, escorted by two battleships, two heavy cruisers and one light, and nine destroyers—put to sea from Tankan Bay in the southern Kurile Islands. Eight tank ships trailed it. Screening the advance were twenty-eight submarines which had left Kure a few days earlier.*

This powerful naval striking force had long been preparing for a surprise attack on the United States Pacific Fleet at Pearl Harbor. It did not, however, have a final directive to carry it out. The First Air Fleet was to leave the Kurile Islands and steam slowly east into the North Pacific to await orders either to attack or, if negotiations with the United States reached a conclusion satisfactory to Japan, to return home.]

Washington, Wednesday, November 26

Before attending a meeting of the Army-Navy Joint Board, both General Marshall and Admiral Stark had learned that Secretary of State Hull, with the full approval of the President, had made a momentous decision.

During the evening of the twenty-fifth and the early hours of the twenty-sixth, the State Department received the comments of our allies on the *modus vivendi* reply to the Japanese ultimatum. The British, Australians, and Dutch gave lukewarm approval to the proposal for a three-month truce, though in a personal message to the President, Prime Minister Winston Churchill remarked pointedly, "What about Chiang Kai-shek? Is he not having a very thin diet?"

Chiang, in fact, had protested violently against the truce proposal, which, with its relaxation of economic pressure on Japan, could only work to the psychological and military disadvantage of China. The protest, as well as information gleaned from more intercepted messages indicating that the Japanese would accept nothing less than complete agreement to their demands of November 20, caused Secretary Hull to doubt the wisdom of the *modus vivendi*. Obviously, these concessions were inadequate to satisfy Japanese demands, yet, because they would seem like American appeasement they would strike a major blow to Chinese morale.

Hull therefore recommended a different reply, which the President approved. After a calm but firm restatement of the principles which had guided the American negotiations, the new note proposed, in essence: withdrawal of Japanese military forces from China and Indochina, recognition of the territorial integrity of those countries, unqualified acceptance of the National Government of China, and, finally, negotiation of a liberal U.S.-Japanese trade treaty once the other conditions had been met.

At 5 P.M. on November 26 Secretary Hull met with the two Japanese ambassadors and presented this reply to them. Special envoy Kurusu read the note, then commented that his government would "throw up its hands" and that the American position practically "put an end to the negotiations."

By frequent phone calls, Secretary Hull had kept both Stimson and Knox informed of these rapid developments, and the two service secretaries had passed on the information to their senior military subordinates. So it was that when they met at a Joint Board conference that same day, Marshall and Stark were well aware of the course of the events still in progress at the State Department. Agreeing that war was now almost certain, they both felt that it was incumbent upon them to remind the President once more of the dangerous weakness of the Army and the Navy and particularly the grave danger of disaster in the Philippines if war were to break out before further reinforcements of men and matériel could reach General MacArthur. They directed their subordinates to have ready for their signatures the next day a joint memorandum to the President which would urge avoidance of hostilities for as long as possible consistent with national policy and national honor.

Late in the afternoon General Marshall held a conference with Major General Leonard T. Gerow, Chief of the War Plans Division, to discuss what should be done the next day, November 27. Marshall had planned to be in North Carolina that day to observe the final phases of the largest maneuvers in the Army's peacetime history; he felt he should carry out that intention, despite his concern about a report that a large Japanese troop convoy had moved into the South China Sea. The two officers discussed the grave implications of the growing Japanese concentrations in the Southeast Asia region. Even though he intended to be back at his desk on the twenty-eighth, General Marshall authorized Gerow to send overseas commanders a warning in his name if further information next day—the twenty-seventh—

should point to the possibility of a surprise Japanese attack.

Honolulu, Wednesday, November 26

Admiral Kimmel received a report from the radio intelligence unit in Hawaii of a strong concentration of Japanese submarines and carrier aircraft in the Marshall Islands. This implied, but did not definitely prove, that some Japanese carriers were there as well. This information was perhaps inconsistent with a somewhat more definite report from the Philippines saying that radio traffic indicated all known Japanese carriers to be in home waters. Neither Admiral Kimmel nor members of his staff saw any need to inform General Short of these reports.

Short, meanwhile, had received an official message directing him to send two long-range B-24 bombers—due from the mainland—to photograph and observe the Japanese bases of Truk in the Caroline Islands and Jaluit in the Marshalls, reporting the number and locations of all Japanese naval vessels. He was to make sure both planes were "fully equipped with gun ammunition." But neither mission was ever flown: only one B-24 reached Short, and it was not properly equipped.

[*On the high seas, their bleak rendezvous at Tankan far astern, Nagumo's task force was steaming eastward. Radio silence was absolute. High-grade fuel kept smoke to a minimum. No waste was thrown overboard to leave telltale tracks; blackout on board was complete. Only the Admiral and a handful of his staff knew their orders; the rest of the command buzzed with speculation like so many hornets.*]

Washington, Thursday, November 27

General Gerow, summoned to Mr. Stimson's office, found Secretary Knox and Admiral Stark already there. The Secretary of War felt the time had come to alert General MacArthur in the Philippines. He told his listeners that Secretary Hull had warned him no peaceful solution was apparent. "I have washed my hands of it," Hull had said, "and it is now in the hands of you and Knox, the Army and the Navy."

Stimson added word of a telephone discussion with the President, who, agreeing that an alert order be sent out, desired all commanders to be cautioned that Japan must commit the first overt act of war. All four in Stimson's office then prepared drafts of alert messages to be sent to General MacArthur and Admiral Hart in the Philippines and to Army and Navy commanders in Hawaii, Panama, and on the West Coast.

Early in the afternoon Gerow sent out the warning:

Negotiations with Japan appear to be terminated to all practicable purposes with only the barest possibilities that the Japanese Government might . . . offer to continue.

The message then reiterated Mr. Roosevelt's desire that Japan commit the first overt act. But this, it was pointed out,

should not repeat not be construed as restricting you to a course . . . that might jeopardize your defense. *Prior to hostile Japanese action you are directed to undertake such reconnais-*

sance and other measures as you deem necessary [italics supplied], but these measures should be carried out so as not repeat not to alarm civil population or disclose intent. Report measures taken . . .

The message further directed that, should hostilities occur, commanders would undertake offensive tasks in accordance with existing war plans. It concluded with the caution that dissemination of "this highly secret information" should be limited to the essential minimum.

Stark's message to Navy commanders (as well as to our special naval observer in London, who was to advise the British) was sent at the same time; it opened bluntly: "This dispatch is to be considered a war warning." It related the end of negotiations and the expectation that "an aggressive move" might come within the next few days. Then, in contrast to the more general Army warning, it added the information that known military activities of the Japanese indicated they probably intended to launch "an amphibious expedition against either the Philippines, Thai or Kra peninsula or possibly Borneo." Like the Army warning, it directed execution of existing war plans in the event of hostilities. Naval commanders in the continental United States, Guam, and Samoa were cautioned to take antisabotage measures.

If read together, these two messages definitely pointed a finger at Southeast Asia as the expected enemy target. This, of course, in no way excuses any of the subsequent actions of our commanders in Hawaii, whose paramount responsibility was the security of their post. But it must have influenced their thinking.

Honolulu, Thursday, November 27

The official warnings from Washington confirmed to Short and Kimmel the seriousness of the international situation. Short, who noted that he was expected to report the measures he was taking, sent the following reply: "Report Department alerted to prevent sabotage. Liaison with the Navy."

The Hawaiian Department plans provided for three kinds of alert. Number 1, which was what Short had ordered, was to guard against sabotage and uprisings—long a preoccupation of all Hawaiian commanders because of the high proportion of Japanese in the Islands. Number 2 included security against possible isolated, external air or naval attacks. Number 3 was a full-scale deployment for maximum defense of the Islands, and particularly of Oahu—heart of the military organization. Only in the two higher stages of alert was ammunition to be distributed to the antiaircraft batteries; in Alert No. 1 all ammunition was to be kept stored in the dumps. Under Alert No. 1, planes would be parked closely for easy guarding; under the others they would be dispersed.

General Short felt he was confirmed in his concern over sabotage when his intelligence officer—or G-2—presented a message from the War Department G-2, warning that "subversive activities may be expected."

In obedience to the instruction to make such reconnaissance as he might "deem necessary," Short did, however, order his newly installed radar stations to operate daily from 4 A.M. to 7 A.M.; these were the dawn hours when surprise attack was most likely. Further reconnaissance, he felt, was the Navy's responsibility. He didn't know that Kimmel was having troubles of his own in attempting any sustained offshore reconnaissance. Nor was Kimmel aware that Short's radar was operating only on a curtailed basis.

Kimmel pondered over what steps he should take. Though he was already alerted to some extent, he knew that for the moment he could do little in the way of "defensive deployment" in his war plan tasks—most specifically, raids into the Japanese mandated islands. Should he then prepare for an attack against Oahu? The Washington message implied that this was not a probability. Even so, he didn't have sufficient planes for a 360 degree, distant reconnaissance from Oahu.

In compliance with instructions from Washington, Kimmel was sending some Marine planes to Wake and Midway islands. He decided that the two carrier task forces he was ordering to carry out this instruction could, en route, conduct long-range searches to the west, over the direct route from Japan to Oahu.

Task Force 8, under Vice Admiral William F. Halsey, including the carrier *Enterprise* and three cruisers, was leaving that day. In conference with Halsey before departure, Kimmel showed him the "war warning" message. Halsey asked how far he should go if he met any Japanese ships while searching. "Use your common sense," was Kimmel's reply. Halsey, it is understood, commented that these were the best orders he could receive, adding that if he found as much as one Japanese sampan, he would sink it. Kimmel, by making no further comment, apparently acquiesced.

Pending the arrival of Halsey at Wake, Kimmel sent orders to a patrol plane squadron based on Midway to proceed to Wake and return, searching ocean areas and covering a 525-mile area around Wake itself.

Kimmel felt that he had done all he could in that line without completely halting fleet training and exhausting the pilots of his relatively weak air command. But he did order immediate attack on any and all unidentified submarines discovered in the vicinity of Oahu and other fleet operating zones. Neither then nor later, apparently, did he check on the local security measures undertaken by Admiral Bloch's command, nor did he suggest any co-ordination between Bloch and Short.

[*Nagumo's force was steady on a course laid between the Aleutians and Midway Island, the carriers in two parallel rows of three each. Battleships and cruisers guarded the flanks, destroyers screened wide, and submarines were scouting far ahead.*]

Washington, Friday, November 28

General Marshall, back from his North Carolina inspection, was briefed by Gerow on the previous day's happenings. He read and approved the joint memorandum, already signed by Admiral Stark, which urged on the President the need for gaining time, particularly until troops—some already at sea and nearing Guam, others about to embark on the West Coast—could reach the Philippines. He also approved the warning message Gerow had sent to the overseas commanders.

At noon he attended the President's "War Council" meeting at the White House. The implications of a large Japanese amphibious force, known to be sailing southward through the South China Sea, were discussed. British Malaya, the Netherlands East Indies, and the Philippines were potential targets, the invasion of which would immediately involve us in war. But unless Congress should previously declare war, the United States could not attack this force. It was agreed that the President should send a message to Emperor Hirohito urging him to preserve peace, and that Mr. Roosevelt should also address Congress, explaining the dangers being created by this Japanese aggressive action. The President then left for a short vacation at Warm Springs, Georgia, directing his advisers to have the two documents prepared in his absence.

Marshall, back at his desk, thumbed through a sheaf of radio replies to the "war warning" message. Lieutenant General John L. DeWitt, commanding on the Pacific Coast, reported instituting a harbor alert at San Francisco and similar precautions in Alaska in liaison with naval authorities. He requested permission to direct air as well as ground deployment of his far-flung command. It was a long message, contrasting sharply with Short's succinct report of sabotage defense measures in Hawaii. But the Chief of Staff didn't pay much attention; it would be Gerow's job to handle any necessary responses. So Marshall initialed most of the messages and then forgot about them.

Short's message, however, was not initialed by Marshall. He would later testify he had no recollection of ever having seen it, although it bore the routine rubber stamp, "Noted by Chief of Staff."

As for Admiral Stark, he was pushing off a long message to Navy commanders on the West Coast, and to Admiral Kimmel, quoting the Army alert message of the twenty-seventh, including its admonition that Japan must commit the first "overt act."

Honolulu, Friday, November 28

Kimmel read Stark's long quote of the Army's alert message. He was particularly interested in its stress that "if hostilities cannot . . . be avoided the United States desires that Japan commit the first overt act." This appeared to confirm his decision of the previous day: limiting defensive deployment to one patrol squadron cruising from Wake to Midway and sending carrier task forces for local defense of those outposts.

Admiral Kimmel received several other interesting reports. The U.S.S. *Helena* reported contact with an unidentified submarine. An intelligence estimate based on radio intercepts indicated Japanese carriers were still in their own home waters. Another report on intercepted Japanese messages established a "winds code," by means of which Japan would notify its diplomatic and consular representatives abroad of a decision to go to war: "east wind rain" meant war with the United States; "north wind cloudy," war with Russia; "west wind clear," war with England and invasion of Thailand, Malaya, and the Dutch East Indies.

It was all very interesting. However, the Admiral never thought of mentioning any of these reports during his conference with General Short that day. They discussed mutual responsibility for security of Wake and Midway—in light of the mixed Army-Navy garrisons at both places. But neither thought of asking the other what action he had taken on the November 27 warnings, nor did either volunteer any information on matters he considered to be of interest to his own individual service only.

[Admiral Nagumo's fleet spent the day in attempts to refuel in a plunging sea—an operation which, as it turned out, would continue for several days under almost heartbreaking conditions of bad weather.]

Washington, Saturday, November 29

Both General Marshall and Admiral Stark received Magic copies of more intercepted Japanese messages. One of these from Premier Tojo in Tokyo to the ambassadors in Washington was quite ominous:

> The United States' . . . humiliating proposal . . . was quite unexpected and extremely regrettable. The Imperial Government can by no means use it as a basis for negotiations. Therefore . . . in two or three days the negotiations will be de facto ruptured. . . . However, I did not wish you to give the impression that the negotiations are broken off. Merely say to them that you are awaiting instructions. . . . From now on, do the best you can.

To Marshall and Stark this was clear evidence indeed that the Japanese were stalling for time only long enough to get their forces ready to attack in the Indonesia-Southeast Asia area. It seemed now only a question of time, as more reports streamed in about Japanese convoys moving into the South China Sea.

For a good part of the morning Stark and Marshall were working closely with Secretaries Knox and Stimson in preparing and revising drafts of the presidential messages to Congress and to Emperor Hirohito, in accordance with the agreement at the previous day's meeting of the War Council. Finally, about noon, the two secretaries were satisfied, and their proposed drafts were sent to Secretary Hull.

Late in the afternoon both read with considerable interest reports of a warlike speech which Premier Tojo had delivered that day (November 30, Tokyo time). The twenty-ninth had been the deadline established in the messages from Tokyo to the ambassadors. The speech, while warlike, failed to give any indication of Japanese intentions.

Honolulu, Saturday, November 29

Things were generally quiet on Oahu and in the outlying waters, as the Army and Navy both began a weekend of relaxation after five days of stenuous training. There was considerable bustle, however, at the Army's headquarters at Fort Shafter, as well as at Navy headquarters at nearby Pearl Harbor. General Short approved a message in reply to the latest sabotage warning from Washington, outlining in detail the security measures which had been taken. Admiral Kimmel received another message from Washington reminding him once more that he was to be prepared to carry out existing war plans in the event of hostilities with Japan. Thus, once again, the two commanders were reminded of the alert messages they had received on the twenty-seventh, and once again they found themselves satisfied with the actions they had then taken.

[*In the North Pacific Admiral Nagumo's fleet continued refueling.*]

Washington, Sunday, November 30

General Marshall, returning from his usual Sunday morning horseback ride at Fort Myer, found another intercepted Japanese message awaiting him; the Foreign Ministry was cautioning its envoys in Washington to keep talking and "be careful that this does not lead to anything like a breaking-off of negotiations." He agreed with G-2's conclusion that the Japanese were stalling until their South China Sea assault was ready.

Stark, at his desk, was called that morning by Secretary of State Hull, gravely concerned about Premier Tojo's warlike speech. The Secretary told him he was going to urge the President's return from Warm Springs. A later call from Hull informed Stark that President Roosevelt would be back Monday morning; Stark must see the President and report on the naval developments in the Far East.

Honolulu, Sunday, November 30

General Short, in light of his instructions "not to alarm the civil population," must have been annoyed to read the Honolulu *Advertiser* headlines that morning: "Hawaii Troops Alerted." There wasn't anything he could do about it, however; even the limited nature of his Alert No. 1 would draw newspaper attention in a critical time such as this. He also read that "Leaders Call Troops Back in Singapore—Hope Wanes as Nations Fail at Parleys" and "Kurusu Bluntly Warned Nation Ready for Battle."

Kimmel ordered a squadron of patrol planes to Midway, to replace temporarily the squadron which he had ordered to reconnoiter about Wake. He was also interested in an information copy of a Navy Department message to Admiral Hart, commanding our Asiatic Fleet at Manila, directing him to scout for information as to an intended Japanese attack on the Kra Isthmus of Thailand, just north of Malaya.

Kimmel didn't think that war could be delayed much longer. He wrote on the top of a piece of paper the words—"Steps to be taken in case of American-Japanese war within the next twenty-four hours," an *aide-mémoire* of the orders he must issue to his fleet.

[*The Japanese First Air Fleet was still engaged in the arduous refueling job, while continuing its eastward course at slow speed.*]

Washington, Monday, December 1

A busy day. Stark learned from his intelligence staff that the Japanese Navy had changed service radio frequencies and call letters for all units afloat—a normal prewar step. He went to the White House with Secretary Hull and briefed the President.

In the afternoon both Stark and Marshall digested an unusual number of important Magic intercepts of Japanese messages. Japan's Foreign Minister was urging his ambassadors to prevent the United States "from becoming unduly suspicious," emphasizing that it was important to give the impression to the Americans that "negotiations are continuing." Tokyo also had ordered its diplomatic offices in London, Hong Kong, Singapore, and Manila "to abandon the use of code machines and to dispose of them." Japan's ambassador at Bangkok reported his intrigues to maneuver Thailand into a declaration of war on Great Britain.

But most significant was an exchange between Japan's ambassador to Berlin and his foreign office. The ambassador reported that Foreign Minister von Ribbentrop had given him Hitler's unequivocal assurance that "should Japan become engaged in a war against the United States, Germany, of course, would join the war immediately." Tojo promptly told the ambassador to inform the German government that "war may suddenly break out between the Anglo-Saxon nations and Japan through some clash of arms. . . . This war may come quicker than anyone dreams."

And how quickly would that be? This was the question which sprang immediately to the minds of Admiral Stark and General Marshall, the men responsible for readying the armed forces of the United States for the coming clash of arms. They had no way of knowing that the answer lay in a brief uncoded message picked up by several American radio intelligence intercept stations just a few hours earlier. "Climb Mount Niitaka," was the message. No significance could be attached to it, so it never came to the attention of Marshall or Stark. Nor would it have meant anything to either of them.

Honolulu, Monday, December 1

Kimmel and Short held another routine conference. Presumably they discussed at some length the grave international situation. Supplementing the cryptic but alarming official intelligence reports and warnings were the headlines blazoning the Honolulu newspapers.

But neither Kimmel nor Short in their conversation discussed local security precautions or a possible threat to Oahu. Politely but inconclusively they continued discussion of the divided responsibility at Wake and Midway. Kimmel never thought to mention to Short that he had received another Washington warning about the "winds code" and that he had also been informed of the change in Japanese military frequencies and call letters. It never occurred to Kimmel that Short might not have been told about either matter.

Routine training continued in Army posts. General Short was quite pleased that his limited alert—which the War Department had apparently approved—had not interfered noticeably with training programs.

[*"Climb Mount Niitaka!"*

Admiral Nagumo sucked in his breath as the message was laid before him this day. This was it; the prearranged code which meant "Proceed with attack."

Obedient to the signal flags broken out aboard the flagship, the gray ships came foaming about to a southeasterly course, vibrating to the thrust of increased propeller speed. Inside the steel hulls the mustered crews, learning the news, cheered, quaffed sake, and burned incense to the spirits of their ancestors.]

Washington, Tuesday, December 2

Additional Magic intercepts indicated further Japanese preparations for war, with the enemy's known offensive weight still massing in Southeast Asia.

Honolulu, Tuesday, December 2

Kimmel, discussing intelligence reports with his staff, noted the change in Japanese radio frequencies as related in the Navy Department's fortnightly intelligence summary, received late the previous day. The gist of it was that Tokyo was preparing for "operations on a large scale."

Then Kimmel called for intelligence estimates on the location of Japanese aircraft carriers. Captain Edwin T. Layton, his intelligence officer, gave estimated locations for all except Divisions 1 and 2—four carriers.

"What!" exclaimed Kimmel, "you don't know where [they] are?"

"No, sir, I do not. I think they are in home waters, but—"

Sternly, but with a suspicion of a twinkle in his eyes, Kimmel delivered himself of a masterpiece of unconscious irony.

"Do you mean to say they could be rounding Diamond Head and you wouldn't know it?"

The conference ended after a discussion on the difficulty of locating a force operating under sealed orders while preserving radio silence.

Short met Kimmel that day again. They continued debate over jurisdiction at Wake and Midway.

[*Nagumo's fleet was steadily driving south toward Oahu. In prearranged code—unintelligible to American Magic interceptors— Tokyo had confirmed the target date: "X-Day will be 8 December" —December 7, Honolulu time.*]

Washington, Wednesday, December 3

Along with the other recipients of Magic information, General Marshall and Admiral Stark noted but attached no particular significance to a pair of intercepted messages made available to them that day.

One, dated November 15, was already old; its translation had been deferred for several days in order to take care of messages considered more urgent. It referred to an earlier message directing the Japanese consulate at Honolulu to make periodic reports on the location of American warships in Pearl Harbor, and requested the Honolulu consulate to step up these reports to twice a week.

No particular importance was attributed to this by Admiral Stark or his senior naval intelligence officers, since the Japanese had long been making efforts to obtain information about the activities and number of ships in harbor at other naval bases on the West Coast and at Panama. The fact that the Japanese wanted more complete data, including exact locations of specific vessels in Pearl Harbor, was assumed to be merely an indication of their thoroughness in evaluating intelligence on America's main Pacific combat force.

The other message was a reply by Prime Minister Tojo to the suggestion of his ambassadors at Washington that peace could perhaps be preserved through a high-level conference—they had proposed former Premier Prince Konoye as the Japanese envoy and Vice President Henry Wallace or Presidential Assistant Harry Hopkins for the United States—at "some midway point, such as Honolulu." Tojo's response, that "it would be inappropriate for us to propose such a meeting," seemed a less significant indication of Japan's immediate intentions than the continuing reports of her movements in and near Indochina.

Honolulu, Wednesday, December 3

Admiral Kimmel noted the continuing and surprising lack of information on Japanese carriers contained in the latest daily radio intelligence summary, which stated that "carrier traffic is at a low ebb."

That day, too, he received Admiral Stark's letter of November 25. He agreed with Stark's view that "an attack on the Philippines" might be embarrassing, but that "an advance into Thailand, Indochina, Burma Road area [was] most likely."

In the afternoon Short and Kimmel conferred. They soon got into a grim discussion of what they could do to carry out assigned war plans when and if war broke out. Both were thinking, of course, of planned naval and air raids into the Marshall Islands and of security measures for Wake and Midway. There was no mention of like measures for Oahu. Nor did Admiral Kimmel think to mention to General Short his latest intelligence reports about the burning of Japanese codes or the missing aircraft carriers.

[Nagumo's planners on the high seas were busy marking on their charts of Pearl Harbor the exact locations of six of the U.S. battle

fleet—the Pennsylvania, Arizona, California, Tennessee, Maryland, *and* West Virginia. *The data came from Honolulu, relayed by radio through Imperial Navy Headquarters in Tokyo.*]

Washington, Thursday, December 4

A mixed bag of Magic intercepts available to both Stark and Marshall gave clear indication of Japanese intentions to go to war. Instructions came to Ambassador Nomura to completely destroy one of the two special machines for secret coding, but to hold the other and its cipher key—which should be in his personal possession—"until the last minute." One intercepted message, considered to be relatively insignificant, was to the Japanese consul at Honolulu; he was to "investigate completely the fleet-bases in the neighborhood of the Hawaiian military reservation."

Stark and Marshall concerned themselves with routine activities.

Honolulu, Thursday, December 4

Admiral Kimmel conferred with two of his senior task-force commanders, scheduled to sail the next day on combined training-alert missions. One, under Vice Admiral Wilson Brown, was to proceed to Johnson Island, 700 miles southwest of Oahu, on a joint Navy-Marine bombardment and landing exercise. The other, under Rear Admiral T. H. Newton, included the carrier *Lexington*. This force was to go to Midway Island, fly off a squadron of Marine planes to reinforce the local garrison, and then rendezvous with Brown at Johnson Island. En route the *Lexington*'s planes would conduct routine scouting flights.

Kimmel's intention was that, should war break out, these forces would be available for raids into the Marshall Island group in accordance with existing war plans. Both task-force commanders understood their war-plan missions; both were aware in general of the tense international situation. Kimmel, therefore, felt he was under no obligation to inform either of Washington's November 27 "war warning" message.

The net naval situation on Oahu now was that the entire carrier force of the Pacific Fleet was either at sea or about to steam and that the approaches to the island from the west would be scouted for several days to come.

Kimmel felt that these steps would ensure a reconnaissance search of a large portion of the central Pacific Ocean, as extensive as his limited aircraft strength would permit. But, from the Hawaiian Islands north to the Aleutians, both sea and air were still bare of American reconnaissance.

Kimmel and Short did not meet that day.

[*Admiral Nagumo, watching the intermittent refueling being carried on during the day, was intrigued to learn from Honolulu, via Tokyo, that watchful Japanese eyes were "unable to ascertain whether air alert had been issued. There are no indications of sea alert. . . ."*]

Washington, Friday, December 5

Both War and Navy departments were busy compiling data for President Roosevelt on Japanese sea, land, and air strength concentrating in French Indochina and adjacent areas. In an intercepted Japanese message from Washington, Ambassador Nomura told Tokyo that in case of Japanese invasion of Thailand, joint military action by Great Britain and the United States "is a definite certainty, with or without a declaration of war." Another, from Tokyo, reiterated the previous instructions about destruction of codes and coding machines.

Admiral Stark, conferring with staff officers, decided no further warning orders need be sent to overseas naval commanders; the message of November 27 was adequate. All concurred.

Honolulu, Friday, December 5

General Short read with interest a cryptic message from G-2 in Washington to his intelligence officer, directing him to get in touch with the Navy immediately "regarding broadcasts from Tokyo reference weather." So Lieutenant Colonel George W. Bicknell, assistant G-2, gave the General all facts obtainable from his own office and from Kimmel's headquarters. Short was informed by Kimmel of the departure of the two naval task forces of Admirals Brown and Newton.

[*While pilots and squadron leaders on board Nagumo's fleet studied and restudied their coming roles, the ships—900 miles north of Midway and 1,300 miles northwest of Oahu—slid slowly down the North Pacific rollers, still far beyond the range of any American search plane.*]

Washington, Saturday, December 6

Reports of increasing Japanese concentration and movements in Indochina, South China, and the South China Sea absorbed Stark and Marshall, as well as all the other members of the War Cabinet from the President down. Mr. Roosevelt, the service chiefs were glad to learn, had decided that he would personally warn Emperor Hirohito that further aggressions might lead to war and urge the Japanese ruler that withdrawal of his forces from Indochina "would result in the assurance of peace throughout the whole of the South Pacific area."

Late in the afternoon Magic plucked out of the air thirteen parts of a fourteen-part memorandum from Tokyo to the Japanese envoys. This much of the message summarized negotiations from the Japanese viewpoint, concluding that the American note of November 26 was not "a basis of negotiations." The envoys were instructed to handle it carefully, since "the situation is extremely delicate."

Distribution of this intercept was curious. Decoding was completed after office hours. General Sherman A. Miles, Army G-2, saw no need to disturb either the Secretary of War, General Marshall, or General Gerow at their homes. (In passing it might be mentioned that one didn't disturb General Marshall at home without extremely good reason.) Some Navy people saw the message. Stark, who was at the theater, learned of it when he returned home and found that he was expected to call the White House. The President had received the intercept, as had the State Department. The details of the conversation are not known, but presumably the President told Stark, as he had earlier said to Harry Hopkins: "This means war!"

Honolulu, Saturday, December 6

In the daily radio intelligence summary received that morning from Washington, Admiral Kimmel was again struck by lack of information on the location of Japanese carriers. In other dispatches, however, there was considerable information about different kinds of Japanese activity. He received a copy of Admiral Hart's message reporting on the movement of the two convoys south of Indochina. And he received a message from Washington authorizing him, "in view of the international situation and the exposed position of our outlying Pacific Islands," to order the destruction of classified documents at these islands, "now or under later conditions of greater emergency." Neither the Admiral nor any member of his staff saw any need to pass on any information to the Army. Presumably General Short was getting it all through Army channels.

Carefully checking the reported locations of all fleet units and projecting their planned routes for the next twenty-four hours, Admiral Kimmel again made his daily revision of his personal check-list memorandum: "Steps to be taken in case of American-Japanese war within the next twenty-four hours."

Over at Fort Shafter, Army headquarters, the daily staff conference was as usual presided over by Colonel Walter C. Phillips, chief of staff. General Short did not normally attend these meetings. Bicknell, assistant G-2, who seems to have been on his toes those days, reported the Japanese consulate in Honolulu was busily burning and destroying secret papers, significant in light of similar reports throughout the world already noted in the intercepts. The chief of staff and G-2 reported this information later to General Short.

And so Oahu drifted into another weekend: a time of relaxation for both Army and Navy. Short, however, was interrupted by Bicknell early that evening at his quarters while he and his G-2—Colonel Kendall Fielder—and their wives were about to drive to a dinner dance.

Bicknell, with some sense of urgency, reported that the local FBI agent had passed to him and to Navy intelligence a transcript of a suspicious long-distance telephone message. A Japanese named Mori, talking to someone in Tokyo, mentioned flights of airplanes, searchlights, and the number of ships in Pearl Harbor, along with cryptic reference to various flowers—apparently part of some sort of code.

Both the FBI man and Bicknell were alarmed at the implications of this flower code. Neither Short nor Fielder, however, was disturbed. Short, before they hurried to the car where their wives awaited them impatiently, told Bicknell he was, perhaps, "too intelligence-conscious." In any event they could talk about it again in the morning.

The district intelligence officer of the Navy decided that the transcript should be studied further by a Japanese linguist and so put the FBI report away until Monday morning. Admiral Kimmel was not informed.

[*Nagumo's fleet, the wallowing tankers now left behind, was churning southward at twenty-four-knot speed. By 6 A.M. next day it would be 230 miles north of Oahu with its planes thrusting skyward. And at dawn, five midget two-man submarines—disgorged from five large Japanese submarines gathered offshore that night—poked their way around Diamond Head, Pearl Harbor-bound.*]

Washington, Sunday, December 7

By 8 A.M. the last part of the Japanese memorandum—Part Fourteen—had been intercepted, transcribed, and was ready for distribution. Both Army and Navy intelligence officers were slightly surprised at its mild tone: "The Japanese Government regrets . . . that it is impossible to reach an agreement through further negotiations."

Stark got it in his office. Marshall was taking his Sunday morning recreational ride at Fort Myer: the message would await his arrival—usually at about 11 A.M. All others concerned got it. Meanwhile two other messages had been intercepted by Magic, and Colonel Rufus Bratton, executive officer in G-2, was so upset by them he tried vainly to get them to the Chief of Staff.

One of the messages ordered the embassy to destroy immediately its one remaining cipher machine plus all codes and secret documents. The other read:

"Will the Ambassador please submit to the United States Government (if possible to the Secretary of State) our reply to the United States at 1 P.M. on the 7th, your time."

It will be remembered that General Marshall did not take kindly to interruptions in his off-duty hours. So, despite the limited area of his ride—an automobile or motorcycle from Fort Myer headquarters could have intercepted him in fifteen minutes at most—not until his return to his quarters at ten-thirty did Marshall learn that an important message was awaiting him. He reached his office in the Munitions Building at about 11:15, to find General Gerow, General Miles, and Colonel Bratton there. Bratton handed him the three intercepted messages—the memorandum, the instructions to destroy codes and papers, and the instruction to deliver the Japanese answer at 1 P.M. precisely. Marshall read quickly but carefully, as was usual with him. Then—

"Something is going to happen at one o'clock," he told the officers. "When they specified a day, that of course had significance, but not comparable to an hour."

He immediately called Stark, who had read all three messages. A warning should be sent at once to all Pacific commanders, Marshall felt. Stark hesitated; he felt all had already been alerted. Marshall stated that in view of the "one o'clock" item he would apprise Army commanders anyway.

Hanging up, he reached for a pencil and drafted his instruction to DeWitt, Western Defense Command; Andrews, Panama Command; Short, Hawaiian Command; and MacArthur, Philippine Command. It took him about three minutes. He read it to the group:

"The Japanese are presenting at 1 P.M. E.S.T. today, what amounts to an ultimatum. Also they are under orders to destroy their code machine immediately. Just what significance the hour set may have, we do not know, but be on alert accordingly."

As he was ordering Bratton to send it out at once, Stark telephoned back. Would Marshall please include in his dispatch the "usual expression to inform the naval officer?" Marshall quickly added the words "Inform naval authorities of this communication." He sent Bratton on his way, instructing him to return as soon as the message had been delivered to the message center.

Bratton was back in five minutes; he had delivered the message personally to the officer in charge of the message center, Colonel French.

Marshall, obviously more perturbed than any of those present had ever before seen him, asked Bratton how much time would be consumed in enciphering and dispatching the message. Bratton didn't know. So back he was rushed to find out.

Marshall, it developed, was pondering whether or not he should telephone a warning—especially to MacArthur. Time was running out; not much more than one hour remained. Marshall had a "scrambler" phone on his desk, which permitted secure long-distance conversations with similar phones in the headquarters of overseas commanders; eavesdroppers would hear only unintelligible gibberish. Marshall, however, must have had some private reservations as to the efficacy of the scrambler mechanism, and apparently feared that the Japanese might have some way of deciphering the conversation. A telephone call which could not be kept secret might precipitate Japanese action; it would almost certainly indicate we had broken their secret code. Would it be worth it?

Bratton reported back that the process would take about thirty minutes.

"Thirty minutes until it is dispatched, or thirty minutes until it is received and decoded at the other end?"

Business of rushing back to the message center again, while the big office clock ticked away. Bratton, charging back, announced that the message, decoded, would be in the hands of the addressees in thirty minutes. It was now precisely noon. In Hawaii it was only 6:30 A.M. Marshall, satisfied, made no further follow-up.

Had he done so he would have found out that Colonel French at the message center was having some troubles. To San Francisco, Panama, and Manila the warning sped without delay. But the War Department radio, so Colonel French was informed, had been out of contact with Hawaii since 10:20 that morning. French decided to use commercial facilities: Western Union to San Francisco, thence commercial radio to Honolulu. This was a normal procedure; usually it would mean but little further delay. French never dreamed of disturbing the Chief of Staff by reporting such trivia. So Marshall's warning was filed at the Army Signal Center at 12:01 P.M. (6:31 A.M. in Hawaii); teletype transmission to San Francisco was completed by 12:17 P.M. (6:47 A.M. in Hawaii), and was in the Honolulu office of RCA at 1:03 P.M. Washington time (7:33 A.M. in Hawaii). Since that was too early for teletype traffic to Fort Shafter, RCA sent it by motorcycle messenger. He would, as it turned out, be delayed through extraordinary circumstances.

Honolulu, Sunday, December 7

Extraordinary circumstances had become almost commonplace on and near Oahu as early as 3:42 A.M. At that hour the mine sweeper *Condor,* conducting a routine sweep of the harbor entrance, sighted a submarine periscope. This was a defensive area where American submarines were prohibited from operating submerged. The *Condor* flashed a report of the sighting to the destroyer *Ward,* of the inshore patrol. For two hours the *Ward* searched the harbor entrance in vain; meanwhile the *Condor* and another mine sweeper had entered the harbor at about 5 A.M.; for some reason the antisubmarine net, opened to permit the entrance of the mine sweepers, was not closed.

At 6:30 the U.S.S. *Antares*—a repair ship towing a steel barge— was approaching the harbor entrance when she sighted a suspicious object, which looked like a midget submarine. The *Antares* immediately notified the *Ward.* At 6:33 a Navy patrol plane sighted the same object and dropped two smoke pots on the spot. The *Ward* hastened to the scene, spotting the sub—her superstructure just above the surface—at 6:40, and promptly opened fire. At the same time the patrol plane dropped bombs or depth charges. The submarine keeled over and began to sink, as the *Ward* dropped more depth charges. Shortly after 6:50 the destroyer sent a coded message that it had attacked a submarine in the defensive sea area.

At about 7:40 Admiral Kimmel received a telephone call from the staff duty officer, reporting the *Ward*-submarine incident. Kimmel replied, "I will be right down." Quickly he completed dressing and left for his headquarters.

Meanwhile, the Army's six mobile radar stations on Oahu had been on the alert since 4 A.M. in compliance with General Short's Alert No. 1 instructions. At 7 A.M. five of these stations ceased operations, in accordance with these same instructions. At the remote Opana station at the northern tip of the island, Privates Joseph Lockard and George Elliott kept their set on while waiting for the truck which was to pick them up to take them to breakfast. Lockard, an experienced radar operator, planned to use this time to give Elliott a bit more instruction. At this moment an unusual formation appeared at the edge of the screen; Lockard checked the machine, found it operating properly, and at 7:02 A.M. concluded that a large number of aircraft, approximately 130 miles distant, was approaching Oahu from the north. For fifteen minutes Lockard and Elliott observed the approach of the

Left: A Zero fighter takes off from one of the Japanese carriers on December 7, 1941. The picture at right was taken from a Japanese plane during the attack. An oil slick spreads from the torpedoed ships in Battleship Row. Smoke rises from bombed installations in the Navy Yard.

formation, debating whether they should report it. Finally, at 7:20, Lockard called the radar information center. The switchboard operator informed him that the center had closed down twenty minutes before, that everyone had left except one Air Corps officer, First Lieutenant Kermet Tyler. Lockard reported the approaching flight to Tyler, who thought for a moment; the flight was undoubtedly either a naval patrol, a formation of Hickam Field bombers, or—most likely—a number of B-17's due from the mainland. "Forget it," he told Lockard.

Twenty minutes later—about 7:50—there was a bustle of activity on the decks of the ninety-four vessels of the Pacific Fleet in Pearl Harbor. It was almost time for morning colors on each vessel, and white-garbed sailors were briskly preparing for the daily flag-raising ceremony. Except for one destroyer, moving slowly toward the entrance, each ship was motionless at its moorings.

At 7:55 boatswains' whistles piped, and the preparatory signal for the colors ceremony was hoisted on each ship. At the same moment a low-flying plane, approaching over the hills to the northeast, swooped low over Ford Island, in the middle of the harbor. A bomb dropped on the seaplane ramp, close by the eight battleships moored next to the island. As the plane zoomed upward, displaying the red sun emblem of Japan, it was followed closely by others. By 9:45 some 260 Japanese planes had flashed that emblem over Oahu, and when the dreadful 110 minutes were over, 2,403 Americans—mostly sailors on the battleships—were dead or dying; 1,178 more had been wounded; the battle force of the Pacific Fleet had been destroyed, with four battleships sunk or capsized and the remaining four damaged, while several smaller vessels were sunk or damaged severely. The Japanese lost twenty-nine planes, five midget submarines, and less than a hundred men.

One small further incident is pertinent to our assessment of United States leadership in high places just before Pearl Harbor.

The Nisei RCA messenger boy carrying General Marshall's message speedily found himself involved in trouble. Not until 11:45 could he thread his way through traffic jams, road blocks, and general confusion to reach the Fort Shafter signal office, which was itself swamped in traffic by this time.

Not until 2:58 P.M. Hawaiian time—9:58 that evening in bewildered Washington—was the message decoded and placed on Short's desk. He rushed a copy to Admiral Kimmel, who read it, remarked—perhaps unnecessarily—that it was not of the slightest interest any more, and dropped it into the wastebasket.

It had been a pretty long thirty minutes.

Who was responsible?

No disaster of the magnitude of Pearl Harbor could have occurred without the failure—somewhere and somehow—of leadership. A total of eight separate official investigations searched for scapegoats, and found them. The disaster remained a political football long after the last three of these investigations. And much confusion and argument still exist.

Yet through this welter of discord, some facts and conclusions stand out. Today, nearly thirty years later, in another time of crisis, they hold important lessons.

It makes no difference, in assessing responsibility, that exceptional Japanese military skill, shrouded by deceit and assisted by almost incredible luck, accomplished its mission. Nor, indeed, does it matter that —as adjudicated in the always brilliant light of afterthought—Japan might well have inflicted defeat upon our Pacific Fleet and our Army forces in Hawaii regardless of how well alerted they may have been on December 7, 1941.

It makes no difference, so far as responsibility for the disaster itself was concerned, whether the war could have been prevented by wiser statesmanship or more astute diplomacy—though this would have required a wholehearted and unified national determination which did not exist in America in 1941 and the years before. It makes no difference that on December 7 the President and the Secretary of State—like the civilian Secretaries of War and Navy—had their eyes fixed on the Japanese threat in Southeast Asia. They had repeatedly warned the military men that war had probably become unavoidable.

What *does* matter is that the civilian statesmen—however deft or clumsy, shrewd, or shortsighted—performed their difficult tasks of diplomacy and of administration confident that the military men would carry out their professional responsibilities by doing everything humanly possible to prepare for a war so clearly impending. They had every right to expect that—within the limits of scanty means available —the Armed Forces would be ready for any contingency.

The confidence and expectations of civilian leadership and of the nation were tragically dashed that Sunday almost thirty years ago.

Military failures were responsible for Pearl Harbor.

In Washington the most important of these were the following:

1. The War Department staff, over which General Marshall presided, was at the time a complicated but "one-man" shop, where delegation of responsibility was the exception rather than the rule. When Marshall was absent, the operational wheels tended to freeze. This situation was to some extent due to cumbersome organization, to some extent due to the personality of the Chief of Staff.

2. General Marshall, in a letter to General Short on February 7, 1941, stressed that "the risk of sabotage and the *risk involved in a surprise raid by air and submarine* [italics supplied] constitute the real perils of the [Hawaiian] situation." Yet, although definitely warning General Short on November 27 of the threat of war, and ordering him to report the measures he would take in response, Marshall did not check up on those measures; moreover, he was unaware that Short had done no more than to take routine precautions against sabotage. And General Gerow, heading the War Plans Division of General Marshall's General Staff—as he testified later in taking full responsibility for this slip—had not made any provision for following up operational orders. The net result was that both Marshall and Short remained the whole time in blissful ignorance of a vital misinterpretation of orders.

3. Marshall and Admiral Stark—and indeed all members of their staffs who knew the situation—permitted themselves to be hypnotized by the concrete evidence of the aggressive Japanese build-up in Southeast Asia which threatened our Philippines outpost. This theme, it will be remembered, ran as background to nearly all the warnings sent Hawaii. Thus succumbing to the illusory diagnosis of "enemy probable intentions," both top commanders ignored the danger implicit in our inability to locate at least four Japanese carriers.

4. Finally, on December 7, having indicated his full realization of the significance of the "one o'clock" intercept—that less than two hours now separated peace and war—and having decided not to use his "scrambler" telephone, Marshall failed to require surveillance and positive report on the delivery of his final warning.

These certainly were grave lapses in leadership. Yet in fairness, it

Her back broken by bombs and torpedoes, the battleship Arizona *rests on the bottom of the shallow harbor.*

should be noted that the consequences might not have been disastrous if all subordinate commanders had taken adequate security measures on the basis of the instructions, information, and warnings which they had received. To General Marshall's credit one must also chalk up his ability to profit by his mistakes. In less than three months after Pearl Harbor, he completely reorganized the War Department, decentralizing the mass of relatively minor administrative and executive matters that choked major strategical and tactical decisions. His newly created Operations Division of the General Staff—which he aptly termed his "command post"—ensured co-ordinated action and direction of Army activities in theaters of war all around the globe. On Oahu the situation was less ambiguous: military leadership at the top failed utterly.

Almost three decades later, with war clouds still lowering over most of the world, the story of the Pearl Harbor disaster has more significance than mere passing memorials to the brave men who lost their lives that day. If the lessons are heeded, our surviving descendants may never again have to commemorate another "day of infamy."

William Harlan Hale

The Road
to Yalta

The stormy, mercurial course of American relations with Russia over the past fifty years has been shaped primarily by great events such as the communist revolution, the Great Depression, the German invasion of Russia during World War II, and the complex of controversies that have given shape to the Cold War. However, it has also been shaped by the personal relations of individuals—not only of the great leaders (Roosevelt and Stalin; Kennedy and Khrushchev) but of ambassadors, minor diplomats, propagandists, and many others. It is the virtue of this essay by William Harlan Hale that, while paying full attention to the major events and leaders, it delves into the character and behavior of many of these lesser figures who influenced American-Soviet relations and shows how they (their strengths and their foibles) affected the course of history.

Mr. Hale draws upon personal experience as a foreign service officer as well as historical research in this essay, which appeared in American Heritage *as part of a series which he edited on "America and Russia." Mr. Hale has also written* Horace Greeley: Voice of the People *and numerous other books.*

O n a wintry November day in Washington in 1933, two quite spare, tall American officials of high rank and collected demeanor emerged from under the mansards of the old State Department building to journey to Union Station and there greet a squat, rotund, grinning foreigner who in the eyes of many of their compatriots was a dangerous revolutionary. The moment itself was revolutionary, even in a sartorial sense. Protocol prescribed that when our Secretary of State and his assistants received the visiting foreign minister of another sovereign power, formal morning dress be worn. Yet on this occasion, so Under Secretary William Phillips recorded of the trip across town that he and his chief, Secretary of State Cordell Hull, undertook that day to welcome Soviet Foreign Commissar Maxim Litvinov, "None of us wore top hats because [Litvinov] came as the representative of a government not yet officially recognized by the United States."

The affable Russian, speaking excellent English and himself wearing a snap-brim felt hat, had come here to achieve exactly that recognition, and thus to restore the American-Russian relations that had been broken off in 1918 with the United States' refusal to deal with the atheistic, debt-repudiating, proselytizing new Bolshevik regime of Lenin and Trotsky. The breach had left the world's two potentially greatest powers, after more than a century of mutual cordiality, not speaking to each other for the next fifteen years. Yet now suddenly, it seemed, America's mood had changed. On the very afternoon of his arrival, Litvinov was taken in to see President Franklin D. Roosevelt, also eager to resolve what he called "this anomalous situation." After barely a week of discussions the United States—the one great nation still refusing to accept what Lenin had wrought—agreed to do business with his heir, Joseph Stalin.

In return, the Soviets agreed to mend some ways of theirs that had been particularly offensive to us. They promised to honor at least some of the debts Russia owed America and its citizens, to refrain from fomenting subversive agitation in our midst through their Communist International (or Comintern), and to protect the religious and other civil rights of American nationals in Russia. Ambassadors and a growing wealth of goods would be exchanged, and all or nearly all would now be well between our contrasting fellow republics.

Along this new route to reconciliation, however, traveling conditions were to be as subarctic as northern Russia itself: protracted deep freezes suddenly followed by brief, torrid summer; bright sunshine giving way to violent squalls and sudden darkness. The route, moreover, led over treacherous terrain, with every step along the way a challenge to the most surefooted and imaginative of explorer-diplomats.

Alas! Again, as during America's most demanding previous test —the erupting Russia of the winter of 1917–18—we had painfully few men equal to the task at hand. We had floundered then in Petrograd because we had been amateurish, indecisive, and entangled in cross-purposes. What had we learned during the intervening years about how to comport ourselves when returning to the land of the Great Bear? As in 1917–18, we now proceeded to send to Russia a series of emissaries of sharply contrasting backgrounds, commitments, and beliefs. Moreover, on occasion we again sent several simultaneously, thereby further blurring our "image."

America found itself represented in Moscow first by a millionaire, William C. Bullitt, who had been greatly taken with the Soviets at the outset and ended totally at odds with them; next by a multimillionaire, Joseph E. Davies, who became greatly taken with the Soviets and remained that way for the rest of his days; later by a crusty, retired admiral, William H. Standley, who talked back firmly to the Soviets but also to President Roosevelt, and fell out with both. And these were but a few of the contrasting American visitors to face the Russian monolith.

In the Petrograd of 1917–18 our affairs had become snarled through the presence of proliferating, independent American missions —military, Red Cross, propaganda, etc.—all bypassing our ambassador and feuding with one another. In Moscow, during a second wartime, we were to enlarge upon those precedents by establishing massive lend-lease and military-aid missions also independent of our principal envoy and, moreover, headed by successive chiefs—Generals Philip R. Faymonville and John R. Deane—of wholly diverging viewpoints. The President's personal bright star, Harry L. Hopkins, flew in briefly through the early wartime Moscow sky, as did Averell Harriman, later to return as America's able regular ambassador. Ex-Ambassador Davies oddly reappeared, too, and both a would-be President, Wendell Willkie, and an itinerant Vice President, Henry Wallace, showed up. While we spoke with multiple voices, the Kremlin talked back with one.

Clearly the President was of a divided and changing mind when confronting the heirs of Marx and Lenin. He was not alone. Our whole nation was uncertain how to deal, if deal we must, with this vexing, frightening, secretive colossus. Hence we exported to Moscow during the 1930's and the war years all our own domestic ideological differences about it—every emissary representing his own faiths or fears.

In 1933, though, when the proposal to strike up official relations with the Soviet pariahs received the new President's attention, there was widespread agreement to this much at least: let's give it a try. Times had changed radically since 1918—had been changing, so far as American estimation of Russia was concerned, for quite a number of years. For one thing, the Soviet regime had proved itself stable and responsible (save when it came to that matter of debts); it had emerged far enough from its seclusion to confer with the West at Geneva about disarmament and to ring general alarms about the new menace of militarist Japan. For another, the new, industrializing Russia had become a natural American market—an increasingly desirable and important one as the onset of world-wide depression shriveled every other.

Thus encouraged—and kept up to date on Russian affairs by

William C. Bullitt in 1918, when the twenty-eight-year-old Philadelphian was an attaché of the American Peace Commission at Versailles. In 1933 he became America's first ambassador to Soviet Russia.

journalists like Walter Duranty, William Henry Chamberlin, and Vincent Sheean—Americans had become increasingly fascinated by what they called the "Soviet experiment," even while preserving varying degrees of distaste for it. No man had been more fascinated all along than the wealthy Philadelphian William C. Bullitt, who in 1919, at twenty-eight, had persuaded President Wilson to send him on an unofficial mission to the Bolsheviks to sound out possible conciliatory sentiments among them. Angered by Wilson's abrupt dismissal of his hopeful report, Bullitt had denounced what he held to be American folly, and subsequently resumed his ardent advocacy of American Soviet *rapprochement.* Intense, articulate, a polished Main Line aristocrat but also a maverick, Bullitt had at once attracted the attention of the incoming President Roosevelt—a man often drawn to such mixtures—with the result that early in 1933 he was sent to Moscow to repeat, in effect, his exploratory mission of 1919. And when this time the response brought Litvinov to Washington with powers to conclude an agreement on very broad terms, it seemed only logical to dispatch the enthusiastic Bullitt to Moscow as America's first ambassador to the Soviet Union.

He arrived there that December, bringing with him as Third Secretary a very young Foreign Service officer named George F. Kennan (soon to be joined by another named Charles E. Bohlen), and established himself across Red Square from the Kremlin in the National Hotel, the grubby capital's cavernous refuge for foreigners. Immediately Bullitt found himself receiving, over and beyond the respect due an envoy, the regime's marks of favor as a special friend. Litvinov staged for him a "tremendous" reception; and Stalin, who "until my arrival had never received any ambassador," summoned Bullitt and assured him that "At any moment, day or night, if you wish to see me you have only to ask and I will see you at once."

Yet the honeymoon begun so deliriously lasted only a very few months. By March, 1934, Bullitt was sending home flustered, disappointed cables about "misunderstandings" on matters ranging from Litvinov's debt agreement (which was not being fulfilled) to Moscow's permission for an American Embassy building to be erected there (which was now being blocked). "Oral promises of members of the Soviet government are not to be taken seriously," the veteran proponent of closer ties sourly concluded. By October, infuriated by the Kremlin's default on still another promise—that of curbing the activities of the Comintern within American borders—Bullitt reached the point of cabling Washington. "I think I might go so far as to intimate to Litvinov verbally that we might sever diplomatic relations if the Comintern should be allowed to get out of hand."

The falling out reflected underlying antagonisms between the two nations which the first genial meetings in Washington and Moscow had covered over, not resolved. It was also America's introduction to a typical Soviet tactic: demanding a foot when given an inch. Having received the accolade of recognition, the Kremlin now wanted speedy American credits and support of its drive for "collective-security" pacts against the rising threats of Nazi Germany, Fascist Italy, and Japan; America, on the other hand, insisted on settlement of at least some of Russia's debts to us before there could be talk of going further (and collective security was something that our still-isolationist republic especially did not wish to pursue). So a new freeze set in between the two capitals—coldest in Moscow as between Bullitt and Litvinov. The Kremlin had erred in assuming that its American friend Bullitt would be all-compliant. Bullitt had erred in assuming that the Russians, whom he had trusted, would live up to their word. Stalin's promised "open door" slammed shut in Bullitt's face (during a whole year, the two conferred only once), and the American who in 1933 had entered Moscow in triumph as its favored guest quit it in 1936 in frustration as one of Soviet Russia's embittered critics.

The Kremlin had learned a lesson too: never again an American liberal, with all the mercurial tendencies of the breed! Far better to have from America a hardheaded, stalwart capitalist—a "class enemy" to be sure, but at least one whose reactions you could predict. So the Soviets were relieved when President Roosevelt chose as his next envoy to them the prominent corporation lawyer Joseph E. Davies, financier, politician, and sharer—through his marriage to Mrs. Marjorie Post Close Hutton, the daughter of C. W. Post of Post Toasties—in an immense fortune. Yet Moscow was due for some surprises at Davies' hand. So was America.

A handsome, gregarious figure of many-sided accomplishment and charm, Davies had early begun moving in leading Democratic circles. He had turned down President Wilson's offer of the ambassadorship to czarist Russia in 1913, but later served Wilson as chairman of the

Federal Trade Commission and as economic adviser at the Versailles peace conference. A close friend and political backer of Franklin D. Roosevelt since Wilsonian days, he was going forth now to Moscow as the President's immediate confidant (with the result, as Secretary of State Hull was to complain, that Davies, like Bullitt before him, frequently communicated with Roosevelt directly, "over my head").

All this was impressive. But what seemed to impress the Soviets most of all was the regal state in which Ambassador and Mrs. Davies commenced their expedition to darkest Moscow. Thirty trunks, fifty smaller pieces of luggage, and six personal servants accompanied them. ("We are going to live in Moscow very quietly, very simply," explained Davies; "'When in Rome,' you know . . .") Mistrusting Soviet produce, they also took along some two thousand pints of frozen American cream (Birds Eye process, owned by Mrs. Davies' General Foods), together with twenty-five freezers in which to store it. "Contrary to popular belief," said a Soviet spokesman in New York, "there are cows in Russia."

Half a year later, when supplies ran low, Mrs. Davies was to order another two thousand pints, along with *two tons* of frozen meats, fruits, and vegetables from home. Yet Soviet leaders, far from being affronted by this swollen self-indulgence amid Russia's lean times, were fascinated by it. Coming from below, they had tasted enough of power to like to indulge themselves, too—and the most Lucullan table to be seen in Moscow since the revolution now beckoned them. It soon appeared that the master of Spasso House (the stately mansion of a czarist grandee acquired as the American Embassy) was surprisingly hospitable to their minds as well.

The paunchy Litvinov, restored to amiability now that the demanding Bullitt was gone and this expansive capitalist was here, flattered Davies by telling him (as Davies promptly reported to Washington) that "I had acquired more information and knowledge of Russia in the three months I was here than any other ambassador had obtained in two years." He then went on to ask the new ambassador's general impressions. "I told him briefly that I was very much impressed with what they were doing, with the strength of their leadership, the difficulties they were overcoming; that I felt they were presently sincerely devoted to peace . . ." Meanwhile the colorful Mrs. Davies, to the astonishment of the British ambassador ("I have been here seven years and haven't been able to get so much as a toe in their house!"), was invited to lunch at the country *dacha* of Mme. Molotov, the Premier's consort.

It was a new thaw, evidently—passing at once into balmy summer. Then what, amid all this sweetness and light, was a secret, nocturnal Soviet agent doing in the attic of Spasso House? We come to the incident of Second Secretary Kennan and the night the Davies' cream turned sour. It is recounted by Charles W. Thayer, a young Philadelphian who had become the assistant to the gifted, Russian-speaking Kennan-Bohlen team that often had to pull ambassadorial chestnuts out of the fire.

As Thayer tells it in *Bears in the Caviar*, they had discovered that a Soviet spy was in the process of "bugging" Mr. Davies' office with a microphone run down from the attic. After several fruitless nights of vigil up there to try to observe him, they retired to more comfortable quarters below, leaving a net of cross-wire alarms to alert them at his next visit. But when the intruder returned, he got away in the night—after knocking out the entire Spasso House electrical system. Two days later, Ambassador Davies' butler reported to Thayer: "Two of the deep-freezes seem to have failed to get back into action after we reconnected the current."

"What was in them?"

"The frozen cream, and it's passed all saving."

There were indeed several hundred pints of well-publicized Davies cream rotting in the basement, and there was only one way of getting rid of them so as not to damage the Davies prestige. Since all regular Embassy employees were under close Soviet surveillance, the only thing for Thayer to do was to round up some Russian workmen to help him dump a truckload of the stuff in a deserted pine forest.

There were more hazards facing Davies than espionage and sour cream. As Kennan was to point out in a searching memorandum, "The Position of an American Ambassador in Moscow," there was Soviet evasion, double talk, secrecy, dilatoriness, and a tactic of isolating the American envoy and his staff from all but the most superficial contacts with Russians. But greatest of all (though Kennan did not bring this up) was the danger of impressionable and gullible thinking on the part of the envoy himself—and of this, Davies is one of diplomacy's classic exhibits.

In setting out, as he tells us in *Mission to Moscow* (the best-selling memoir that was to be made into one of the most debated movies of the war years), his verbal instructions from the President were to seek to persuade the Soviets to break the debt and trade impasse, meanwhile assuming a posture of "dignified friendliness" qualified by "definite reserve." Reserve, however, flew out the window at his first meeting with Soviet President Kalinin. "A fine type," Davies called him, "a kind, good man." But this was nothing compared to the Ambassador's enthusiasm on meeting Stalin himself: "His brown eye is exceedingly kindly and gentle. A child would like to sit in his lap and a dog would sidle up to him. . . . Throughout [the interview] he joked and laughed at times. He has a sly humor."

Yet there was little to laugh about during Davies' first year in Moscow. For his arrival there coincided with the start of the second and greatest of the series of "purge" trials that bewildered the world and bitterly divided those until then inclined to befriend the "Soviet experiment." A long procession of hitherto high-ranking Communist ministers, intellectuals, ideologues, and generals were quickly tried for counterrevolutionary conspiracy and duly led off to execution. Were the trials a frame-up? Had the accused been tortured in some mysterious fashion, and was this Stalin's Oriental way of disposing of his rivals?

Many observers of the macabre spectacle were torn by doubt, but Davies, watching from one of the best diplomatic seats in the Soviet Supreme Court as the ''Old Bolshevik'' editor Karl Radek and nearly a score of others went under, seemed untroubled. He wrote home that he accepted at face value Public Prosecutor Andrei Vishinsky's thesis of a dark terrorist plot and blandly concluded after the prisoners had been condemned: ''The purge . . . cleansed the country and rid it of treason.'' This view he also maintained when visiting London. Dining in company with Winston Churchill, Davies was chagrined to find that it did not go down well there, ''so violent is the prejudice. . . . I gave the facts as interpreted from the Soviet viewpoint.''

An American ambassador handing out in London the ''facts'' as interpreted by Stalin: What next?

Early in 1938 President Roosevelt realized that his man in Moscow was a liability—for all his popularity there, he still had not achieved that debt settlement—and withdrew him to the safer post of Brussels. Litvinov threw Davies a great farewell dinner, and the amiable visitor left trailing such pronouncements as ''I do not think that the world is in any real danger from communism for many years to come,'' and, later, ''It is not [the Soviets'] intent to seek to project communism in the United States.''

The Soviet Union was, however, embarking on a course that would once more lead to a freeze in Russo-American relations. For fully three years we would again be barely on speaking terms; for many months on end—particularly those of the Munich crisis, the height of Western humiliation and distress—we were to be without an ambassador in Moscow at all.

For while the Soviets had been clamoring for joint opposition to Hitler, Mussolini, the aggressive Japanese, and then Franco, America (like its old European partners, Britain and France) had avoided doing anything effective about it—a fact that had enormously increased Communist prestige among all those aroused to resistance. Roosevelt in the fall of 1937 had tried to reverse America's position by his historic ''quarantine-the-aggressors'' speech, but when he was unable to prevail, it next became the turn of the Soviets to reverse their own: by the next summer they were threatening to retreat into isolation unless we came out of ours, and by the spring of 1939, in the aftermath of Munich, they did precisely that, furthermore denouncing the Western allies as ''warmongers'' just when these at last were arming against the general danger.

In August came Russia's second turnabout—alliance with the former enemy, in the pact that helped unleash Hitler's forces and win for Russia a share of Poland. This was followed by Russia's ''dreadful rape of Finland,'' as Roosevelt termed it, which led us to place an embargo on many exports to this latest aggressor, while at home sentiment was rising in favor of aiding embattled France and Britain. In Moscow an appropriately chilly Foreign Service professional, Ambassador Laurence A. Steinhardt, represented us, engaged largely in delivering messages of protest over such incidents as the Soviet detention of the American freighter *City of Flint*.

Then on June 22, 1941, Hitler performed *his* fateful turnabout: he invaded Russia with 175 divisions. Overnight the whole configuration of affairs changed again: the Western "warmongers" of yesterday became in Russia's eyes partners in her "Great Patriotic War," while a hitherto lonely Britain and a defensive America set out to build with Russia the Grand Alliance. In barely a month, the President's personal adviser, Harry L. Hopkins, was on the Moscow scene with an introduction from Roosevelt asking Stalin to treat Hopkins with "the identical confidence you would feel if you were talking directly to me." Cordially welcomed at the Kremlin, he declared to Stalin "the determination of the President and our government to extend all possible aid to the Soviet Union at the earliest possible time."

It was characteristic of Roosevelt under pressure that he conveyed this vital message not through his regular ambassador on the ground or through a visit by Secretary of State Hull (with whom his own relations had become distant) but by a special emissary. Hopkins, for his part, hastened to point out to Stalin that his mission was "not a diplomatic one" in the usual sense. In title, Hopkins was Roosevelt's administrator of lend lease. In fact, he was his Colonel House and closest friend; and the skill of this extraordinary expediter, sensitive yet durable, often ill and nerve-racked yet searching and thorough, was never greater than during the crucial sessions—lasting only two days—in which he won the inscrutable Stalin's confidence, gained from him a complete picture of Soviet military strengths and weaknesses, placed Soviet-American relations upon an entirely new footing, and did all this so circumspectly as to draw from the sidetracked Hull and Steinhardt no audible murmur of criticism. As Hopkins' biographer, Robert E. Sherwood, remarks: "This was indeed the turning point in the wartime relations of Britain and the United States with the Soviet Union."

It also marked a point from which there was to be no turning back. Stalin, whose armies were reeling under German impact across the Ukraine toward Moscow, needed immediately great supplies of guns and aircraft metal. Many expert Western observers on and around the scene were pessimistic; why, asked Major Ivan Yeaton, the American military attaché at Moscow, lend aid to a doomed cause? Yet when Hopkins reported to Roosevelt, "I feel ever so confident about this front . . . There is unbounded determination to win," his word tilted the scales. Within a few days, at their seaborne conference in Newfoundland's Argentia Bay at which the Atlantic Charter was framed, Roosevelt and Churchill determined to rush all possible equipment to Stalin even at some risk to their own arsenals, and to send at once a joint supply mission to explore his needs. This was the occasion that brought Averell Harriman for the first time to Moscow, along with England's Lord Beaverbrook. Two weeks after they arrived, German spearheads had pushed to within thirty miles of the capital, government offices were being evacuated to Kuibyshev

*In September of 1941 Roose-
velt sent Harry Hopkins as his
special emissary to Stalin.*

in the rear, and Major Yeaton was reporting that the end of Russian resistance might not be far away.

Yet while Americans were concentrating on first things first—to help Russia stave off defeat—Stalin was already thinking far ahead to the shape that Europe should take after the victory. Here was the great misstep on our road to Yalta: not only did Western leaders seem to fail to realize how large the Soviets might loom in the event of victory, but they refused to discuss the future with Stalin at a time advantageous to themselves, when he was so hard-pressed and weak. Thus it happened that soon after Pearl Harbor, Roosevelt, though aware of Soviet territorial demands in Poland and the Baltic area, specifically asked Stalin to omit such questions from the treaty of alliance then being negotiated. The absence of territorial discussion now left the new alliance a one-way street—we were giving the Russians more and more aid against Hitler's onslaught, without pressing them to surrender some of their aspirations in return.

How much aid—and when? How soon are you going to open a "second front" to relieve us? When are you going to recognize our just claims in eastern Europe? These were the constant calls from Moscow, and each brought new East-West collisions. Only a few months after Hopkins' warm reception at the Kremlin, the visiting Harriman was given a brusque one: Stalin showed impatience at the slowness of Western aid and warmed only when Harriman promised him five thousand jeeps. The President, aware how tough a customer we were dealing with, now thought we had better send him as resident ambassador a markedly tough personality of our own, and so Stalin got a battleship admiral.

The President had a particular fondness for the Navy and its proven leaders—and William H. Standley had served him outstandingly as Chief of Naval Operations. A square-jawed, sharp-spoken quarter-deck disciplinarian with forty-five years in the service, Standley had no experience of Russia except for a brief ceremonial visit to Vladivostok in 1896 as a midshipman. But upon retirement he had become one of Roosevelt's staunchest supporters in the long domestic battle for aid to the Allies before Pearl Harbor; such a man might serve with insight and muscle.

His first reaction to Stalin differed noticeably from that of Davies. Standley found the Soviet dictator "a cocky, healthy-looking individual, with swarthy complexion and an Oriental cast of countenance . . ." A man of stalwart build himself, Standley carried chips on both broad shoulders: he was easily offended when Stalin kept him waiting or when Washington failed to brief him fully or when visiting firemen from home intruded. He wanted to run his Embassy as a "taut ship" in perilous waters with himself in sole command—a logical aspiration, but quixotic in view of the Rooseveltian way of conducting wartime affairs abroad. Messages passed directly between Roosevelt and Stalin, "leapfrogging over my tophatted head," Standley complained; summit conferences were arranged and second-front commitments entered into without his being the wiser; and Hopkins' and Harriman's lend-lease man on the spot, Colonel (later Brigadier General) Faymonville, pursued his own quite independent course. The old admiral finally exploded when two further visiting emissaries, Wendell Willkie and the familiar Joe Davies, arrived on the scene with powers to go over his head to the Kremlin.

Willkie, the President's 1940 electoral opponent who had subsequently been enlisted into the bipartisan war effort, touched down in Moscow during his globe-girdling "One World" tour in the fall of 1942. He delivered himself of statements declaring America's unqualified friendship for Soviet Russia, and after closeting himself alone with Stalin went so far as to remark to Standley that some of the things he had learned there were too secret for even the ambassador to know. As if this were not galling enough, Willkie made a point of telling the world that Soviet Russia had been misrepresented in the United States and that he wished to "put over a more favorable picture" of it. "Many among the democracies fear and mistrust Soviet Russia . . ." he wrote. "Such fear is weakness . . ." He issued in Moscow a call, echoing Stalin's, for the early opening of a second front.

"Mr. Willkie, I have been very patient," Standley finally exploded. "Now I feel it my duty to remind you that there is only one United States representative in the Soviet Union, and I, the American Ambassador, am that representative."

But Standley's patience was to be tried even more by the brief return engagement of Davies, who arrived the following spring on a 10,000-mile round trip from Washington—in a special plane, with a crew of nine plus his personal staff and physician—simply to deliver a letter from Roosevelt to Stalin proposing a top-level meeting. It was a message that conceivably could have been delivered to the Kremlin by Standley himself from his office four blocks away. Welcomed at the airport by Soviet dignitaries as a returning hero, Davies insisted on delivering his letter alone. He had also brought along an advance print of the Warner Brothers movie made from his *Mission to Moscow* (Stalin was flatteringly portrayed by Manart Kippen, Davies by Walter Huston), which he prevailed upon the dictator to show after dinner in the Kremlin projection room. Stalin was visibly bored by it, and diplomatic guests went up in arms over its obvious distortions of the history of the purge trials and acceptance of the Soviet line on them. Next, Davies met the American press corps, and on hearing its complaints that the Soviets were failing to show appreciation for American aid, tongue-lashed the correspondents and accused them of "non-co-operation." "His lack of knowledge regarding Russia," wrote Quentin Reynolds, "shocked us all."

The reason behind the Willkie-Davies visits was that the President had lost confidence in his newest ambassador, while Standley had taken to grumbling about the President. Standley felt himself alone in a hostile environment and at odds with Washington, which he felt was playing the game on Stalin's terms. Our policy, he snorted, was only "Do not antagonize the Russians, give them everything they want, for, after all, they are killing Germans . . ."

Increasingly suspicious, Standley fell out particularly with General Faymonville, the gifted, Russian-speaking Regular Army officer who was managing lend-lease from an office down the corridor, and whose predictions as to the staying power of the Red Army when others had given up hope in it had been amply borne out. Feeling that Faymonville was working too closely and enthusiastically with the Russians, Standley made direct representations to Roosevelt and Hopkins that the general be placed under Standley's orders. He got him reduced in size and then banished—though at the cost of any remaining White House good will toward himself.*

Standley had the ill fortune to represent us in Moscow during our hardest times there. During 1942 and most of 1943 the promised American aid never lived up to expectations, due first to enormous convoy losses and then to our own build-up for the second front that Stalin had demanded. But the Soviet chieftain kept upbraiding us

---

*A personal recollection: While at the Office of War Information in 1942, in charge of broadcasts to Germany, I was assigned by Robert E. Sherwood to go to Moscow on a mission arising from an offer made by Foreign Minister Vishinsky—that of my speaking nightly from there to eastern-front Germans in the name of the Voice of America. At that time, when American troops had not yet come to grips with Germans, it seemed a promising idea to convey in this fashion the message of Allied unity, and Vishinsky had promised that, apart from sheer military censorship, what I said over the Moscow radio would be subjected to no surveillance whatsoever. After I had waited several months with packed suitcases for travel orders, though, the mission was finally vetoed by Ambassador Standley on the ground that this, too, might lead to too-close collaboration with the Russians.

for our delays in respect to both. When Allied armies streaked across Sicily and landed on the Italian mainland, though, the Bear warmed once more; and when in October, 1943, Standley having been retired to the shades, Secretary Hull arrived in Moscow for a four-power foreign ministers' conference accompanied by a new ambassador (Harriman) and a new military-aid chief (General Deane), Stalin was genial. With enormous forces now building up for OVERLORD (the Anglo-American descent upon Normandy) and supplies flowing to Russia over several seas, broad pledges of mutual aid and confidence were exchanged. Harriman was particularly elated when, in a daring mood, he proposed a toast at the Kremlin to the day "when we would be fighting together against the Japs," and Molotov suddenly responded: "Why not—gladly—*the time will come.*"

Yet Harriman was not so elated as to lose perspective. A shrewd observer and Presidential trouble shooter, he had known all the ups and downs of American-Soviet relations, and the reassuring atmosphere of the Moscow foreign ministers' conference had not concealed from him its lack of real achievement.

Now the final stage of the road led via Teheran and Moscow to Yalta—conferences marked by increasing inter-Allied warmth as the outlines of military victory became clearer, although the ultimate political consequences remained hidden in the veil. It was as if the civil plenipotentiaries, having failed to lay a basis of searching diplomacy with each other at the start, had come to feel that the soldiers would resolve their problems for them by providing a smashing triumph that would leave everyone happy—if exhausted. Stalin was enormously impressed by the prospects of OVERLORD. Churchill was equally impressed by the avenging progress of the Red armies and supported Stalin's claim for territory to protect Russia from future German invasions, even though this meant shifting Poland several hundred miles westward. Roosevelt, though he said he wanted no part of the

In 1943 Americans cheered the wartime alliance of Roosevelt, Stalin, and Churchill. This cartoon from the Arizona Republic *questioned Stalin's intentions.*

Polish wrangle—not until after the 1944 elections, in any case—was inclined to support the Anglo-Soviet understanding reached on this point during the summit meeting at Teheran at the end of 1943.

Harriman, though a devoted admirer of Roosevelt and a believer in mobility in dealing with the Soviets, was not quite so sure. Shouldn't we, he asked, try to awaken them to the fact that we expected them to give as well as receive? In this he was supported by his top military-aid man, General Deane, a newcomer constituted very differently from his predecessor, General Faymonville. Deane demanded detailed information from the Soviets as to just what they were doing with supplies, even as Harriman kept requiring of them more specific knowledge of their political plans as Hitler's legions fell back. But then came the great convergence of Anglo-American armies upon Germany, (simultaneously with the Soviet armies' even greater one); the knowledge that the Soviets would join our hard-won march against Japan; and a profound feeling that amid so many mutual sacrifices made and joint victories won, the problems remaining between us—the fate of eastern Europe, the control of Germany, the level of reparations, the structure of the Balkans, the ratio of representation in the new United Nations—could be amicably resolved.

This was the immense agenda that faced the Big Three chiefs of government when they met at Yalta in the Crimea in February, 1945, for a week of breathless negotiating and climactic banqueting that would give new shape to the world. Time was short at Yalta—too short; the chieftains had to hurry home to direct the closing scenes of the military drama in Europe and stage its last act in Asia. Moreover, Roosevelt and Hopkins were both ailing; the new Secretary of State who accompanied them, Edward R. Stettinius, was inexperienced; and our standing representation in Russia itself had been so assorted and at times discredited that the President found himself with little in the way of a concerted body of first-hand experience there on which to draw. In our massive delegation at the Livadia Palace, the effective "Russian experts" were just two—the overburdened Harriman and young "Chip" Bohlen, serving as interpreter.

Many settlements, or what passed for settlements, were reached. The westward shift of Poland was confirmed; pledges as to the self-determination of liberated peoples were renewed; the Soviet Union, about to enter the war against Japan, was recognized as a major power in the Pacific, with legitimate aspirations there. The Soviets, in turn, recognized America's particular interest in succoring the regime of Chiang Kai-shek, gave ground on some points concerning joint occupation of Germany, and seemed willing to forego crushing reparations if it could obtain American reconstruction aid. The debate over seating at the United Nations also resulted in what both sides then regarded a fair draw; and such was Yalta's resulting mood that Prime Minister Churchill spoke in exalted terms of "the glories of future possibilities . . . before us," while Harry Hopkins reported a deep sense of accomplishment there. "We really believed in our hearts," Hopkins said, "that this was the dawn of the new day we had all been praying

The diplomats behind the Big Three at Yalta are (from left) Britain's Eden, America's Stettinius, Russia's Molotov, and (far right)Averell Harriman.

for . . . We were absolutely certain that we had won the first great victory of the peace."

Perhaps, then, all—or almost all—would be well at last. Yet it was not to be so; and bitter blame has been heaped upon the Yalta Conference, as if it were the author of all our woes with Russia since. Yet perhaps it was culpable not so much for what it did as for what it did not do. Yalta left more matters unresolved than settled. In its headlong haste to catch up with the facts of military success, it was a political convocation that came too late. Moreover, it was one to which the warring partners came as unequals in the sense that they harbored very different political intentions, clothe them as they might. All spoke of liberation, but to the Soviets this meant also annexation of the liberated. On the other hand, the Western allies had no ulterior territorial motives: true, the British were willing to bargain with the Russians over spheres of influence so as to preserve their own, but the United States had no thought—and, it was agreed by all sides at home, no need—of aggrandizement at all.

America's position all along had been to avoid making postwar commitments until the war itself was nearly won. As late as October, 1944, Roosevelt had cabled Harriman (then sitting in on the Churchill-Stalin meetings at Moscow that prefaced Yalta), "It is important that I retain complete freedom of action after this conference is over." Yet the area of such freedom was narrowing fast as Red armies swarmed over southeastern and central Europe, pushing borders westward on their own. The most that could now be done about displaced Poland was an ambiguous formula calling for "reorganization" of the provisional Warsaw regime—by which the West meant a new government based on democratic elections, while Moscow meant one firmly attached to itself. The West asked for free ballot boxes all over eastern Europe; Moscow promised, but at the same time began converting once-free nations into satellites.

The ailing President, returning homeward across calm seas aboard the U.S.S. *Quincy* in the trust that Yalta's promise of freedom and equity would be fulfilled, was not to be spared disillusionment in the few weeks of life remaining to him. A mere fortnight later, Ambassador Harriman in Moscow was protesting sharply against Soviet moves to make defeated Rumania a captive state, and the West flatly refused to recognize the puppet regime set up there. More trouble was in store for our ambassador when an inter-Allied commission began to work out Yalta's indecisive plan for Poland. On April 2, after wrangling sessions in which Molotov had become more and more intransigent, Harriman reported flatly, "No agreement was reached on any point." Stalin himself, on the wire to Roosevelt, concurred. Harriman, for his part, was now reaching the point of recommending to Washington that further aid to Russia be suspended until Moscow ceased violating Yalta agreements. Then Stalin, suspicious because he had not been made party to the parleys between surrendering German commanders and advancing Anglo-American troops in Italy, cabled Roosevelt to charge deception and trickery. Roosevelt, aroused to the core, expressed "bitter resentment" at such "vile misrepresentations of my actions or those of my trusted subordinates." This and Stalin's reply were the last communications that passed between the two most powerful leaders of what had briefly been a common cause.

So the bright day dimmed even when the sun seemed to stand high. Roosevelt died, and Harriman in Moscow was alone in the gathering darkness. Once again, the modern world's two titans, so different in their ways and make-up, so subject to alternating currents of mutual attraction and repulsion, drew apart. We had been by turns cordial friends over great distances (never more so than during our own Revolution and the Napoleonic wars), far-removed yet mutually amenable expansionists through the later nineteenth century, uneasy allies in two world wars, and profound ideological antagonists in the aftermath of each. Yet we had never, despite all our differences, become declared enemies on the battlefield; in fact, we were the only two great powers to have preserved peace—or what passed for it—with one another during all this long span of modern time. We did not speak one another's language; perhaps in the deepest sense we never quite would. Yet some recognition of the madness of ever making war upon one another in the name of our two immense and kindred humanities on opposite sides of the globe seemed to have been borne in upon us both. Will the time now come when, if nuclear war is unimaginable and the sheer absence of war not enough, we may proceed with firmer skill to the building of peace?

Cornell Capa's 1969 photo-graph peers down Wall Street's glass and stone canyon toward the southern tip of Manhattan.

*Part
Five*

MODERN
AMERICA

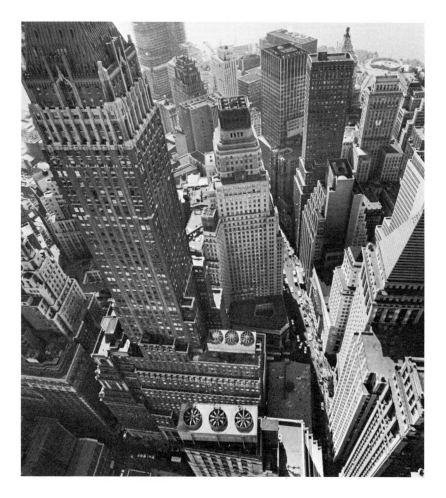

John Kenneth Galbraith

The Causes
of the
Great Crash

*The following essay is an example of analytical history at its best.
Without relying on narrative techniques, the Harvard economist
John Kenneth Galbraith takes apart the economy of the 1920's and
shows us how its weaknesses led to the Great Depression of the 1930's.
In the course of doing so, he also "takes apart," in the colloquial sense
of that expression, the Presidents of the 1920's and a number of their
leading advisers.*

*The effectiveness and power of the essay depend upon a number
of factors. One is Galbraith's mastery both of the facts he deals with
and of the economic mechanisms of the society; he discusses few events
that are not thoroughly familiar to students of the subject, but he has
an unfailing eye for what is significant. Another is his gift for anecdote
and the pithy phrase. As he says, the epigram that Elbert H. Gary
of U. S. Steel "never saw a blast furnace until his death" is well
known; but not everyone who writes about Gary knows enough to
use it. Still a third is Galbraith's ability to state his own opinions
without qualification and at the same time without passion, to make
the kind of calm, reasoned judgments that are characteristic of a
convinced but unprejudiced and intelligent mind. All these qualities
explain why his books, such as* American Capitalism, The Affluent
Society, *and* The Great Crash, 1929 *(a fuller treatment of the subject
of this essay), have been both popular and critical successes.*

*T*he decade of the twenties, or more exactly the eight years between the postwar depression of 1920–21 and the sudden collapse
of the stock market in October, 1929, were prosperous ones
in the United States. The total output of the economy increased by
more than 50 per cent. The preceding decades had brought the automobile; now came many more and also roads on which they could
be driven with reasonable reliability and comfort. There was much
building. The downtown section of the mid-continent city—Des
Moines, Omaha, Minneapolis—dates from these years. It was then,
more likely than not, that what is still the leading hotel, the tallest
office building, and the biggest department store went up. Radio
arrived, as of course did gin and jazz.

These years were also remarkable in another respect, for as time
passed it became increasingly evident that the prosperity could
not last. Contained within it were the seeds of its own destruction.
The country was heading into the gravest kind of trouble. Herein lies
the peculiar fascination of the period for a study in the problem of
leadership. For almost no steps were taken during these years to
arrest the tendencies which were obviously leading, and did lead,
to disaster.

At least four things were seriously wrong, and they worsened
as the decade passed. And knowledge of them does not depend on
the always brilliant assistance of hindsight. At least three of these
flaws were highly visible and widely discussed. In ascending order,
not of importance but of visibility, they were as follows:

First, income in these prosperous years was being distributed with
marked inequality. Although output per worker rose steadily during
the period, wages were fairly stable, as also were prices. As a result,
business profits increased rapidly and so did incomes of the wealthy
and the well-to-do. This tendency was nurtured by assiduous and
successful efforts of Secretary of the Treasury Andrew W. Mellon
to reduce income taxes with special attention to the higher brackets.
In 1929 the 5 per cent of the people with the highest incomes received
perhaps a quarter of all personal income. Between 1919 and 1929
the share of the one per cent who received the highest incomes increased by approximately one seventh. This meant that the economy
was heavily and increasingly dependent on the luxury consumption
of the well-to-do and on their willingness to reinvest what they did
not or could not spend on themselves. Anything that shocked the
confidence of the rich either in their personal or in their business
future would have a bad effect on total spending and hence on the
behavior of the economy.

This was the least visible flaw. To be sure, farmers, who were not
participating in the general advance, were making themselves heard;
and twice during the period the Congress passed far-reaching relief
legislation which was vetoed by Coolidge. But other groups were
much less vocal. Income distribution in the United States had long
been unequal. The inequality of these years did not seem exceptional.
The trade-union movement was also far from strong. In the early

twenties the steel industry was still working a twelve-hour day and, in some jobs, a seven-day week. (Every two weeks when the shift changed a man worked twice around the clock.) Workers lacked the organization or the power to deal with conditions like this; the twelve-hour day was, in fact, ended as the result of personal pressure by President Harding on the steel companies, particularly on Judge Elbert H. Gary, head of the United States Steel Corporation. Judge Gary's personal acquaintance with these working conditions was thought to be slight, and this gave rise to Benjamin Stolberg's now classic observation that the Judge "never saw a blast furnace until his death." In all these circumstances the increasingly lopsided income distribution did not excite much comment or alarm. Perhaps it would have been surprising if it had.

But the other three flaws in the economy were far less subtle. During World War I the United States ceased to be the world's greatest debtor country and became its greatest creditor. The consequences of this change have so often been described that they have the standing of a cliché. A debtor country could export a greater value of goods than it imported and use the difference for interest and debt repayment. This was what we did before the war. But a creditor must import a greater value than it exports if those who owe it money are to have the wherewithal to pay interest and principal. Otherwise the creditor must either forgive the debts or make new loans to pay off the old.

During the twenties the balance was maintained by making new foreign loans. Their promotion was profitable to domestic investment houses. And when the supply of honest and competent foreign borrowers ran out, dishonest, incompetent, or fanciful borrowers were invited to borrow and, on occasion, bribed to do so. In 1927 Juan Leguia, the son of the then dictator of Peru, was paid $450,000 by the National City Company and J. & W. Seligman for his services in promoting a $50,000,000 loan to Peru which these houses marketed. Americans lost and the Peruvians didn't gain appreciably. Other Latin American republics got equally dubious loans by equally dubious devices. And, for reasons that now tax the imagination, so did a large number of German cities and municipalities. Obviously, once investors awoke to the character of these loans or there was any other shock to confidence, they would no longer be made. There would be nothing with which to pay the old loans. Given this arithmetic, there would be either a sharp reduction in exports or a wholesale default on the outstanding loans, or more likely both. Wheat and cotton farmers and others who depended on exports would suffer. So would those who owned the bonds. The buying power of both would be reduced. These consequences were freely predicted at the time.

The second weakness of the economy was the large-scale corporate thimblerigging that was going on. This took a variety of forms, of which by far the most common was the organization of corporations to hold stock in yet other corporations, which in turn held stock in yet other corporations. In the case of the railroads and the utilities, the purpose of this pyramid of holding companies was to obtain control of a very large number of operating companies with a very small investment in the ultimate holding company. A $100,000,000 electric utility, of which the capitalization was represented half by bonds and half by common stock, could be controlled with an investment of a little over $25,000,000—the value of just over half the common stock. Were a company then formed with the same capital structure to hold *this* $25,000,000 worth of common stock, it could be controlled with an investment of $6,250,000. On the next round the amount required would be less than $2,000,000. That $2,000,000 would still control the entire $100,000,000 edifice. By the end of the twenties, holding-company structures six or eight tiers high were a commonplace. Some of them—the utility pyramids of Insull and Associated Gas & Electric, and the railroad pyramid of the Van Sweringens—were marvelously complex. It is unlikely that anyone fully understood them or could.

In other cases companies were organized to hold securities in other companies in order to manufacture more securities to sell to the public. This was true of the great investment trusts. During 1929 one investment house, Goldman, Sachs & Company, organized and sold nearly a billion dollars' worth of securities in three interconnected investment trusts—Goldman Sachs Trading Corporation; Shenandoah Corporation; and Blue Ridge Corporation. All eventually depreciated virtually to nothing.

This corporate insanity was also highly visible. So was the damage. The pyramids would last only so long as earnings of the company at the bottom were secure. If anything happened to the dividends of the underlying company, there would be trouble, for upstream companies had issued bonds (or in practice sometimes preferred stock) against the dividends on the stock of the downstream companies. Once the earnings stopped, the bonds would go into default or the preferred stock would take over and the pyramid would collapse. Such a collapse would have a bad effect not only on the orderly prosecution of business and investment by the operating companies but also on confidence, investment, and spending by the community at large. The likelihood was increased because in any number of cities—Cleveland, Detroit, and Chicago were notable examples—the banks were deeply committed to these pyramids or had fallen under the control of the pyramiders.

Finally, and most evident of all, there was the stock market boom. Month after month and year after year the great bull market of the twenties roared on. Sometimes there were setbacks, but more often there were fantastic forward surges. In May of 1924 the New York *Times* industrials stood at 106; by the end of the year they were 134; by the end of 1925 they were up to 181. In 1927 the advance began in earnest—to 245 by the end of that year and on to 331 by the end of 1928. There were some setbacks in early 1929, but then came the fantastic summer explosion when in a matter of three months the averages went up another 110 points. This was the most frantic summer in our financial history. By its end, stock prices had nearly quadrupled as compared with four years earlier. Transactions on the New York Stock Exchange regularly ran to 5,000,000 or more shares a day. Radio Corporation of America went to 573¾ (adjusted) without ever having paid a dividend. Only the hopelessly eccentric, so it seemed, held securities for their income. What counted was the increase in capital values.

And since capital gains were what counted, one could vastly increase his opportunities by extending his holdings with borrowed funds—by buying on margin. Margin accounts expanded enormously, and from all over the country—indeed from all over the world— money poured into New York to finance these transactions. During the summer, brokers' loans increased at the rate of $400,000,000 a month. By September they totaled more than $7,000,000,000. The rate of interest on these loans varied from 7 to 12 per cent and went as high as 15.

This boom was also inherently self-liquidating. It could last only so long as new people, or at least new money, were swarming into the market in pursuit of the capital gains. This new demand bid up the stocks and made the capital gains. Once the supply of new customers began to falter, the market would cease to rise. Once the market stopped rising, some, and perhaps a good many, would start to cash in. If you are concerned with capital gains, you must get them while the getting is good. But the getting may start the market down, and this will one day be the signal for much more selling—both by those who are trying to get out and those who are being forced to sell securities that are no longer safely margined. Thus it was certain that the market would one day go down, and far more rapidly than it went up. Down it went with a thunderous crash in October of 1929. In a series of terrible days, of which Thursday, October 24, and Tuesday, October 29, were the most terrifying, billions in values were lost, and thousands of speculators—they had been called investors—were utterly and totally ruined.

This too had far-reaching effects. Economists have always deprecated the tendency to attribute too much to the great stock market collapse of 1929: this was the drama; the causes of the subsequent depression really lay deeper. In fact, the stock market crash was very important. It exposed the other weakness of the economy. The overseas loans on which the payments balance depended came to an end. The jerry-built holding-company structures came tumbling down. The investment-trust stocks collapsed. The crash put a marked crimp on borrowing for investment and therewith on business spending. It also removed from the economy some billions of consumer spending that was either based on, sanctioned by, or encouraged by the fact that the spenders had stock market gains. The crash was an intensely damaging thing.

And this damage, too, was not only foreseeable but foreseen. For months the speculative frenzy had all but dominated American life. Many times before in history—the South Sea Bubble, John

Cartoonist Forbell titled this 1929 drawing
"Club Life in America—The Stock Brokers."

Law's speculations, the recurrent real-estate booms of the last century, the great Florida land boom earlier in the same decade—there had been similar frenzy. And the end had always come, not with a whimper but a bang. Many men, including in 1929 the President of the United States, knew it would again be so.

The increasingly perilous trade balance, the corporate buccaneering, and the Wall Street boom—along with the less visible tendencies in income distribution—were all allowed to proceed to the ultimate disaster without effective hindrance. How much blame attaches to the men who occupied the presidency?

Warren G. Harding died on August 2, 1923. This, as only death can do, exonerates him. The disorders that led eventually to such trouble had only started when the fatal blood clot destroyed this now sad and deeply disillusioned man. Some would argue that his legacy was bad. Harding had but a vague perception of the economic processes over which he presided. He died owing his broker $180,000 in a blind account—he had been speculating disastrously while he was President, and no one so inclined would have been a good bet to curb the coming boom. Two of Harding's Cabinet officers, his secretary of the interior and his attorney general, were to plead the Fifth Amendment when faced with questions concerning their official acts, and the first of these went to jail. Harding brought his fellow townsman Daniel R. Crissinger to be his comptroller of the currency, although he was qualified for this task, as Samuel Hopkins Adams has suggested, only by the fact that he and the young Harding had stolen watermelons together. When Crissinger had had an ample opportunity to demonstrate his incompetence in his first post, he was made head of the Federal Reserve System. Here he had the central responsibility for action on the ensuing boom. Jack Dempsey, Paul Whiteman, or F. Scott Fitzgerald would have been at least equally qualified.

Yet it remains that Harding was dead before the real trouble started. And while he left in office some very poor men, he also left some very competent ones. Charles Evans Hughes, his secretary of state; Herbert Hoover, his secretary of commerce; and Henry C. Wallace, his secretary of agriculture, were public servants of vigor and judgment.

The problem of Herbert Hoover's responsibility is more complicated. He became President on March 4, 1929. At first glance this seems far too late for effective action. By then the damage had been done, and while the crash might come a little sooner or a little later, it was now inevitable. Yet Hoover's involvement was deeper than this—and certainly much deeper than Harding's. This he tacitly concedes in his memoirs, for he is at great pains to explain and, in some degree, to excuse himself.

For one thing, Hoover was no newcomer to Washington. He had been secretary of commerce under Harding and Coolidge. He had also been the strongest figure (not entirely excluding the President) in both Administration and party for almost eight years. He had a clear view of what was going on. As early as 1922, in a letter to Hughes, he expressed grave concern over the quality of the foreign loans that were being floated in New York. He returned several times to the subject. He knew about the corporate excesses. In the latter twenties he wrote to his colleagues and fellow officials (including Crissinger) expressing his grave concern over the Wall Street orgy. Yet he was content to express himself—to write letters and memoranda, or at most, as in the case of the foreign loans, to make an occasional speech. He could with propriety have presented his views of the stock market more strongly to the Congress and the public. He could also have maintained a more vigorous and persistent agitation within the Administration. He did neither. His views of the market were so little known that it celebrated his election and inauguration with a great upsurge. Hoover was in the boat and, as he himself tells, he knew where it was headed. But, having warned the man at the tiller, he rode along into the reef.

And even though trouble was inevitable, by March, 1929, a truly committed leader would still have wanted to do something. Nothing else was so important. The resources of the Executive, one might expect, would have been mobilized in a search for some formula to mitigate the current frenzy and to temper the coming crash. The assistance of the bankers, congressional leaders, and the Exchange authorities would have been sought. Nothing of the sort was done. As secretary of commerce, as he subsequently explained, he had thought himself frustrated by Mellon. But he continued Mellon in office. Henry M. Robinson, a sympathetic Los Angeles banker, was commissioned to go to New York to see his colleagues there and report. He returned to say that the New York bankers regarded things as sound. Richard Whitney, the vice-president of the Stock Exchange, was summoned to the White House for a conference on how to curb speculation. Nothing came of this either. Whitney also thought things were sound.

Both Mr. Hoover and his official biographers carefully explained that the primary responsibility for the goings on in New York City rested not with Washington but with the governor of New York State. That was Franklin D. Roosevelt. It was he who failed to rise to his responsibilities. The explanation is far too formal. The future of the whole country was involved. Mr. Hoover was the President of the whole country. If he lacked authority commensurate with this responsibility, he could have requested it. This, at a later date, President Roosevelt did not hesitate to do.

Finally, while by March of 1929 the stock market collapse was inevitable, something could still be done about the other accumulating disorders. The balance of payments is an obvious case. In 1931 Mr. Hoover did request a one-year moratorium on the inter-Allied (war) debts. This was a courageous and constructive step which came directly to grips with the problem. But the year before, Mr. Hoover, though not without reluctance, had signed the Hawley-Smoot tariff. "I shall approve the Tariff Bill. . . . It was undertaken as the result of pledges given by the Republican Party at Kansas City. . . . Platform promises must not be empty gestures." Hundreds of people—from Albert H. Wiggin, the head of the Chase National Bank, to Oswald Garrison Villard, the editor of the *Nation*—felt that no step could have been more directly designed to make things worse. Countries would have even more trouble earning the dollars of which they were so desperately short. But Mr. Hoover signed the bill.

Anyone familiar with this particular race of men knows that a dour, flinty, inscrutable visage such as that of Calvin Coolidge can be the mask for a calm and acutely perceptive intellect. And he knows equally that it can conceal a mind of singular aridity. The difficulty, given the inscrutability, is in knowing which. However, in the case of Coolidge the evidence is in favor of the second. In some sense, he certainly knew what was going on. He would not have been unaware of what was called the Coolidge market. But he connected developments neither with the well-being of the country nor with his own responsibilities. In his memoirs Hoover goes to great lengths to show how closely he was in touch with events and how clearly he foresaw their consequences. In his *Autobiography*, a notably barren document, Coolidge did not refer to the accumulating troubles. He confines himself to such unequivocal truths as ''Every day of Presidential life is crowded with activities'' (which in his case, indeed, was not true); and ''The Congress makes the laws, but it is the President who causes them to be executed.''

At various times during his years in office, men called on Coolidge to warn him of the impending trouble. And in 1927, at the instigation of a former White House aide, he sent for William Z. Ripley of Harvard, the most articulate critic of the corporate machinations of the period. The President became so interested that he invited him to stay for lunch, and listened carefully while his guest outlined (as Ripley later related) the ''prestidigitation, double-shuffling, honey-fugling, hornswoggling, and skulduggery'' that characterized the current Wall Street scene. But Ripley made the mistake of telling Coolidge that regulation was the responsibility of the states (as was then the case). At this intelligence Coolidge's face lit up and he dismissed the entire matter from his mind. Others who warned of the impending disaster got even less far.

And on some occasions Coolidge added fuel to the fire. If the market seemed to be faltering, a timely statement from the White House—or possibly from Secretary Mellon—would often brace it up. William Allen White, by no means an unfriendly observer, noted that after one such comment the market staged a 26-point rise. He went on to say that a careful search ''during these halcyon years . . . discloses this fact: Whenever the stock market showed signs of weakness, the President or the Secretary of the Treasury or some important dignitary of the administration . . . issued a statement. The statement invariably declared that business was 'fundamentally sound,' that continued prosperity had arrived, and that the slump of the moment was 'seasonal.' ''

Such was the Coolidge role. Coolidge was fond of observing that ''if you see ten troubles coming down the road, you can be sure that nine will run into the ditch before they reach you and you have to battle with only one of them.'' A critic noted that ''the trouble with this philosophy was that when the tenth trouble reached him he was wholly unprepared. . . . The outstanding instance was the rising boom and orgy of mad speculation which began in 1927.'' The critic was Herbert Hoover.

Plainly, in these years, leadership failed. Events whose tragic

*March 4, 1929: President
Coolidge (left) and President-
Elect Hoover drive from
the White House to Hoover's
inauguration at the Capitol.*

culmination could be foreseen—and was foreseen—were allowed to
work themselves out to the final disaster. The country and the world
paid. For a time, indeed, the very reputation of capitalism itself was
in the balance. It survived in the years following perhaps less because
of its own power or the esteem in which it was held, than because
of the absence of an organized and plausible alternative. Yet one
important question remains. Would it have been possible even for
a strong President to arrest the plunge? Were not the opposing forces
too strong? Isn't one asking the impossible?

No one can say for sure. But the answer depends at least partly
on the political context in which the Presidency was cast. That of
Coolidge and Hoover may well have made decisive leadership impossible. These were conservative Administrations in which, in addition, the influence of the businessman was strong. At the core of
the business faith was an intuitive belief in *laissez faire*—the benign
tendency of things that are left alone. The man who wanted to
intervene was a meddler. Perhaps, indeed, he was a planner. In any
case, he was to be regarded with mistrust. And, on the businessman's
side, it must be borne in mind that high government office often nur-
tures a spurious sense of urgency. There is no more important public
function than the suppression of proposals for unneeded action. But
these should have been distinguished from action necessary to economic survival.

A bitterly criticized figure of the Harding-Coolidge Hoover era
was Secretary of the Treasury Andrew W. Mellon. He opposed all
action to curb the boom, although once in 1929 he was persuaded
to say that bonds (as distinct from stocks) were a good buy. And

when the depression came, he was against doing anything about that. Even Mr. Hoover was shocked by his insistence that the only remedy was (as Mr. Hoover characterized it) to ''liquidate labor, liquidate stocks, liquidate the farmers, liquidate real estate.'' Yet Mellon reflected only in extreme form the conviction that things would work out, that the real enemies were those who interfered.

Outside of Washington in the twenties, the business and banking community, or at least the articulate part of it, was overwhelmingly opposed to any public intervention. The tentative and ineffective steps which the Federal Reserve did take were strongly criticized. In the spring of 1929 when the Reserve system seemed to be on the verge of taking more decisive action, there was an anticipatory tightening of money rates and a sharp drop in the market. On his own initiative Charles E. Mitchell, the head of the National City Bank, poured in new funds. He had an obligation, he said, that was ''paramount to any Federal Reserve warning, or anything else'' to avert a crisis in the money market. In brief, he was determined, whatever the government thought, to keep the boom going. In that same spring Paul M. Warburg, a distinguished and respected Wall Street leader, warned of the dangers of the boom and called for action to restrain it. He was deluged with criticism and even abuse and later said that the subsequent days were the most difficult of his life. There were some businessmen and bankers—like Mitchell and Albert Wiggin of the Chase National Bank—who may have vaguely sensed that the end of the boom would mean their own business demise. Many more had persuaded themselves that the dream would last. But we should not complicate things. Many others were making money and took a short-run view—or no view—either of their own survival or of the system of which they were a part. They merely wanted to be left alone to get a few more dollars.

And the opposition to government intervention would have been nonpartisan. In 1929 one of the very largest of the Wall Street operators was John J. Raskob. Raskob was also chairman of the Democratic National Committee. So far from calling for preventive measures, Raskob in 1929 was explaining how, through stock market speculation, literally anyone could be a millionaire. Nor would the press have been enthusiastic about, say, legislation to control holding companies and investment trusts or to give authority to regulate margin trading. The financial pages of many of the papers were riding the boom. And even from the speculating public, which was dreaming dreams of riches and had yet to learn that it had been fleeced, there would have been no thanks. Perhaps a President of phenomenal power and determination might have overcome the Coolidge-Hoover environment. But it is easier to argue that this context made inaction inevitable for almost any President. There were too many people who, given a choice between disaster and the measures that would have prevented it, opted for disaster without either a second or even a first thought.

On the other hand, in a different context a strong President might have taken effective preventive action. Congress in these years was becoming increasingly critical of the Wall Street speculation and corporate piggery-pokery. The liberal Republicans—the men whom Senator George H. Moses called the Sons of the Wild Jackass— were especially vehement. But conservatives like Carter Glass were also critical. These men correctly sensed that things were going wrong. A President such as Wilson or either of the Roosevelts (the case of Theodore is perhaps less certain than that of Franklin) who was surrounded in his Cabinet by such men would have been sensitive to this criticism. As a leader he could both have reinforced and drawn strength from the contemporary criticism. Thus he might have been able to arrest the destructive madness as it became recognizable. The American government works far better—perhaps it only works— when the Executive, the business power, and the press are in some degree at odds. Only then can we be sure that abuse or neglect, either private or public, will be given the notoriety that is needed.

Perhaps it is too much to hope that by effective and timely criticism and action the Great Depression might have been avoided. A lot was required in those days to make the United States in any degree depression-proof. But perhaps by preventive action the ensuing depression might have been made less severe. And certainly in the ensuing years the travail of bankers and businessmen before congressional committees, in the courts, and before the bar of public opinion would have been less severe. Here is the paradox. In the full perspective of history, American businessmen never had enemies as damaging as the men who grouped themselves around Calvin Coolidge and supported and applauded him in what William Allen White called ''that masterly inactivity for which he was so splendidly equipped.''

Poverty makes strange bedfellows: in Everett
Shinn's depression drawing of a breadline,
former businessmen and bums queue up.

Allan Nevins

The Place of Franklin D. Roosevelt in History

This essay, like Lewis Mumford's analysis of Emerson in Volume I, brings together a great historian and a great subject. Allan Nevins' estimation of Franklin D. Roosevelt is complicated. He says as much about Roosevelt's weaknesses as about his strengths. He looks at Roosevelt through the eyes of the President's friends and his enemies; he refers to his personal observations of the man and also makes the broadest of generalizations, based on his amazing under-standing not only of the whole course of American history but of much of the history of the western world. He tells us funny stories that re-veal Roosevelt in moments of relaxation and quotes from formal state papers which show him center stage at crucial points in his career. Above all, like a great conductor interpreting a symphony, he is at every stage absolute master of his subject and his materials, devoting exquisite care to every detail yet never forgetting that each separate passage contributes vitally to the total effect.

That effect is, in a word, sunny. Nevins, despite his awareness of Roosevelt's limits and defects, admires the man because of what he calls his "effective greatness," which he believes was produced by qualities of spirit rather than of intellect or even of moral fiber.

*S*eldom has an eminent man been more conscious of his special place in history than was Franklin D. Roosevelt. He thought of history as an imposing drama and himself as a conspicuous actor. Again and again he carefully staged a historic scene: as when, going before Congress on December 8, 1941, to call for a recognition of war with Japan, he took pains to see that Mrs. Woodrow Wilson accompanied Mrs. Roosevelt to the Capitol, thus linking the First and Second World Wars. As governor and as President, he adopted for the benefit of future historians the rule that every letter addressed to him, however insignificant, and copies of every document issued from his office, should be preserved. This mass of papers, mounting into the millions, soon became almost overwhelming. It might have been added, with some difficulty, to the many other official collections in the Library of Congress. But, with a strong sense of his special place in history, Roosevelt wanted a memorial all his own, a place of resort for scholars, connected uniquely with his name and his administrations. He announced the gift of his papers to the nation; his mother gave sixteen acres of land for a building at Hyde Park; some 28,000 donors subscribed $400,000 for an edifice; and Congress made the Roosevelt Library a federal institution.

In this Library at Hyde Park, as a token of his place in history, he took an almost naïve pride. I well recall the dinner he gave early in 1939 to the trustees and a select number of historians to discuss plans for its management. It took place at the Mayflower Hotel in Washington; he was wheeled up an inclined ramp to his place at a central table; he waved joyously to everyone; he enjoyed his stewed mulligatawny turtle—a favorite dish—his companions, his sense of launching another original enterprise. In a long informal speech he talked of certain predecessors: of Lincoln, of Grover Cleveland, whom he had known, and of his cousin Theodore Roosevelt; he dwelt on Woodrow Wilson's sense of history—Wilson in 1917 had forbidden young Roosevelt, then Assistant Secretary of the Navy, to bring warships up from Cuban waters to the United States lest future historians should accuse him of making a provocative gesture on the eve of our first war with Germany. I well recall, too, the still more interesting occasion when he laid the cornerstone of the Hyde Park Library on November 19, 1939. Trustees, historians, and editors lunched with him; he gaily drove his own specially equipped car to the site; he chatted blithely with everyone; and he watched the cornerstone slip into place with a gratified smile.

Today his grave lies close by that Library, and by the family home that has become a national shrine, visited by hundreds of thousands every year. To the collections there shelved, multitudes of scholars annually repair, for they are open to all. Roosevelt's own deposits, including letters, documents, books, pamphlets, films, photographs, speeches, and museum pieces, have exceeded a total of fifty million items; and to them are being added the papers of Cabinet officers and other official associates. The career of no other American President has so vast a documentation for history.

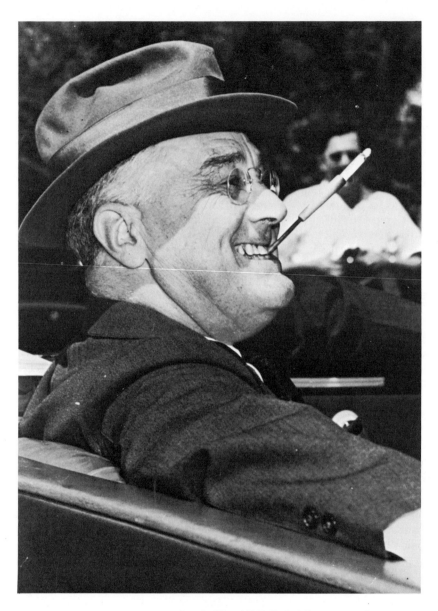

An ebullient F.D.R. holding an outdoor press conference at Warm Springs, Georgia, in 1939.

Is it too soon to estimate the place of Franklin D. Roosevelt in the stream of American and world events? It is never too soon for such a task. History is not a remote Olympian bar of judgment, but a controversial arena in which each generation must make its own estimate of the past. We have every right to fix the historical position of Roosevelt as we see it today, knowing that it will be reassessed from the vantage point of a longer perspective and fuller knowledge in 1975, and re-estimated again in 2065. That it will be a great place we may already be certain. A statue to Roosevelt has been reared in Oslo. When a statue was proposed in London, five-shilling subscriptions were opened one morning; they were closed that night with the sum oversubscribed; had they been kept open a few days money would have poured in for five statues. Streets have been named for him around the world. Fifty American historians, interrogated by Arthur M. Schlesinger, Sr., of Harvard, have all but unanimously agreed that in the roster of Presidents Lincoln stands first, Washington second, and Franklin D. Roosevelt third. Hearing of that verdict, Winston Churchill declared that in impact upon world history Roosevelt unquestionably stood first.

We have this advantage in attempting the task, that a great part of the necessary evidence is already at hand. Never before in human annals has so huge a volume of reminiscences, autobiographies, impressions, letters, official documents, and other data bearing on one man been issued within twenty years of his death. The thirteen volumes of Roosevelt's official papers edited by Judge Samuel I. Rosenman and the four volumes of personal letters edited by Elliot Roosevelt; the memoirs of Cordell Hull, Harry Hopkins, Henry Morgenthau, Harold Ickes, Henry L. Stimson, James Farley, Edward J. Flynn, Mrs. Franklin D. Roosevelt, Frances Perkins, Grace Tully, Hugh Johnson, Dwight Eisenhower, Omar Bradley, and a hundred others; the mass of comment by Washington reporters and war correspondents who watched history being made; the procession of European histories and memoirs so impressively headed by Winston Churchill's volumes —this already forms a corpus too great for one student to explore fully in a lifetime. But while we shall have immense fresh accretions of detail, it is unlikely that we shall receive any startling new "revelations," any facts that will offer a basis for sweeping revisions of judgment.

In dealing with every commanding figure of history, a fundamental question presents itself: To what extent did greatness inhere in the man, and to what degree was it a product of the situation? If great men have their stars, as Napoleon said he did, it is often because a national or world crisis favors greatness. The reason why fifty American historians did not wholly agree with Winston Churchill upon Roosevelt's rank among the nation's Presidents is, I think, simple. Washington had indisputable greatness in himself. "The first, the last, the best, the Cincinnatus of the West," as Lord Byron called him, he was great in character, great in traits of leadership, great in insight and wisdom. Lincoln had an even more manifest and appealing personal greatness. His public utterances, from the House Divided address to the Gettysburg Address, his state papers, from the First Inaugural to the final pronouncements on Reconstruction, attest a rare intellectual power. The wisdom of his principal public acts, his magnanimity toward all foes public and private, his firmness under adversity, his elevation of spirit, his power of strengthening the best purposes and suppressing the worst instincts of a broad, motley democracy, place him in the front rank of modern statesmen.

But with Franklin D. Roosevelt we feel no such assurance of transcendent personal eminence. We feel that he lacked the steadfast elevation of character exhibited by George Washington. We find in him distinctly less intellectual power than in Jefferson, Lincoln, or perhaps Woodrow Wilson. We conclude, in short, that his tremendous place in history was in lesser degree the product of his special personal endowments, and in larger degree the handiwork of his stormy times, than that occupied by George Washington or Abraham Lincoln.

That Roosevelt had remarkable intellectual gifts is plain; but these gifts fell short of the highest distinction. He possessed a quick, resourceful, and flexible mind. This fact is illustrated on an elevated level by his ability to deal with fifty important issues in a day, making shrewd decisions on each; by his power in wartime of efficiently coordinating departments, industries, and armies, of gaining the teamwork of generals, admirals, and business leaders, as no other President has ever done. He organized the national energies with unique success. His intellectual proficiency is illustrated on a lower plane by almost any of the press conferences recorded in Judge Rosenman's volumes; by his deft tact in handling two-score quickwitted newspapermen, evading some questions, dissecting the fatuity of others, using a few to touch a needed chord of publc opinion, and responding to many with concise, expert answers. Like his cousin Theodore Roosevelt, he had an insatiable curiosity about books, about men, about events. It was linked with an unquenchable zest for experience; the zest expressed in his famous wartime message to Churchill, "It is fun to be in the same century with you."

He had a talent for quick parliamentary hits. He could make his enemies ridiculous by a few pungent words, as in the happy rhythmical phrase about "Martin, Barton, and Fish" that, recited over the radio, exposed these three reactionary congressmen to a continental gale of laughter in 1940; or by a lambent flare of humor, as in his speech of 1944 picturing the Scottish unhappiness of his dog Fala over an accusation of extravagance. He had flashes of daring imagination. He had a remarkable gift of rapid improvisation, as he showed in all the recurrent crises of his twelve crowded years in office. In part this consisted of his ability to use other men's thought; "he is the best picker of brains who ever lived," his intimates used to say. His power of application was remarkable even among our overworked Presidents. He had an average working day of fourteen hours (Truman later boasted of sixteen), and he told Governor James M. Cox: "I never get tired."

But of pre-eminent intellectual talent he had little. I recall Walter Lippmann saying in the second administration: "He has never written a real state paper." In a sense that is true. No paper signed by him equals Washington's Farewell Address, Lincoln's great papers, Theodore Roosevelt's first annual message, or Woodrow Wilson's nobler productions. Nearly all his speeches were in fact largely written for him by others. Robert Sherwood describes a typical scene: Judge

As this 1938 cartoon from the Columbus Dispatch *suggests, Roosevelt was exceedingly interested in assuring himself a place among the outstanding Presidents of American history.*

Rosenman, Harry Hopkins, and Sherwood gathered about a table discussing the material for an imminent presidential address, and threshing it over and over until Judge Rosenman impatiently flung down a pencil with the words, "There comes a time in the life of every speech when it's got to be *written!*" Roosevelt wrote no books; he was probably incapable of matching such a work as Theodore Roosevelt's *The Winning of the West.* He threw out no such immortal epigrams as Churchill's sentence challenging Britons to face a future of "blood, sweat, and tears." His best phrases, like "the forgotten man" and "the new deal," were borrowed from other men.

A capacity for abstract thought was largely omitted from his equipment. The idea once current that he had a special intimacy with Maynard Keynes was obviously erroneous, for he was simply incapable of following a mind so analytical, an intellect so subtle, as that of Lord Keynes. When John Gunther asked one of Roosevelt's friends, "Just how does the President think?" he met the reply: "The President never *thinks.*" Like Theodore Roosevelt, he was primarily a man of action. His mental processes, as many friends have said, were intuitive rather than logical. He reacted rather than reflected. A President is not necessarily too busy to do abstract thinking. Newton D. Baker, who held a minor post in Grover Cleveland's administration and a major office under Woodrow Wilson, once observed to me that while Cleveland shouldered his way through difficulties like a buffalo charging a thicket, Wilson "dissolved his problems by an acid process of thought." This acid process was beyond Roosevelt. All that is told us of his reading suggests that it was rather adolescent: either escapist, like the detective stories carried on every long trip; or attached to a hobby, like naval history; or journalistic. His humor lacked the philosophic overtones of Lincoln's, or even the saltiness of Harry Truman's; it too was somewhat adolescent. It was usually the humor of the quip, as when he said to his secretary, Grace Tully, over-addicted to punctuation, "Grace, how often do I have to tell you not to waste the taxpayer's commas?" Or it was the humor of the wise-crack, as when he remarked to the six New England governors who startled him in 1933 by suddenly appearing at the White House in a body: "What, all six of you? You're not going to secede from the Union, are you?"

We all know what Lord Bacon said makes a ready man; and intellectually, the talkative Roosevelt was a ready leader—perhaps the readiest of all the world's leaders in his exigent time. This power to act quickly, shrewdly, and earnestly was a gift that served the nation and the free world with unforgettable dexterity and force. Honoring this princely capacity, we can afford to give minor weight to the fact that his mind, compared with that of Woodrow Wilson, sometimes appears superficial, and that he possessed no such intellectual versa-tility as Thomas Jefferson—to say nothing of Winston Churchill.

In respect to character, similarly, he had traits of an admirable kind; but we must add that even in combination, they fell short of a truly Roman weight of virtue. He held sincere religious convictions, and it was no mere gesture that led him to take his Cabinet, on the morn of his first inauguration, to divine service at St. John's. "I think," writes Mrs. Roosevelt in *This I Remember*, "he actually felt he could ask God for guidance and receive it. That was why he loved the Twenty-third Psalm, the Beatitudes, and the thirteenth chapter of First Corinthians." He was one of the unflinching optimists of his time. Having conquered a prostrating illness and horrible physical handicap, he felt an inner faith in man's power to conquer anything. When his aides made estimates of American industrial capacity, he raised them; when the Combined Chiefs of Staff set down dates for the various goals in the invasion of Europe, he revised them forward. Because of his religious faith and his ingrained optimism, he possessed an unfailing serenity. In the stormiest of hours his nerve was never shaken.

On his first day in the Presidency in 1933, with the banks of the nation closed down and the country almost prostrate with anxiety, he found his desk at six o'clock in the afternoon quite clear. He pressed a button. Four secretaries appeared at four doors to the room. "Is there anything more, boys?" he inquired. "No, Mr. President," they chorused. And Roosevelt remarked with his happy smile: "This job is a cinch!"

Equally admirable were his idealism, his consciousness of high objectives, and his frequent nobility of spirit. He was willing to sacrifice himself for the public weal. When in 1928 Alfred E. Smith, the Democratic presidential candidate, asked him to run for governor of New York, he was told by physicians that if he kept out of public life another year or two, he could regain the use of his left leg, while if he did not he would be incurably lame; but he answered the call of duty. His concern for the poor, the friendless, the unfortunate, was more keenly humane than that of any leader since Lincoln. "I see one-third of a nation," he said in his Second Inaugural, "ill-housed, ill-clad, ill-nourished''—and meant to do something about it. Moderately rich himself, he disliked those who were too rich. The steel magnate Eugene Grace, who took a bonus of a million dollars a year without the knowledge of his stockholders, aroused his bitter scorn. ''Tell Gene he'll never make a million a year again!'' was the angry message he sent the man. Frances Perkins, who had known him as a rather arrogant, snobbish young man before his seizure by infantile paralysis, and who knew him as a battler for social justice afterward, believed that this physical ordeal taught him sympathy for the afflicted and underprivileged.

Yet, we must add, these impressive virtues were flawed by certain grievous defects. He had flashes of insincerity which sometimes impaired the confidence even of close friends. Henry L. Stimson mentions in his memoirs the fact that, having found out Roosevelt in a quite needless bit of duplicity, for several years he avoided all contact with him. Henry A. Wallace committed to paper an account of Roosevelt's double-dealing (as Wallace saw it) in handling the Vice Presidential nomination in 1944. Other men have penned different stories. Even the President's defenders could not deny that his treatment of that critical problem showed a certain irresponsibility, to be excused perhaps by the fact that he was already more ill than he realized. Because of this instability, Roosevelt was ready at times to abandon principle for expediency. Cordell Hull has described how unfortunate were the results of such an abandonment in the Neutrality Acts. And Mrs. Roosevelt writes: ''While I often felt strongly on various subjects, Franklin frequently refrained from supporting causes in which he believed, because of political realities. There were times when this annoyed me very much. In the case of the Spanish Civil War, for instance, we had to remain neutral, though Franklin knew quite well he wanted the democratic government to be successful. But he also knew he could not get Congress to go along with him. To justify his action, or lack of action, he explained to me, when I complained, that the League of Nations had asked us to remain neutral. . . . He was simply trying to salve his own conscience. It was one of the many times I felt akin to a hair shirt.''

Edward J. Flynn writes flatly: ''The President did not keep his word on many appointments.'' There exists no question that he promised to make Louis Johnson Secretary of War, and broke the promise. All statesmen have to adjust principle to events and to public sentiment, and are sometimes compelled to revoke promises. But Roosevelt was at times indefensibly evasive even with intimates like Flynn and Louis Johnson, and lacked straightforwardness. It can be said, too, that he often followed a Machiavellian technique in administration. He liked, for example, to put two or three men in positions of conflicting authority, so that they worked at loggerheads, with himself as ultimate arbiter. It was in part his fault that Sumner Welles and Cordell Hull made the State Department for several years a maelstrom of rival policies and ambitions—although this is a complex story; it was in part his fault that Jesse Jones and Henry Wallace engaged at one time in a feud which sadly injured both the administration and the country.

Other unhappy traits might be copiously illustrated. Roosevelt could seem dismayingly casual about everything from a political speech to some of the issues at Yalta. He could be reprehensibly secretive; he kept the minutes of the Teheran Conference from Secretary of State Hull, and withheld from the American people the concession he made at Yalta to Russia on votes in the United Nations Assembly. He was pettily vindictive toward some opponents, as Raymond B. Moley and James Farley testify in detail, and his attempted purge of certain southern leaders in 1938 is far from the happiest chapter in his career. All in all, we must repeat our conclusion that his character lacked the symmetry, harmony, and weight found in that of Washington and of Lincoln.

Yet without the highest inner greatness Roosevelt had an effective greatness of action, in relation to his time, which will cause him to be remembered as happily as any American leader. It is significant that Churchill, intellectually so much superior, always treated him with manifest deference, as a lesser man bowing to a greater. Was this simply because Roosevelt headed the more powerful state? I think not. We must here face what seems to me a salient fact of history. A leader who puts second-rate qualities of intellect and character into first-rate application to the needs of his time may be a greater man than the leader who puts first-rate qualities into a second-rate application. Roosevelt signally illustrates this aphorism. He had, to begin with, the gift of address: a gift for doing the right thing at just the right time. He had, in the second place, the greater gift of being able to put his personal forces into harmony with the best forces of his era.

Roosevelt's effective greatness included an unrivalled power of matching the urgent crisis with the adequate act; a power of timing an impressive measure to meet a desperate need. Take the first days of 1933, after his election. Never in a period of peace—never since the days of British invasion in 1814, or Confederate victory in 1863—had the nation been in such straits. Between twelve and fifteen million men were out of work. Five million families, one seventh of the population, were supported by public relief or private charity. Since the beginning of the depression, 4,600 banks had failed. Travellers through the broad industrial belt from Chicago to New York seemed to pass nothing but closed factory gates. Half the automobile plants of Michigan had shut down. Along the Great Lakes, path of the largest marine commerce of the world, ships had almost ceased to move. In the iron beds of the Mesabi and Vermilion ranges scarcely a shovel dipped into the richest ores of the globe; in the copper mountain at Butte scarcely a drill was at work. The looms of southern textile factories were cobwebbed. On railway sidings locomotives gathered rust in long rows; behind them huddled passenger and freight cars in idle hundreds, their paint fading. Middle-western farmers gazed bitterly at crops whose market value was less than the cost of harvesting; on the high plains, ranchers turned cattle loose to graze at will because it did not pay to send them to the stockyards. In Pennsylvania and New England desperate men and women offered to work for anything, and some did work for a dollar a week.

Worst of all was the fear which gripped the nerves of the nation. To observers who travelled across the country in trains almost empty, through factory districts with hardly a wisp of smoke, the helpless populations sent up an almost audible cry of anger, bewilderment, and panic. The day before Roosevelt took office the crisis gathered to a climax. By midnight of March 3 the closing of all remaining banks had been or was being ordered in every state. Never before had a change of Presidents taken place against a background so dramatic. The people, awakening on March 4 to read that their financial system was prostrate, gathered at noon by millions about their radios to listen in anguish, in anxiety, but in hope, to the voice of their new national leader.

There ensued four of the most brilliantly successful months in the history of American government. Roosevelt's first words promised energy: "I assume unhesitatingly the leadership of this great army of our people, dedicated to a disciplined attack upon our common problems." He improvised a series of policies, and mobilized an administrative machine, with a vigor that would have done credit to any wartime executive. Within thirty-six hours he had taken absolute control of the currency and banking system, and called Congress in extraordinary session. He forthwith launched an aggressive attack along half a dozen fronts; upon banking problems, industrial prostration, farm distress, unemployment, public works, the burden of public and private debt. One reporter wrote that the change in Washington was like that from oxcart to airplane. Congress labored for ninety-nine days under the President's all-but-complete sway. Almost his every wish was obeyed by immediate votes. One staggered member said of the program: "It reads like the first chapter of Genesis."

And as Roosevelt took these steps his courage, his resourcefulness, his blithe optimism, infected the spirit of the people; he gave Americans new confidence and the *élan* of a new national unity. When he gaily signed his last bills and departed for a brief sail up the Atlantic coast as skipper of a 45-foot sailing boat, the nation realized that it had turned from stagnation to a bright adventure. As the President put it, we were "on our way."

Nor was this an isolated spasm of leadership; for each recurrent crisis found the same resourcefulness called into effective play. When France fell, when the British Commonwealth stood alone against the deadliest foe that modern civilization had known, Americans gazed at the European scene in fear, in gloom, in perpexity. With a sense of dumb helplessness, tens of millions put their intensest feeling into the hope for Britain's survival. Those tens of millions never forgot the morning of September 3, 1940, when they read the headlines announcing that Roosevelt had told a startled Congress of the transfer of fifty destroyers to embattled Britain; a defiance of Hitler, a defiance of home isolationists, a first long stride toward ranging America against the Fascist despots. Nor could lovers of world freedom ever forget the dramatic steps that followed hard upon British victory over Hitler's air force and upon Roosevelt's re-election: the Four Freedoms speech of January 6, 1941; the introduction of the Lend-Lease Bill four days later, a measure which completely transformed American foreign policy; the establishment of naval and military posts in Greenland and Iceland; the proclamation of an unlimited national emergency; the seizure of all Axis ships and Axis credits; the Atlantic Charter meeting with Churchill off Newfoundland; the establishment of convoys for American ships carrying aid to Britain; and, in the background, the stimulation of American production to an unprecedented flow of guns, tanks, shells, and airplanes, with factories roaring day and night for the defense of democracy.

These years 1940–41 were, as we see now, among the greatest crises in modern history. They were met with an imagination, boldness, and ingenuity that can hardly be overpraised. Parochialism, timidity, or fumbling might have been fatal; even a pause for too much reflection might have been fatal. We knew then that Roosevelt was determined to face the exigency with an intrepidity worthy of the republic. But his intention was even more courageous than we supposed. For we know now that Harry Hopkins told Churchill in London early in 1941: "The President is determined that we shall win the war together. Make no mistake about it. He sent me here to tell you that at all costs and by all means he will carry you through."

Roosevelt's second quality of effective greatness was his ability to vindicate the American method of pragmatic experiment, of practical *ad hoc* action, step by step. He was essentially a Jeffersonian. He belonged to the school which, following the historic Anglo-American bent of mind, is attached to facts rather than ideas, to the enlargement of precedents rather than the formulation of dazzling visions. Like all Anglo-American statesmen, he disliked sweeping generalizations of an intolerant, exclusive nature. He loved experimental advance, and was wont to say that if he were right sixty per cent of the time, he would be satisfied. Like Jefferson, he was willing to scrap a theory the moment a brute fact collided with it; he trusted experience, and distrusted flights into the empyrean. His so-called revolution, though unprecedentedly broad and swift, was like Jefferson's "revolution"; it was simply a combination of numerous practical changes, the main test of which was whether or not they worked.

The Rooseveltian changes did work. They did transform American life and the American outlook in two distinct ways. They converted a nation of aggressive individualists into a social-minded nation accepting the principles of the welfare state. They changed an isolationist or largely isolationist nation into one committed to world partnership and world leadership. The New Deal in home affairs was empirical, not ideological. The emergency program I have sketched was a stopgap affair put together to tide over a crisis, and as Mrs. Roosevelt once put it, "give us time to think." It succeeded. Taken as a whole, the New Deal passed through two phases. In the first, 1933–35, the government tried scarcity economics, reducing factory production, farm output, and hours of work, and doing what it could to cut off the American economy from the outside world. In the second and better phase, 1935–50, it tried full employment, full production, enlarged distribution of goods, and freer international trade. This led directly toward the acceptance of Cordell Hull's ideal of co-operative internationalism. American participation in world affairs after 1938 similarly passed through two phases. In the first, all the nation's energies were devoted to the defeat of the Axis. In the second, Roosevelt, Hull, Welles, and Stettinius moved step by step to construct a new world order, an enduring fabric of the United Nations. In home and foreign affairs alike action was always direct, experimental, and pragmatic.

It gave America a new social order at home, and a new orientation in global affairs. It worked; it is still working. But because it never approached a sweeping ideological revolution of the Marxist or totalitarian type, it was the despair of certain impractical theorists *pur sang*.

For example, readers of that brilliant but extraordinarily half-informed and error-streaked book, Harold Laski's *The American Democracy*, will find an almost incredible analysis of what the author regards as Mr. Roosevelt's fundamental failure. This was his failure to smash the old America completely, and build a quite new America on the theories that pleased Mr. Laski. The author draws an illuminating comparison between Lenin and Roosevelt. Lenin, it appears, made a marvelously precise and correct analysis of the maladies of modern society and economics; and he applied it with revolutionary courage. Roosevelt, on the other hand, was never converted—he never learned that "the foundations of the Americanism he inherited were really inadequate to the demands made upon its institutional expression." In particular, writes Laski, he failed to see that he should destroy "private ownership of the means of production"; that is, that the state should take over all mines, factories, transport, workshops, and farms. Roosevelt, as a result of his faulty analysis, unhappily failed to carry through a real revolution. What was the upshot? In Russia, admits Laski, life became nearly intolerable. The price of revolution proved "almost overwhelming"—starvation of millions, wholesale executions, vast concentration camps, the extinction of freedom. In America, Laski admits, life was immensely improved. Industrial production became enormous; farm output grew tremendous; the standard of living steadily rose. But theory (says Mr. Laski) is everything. Lenin with his ideology was right; Roosevelt with his practical experimentalism was a failure!

This view of the matter would be emphatically rejected by all but a handful of Americans, including those who do not admire Roosevelt. Like Jefferson, like Lincoln, like Wilson, he was innovator and conservator at once; he made daring new additions to the American fabric, but he kept the best of the old structure. While he converted

Americans to the new ideal of social security, he strengthened their old faith in individual opportunity. He proved again that America needs no ideological revolution. He vindicated our traditional method of solving problems one at a time by pragmatic trial and error. As one journalist wrote: ''One remembers him as a kind of smiling bus driver, with that cigarette holder pointed upward, listening to the uproar from behind as he took the sharp turns. They used to tell him that he had not loaded his vehicle right for all eternity. But he knew that he had stacked it well enough to round the next corner, and he knew when the yells were false, and when they were real, and he loved the passengers.''

Roosevelt's third and most important quality of effective greatness lay in his ability to imbue Americans, and to some extent even citizens of other lands, with a new spiritual strength. Well into the twentieth century, most men in the New World had shared a dream of ever-widening adventure, a sense of elated achievement. They had dared much in coming to the new continent, and still more in mastering it. They were optimistic, self-confident, exuberant. The heavy costs of the First World War, the disillusionments of its aftermath, the pressure of complex new social problems, and above all the staggering blows of the Great Depression darkened our horizons. We had entered the Shadow Belt which Bryce predicted in his book on *The American Commonwealth*. From that zone of gloom, that numbed consciousness of frustration and failure, Roosevelt lifted Americans on the wings of his great new adventures—the alphabetical adventures of the AAA, the NRA, the TVA; above all, on the wings of the greatest adventure in our history, the effort to rescue democracy from totalitarianism, and to organize the world to safeguard freedom.

For a few years Americans had felt lost, bewildered, paralyzed. Roosevelt carried them to a Moabite peak whence once more they saw promised lands. They threw off their frustrations; he gave them a feeling that they were participating in a life far wider than their everyday parochial concerns. His self-confidence, his enthusiasm, his happy faculty of obliterating old failures by bold new plans, taught them that they were not imprisoned in a dead past but were helping build a living future. In the three centuries 1607–1907 Americans had triumphantly mastered their physical environment. Just so, in the next century to come, they would master their social and economic environment at home, and join other nations in a mastery of the world environment. As the storm thickened after 1940, Roosevelt's rich voice grew more urgent—''bidding the eagles of the West fly on.'' Here at last, he seemed to say, is a task worthy of you; tyranny like Hell is not easily conquered. Lincoln had once used a phrase which haunts his countrymen. ''Thanks to all,'' he exclaimed after Gettysburg and Vicksburg, ''thanks to all: for the great republic—for the principle it lives by and keeps alive—for man's vast future—thanks to all.'' A sense of man's vast future, a hope of shaping it for the better, never left Roosevelt's cheerful heart.

It is not often realized to what a degree the spirit of adventure kindled at home under the New Deal was carried over into world affairs when the United States faced the Axis menace. The defeatism of Hoover's day was gone. A hundred and sixty million citizens had been morally prepared to undertake unprecedented tasks. They grumbled; they cursed the hard luck of their grim era; they shuddered over the mounting costs—the colossal debt, the wasted resources; but they never doubted their ability to put the job through. That change in temper was primarily Roosevelt's accomplishment. It threw open, temporarily, the portals of a wider world. The change from oxcart was a spiritual, not a material, change. Never in our history have the emotion and resolution of the American people been so completely fused as when, as the first waves of American and British troops stormed across the Normandy beaches, Roosevelt sat at the radio leading the nation in prayer.

Effective greatness—that is Roosevelt's title to a high place in the world's history. Intellect and character are not enough; to them must be added personality, energy, and an accurate sense for the proper timing of action. Roosevelt was not an intellectual giant; but what of the personality that made the Arkansas sharecropper and the Harlem Negro feel they shared all the destinies of the republic? His character did not awe men by its massive strength; but what of the gifts that made him so efficient in harmonizing labor, capital, and agriculture at home, and getting discordant nations to pool their wartime efforts? He lacked the iron traits of Cromwell—but how incomparably more successful he was! He did not have the powerful grasp of Bismarck, but how much more beneficent was his career! In time his specific achievements may be blurred, but the qualities of his spirit will be remembered. For centuries Americans will think of him as one of those spirits who ride in front; we shall see his jaunty figure, his gaily poised head, still in advance of us. We shall hear his blithe voice in his words just before his death at Warm Springs on April 12, 1945:

"The only limit to our realization of tomorrow will be our doubts of today. Let us move forward with strong and active faith."

Daniel P. Moynihan

The American City: Continuity and Change

Current concerns always produce "new" history; they lead us to reconsider the past in our search for an understanding of the present. This essay by Daniel P. Moynihan illustrates this principle perfectly. Moynihan has devoted most of his adult life to what may generally be called urban problems—as a government official, as a university professor, and as a writer. He served in the United States Department of Labor from 1961 to 1965, rising to the post of Assistant Secretary. He then became a professor at Harvard and director of Harvard and M.I.T.'s Joint Center for Urban Studies. He is currently Special Assistant for Urban Affairs to President Nixon. His book Beyond the Melting Pot, *written with Nathan Glazer, has been a major force in shaping liberal attitudes toward the problems of ethnic minorities in America.*

In the following pages Moynihan takes a hard look at American cities today. His essay bristles with references to modern social science studies of urban life. But in attempting to place urban problems in perspective, he refers repeatedly to history, showing how present-day difficulties are similar to—and different from—those of earlier times. He ends on a note of uncertainty. Avoiding the easy tendency of many historians to justify social evils by "proving" that they have always existed, he concludes by admitting "we do not know" the prescription for curing America's sick cities. But surely, if urban problems are ever to be solved or even mitigated, it will be by considering them in the thoughtful, learned, yet modest way that Moynihan here employs.

*T*here is to be encountered in a Benjamin Disraeli novel a gentleman described as a person "distinguished for ignorance" as he had but one idea and that was wrong. It is by now clear that future generations will perforce reach something of the same judgment about contemporary Americans in relation to their cities, for what we do and what we say reflect such opposite poles of judgment that we shall inevitably be seen to have misjudged most extraordinarily either in what we are saying about cities or in what we are doing about them. We are, of course, doing very little, or rather, doing just about what we have been doing for the past half century or so, which can reflect a very great deal of activity but no very considerable change. Simultaneously, and far more conspicuously, we are talking of crisis. The word is everywhere: on every tongue; in every pronouncement. The President has now taken to sending an annual message to Congress on urban subjects. In 1968 it was bluntly titled *The Crisis of the Cities*. And indeed, not many weeks later, on Friday, April 5, to be exact, he was issuing a confirming proclamation of sorts:

> Whereas I have been informed that conditions of domestic violence and disorder exist in the District of Columbia and threaten the Washington metropolitan area, endangering life and property and obstructing execution of the laws, and the local police forces are unable to bring about the prompt cessation . . . of violence and restoration of law and order. . . .

The excitement is nothing if not infectious. In a recent joint publication, *Crisis: The Condition of the American City*, Urban America, Inc. and the League of Women Voters noted that during 1967 even the Secretary of Agriculture devoted most of his speeches to urban problems. At mid-1968, the president of the University of California issued a major statement entitled, "What We Must Do: The University and the Urban Crisis." The bishops of the United States Catholic Conference came forth with their own program, entitled "The Church's Response to the Urban Crisis." At its 1968 convention the Republican party, not heretofore known for an obsession with the subject, adopted a platform plank entitled "Crisis of the Cities," while in an issue featuring a stunning black coed on the cover, *Glamour* magazine, ever alert to changing fashions, asked in appropriate form the question many have posed themselves in private—"The Urban Crisis: What Can One Girl Do?"

Academics who have been involved with this subject might be expected to take some satisfaction that the alarums and jeremiads of the past decades seem at last to have been heard by the populace, and yet even those of us most seized with what Norman Mailer has termed the "middle-class lust for apocalypse" are likely to have some reservations about the current enthusiasm for the subject of urban ills. It is not just a matter of the continued disparity between what we say and what we do: it is also, I suspect, a matter of *what* we are saying, and the manner of our saying it. A certain bathos comes through. One thinks of Sean O'Casey's Captain Boyle and Joxer in that far-off Dublin tenement: no doubt the whole world was even then in a "state of chassis" but precious little those two could or would do about it, save use it as an excuse to sustain their own weakness, incompetence, and submission to the death wishes of the society about them. One wonders if something not dissimilar is going on in this nation, at this time. Having persistently failed to do what it was necessary and possible to do for urban life on grounds that conditions surely were not so bad as to warrant such exertion, the nation seems suddenly to have lurched to the opposite position of declaring that things are indeed so very bad that probably nothing will work anyway. The result either way is paralysis and failure. It is time for a measure of perspective.

I take it Lewis Mumford intended to convey something of this message in his most recent book, *The Urban Prospect*, which he begins with a short preface cataloguing the ills of the modern city with a vigor and specificity that command instant assent from the reader. Exactly! one responds. That is precisely the way things are! Mumford is really "telling it like it is." (A measure of *négritude* has of late become the mark of an authentic urban-crisis watcher.) One reads on with increasing recognition, mounting umbrage, only to find at the end that this foreword was in fact written for the May, 1925, edition of *Survey Graphic*. Things have changed, but not that much, and in directions that were, in a sense, fully visible to the sensitive eye nearly a half century ago. To be sure, at a certain point a matter of imbalance becomes one of pathology, a tendency becomes a condition, and for societies as for individuals there comes a point when mistakes are no longer to be undone, transgressions no longer to be forgiven. But it is nowhere clear that we have reached such a point in our cities.

Continuity and change. These are the themes of all life, and not less that of cities. However, as in so many aspects of our national experience, Americans seem more aware of, more sensitive to modes of change than to those of continuity. This is surely a survival from the frontier experience. There has not, I believe, ever been anything to match the rapidity, nay, fury with which Americans set about founding cities in the course of the seventeenth, eighteenth, and nineteenth centuries. Only just now is the historical profession beginning to catch up with that breathless undertaking. Before long we are likely to have a much clearer idea than we do now as to how it all began. But it is still possible at this early state, as it were, to identify a half dozen or so persistent themes in the American urban experience which seem to evolve from earlier to later stages in a process that some would call growth, and others decay, but in a manner that nonetheless constitutes change.

The first theme is that of violence. Through history—the history, that is, of Europe and Asia and that great bridge area in between—cities have been, nominally at least, places of refuge, while the countryside has been the scene of insecurity and exposure to misfortune and wrongdoing. Obviously the facts permit of no generalization, but there is at least a conceptual validity, a persistence over time, of the association of the city with security. In the classical and feudal world, to be without the gates was to be in trouble. Writing of the destruction of Hiroshima and Nagasaki, the critic George Steiner evokes the ancient certainty on this point, and suggests the ways in which it lives on.

In these two cities, the consequences have been more drastic and more specialized. Therein lies the singularity of the two Japanese communities, but also their symbolic link with a number of other cities in history and with the role such cities have played in man's consciousness of his own vulnerable condition—with Sodom and Gomorrah, visited by such fiery ruin that their very location is in doubt; with Nineveh, raked from the earth; with Rotterdam and Coventry; with Dresden, where in 1944, air raids deliberately kindled the largest, hottest pyre known to man. Already, in the "Iliad," the destruction of a city was felt to be an act of peculiar finality, a misfortune that threatens the roots of man. His city smashed, man reverts to the unhoused, wandering circumstance of the beast from which he has so uncertainly emerged. Hence the necessary presence of the gods when a city is built, the mysterious music and ceremony that often attend the elevation of its walls. When Jerusalem was laid waste, says the Haggada, God Himself wept with her.

Little of this dread is to be encountered in the United States, a society marked by the near absence of internal warfare once the major Indian conflicts were over. Warfare, that is to say, between armies. We have, on the other hand, been replete with conflict between different groups within the population, classified in terms of race, class, ethnicity, or whatever, and this conflict has occurred in our cities, which in consequence have been violent places.

An account of the draft riots in New York City in 1863 strikes a surpassingly contemporary note.

Nothing that we could say, could add to the impressiveness of the lesson furnished by the events of the past year, as to the needs and the dangerous condition of the neglected classes in our city. Those terrible days in July—the sudden appearance, as if from the bosom of the earth, of a most infuriated and degraded mob; the helplessness of property-holders and the better classes; the boom of cannon and rattle of musketry in our streets; the skies lurid with conflagrations; the inconceivable barbarity and ferocity of the crowd toward an unfortunate and helpless race; the immense destruction of property—were the first dreadful revelations to many of our people of the existence among us of a great, ignorant, irresponsible class,

During New York's draft riots in 1863, looters did not hesitate to put homes to the torch.

who were growing up here without any permanent interest in the welfare of the community or the success of the Government—the *proletaires* of the European capitals. Of the gradual formation of this class, and the dangers to be feared from it, the agents of this Society have incessantly warned the public for the past eleven years.

—Eleventh Annual Report
Children's Aid Society, New York

In some degree this violence—or the perception of it—seems to have diminished in the course of the 1930's and 1940's. James Q. Wilson, a professor of government at Harvard, has noted the stages by which, for example, the treatment of violence as an element in American politics steadily decreased in successive editions of V. O. Key's textbook on American politics that appeared during the latter part of this period. It may be that depression at home and then war abroad combined to restrict opportunity or impulse. In any event, there was a lull, and in consequence all the more alarm when violence reappeared in the mid-1960's. But it was only that: a reappearance, not a beginning.

Yet with all this it is necessary to acknowledge a transformation howsoever subtle and tentative. The tempo of violence seems to have speeded up, the result, more or less direct, of change in the technology of communications, which now communicate not simply the fact but also the spirit of violent events, and do so instantaneously. More ominously, there appears to have been a legitimation of violence, and

*Four Detroit policemen drag
a handcuffed man during the
riot of July 24, 1967.*

a spread of its ethos to levels of society that have traditionally seen themselves, and have been, the repositories of stability and respect for, insistence upon, due process. It is one thing to loot clothing stores —Brooks Brothers was hit in 1863—to fight with the police, to seize sections of the city and hold out against them. It is another thing to seize university libraries, and that is very much part of the violence of our time, a violence that arises not only among the poor and disinherited, but also among the well-to-do and privileged, with the special fact that those elements in society which normally set standards of conduct for the society as a whole have been peculiarly unwilling, even unable, to protest the massive disorders of recent times.

A second theme is migration. The American urban experience has been singular in the degree to which our cities, especially those of the North and East, have been inundated by successive waves of what might be called rural proletarians, a dispossessed peasantry moving— driven from—other people's land in the country to other people's tenements in the city. American cities have ever been filled with unfamiliar people, acting in unfamiliar ways, at once terrified and threatening. The great waves of Catholic Irish of the early nineteenth century began the modern phase of this process, and it has never entirely stopped, not so much culminating as manifesting itself at this time in the immense folk migration of the landless southern Negro to the northern slum. In small doses such migrations would probably have been easily enough absorbed, but the sheer mass of the successive migrations has been such as to dominate the life of the cities in their immediate aftermath. The most dramatic consequence was that popular government became immigrant government: in the course of the nineteenth century, great cities in America came to be ruled by men of the people, an event essentially without precedent in world history —and one typically deplored by those displaced from power in the course of the transformation. Let me cite to you, for example, a schoolboy exercise written in 1925 by a young Brahmin, the bearer of one of Boston's great names, on the theme ''That there is no more sordid profession in the world than *Politics*.''

> The United States is one of the sad examples of the present form of government called democracy. We must first remember that America is made up of ignorant, uninterested, masses, of foreign people who follow the saying, ''that the sheep are many but the shepards are few.'' And the shepards of our government are wolves in sheeps clothing. From Lincoln's Gettysburg address let me quote the familiar lines ''a government of the people, for the people, and by the people.'' In the following lines I shall try and show you how much this is carried out in modern times.
>
> Let us take for example the position of our mayors. They are elected by majority vote from the population in which they live. Let us take for a case Mayor Curley of Boston. He tells the Irish who make up the people of Boston that he will lower their taxes, he will make Boston the greatest city in America. He is elected by the Irish mainly because he is an Irishman. He is a remarkable politician: he surrounds himself by Irishmen, he bribes the Chief Justice of the court, and although we know that the taxes that we pay all find a way into his own pocket we cannot prove by justice that he is not a just and good mayor.

But such distaste was not wholly groundless. The migrant peasants did and do misbehave: as much by the standards of the countryside they leave behind, as of the urban world to which they come. The process of adapting to the city has involved great dislocations in personality and manners as well as in abode. From the first, the process we call urbanization, with no greater specificity than the ancient medical diagnosis of ''bellyache'' or ''back pain,'' has involved a fairly high order of personal and social disorganization, almost always manifesting itself most visibly in a breakdown of social controls, beginning with the most fundamental of controls, those of family life. The Children's Aid Society of New York was founded in response to the appearance of this phenomenon among the immigrant Irish. Let me quote from their first annual report:

> It should be remembered, that there are no dangers to the value of property or to the permanency of our institutions, so great as those from the existence of such a class of vagabond, ignorant, ungoverned children. This ''dangerous class'' has not begun to show itself, as it will in eight or ten years, when these

boys and girls are matured. Those who were too negligent or too selfish to notice them as children, will be fully aware of them as men. They will vote. They will have the same rights as we ourselves, though they have grown up ignorant of moral principle, as any savage or Indian. They will poison society. They will perhaps be embittered at the wealth, and the luxuries, they never share. *Then let society beware, when the outcast, vicious, reckless multitude of New York boys, swarming now in every foul alley and low street, come to know their power and use it!*

Mumford in his new book speaks of precisely the same phenomenon:

One of the most sinister features of the recent urban riots has been the presence of roaming bands of children, armed with bottles and stones, taunting and defying the police, smashing windows and looting stores. But this was only an intensification of the window-breakings, knifings, and murders that have for the past twenty years characterized "the spirit of youth in the city streets."

And note the continuity of his last phrase, which alludes, of course, to Jane Addams' book *The Spirit of Youth and the City Streets*, in which she describes just those conditions at the turn of the century in terms that William James declared "immortal" and which, we must allow, were hardly ephemeral.

Yet here, too, technology seems to have been playing us tricks, accentuating and exacerbating our recent experience. The newest migrants come upon an urban world that seems somehow to need them less, to find them even more disturbing and threatening, and to provide them even less secure a place in the scheme of things than was ever quite the case with those who preceded them. I take this to be almost wholly a function of changing employment patterns consequent upon changing technology. But this very technology has also provided an abundance of material resources—and a measure of social conscience—so that people who are not especially needed are still provided for: by 1968, after seven years of unbroken economic expansion, there were 800,000 persons living on welfare in New York City, with the number expected to reach 1,000,000 in 1969. In part this is a phenomenon of birth rates. One person in ten, but one baby in six today is Negro. The poor continue to get children, but those children no longer succumb to cholera, influenza, and tuberculosis. Thus progress more and more forces us to live with the consequences of social injustice. In a more brutal age the evidence soon disappeared!

A third theme of the American urban experience has been the great wealth of our cities. Those who have moved to them have almost invariably improved their standard of life in the not-very-long run. Nor has this been wholly a matter of the consumption of goods and services. "City air makes men free," goes the medieval saying, and this has not been less true for industrial America. The matter was settled,

Urban traffic congestion has a long history.
This is New York's Fifth Avenue in 1921.

really, in an exchange between Hennessey and Dooley at the turn of the century. The country, said that faithful if not always perceptive patron, is where the good things in life come from. To which the master responded, "Yes, but it is the city that they go to." Technology is at the base of this process. The standard of life in American cities rises steadily, and there are few persons who do not somehow benefit. And yet this same technology—wealth—takes its toll. More and more we are conscious of the price paid for affluence in the form of manmade disease, uglification, and the second- and third-order effects of innovations which seem to cancel out the initial benefits.

Nathan Keyfitz, a sociologist at the University of Chicago, has nicely evoked the paradox implicit in many of the benefits of technology. Plenty encourages freedom. It also encourages density. Density can be managed only by regulation. Regulation discourages freedom. The experienced, conditioned city dweller learns, of course, to live with density by maintaining, as Keyfitz puts it, "those standards of reserve, discretion, and respect for the rights of others" that keep the nervous system from exhausting itself from the overstimulus available on any city street. The traditional assertion of Manhattan apartment dwellers that they have never met their neighbors across the hall is not a sign of social pathology: to the contrary, it is the exercise of exemplary habits of social hygiene. Borrowing the meter from George Canning's account of the failings of the Dutch, the rule for the modern cliff dweller might be put as follows:

> *In the matter of neighbors,*
> *The sound thing to do,*
> *Is nodding to many*
> *But speaking to few.*

It may be speculated, for example, that a clue to the transformation of the roistering, brawling, Merrie England of tradition into that somber land where strangers dare not speak to one another in trains lies *in the fact of the trains.* Technology—in this case the steam engine that created the vast nineteenth-century complexes of London and Manchester—brought about urban densities which required new forms of behavior for those who wished to take advantage of technology's advances and yet retain a measure of internal balance. The British, having been first to create the densities, were first to exhibit the telltale *sang-froid* of the modern urban dweller.

It may also be speculated that the "disorganized" life of the rural immigrants of today arises in some measure at least from an inability to control the level of stimulus: to turn down the radio, turn off the television, come in off the streets, stay out of the saloons, worry less about changing styles of clothes, music, dance, whatever. Lee Rainwater, a professor of sociology at the University of Washington, has provided us with painful accounts of the feeling of helplessness of the mothers of poor urban families in the face of the incursions from the street: the feeling, literally, that one cannot simply close one's door in the housing project and refuse to allow family, friends, neighbors, and God knows who else to come and go at will. This makes for lively neighborhoods, which from a distance seem almost enviable. But also for very disturbed people.

When such groups became large enough, when densities become ominous, government regulation becomes necessary, or at least all but invariably makes its appearance, so that even for the disciplined urbanite, technology at some point begins to diminish freedom. Keyfitz writes:

> George Orwell's *1984* is inconceivable without high population density, supplemented by closed circuit television and other devices to eliminate privacy. It exhibits in extreme form an historical process by which the State has been extending its power at the expense of the Church, the Family, and the Local Community, a process extending over 150 years.

There are few bargains in life, especially in city life.

A fourth theme of the American urban experience is mobility. Cities are not only places where the standards of life improve, but also very much—and as much now as ever—they are places where men rise in social standing. Otis Dudley Duncan and Peter M. Blau in their powerful study, *The American Occupational Structure,* have made this abundantly clear. American cities are places where men improve their position, as well as their condition. Or at least have every expectation that their sons will do so. The rigidities of caste and class dissolve, and opportunity opens. Yet this has never been quite so universally agreeable an experience as one could be led to suppose from the accounts of those for whom it has worked. In the city men first, perhaps, come to know success. There also men, especially those from the most caste-ridden rural societies, first come to know failure. It seems to me that this is a neglected aspect of the urban experience. I would argue that the rural peasant life of, let us say, the Irish, the Poles, the Slavs, the Italians, the Negro Americans who have migrated over the past century and a half was characterized by a near total absence of opportunity to improve one's position in the social strata, but also it was characterized by the near impossibility of observing others improve theirs. Rarely, in either absolute or relative terms, did individuals or families of the lowest peasant classes experience decline and failure: that in a sense is the law of a non-contingent society. Only with arrival in the city does that happen, and I would argue that for those who lose out in that competition, the experience can be far more embittering than that brought on by the drab constancy of country life.

Again technology—again television, for that matter—plays its part. Stephan Thernstrom in *Poverty and Progress* has noted that the immigrant workers of nineteenth-century New England, earning $1.50 a day when they had work, nonetheless managed in surprising numbers to put aside some money and to buy a piece of property and respectability before their lives were out, despite the fact that their incomes rarely permitted them to maintain what the social workers of the time calculated to be the minimum standard of living. The difference, Thernstrom notes, was that for the migrants a minimum standard of living was potatoes. Period. So long as they did not share the expectations of those about them—even the small expectations of social workers—they were not deprived. But advertising and television, and a dozen similar phenomena, have long since broken down that isolation, and the poor and newly arrived of the American city today appear to be caught up in a near frenzy of consumer emotions: untouched by the disenchantment with consumption of those very well off, and unrestrained by the discipline of household budgets imposed on those in between. The result, as best such matters can be measured, is a mounting level of discontent, which seems to slide over from the area of consumption as such to discontent with levels of social status that do not provide for maximum levels of consumption. Thus, even those who seem to be succeeding in the new urban world feel they are not succeeding enough, while others are suffused with a sense of failure.

A fifth theme of the American urban experience relates not to the experience of the poor and the newly arrived so much as to that of the well-to-do and the comparatively well settled: the persistent, one almost says primal, distaste for the city of educated Americans. In *The Intellectual Versus the City*, Morton and Lucia White point out that "enthusiasm for the American city has not been typical or predominant in our intellectual history. Fear has been the more common reaction." Fear, distaste, animosity, ambivalence. "In the beginning was the farm," or so the Jeffersonian creed asserts. And the great symbol —or perhaps *consummation* would be the better term—of this belief was the agreement whereby in return for the Jeffersonian willingness to have the federal government accept the debts acquired by states during the Revolutionary War, the capital of the new nation would be transferred from the city of New York to a swamp on the banks of the Potomac. Do not suppose that that agreement has not affected American history. New York remains the capital of the nation, as that term is usually understood, in the sense of the first city of the land. It is the capital of finance, art, theatre, publishing, fashion, intellect, industry . . . name any serious human endeavor other than politics, and its center in the United States will be found in New York City. In years of hard-fought presidential primaries, it is even for many purposes the political capital of the nation. But the seat of government is in Washington, which is only just beginning to respond to the fact that for half a century now ours has been a predominantly urban society.

Once again technology seems to be interacting with a pre-existing tendency. As the American city came more and more to be the abode of the machine, the alarm of American intellectuals, if anything, was intensified. And to a very considerable degree legitimated, for surely machines have given a measure of reality to alarums that were previously more fantasy than otherwise. To this has been added an ever more persistent concern for social justice, so that American intellectuals of the present time now conclude their expanding catalogues of the horrors of urban life with ringing assertions that the cities must be saved. But it is to be noted that this comes almost as an afterthought: the conviction that in the cities will be found the paramount threat to the life of the Republic has changed hardly at all. But at long last what they have been saying may be beginning to be true.

A sixth theme of the American urban experience, and the last with which I shall deal, has been and continues to be the singular ugliness of the average American city. That there are great and stunning exceptions is as much a matter of accident as anything. The essential fact is that for all the efforts to sustain and assert a measure of elite concern for urban aesthetics—of the kind one associates with historical preservation societies—and for all the occasional bursts of energy within the urban planning profession, the American city remains an ugly place to live, pretty much because we like it that way. A measure, no doubt, of this persisting condition can be attributed to the business and propertied interests of the nation that have resisted municipal expenditure, notably when it passed through the hands of egalitarian city halls. But it is more than that. Somehow, somewhere, in the course of the development of democratic, or demagogic, tradition in this nation the idea arose that concern for the physical beauty of the public buildings and spaces of the city was the mark of —what?—crypto-deviationist antipeople monumentalism—and in any event an augury of defeat at the polls. The result has been a steady deterioration in the quality of public buildings and spaces, and with it a decline in the symbols of public unity and common purpose with which the citizen can identify, of which he can be proud, and by which he can know what he shares with his fellow citizens. For the past seven years, as an example, I have been involved with efforts to reconstruct the center of the city of Washington, an attempt that begins with the assertion of the validity and viability of L'Enfant's plan of the late eighteenth century. In this effort we have had the tolerant to grudging co-operation of a fairly wide range of public and private persons, but let me say that we have had at no time the enthusiasm of any. And now I fear we may have even less, since of late there has arisen the further belief that to expend resources on public amenities is in effect to divert them from needed areas of public welfare. The very persons who will be the first to demand increased expenditures for one or another form of social welfare will be the last to concede that the common good requires an uncommon standard of taste and expenditure for the physical appointments of government and the public places of the city.

This attitude was perhaps unintentionally evoked by the respected Episcopal bishop of New York who in 1967 announced that in view of the circumstances of the poor of the city he would not proceed with the completion of the Cathedral of St. John the Divine, the largest such building ever begun, situated on a magnificent site overlooking the flat expanse of Harlem. Why? Meaning no disrespect, is it the plan of the church to liquidate its assets and turn them over to the poor? How much would that come to per head? But even so, would not the completed cathedral be an asset? If men need work, could they not be given jobs in its construction? The French—*toujours gai*, as mehitabel would have it—built Sacre Coeur as an act of penance for the excesses of the Commune. Could not the Episcopalians build St. John the Divine—a perfect symbol of rebirth—as a gesture of penance for all that Brahmin disdain which, in one form or another, to use Max Ways's phrase, taught us to despise our cities until they became despicable? If the phenomenon of ugliness, the last of my urban themes, can be thought to have arisen from more or less abstract qualities of American society, in the present and foreseeable future its principal cause is visible, concrete, and ubiquitous, which is to say it is the automobile. More than any other single factor it is the automobile that has wrecked the twentieth-century American city, dissipating its strength, destroying its form, fragmenting its life. So pervasive is the influence of the automobile that it is possible almost not to notice it at all. Indeed, it is almost out of fashion to do so: the men who first sought to warn us have almost ceased trying, while those who might have followed have sought instead formulations of their own, and in that manner diverted attention from the essential fact that in the age of the automobile cities, which had been places for coming together, have increasingly become machines for moving apart, devices whereby men are increasingly insulated and isolated one from the other.

A coda of sorts that has persisted through the elaboration of the themes of this paper has been the recent role of technology in accentuating and in a sense exacerbating long-established tendencies. The impact of technology on human society—on all forms of life—is the pre-eminent experience of the modern age, and obviously of the city as well. But only of late, one feels, has any very considerable appreciation developed that a change in quantity becomes after a point a change in quality, so that a society that begins by using technology can end by being used by it, and in the process, somehow, lose such control of its destiny as past human societies can be said to have had. Technology being so outwardly rational, it has been assumed by many that those who have been concerned about its directions have not really understood it. People easily come to fear what they do not understand, and it has been suspected, not always without foundation, that a certain amount of criticism of technology has been a latter-day form of rick burning.

One begins to think that this may not be so. Take the family automobile: a simple, easily enough comprehended (or seemingly so), unthreatening, and convenient product of folk technology rather than of modern science. Who would imagine any great harm coming from the automobile? Yet consider a moment. With its advent, everyday citizens, for the first time in human history, came into possession of unexampled physical energy: the powers of the gods themselves became commonplace. And from the very outset, violence ensued. It is said, for example, that when there were only four gasoline-powered vehicles in Missouri, two of them were in St. Louis and managed to collide with such impact as to injure both drivers, one seriously. Thus was introduced a form of pathology that was to grow steadily from that year to this. Today, something between one quarter and two thirds of the automobiles manufactured in the United States end up with blood on them. Indeed so commonplace and predictable have collisions become that the U.S. Court of Appeals for the Eighth Circuit recently ruled that a crash must be considered among the "intended uses" of a motor vehicle, and the manufacturers accordingly responsible to provide for such contingency in their design.

It becomes increasingly clear that the major environment, or, if you will, vehicle, in which incidents of uncontrolled episodic violence occur within the population is that of the automobile. Whether access and exposure to this environment have increased the incidence of such episodes, or whether the urban environment now largely created and shaped by the automobile has generally increased the violence level is uncertain at best (there has, of course, been a great decline in violence directed toward animals), but with the number of deaths and injuries at the present ongoing rates, and the number of vehicles in use approaching the one-hundred-million mark, it is a matter worth pondering.

Crashes are but one form of pathology. Each year in the United States automobiles pour eighty-six million tons of carbon monoxide, oxides of nitrogen and sulfur, hydrocarbons, lead compounds and particulates into the air we breathe. Recently my younger son came home with a button that announced, "Clean air smells funny." Dr. Clare C. Patterson of the California Institute of Technology put it another way in testimony before a congressional committee: "The average resident of the United States is being subject to severe chronic lead insult," originating in lead tetraethyl. Such poisoning can lead to severe intellectual disability in children: so much that Patterson feels it is dangerous for youth to live long periods of time near freeways.

But that is only the beginning, hardly the end of the impact of this particular form of technology on the society at this time. In consequence of the management of the automobile traffic system by means of traditional rules of the road, the incidence of armed arrest of American citizens is the highest of any civilization in recorded history. In 1965, for example, the California highway patrol alone made one million arrests. Indeed so commonplace has the experience become that a misdemeanor or felony committed in a motor vehicle is no longer considered a transgression of any particular consequence, and to be arrested by an armed police officer is regarded as a commonplace. That is precisely what Orwell told us would happen, is it not?

There are some 13,600,000 accidents a year, with some thirty million citations for violations issued each twelve months. And at this point, ineluctably, technology begins to have an effect on the most fundamental of civil institutions, the legal system itself. Largely in consequence of the impact of traffic-crash litigation, it now takes an average of 32.4 months to obtain a civil jury trial for a personal injury case in the metropolitan areas of the nation. In Suffolk County, New York, it is 50 months. In the Circuit Court of Cook County, serving Chicago, it is 64 months. This past winter in Bronx County, New York, the presiding judge of the appellate division announced he was suspending civil trials altogether while he tried to catch up with criminal cases. The courts are inundated; the bar is caught up, implicated and confused; the public knows simply that somehow justice is delayed and delayed. All of which is a consequence of this simplest form of technology, working its way on the institutions of an essentially pretechnological society.

It sometimes happens that a work of art appearing at a particular moment in time somehow simultaneously epitomizes and reveals the essential truths of the time. In a most astonishing and compelling way this has happened for the American city, and it has done so, most appropriately, on Forty-second Street in Manhattan, in the persona of the Ford Foundation headquarters, designed by Kevin Roche, John Dinkeloo & Associates—a great firm, successor to Eero Saarinen & Associates whose first large commission was, of course, the General Motors Technical Center outside Detroit. Saarinen, and now Roche, have gathered a group of artist/technicians whose work, from the Dulles Airport at Chantilly, Virginia, to the Trans World Airlines Terminal at Kennedy Airport and the Columbia Broadcasting headquarters in New York City, has evoked the power and purpose of the age of technology as perhaps no other organization has.

Here in the Ford Foundation headquarters is expressed the very highest purposes of modern technological power: compassionate and potent concern for the betterment of man's lot. The building is everything a building could be: a splendid work place, a gift to the city in the form of a public park, a gift to the world simply as a work of imagination and daring. If it is a reproach of sorts to the public and private builders of the nation who by and large show little of either, it is a gentle reproach, more show than tell. In that favored form of foundation giving, it is a kind of demonstration project: an example of what can, and what therefore in an age of technology must, be done.

The exterior of the building is quiet and unassertive: it is not *that* big a building, and it seeks rather to understate both its size and importance. No-nonsense shafts of Cor-ten steel rise from the ground, here and there sheathed with a blue-brown granite and interspersed with large rectangular glass panels. Rather in the mode of a cathedral, the portals do not so much impart as suggest the experience to come. It is only on entering—Chartres, say, or Vézelay—and encountering the incomparable space, shaped and reserved for a single purpose only, that one leaves off observing the building and begins to be shaped by it: the eye rises, the mind turns to last things. So with the Ford Foundation headquarters. One passes through revolving doors to enter a garden. Truly a garden, a small park, like nothing anywhere else to be encountered, a third of an acre, lush and generous, climbing a small hill that follows the terrain of Manhattan at this point, illuminated by the now vast windows that climb nine stories toward heaven itself, and there only to be met by a glass roof. Water moves slightly in a pool—a font? Attendants move quietly, and are helpful. One notices that vegetation sprouts from beams and ledges on the third and fourth and even the fifth floors. One is awestruck by the wealth and power of the foundation, and the sheer authority of its intent to do good. Only the gray-white light is not quite what it should be: as in those French and German cathedrals whose stained glass was lost to war or revolution or Protestantism.

But this is only the entering light. As in any such edifice, there is a light within. In this case a very monstrancelike golden-brown glow that shines forth from the offices of the foundation executives, who from the floor of the park are to be seen at their work behind glass panels formed and reticulated by the same rusted beams that frame the colorless glass of two sides of the building. (Cor-ten steel seals itself by rusting and need not be painted.) At this point one perceives readily enough that the building has been built as a factory. Not precisely as a factory—any more than the Gothic Revival built office buildings precisely as medieval monasteries—but rather to evoke the style and somehow the spirit of a great plant. The huge, heavy lateral beams, from which elsewhere would be suspended the giant hoists that roam back and forth amidst the clatter and roar; the sawtooth roof; the plant managers' eyrie hung from the ceiling, keeping an eye on everything; the perfectly standardized, interchangeable fixtures in each office; the seriousness and competence of it all, even the blue-black, somehow oily granite of the cheerless rest rooms (No Loitering

The Ford Foundation building
at night, as seen from
New York's 42nd Street.

in the Can) magically, stunningly, triumphantly, evoke the style and spirit of the primeval capitalist factory. Cor-ten. Red. Rouge. River Rouge. Of course! And why not, for $16,000,000 of Henry Ford's money? He was that kind of man. Knew how to make automobiles and obviously liked to. Else he could hardly have done it so well. All black, just as the Ford Foundation headquarters is all brown. Same principle. So also the panopticon effect of the exposed offices wherein the presumptively interchangeable officers at their perfectly interchangeable desks labor at their good works in full view of management and public alike. (The public serving, perhaps, as the visitors to Jeremy Bentham's prospective model prison: a "promiscuous assemblage of unknown and therefore unpaid, ungarbled and incorruptible inspectors"?) Critics, at least in the first reviews, seem to have missed most of this, but no matter: the architecture needs no guidebook: the intellectual and aesthetic effect is not to be avoided, even when the intent is least perceived. All in all it is just as McGeorge Bundy proclaimed it in the 1968 annual report of the foundation: "Kevin Roche's triumph."

But it is more than that. Or rather, there is more than is to be perceived at one time. A great work of art has levels of meaning at once various and varying. Standing in the park, gazing upward, following the factory motif, the mind is of a sudden troubled. Something is missing. Noise. Factories are places of noise. Of life. Clatter. Roar.

*A daytime view, looking out
from the two-hundred-foot-
square interior garden.*

There is no noise here. Only quiet. The quiet of the . . .? The mind
oscillates. It is a factory, all right. But a *ruined* factory! The holocaust
has come and gone: hence the silence. The windows have blown out,
and only the gray light of the burned-out world enters. The weather
has got in, and with it nature now reclaiming the ravaged union of
fire and earth. The factory floor has already begun to turn to forest.
Vegetation has made its way to ledges halfway up the interior. The
machine tools are gone. Reparations? Vandalism? Who knows. But
the big machines will no longer be making little machines. Gone too is
the rational, reforming, not altogether disinterested purpose of the
panopticon. One is alone in the ominous gloom of a Piranesi prison,
noting the small bushes taking hold in the crevices of the vast ruined
arches.

Is it the past or the future that has taken hold of the mind? Certainly the ruined steel frame is a good enough symbol of the twentieth
century so far. (Where had one last seen that color? Of course. Pingree
Street in Detroit after the riot. A year later there it was again, on
Fourteenth Street in Washington: the fiery orange-red of the twisted
steel shopping centers' framing after the looting and arson has
passed.) Or is it the future? There is a *sur réal* quality that comes of
standing in the ruined half of the building, watching the life going
on behind the glass walls of the intact half, seemingly oblivious to the
devastation without. Can ruin advance slowly like rot? No. Yes. Did

the automobile start all this? No. Surely it is all this that started automobiles. One quarter to two thirds of which end up with blood on them. Blood. Red. Rouge. River Rouge.

Enough.

But then why has the American architect Joseph Stein built the Ford Foundation headquarters in New Delhi immediately adjacent the Lodi Tombs, symbols of death sensual to the point of necrophilia? Did not Bentham remark that he could legislate wisely for all India from the recesses of his study? There's a panopticon in your future.

No. Enough.

And yet it comes together in a way. "*Le siècle de la machine,*" Le Corbusier wrote in 1924, "*a réveillé l'architecte.*" Not least because the machine destroys so much of that experience of community that the architect seeks to create. A biographer describes Eero Saarinen's purpose thus: "What . . . [he] wished to renew, maintain, and improve was the organic expression of the *civitas* which he found weakened or destroyed virtually everywhere in modern civilization, with one significant exception—the university campus." And so Roche built a ruined machine-for-making-machines as the headquarters of a great philanthropic foundation whose principal concerns have been to support the universities of the nation, and to seek to strengthen the community life of its cities.

The research of James Q. Wilson and Edward C. Banfield at Harvard University is now beginning to produce results surprisingly similar to the visions of the architect/artist. As Wilson puts it, "After a decade or more of being told by various leaders that what's wrong with our large cities is inadequate transportation, or declining retail sales, or poor housing, the resident of the big city is beginning to assert his own definition of that problem—and this definition has very little to do with the conventional wisdom on the urban crisis." Wilson and his colleague asked one thousand Boston homeowners what *they* thought to be the biggest urban problem of this time.

> The "conventional" urban problems—housing, transportation, pollution, urban renewal, and the like—were a major concern of only 18 per cent of those questioned, and these were expressed disproportionally by the wealthier, better-educated respondents. Only 9 per cent mentioned jobs and employment, even though many of those interviewed had incomes at or even below what is often regarded as the poverty level. *The issue which concerned more respondents than any other was variously stated—crime, violence, rebellious youth, racial tension, public immorality, delinquency. However stated, the common theme seemed to be a concern for improper behavior in public places.*
>
> What these concerns have in common, and thus what constitutes the "urban" problem for a large percentage (perhaps a majority) of urban citizens, is *a sense of the failure of community.*

And yet cities, by definition, destroy community. Or is it only when they are too big, too unsettled, that they do this? Is it only when social conditions are allowed to arise which lead inevitably to assaults on the private communities that experienced city dwellers create for themselves, which in turn lead to more collective regulation and, in consequence, less of the self-imposed decision to behave properly and as expected, which is the essence of community?

We do not know. "Them what gets the apple gets the worm," goes an old folk saying. Is that what the Ford Foundation building represents: a shining exterior, rotting from within? A civilization whose cancerous growth has already devoured half its offspring, and is moving toward the unthinking, untroubled other half? We shall see. Hopefully, in the meantime we shall also think about it a bit. Mumford, unfailingly, has sorted out the levels of immediacy and difficulty of the current crisis.

> To go deeper into this immediate situation we must, I suggest, distinguish between three aspects, only one of which is open to immediate rectification. We must first separate out the problems that are soluble with the means we have at hand: this includes such immediate measures as vermin control, improved garbage collection, cheap public transportation, new schools and hospitals and health clinics. Second, those that require a new approach, new agencies, new methods, whose assemblage will require time, even though the earliest possible action is urgent. And finally there are those that require a reorientation in the purposes and ultimate ideals of our whole civilization—solutions that hinge on a change of mind, as far-reaching as that which characterized the change from the medieval religious mind to the modern scientific mind. Ultimately, the success of the first two changes will hinge upon this larger—and, necessarily, later —transformation. So, far from looking to a scientifically oriented technology to solve our problems, we must realize that this highly sophisticated dehumanized technology itself now produces some of our most vexatious problems, including the unemployment of the unskilled.

But something more than thinking will be required. A certain giving of ourselves with no certainty of what will come of it. It is the only known way, and imperfectly known at that.

Attend to Mrs. Boyle at the end of *Juno and the Paycock*, pleading for the return of a simpler life, a life before all things had become political, before all men were committed, before all cities somehow seemed in flames:

> Sacred Heart o' Jesus, take away our hearts o' stone, and give us hearts o' flesh! Take away this murdherin' hate, an' give us Thine own eternal love!

Martin Duberman

Harlem:
The Village That
Became a Ghetto

What Daniel P. Moynihan has done in the previous essay for the history of urban problems in general, in this article Martin Duberman does, in somewhat different fashion, for one city, New York, and one particular problem—the black ghetto. His account is both a study in microcosm of the fate of the northern Negro and a history of a particular urban neighborhood. It throws light also on many broader aspects of city life in the nineteenth and twentieth centuries: the role of urban transportation, of land speculation, of the housing problem in general (for rich and for poor). Above all it reveals the dynamic quality of the city environment and the extraordinary changes that occur one after another when a huge urban complex develops out of a cluster of villages in a relatively short span of time. The history of Harlem, "the village that became a ghetto," is, of course, entirely tragic and ignoble—a reflection of the tragedy of the black man in America and of the ignobility of the majority of white Americans in matters of race relations.

Mr. Duberman, professor of history at Princeton University, is the author of the standard biography of Charles Francis Adams and also a playwright. His In White America, a drama based on letters and other documents dealing with Negro life, first produced in 1963, was both a commercial and critical success.

*M*anhattan Island had Negroes almost as soon as it had settlers. They were slaves, of course, the property of the New Amsterdam Dutch; and very few of them lived in Harlem. That northeastern section of the island, although settled early, remained throughout the colonial period a distant village, a rural outpost of the metropolis. Nearly all of the seven hundred Negroes who were part of New York's population when Peter Stuyvesant surrendered his colony to the English in 1664 lived far downtown, with or near their masters. Under the Dutch, slaves received the rudiments of schooling, were allowed to own land, and in a few cases, were even permitted to obtain their freedom.

The English changed all that, developing a slave code of precise regulations and heightened restrictions. Yet by the end of the eighteenth century, the movement to abolish slavery in New York State had begun. Led by the Quakers, and given further impetus by the egalitarian ideas of the Revolution, it resulted in full emancipation through action of the state legislature on July 4, 1827.

When that date arrived, the Negro population of Manhattan and Brooklyn had grown to about fifteen thousand. The Negro citizens of New York were henceforth free—but hardly equal. They had to meet higher property qualifications than their white counterparts in order to vote; they had to attend separate schools; they were barred from many public facilities; they could hold only the most menial jobs; and they were forced to live in squalid surroundings.

This does not mean that in the pre-Civil War period the Negro was confined to a single area of the city; but within a given neighborhood, segregation was usually complete. Between 1820 and 1840, Negroes were concentrated chiefly in the notorious "Five Points" district, an area that today includes City Hall and its environs. The crowded Negro section known as Stagg Town was vividly described by Charles Dickens in his *American Notes:* ". . . lanes and alleys, paved with mud knee-deep . . . hideous tenements [in] which . . . dogs would howl to lie . . . where women and men . . . slink off to sleep, forcing the dislodged rats to move away."

There was a somewhat brighter side: from 1821 to 1829 a Negro theatre existed, the African Grove, which whites were allowed to attend, but in a partitioned section at the back; the famed "old Mulberry School" produced most of the city's Negro leaders; and there was the beginning of an institutional life in the African Society of Mutual Relief and in the growing number of Negro churches.

Stability, however, was not to be the lot of New York's Negro community. By the time of the Civil War the Five Points had been taken over by the immigrant Irish, and the focus of Negro settlement had shifted to Greenwich Village. This, too, was temporary; by the turn of the century, the Negro population had become most heavily concentrated in two areas: the unsavory "Tenderloin" (today's midtown Manhattan) and "San Juan Hill" (today's west Sixties) so called because of frequent racial battles that took place in the neighborhood.

When this lithograph was done
in 1812, Harlem was a village
of less than one hundred families.

It was by no means only the pressure of foreign immigrant groups that kept Negroes on the move. Probably the most important factor of all was the huge increase of New York's black population itself, caused largely by the arrival of southern Negroes. By 1910 the number of blacks in Manhattan alone had jumped to over 60,000; in another twenty years the figure would more than triple.

They had to go somewhere, and where they went was determined by unpredictable factors. During a real-estate depression, for instance, the more affluent members of the Negro community would grasp at the chance to move to a better neighborhood; their advent would then lead to widespread white desertion, and the poorer Negroes would rapidly move in behind them. The curious fact is that before 1900, Harlem seemed the part of Manhattan least likely to become a black residential section, let alone a black ghetto.

For Harlem was a synonym for elegant living through a good part of the nineteenth century. As late as 1820, it had only ninety-one families, one church, one school, and one library; still a village, it was dominated by the extensive estates of the wealthy farmers known as patroons. A New York City planning commission in 1811 announced its opinion that Harlem would not be "covered with houses for centuries to come."

It is true that in the decades just before and after the Civil War, Harlem went into a temporary decline. Many of the large estates, including Alexander Hamilton's beautiful Grange, were auctioned off because of worn-out soil. Newly arriving Irish immigrants, destitute and unwanted, squatted on the village's abandoned lands, threw up flimsy shantytowns (bringing property values down still further), and thus for the first time, though not the last, turned Harlem into a slum.

But a renaissance was near at hand. The turning point came between 1878 and 1881 when the elevated railroad was extended to 129 Street, thus converting Harlem into a feasible commuting point from downtown Manhattan. Feasible soon meant fashionable, since the improved transportation came at precisely the moment when the island's population and industrial growth were necessitating new expansion—in Manhattan, that could only occur to the north.

And so by the mid-1880's, the Harlem land boom was on. Land speculators and builders seemingly overnight turned a decaying community into the city's most plush residential area. Rows of elegant brownstones (many of which are still occupied) sprang up. A stunning group of one hundred and six was designed by Stanford White; its rents started at the then-astronomical figure of eighty dollars per month (the houses are now known as Striver's Row because of their well-to-do Negro tenants). Into the new mansions moved old-line aristocrats and new-style politicians, and to tend to their needs came theatres, luxurious restaurants, Gothic-revival churches, banks, a Harlem Opera House (built by Oscar Hammerstein I in 1880), a Harlem Yacht Club, a Harlem Literary Society, and a Harlem Philharmonic Orchestra. One of America's first suburban communities had been born—and it was, for a while, one of the most elegant. "It is evident to the most superficial observer," said the *Harlem Monthly Magazine* in 1893, "that the centre of fashion, wealth, culture, and intelligence, must, in the near future, be found in the ancient and honorable village of Harlem." Twenty years later that would read like satire.

A small number of Negroes had always lived in Harlem—as slaves in the seventeenth and eighteenth centuries, and following emancipation, as small farmers or domestic servants. By the 1880's the Negro community had grown to several hundred families and was generally, though not exclusively, confined to the streets of the west 120's. It was a large enough community to provide abundant servants for fashionable white Harlem, but not large enough to create apprehension.

Then, around the turn of the century, came a substantial growth in Manhattan's Negro population and, coincidentally, the swift collapse of the Harlem land boom. Speculators had inflated real-estate values and contractors had overbuilt—the result was the bust of 1904-1905. Faced with ruin, some operators decided to rent their vacant apartments to Negroes. They had no lack of applicants, for many in the black community were eager to pay the higher Harlem rents. In 1905 there had been a brutal race riot in the ghetto of the west Sixties, and at the same time demolition on the site of the new Pennsylvania Station destroyed hundreds of Negro tenements and caused unbelievable crowding in the Negro slums of midtown. In less than a decade, at least 20,000 Negroes had come to live in central Harlem, most of them between 130 and 144 streets, bounded by Park Avenue on the east and by Eighth Avenue on the west.

Needless to say, this new Negro influx into Harlem was protested—bitterly but futilely. Whites tried to halt the "invasion" by pressuring banks not to lend money or to renew mortgages, by forming holding companies to buy up "Negro" houses and evict their tenants, and by agreements between white property owners not to rent or sell to Negroes.

All of these efforts failed. The chief reason, apparently, was that unified action by white property owners could never be won. Some white landlords and speculators could not resist the lure of profit. Indeed, a few actively encouraged the Negro advance: they would buy a building and open it up to black tenants with the purpose of forcing neighboring whites either to sell out at a deflated price or to buy back the "Negro" building at an inflated one. By the end of World War I it became clear that the black influx could not be halted, and the white community shifted its tactics from resistance to flight. House by house, block by block, they fled the black advance. It was not Negro behavior, but white, that turned Harlem into a ghetto.

New York's pattern was hardly unique. In the early years of the twentieth century, ghettos were rising in cities all over the country. This was the result of rural southern Negroes migrating toward "freedom" and industrial opportunity, and of the subsequent decision by whites to isolate the migrants in clearly defined enclaves. New York had its Harlem, Chicago its South Side, Detroit its Paradise Valley, and almost every urban center its "Nigger Rows," "Bronze-

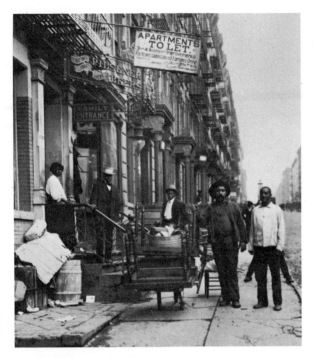

Harlem's fall from elegance took just about a decade. In 1908 it was still the home of fashionable ladies who rode their carriages to the races (left). By about 1918, when the photograph at right was taken, Harlem was on its way to becoming a ghetto.

villes," "Smoketowns," or "Coon Alleys."

Yet the development of city ghettos did not follow identical lines. In Chicago, for example, preexisting Negro neighborhoods simply expanded their boundaries—a pattern in contrast to the dramatic shift of New York's Negro community into a previously all-white area. Harlem, moreover, was unique in the sense that no other black ghetto arose in what recently had been a fashionable white community.

In any case, Harlem was changed in a few decades from a symbol of success to a symbol of defeat, from a gilt-edged white compound to a dilapidated black slum. The combination of high rents and low salaries had much to do with the change. By the end of the twenties, in response to the overwhelming demand by Negroes for apartments and the limited facilities available, rents in Harlem had doubled from what they had been the previous decade; the average Harlem family paid about $9.50 a room monthly compared with the $6.50 paid by the typical white working-class family elsewhere in the city. At the same time, the Negro worker, restricted to menial jobs, was earning less money than his white counterpart—roughly $1,300 a year compared with $1,600.

As a result of high rents and low incomes, families often had to take in lodgers to make ends meet, and this in turn weakened the family structure and led to more crowding and unsanitary living conditions. Another device for raising rent money in the twenties was the famed "rent party," where a twenty-five cent admission ticket bought southern barbecue and piano playing by the likes of Willie "the Lion" Smith, James P. Johnson, Willie Gant, or "Fats" Waller.

All the statistics of birth and death and disease made it clear that Harlem's health problems were the most pronounced in the city. Not all of this, however, could be laid at the door of low incomes or congested living conditions. Many Harlemites were recent arrivals from the rural South, and as "an ignorant and unsophisticated peasant people"—a description given by a Negro scholar, E. Franklin Frazier —they lacked the experience and training needed for survival in an urban environment. They tended to put their money in the hands of quack spiritualists and "healers."

Yet in the twenties, when most white New Yorkers thought of Harlem, they thought of it not as a slum community breeding disease and despair, but as the exotic locale for a night's slumming. To whites, Harlem ("Take the 'A' Train") meant bootleggers and prostitutes, jazz and chitterlings, the numbers racket and dope; it meant the little cellar cabarets and after-hours places where Jelly Roll Morton or Ethel Waters might entertain and where jam sessions might last all night; it meant the Cotton Club, where Duke Ellington's band held forth for five years; it meant the Savoy Ballroom, which took up a whole block on Lenox Avenue and where, on a two-hundred-foot dance floor under klieg lights, the Lindy Hop was born. (Malcolm X reports in his autobiography that when La Guardia closed the Savoy during World War II, Harlemites believed the real reason was to stop Negroes from dancing with white women.)

Throughout the twenties white playboys poured their money and their fantasies into Harlem. A few blacks may have profited from the money, but many more suffered from the fantasies. For most Negroes in Harlem were not swingers, were not joyous primitives or rhythmic giants. They were people struggling to adjust to a strange urban world, struggling to afford enough food and clothing, struggling to persuade the landlord to fix a leak in the ceiling or to cover up rat holes so that their babies would not be bitten at night.

A few whites were willing to face the facts of Harlem life and to try to change them, but only a few. Mary White Ovington, who in 1909 helped to found the National Association for the Advancement of Colored People, was one. John D. Rockefeller, Jr., who gave millions to Harlem charities, was another—although the Paul Laurence Dunbar Apartments, which he financed in the twenties to serve as a model housing development, were priced too high for most Negroes.

Fortunately, Harlem did not put its hopes for a better life solely on the benevolence of whites—slummers or philanthropists. The Negro community developed its own leadership and its own forms of expression. Often that leadership proved distasteful to whites—as with the black nationalist Marcus Garvey, whose Universal Negro Improvement Association flourished during the twenties, and more recently, with Malcolm X and Adam Clayton Powell, Jr. Sometimes the community's leadership, though highly acceptable to whites, was not in the best interest of Harlem itself—as when Negro political boss Ferdinand Q. Morton was recognized by Tammany throughout the

1920's and early 1930's as the head of the Harlem Democracy (often called Black Tammany) even while he dictatorially silenced opposition and used his power chiefly to promote his own rather than the community's interests. Only a few of Harlem's leaders have won and held admiration in both the white and black worlds. Foremost in this regard is A. Philip Randolph, the pioneering civil rights organizer and president of the Brotherhood of Sleeping Car Porters, whose personal integrity and devotion to the interests of the Negro community alike have been unquestionable.

It is paradoxical that the ghetto at one and the same time constricts the possibilities of Negro life and yet forms the base for such black power as has existed—not only political, but fraternal and social as well.

Harlem has changed surprisingly little since the 1920's. The Savoy Ballroom and the Cotton Club no longer exist, but in terms of basic institutional and cultural patterns, Harlem today is much what it was forty years ago. To the extent that change has come, it has often been for the worse.

Central Harlem no longer has, needless to say, a Philharmonic Orchestra or a Yacht Club, but less obvious is the fact that in the entire ghetto there is not one museum or art gallery, and only five libraries (one of which is the superb Schomburg Collection, probably the most important archive in the world devoted to Negro life and history). About all that Harlem does have more of in 1968 than it did in 1928 is churches. There are now 256 of them, the majority belonging to segregated Negro Protestant denominations; many of the rest are evangelical sects.

Economically as well as socially, Harlem is not the viable, self-contained community that it was back at the turn of the century. There are still banks, but with the exception of the Carver Federal Savings and Loan Association (with assets of more than $21,000,000), they are all branches of white-owned downtown banks. There are still thousands of stores (with an annual gross sale of nearly $350,000,000), but they, too, are mostly owned by whites who live outside the community—and who invest their profits outside. Probably the chief reason why so few of Harlem's stores are owned by Harlemites is that in a community that lives on credit, as Harlem does, future wages are already pledged, and thus there is no risk capital available for business investment. (It should be noted, though, that Jackie Robinson, the former baseball star-turned-businessman and adviser to Governor Nelson Rockefeller, recently reported that in the last two years, Negro-owned businesses in Harlem have risen from eighteen per cent to thirty-one per cent of the total.) Harlem's businesses, moreover, provide very little employment for the community's inhabitants, most of whom have to travel downtown for their daily jobs, forty-three per cent of which are in unskilled occupations due to be automated out of existence within the next decade.

In still another sense, central Harlem since World War II has been a community in decline. Many middle- or upper-income Negroes

James Reagan's 1968 drawing, Pool Hall, *expresses what Harlem looks like from the inside to an eighteen-year-old resident of the ghetto.*

have moved to Westchester or Long Island. Even the Negro masses have begun to shift to other ghettos within the city—to the lower Bronx, to Queens, and to Brooklyn's Bedford-Stuyvesant—with the result that central Harlem suffered a ten per cent population loss from 1950 to 1960, a decade in which most metropolitan ghettos were growing.

Many of the elegant brownstones still stand in Harlem and from the outside still give off an air of stability. But their interior condition is far worse than it was forty years ago. More than 230,000 people live within three and one half square miles, packed into tenements of which twenty-five per cent have been judged "overcrowded" and a full forty-nine per cent have been labelled "dilapidated." Rents, moreover, continue to be high; a single room is usually priced from $16 to $28 per month, and it is difficult to find any apartment, let alone a decent one, which rents for less than $75 per month. The city's Buildings Department averages five hundred complaints a day about rats, falling plaster, lack of heat, and unsanitary plumbing.

The disabling personal and social consequences of living under such conditions are, as Kenneth B. Clark has eloquently written in *Dark Ghetto,* beyond mere quantification. Statistics of disease, drug addiction, crime, and prostitution tell us something of these consequences, but we have heard the reports so often that they carry only limited impact. Besides, statistics cannot measure or weigh the frightful emotional costs of living in the ghetto; they cannot convey the irritability and self-alienation which results from lack of privacy, the fury which mounts at an absentee landlord's endless evasions, the anguish which comes when a fourteen-year-old child turns to prostitution or to drugs.

*Expletives and activity, amid the ghetto's
boredom are all expressed in eighteen-year-old
Jeff McDonald's* A Harlem Playground *(1968).*

To get some sense of the ghetto's human cost, one must look not to
the statistics of the social scientists, but to the work of Negro writers
for whom Harlem has been the central experience and the central
metaphor. From the 1920's on, talented black poets and novelists—
Langston Hughes, Countée Cullen, James Baldwin, Jean Toomer,
Claude McKay, Richard Wright, Ralph Ellison—have given us insight
into Harlem's special hell. Most recently of all, we have had Claude
Brown's searing autobiography, *Manchild in the Promised Land.* One
anecdote and one statement in Brown's book does more to sum up
contemporary Harlem than any volume of statistics. The anecdote
relates to Brown's experience as a young teenager hauled into court
for stealing: the judge, after lecturing Brown and his friends, an-
nounces magnanimously that he is "going to give you boys another
chance"; Brown takes even himself by surprise when he yells out,
"Man, you not givin' us another chance. You givin' us the same
chance we had before." Yet at the end of his book, Brown makes this
telling statement: ". . . despite everything that Harlem did to our
generation, I think it gave something to a few. It gave them a strength
that couldn't be obtained anywhere else."

But finally the last word must go to Langston Hughes: Harlem
"has been the subject of innumerable surveys, innumerable reports
published and unpublished, innumerable official and unofficial studies,
hundreds of magazine and newspaper articles, columns, radio and TV
commentaries, plus an unending stream of speeches from men in pul-
pits, at forums and learned seminars. Seemingly all that could conceivably be written or said, has been said—and Harlem is still the
same old Harlem."

Andy Logan

J.F.K.:
The Stained-Glass
Image

It is always difficult to evaluate recent events. Time—the perspective of history—is essential to any sound understanding of their significance. This is especially true where the careers of the main actors in recent events are concerned, and indeed the task becomes next to impossible when the subject is a man cut off in the prime of life by tragic, meaningless circumstances. The tendency to make a martyred saint of the victim, to forget his weaknesses and glorify his strengths, then becomes irresistible. This was true, as Andy Logan, staff writer for the New Yorker and author of The Man Who Robbed the Robber Barons, points out in the following essay, in the case of Abraham Lincoln and also in the recent case of John F. Kennedy.

Logan dissects with candor and critical acuity the shelves of books, many of them best sellers, which have appeared in the years since Kennedy's assassination. She exposes in detail the cant, the sentimentalism, and the obfuscations which they contain, and offers some generalizations about the genre of "Kennedy books" as well. That this essay was written in sorrow rather than anger, however, is clear. It is her own admiration of Kennedy, the belief that Kennedy's long-run reputation will only be harmed by unctuous flattery and self-serving praise, that has motivated her attack on the Kennedy biographers. The historical lesson to be learned, of course, concerns the importance of objectivity. The historian may justly admire and praise his subject; nevertheless, he must be neither an apologist nor a press agent if his work is to have any enduring value as a portrait of the man.

*I*n mid-November, 1963, according to all the major best-seller lists, by far the most popular nonfiction publication in America was a book that portrayed Jack Kennedy as "immature," "arrogant," "snobbish," "glib," "slick," "calculating," "hard as nails," "mealymouthed," "opportunistic," "Machiavellian," "intellectually shallow," "spiritually rootless," "morally pusillanimous," "passionless," "vain," "shifty-eyed," and, for every good reason, nicknamed "Jack the Knife." The book, of course, was *J.F.K.: The Man and the Myth*, by Victor Lasky. By the end of the same month there burned above the grave of the very same man an eternal flame, more often reserved in the protocol of his religion for saints of the first order. Whatever their religious or political persuasion, few Americans were protesting this instant canonization. In the horror, grief, and guilt that overwhelmed the nation following the assassination, the minor Kennedy myth that Lasky had contended against—the fine-liberal-fellow image—had expanded uncountable times, been transformed and purified, burst all mortal bonds, and soared toward the realm of the supernatural. As after the death of Lincoln nearly a hundred years earlier, the common thought of Americans was "How are the fallen mighty!" and John F. Kennedy was on his way to becoming the legendary national hero of his century.

"It is difficult now to comprehend the wave of hero-worship which swept over the country after Lincoln's assassination," Roy P. Basler wrote a generation ago in *The Lincoln Legend*. "Lincoln was suddenly lifted into the sky as the folk-hero, the deliverer, and the martyr who had come to save his people and to die for them . . . the folk mind was enraptured with the stories of how Lincoln had suffered, prayed, dreamed, and loved mankind and conquered his enemies. How he had doubted, despaired, cunningly schemed, and contrived to effect his ends, no one wanted to hear." Thousands of Americans were soon seriously arguing that Lincoln was of divine origin. (After all, in his own words he was the son of an "angel mother"; his father-of-record was a poor carpenter; and he was shot on Good Friday.) This conclusion would have astonished Lincoln only a little more than, in the view of Arthur Krock and some of John Kennedy's other friends, the lighting of the eternal flame would have embarrassed Kennedy nearly a century later. But neither man was by this time making history. It was being made for him.

Until 1872 Lincoln biography was entirely in the hands of spiritual and stylistic descendants of Parson Weems, rather than of men who had known him as he was. Then a book appeared by Ward Hill Lamon, a jovial crony of Lincoln's who had ridden the backwoods legal circuit with him in central Illinois. Lamon was "pre-eminently the Good Fellow," writes Sandburg, and the President's more punctilious associates regarded the long Lincoln-Lamon alliance as evidence of "a certain degree of . . . obtuseness" on Lincoln's part. "Sing me a little song," he often said to Lamon, who would then make him smile with some such nonsensical ballad as "Cousin Sally Downard." "I want you with me, I must have you," Lincoln told his old friend

when he was about to leave for Washington, and he arranged to have
Lamon appointed a city marshal at the capital. Lamon's biography
of Lincoln, pulled together by a ghostwriter, was based largely on
material gathered by Lincoln's onetime law partner, William H.
Herndon. A bald account of the late President's political opportunism
and his often indecorous life during his western years, it was denounced
as "shameless." "Want of delicacy and even decency," wrote a more
worshipful biographer, made its appearance "something close to a
national misfortune." The book did not even reap the traditional
reward of publications charged with indecency; it was a financial
failure. In the first years after the assassination Herndon had delivered
several lectures based on the material he had made available to Lamon,
but it wasn't until 1889 that he published his own biography, *Herndon's Lincoln,* in which Lincoln emerged as an earthy, moody, ir-
religious frontier hero, unrecognizable as the saintly Christian martyr
of prevailing legend. ("Why, Lamon," wrote Herndon, "if you and
I had not told the exact truth about Lincoln he would have been a
myth in a hundred years after 1865.") The Herndon book, which, of
course, launched myths of its own, such as the Ann Rutledge love
story so infuriating to Mary Todd Lincoln, brought Herndon less than

Michael Ramus' mythical cartoon pictures the Kennedy authors surrounding their hero in the White House Rose Garden. From left: Maud Shaw, Pierre Salinger, Paul Fay, Theodore Sorensen, Arthur Schlesinger, Jr., Evelyn Lincoln, Kenneth O'Donnell, David Powers, Lawrence O'Brien, and (with microphone, far right) William Manchester.

five hundred dollars in royalties in the next eight years. Their tedious, circumspect *Abraham Lincoln: A History* proved to be a more profitable venture for Lincoln's two private secretaries, John G. Nicolay and John Hay. Authorized by Robert Todd Lincoln, the President's surviving son (Nicolay and Hay, gibed Herndon, were "afraid of Bob; he gives them materials and they in their turn play *hush*"), the widely admired biography appeared in serial form in the *Century Magazine* during the eighties but was not published as a book until 1890, a quarter of a century after Lincoln's death.

The colleagues of our twentieth-century presidential martyr did not wait so long to be heard from. As we all know, among the nearly two hundred books on Kennedy issued in the thirty-six months after his death (including *The Mind of JFK, The Faith of JFK, The Kennedy Wit, More Kennedy Wit,* and other striking signs of publishers' faith in the selling power of the newly sacred name) were reports by his special counsel (Theodore Sorensen's *Kennedy*), by one of his special assistants (Arthur Schlesinger, Jr.'s *A Thousand Days*), by his chief of press relations (Pierre Salinger's *With Kennedy*), by his private secretary (Evelyn Lincoln's *My Twelve Years with John F. Kennedy*), and by his children's nurse (Maud Shaw's *White*

House Nannie). Besides these, there was *The Pleasure of His Company*, by Paul B. "Red" Fay, Jr., Kennedy's old friend from PT-boat days whom he called "Grand Old Lovable," who could always make him laugh with his uninhibited rendition of "Hooray for Hollywood!" and whom Kennedy brought to Washington by arranging his appointment as Under Secretary of the Navy.

None of these posthumous best sellers was authorized by the surviving Kennedys, of course, in the same sense that they authorized the Manchester account of the assassination. Indeed, the family tried to prevent publication of *White House Nannie*. After the attempt failed, however, they censored only a few paragraphs since it turned out to be in the inane tradition of inside stories by refined nannies who wouldn't dream of telling all ("[Mrs. Kennedy] never likes to put other people out, even the tiniest bit"). *The Pleasure of His Company* is on the family Index, although Fay submitted it for clearance and has said that he deleted 90,000 of about 180,000 words at Mrs. Kennedy's request. His publisher thinks it was not so many. He balked, he said, at removing another 30,000, which would have reduced it to a third of its original length and might have rendered it unpublishable, an outcome the Kennedys may have had in mind. No *passim* cuts could remedy its pervading indiscretion—the evidence throughout the book that Kennedy, the symbol of intellect and culture come to the White House, had chosen to spend a large share of his leisure time during the last twenty years of his life with a good-hearted end man whose mother tongue is Kiwanis Club slang and who cheerfully admits he had to be clued in on Renoir and Cézanne. ("If you have to ask a question like that, do it in a whisper," Kennedy told him. "We're trying to give this administration a semblance of class.") Rejecting Fay's three-thousand-dollar gift to the Kennedy Library, Mrs. Kennedy—for whom those long, recurrent weekends *en famille* with the Fays may have been somewhat of a trial—wrote that she regarded the contribution as "hypocritical." Of all the diarists of the Kennedy era to date, Fay, best man at the Kennedy wedding, had been closest to the Hyannisport-Hickory Hill contingent. Since the appearance of his fond but inelegant view of life with their martyred brother, he and the Kennedys have been, as the columnists say, don't-invite-'ems.

Schlesinger, Sorensen, and Salinger—the S-men—remain decidedly *grata* in the compound, however, nor have diplomatic relations apparently been severed with Mrs. Lincoln, in whose adoring book the Kennedys made no changes. She had relied almost entirely on her personal diary and her trusty notebook; but the long, intensively documented accounts of the Kennedy administration by Sorensen and Schlesinger—and, to an extent perhaps, Salinger's specialized report of those years as seen from the White House press office—could not have been written without access to information and records in Kennedy control. Only nonbelievers would suggest that the authors played "hush" in any respect just because someone named Bob gave them materials. But even before their books were stamped with

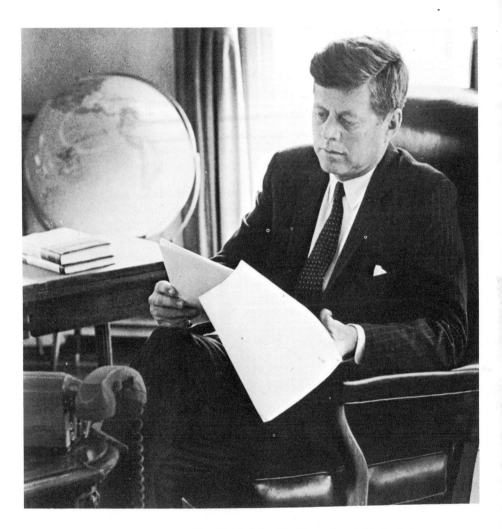

*President John F. Kennedy at his desk in
the Oval Room of the White House in 1963.*

approval, these men were part of the privy council, sworn to serve
the clan that the same nonbelievers have charged with assuming the
prerogatives of an American royal family in temporary exile. Members
of the council (William Manchester must now be inclined to refer
to it as another "tong," the epithet that, in *Death of a President*,
he applies to Johnson's Texas followers) are pledged to rally around
during all Kennedy campaigns,. to run general interference in off-
election years, to squire the widow about on occasion, and to help
the family maintain its dominion over all insiders' published recol-
lections of the Kennedy era—or so it appears to gawkers on the
sidelines. Of course, in the years since the White House was their
second home, they have all made other lucrative professional commit-

ments, but there doesn't seem to be much doubt about where the priorities would lie if a footman should arrive with a summons from Jackie.

During Kennedy's term of office his staff was accused of trying to manage the news. Now, of course, the charge on several fronts is that of managing history. Kennedy himself during his drive for the Presidency had no qualms about attempting to control what appeared in books written about him. In the late fifties he saw to it that some of his father's anti-Semitic remarks were removed from a biography of the family, and at about the same time, according to Sorensen, he "waged an intensive effort with his contacts in the publishing world to prevent a projected biography by a writer inaccurately representing himself to potential publishers as a Kennedy intimate—a man whom Senator Kennedy in fact regarded as uninformed, unobjective and unsound."

The authors of the certified chronicles do not pretend to be objective. Salinger notes that his inability to continue to work for Lyndon Johnson was no fault of Johnson's, whom he liked. He simply came to realize that "the memory of J.F.K. was too overpowering." "Our faith in him and in what he was trying to do was absolute," he writes of Kennedy's cadre of White House assistants, and, in retrospect, Sorensen is moved by their sense of common challenge and dedication to their leader's cause to quote Henry V at Agincourt:

> . . . we . . . shall be remembered—
> We few, we happy few, we band of brothers. . . .
> And gentlemen . . . now abed
> Shall think themselves accurs'd they were not here.

Kennedy once joked with his staff about Evelyn Lincoln's blind devotion to him. "If I had said just now, 'Mrs. Lincoln, I have cut off Jackie's head, would you please send over a box?' she still would have replied, 'That's wonderful, Mr. President, I'll send it right away. . . . Did you get your nap?' " Often, in these approved histories, when a head has been cut off, Schlesinger and company, though they don't run for a box, seem to suggest that somebody else did the dirty deed or anyhow talked Kennedy into it, or that, even if their leader did it himself, it was all, in the long run, for the best—especially if he got his nap. For example, they cite every pragmatic political excuse for Kennedy's trepid record on McCarthyism, and Sorensen himself takes full blame for not pairing him against McCarthy in the Senate vote on censure. (Since Kennedy was incommunicado in the hospital and had not heard the final debate, says his loyal assistant, Sorensen felt it would be in violation of due process to record his vote.) Kennedy, having assailed Eisenhower for failing to issue an executive order forbidding racial discrimination in federally financed housing, then sat on the same order for nearly two years after he took office, but *his* delay is treated as an instance of his shrewd sense of values— even grace under pressure—since the controversial edict would have endangered the rest of his legislative program. The excuse is not extended retroactively to his predecessor.

The band of brothers combines to portray Mrs. Roosevelt as a villainess, as indeed she appeared to Kennedy in the pre-nomination days when she held him in deep distrust and maneuvered her forces in favor of Stevenson and Humphrey. And although Kennedy did once telephone the *New York Times* and suggest a vacation for David Halberstam, whose Vietnam dispatches were rankling, he made the call, argues Salinger, knowing full well that its effect would be to insure Halberstam's continued presence in Southeast Asia. As for the Cuban invasion, some of the press at the time noted that while Kennedy at his own desk was manfully taking entire responsibility for the disaster, his staff in the outer office was plying newspapermen with evidence that the debacle was really the fault of the C.I.A., the Joint Chiefs of Staff, and the previous administration. In their books they are still at it. But then, as Sorensen writes: "This is not . . . a neutral account. An impassioned participant cannot be an objective observer."

Still, if we should not be surprised to find Kennedy's friends giving him the best of it, it's all right, perhaps, to be taken aback when Schlesinger in the *Life* serialization of *A Thousand Days* has the President crying in his wife's arms after the Cuban setback and then removes the scene from his published book, announcing that "it sounded sob-sisterish" and "didn't come off." Apparently where John Kennedy is concerned, the previous winner of the Bancroft, Parkman, and Pulitzer prizes for history thinks of historic material as something that may be tried this way, turned around and tried that way, and balled up and discarded if it doesn't seem entirely becoming to the subject. And then there is the matter of the style sheet that probably didn't need to be sent to these prospective authors since they knew the house rules. Among its apparent proscriptions:

Don't call Bobby "Bobby," as everybody else does. Salinger, Sorensen, Fay, and Mrs. Lincoln dutifully make it "Bob." Schlesinger prefers "Robert Kennedy," even in describing the celebrated occasion when, fully clothed, he jumped or fell into Robert's swimming pool. There are a few exceptions, almost unavoidable since the books are full of remarks by their President in which he used the politically awkward diminutive. Schlesinger breaks ranks all the way on the few pages that cover the events at the 1960 convention after Kennedy offered Johnson the vice-presidential nomination and, apparently to his astonishment, was accepted, and his brother then appeared in the Johnson hotel suite on what Johnson interpreted as a campaign to talk him out of it. In the farrago that followed, right out of the second act of *Three Men on a Horse*, the cast of characters included another Bobby, last name Baker. Possibly Schlesinger won a special dispensation, arguing that to play fair and also call the latter "Robert" struck him as a bit much. However, in the account of the same melee by Sorensen, now quite a formal fellow for a born-and-bred Nebraskan, it is "Robert Baker."

*Pretend you always called the President's wife "Mrs. Kennedy"
or "Jacqueline," not "Jackie,"* as the whole world knows her. Although he complies, this stipulation must have been a particular drag
to Paul Fay, a highly informal type whose own wife the President
always referred to as "the Bride," who knew Kennedy for many
years as "Shafty Boy," and who shared with him a fraternity of
pals called, in middle age as in their youthful Navy days, by such
nicknames as Bitter Bill, Dirty John, and Jim Jam Jumping Jim.

*The President's father is not to be called "Joe," "Old Joe," or
"Big Joe." Refer to him as Mr. Joseph P. Kennedy or "the Ambassador"—and always respectfully.* ("I would like to see Red Fay
write this story if my father was not ill—I think it is an outrage,"
runs a notation on the Fay manuscript beside an anecdote about
Kennedy, Sr., that did not appear in the book.)

Rules having to do with nomenclature need not signify much.
Yet anyone reading a biography of Jack Kennedy that leaves out
characters called "Jackie," "Bobby," and "Big Joe" may be entitled to wonder what else has been omitted to suit his survivors.
The only matters suppressed in his book, says Sorensen, are those
absent "for reasons of security or propriety." One of the men dele-
gated by Mrs. Kennedy to help blue-pencil the Fay as well as the
Salinger efforts is J. Kenneth Galbraith (who once wrote an essay
on the general topic of the political build-up, which he defined as
"synthesizing a public reputation as a matter of deliberate design").
Most of the deletions that were eventually made in the books in
question, he wrote recently, "involved the elimination of language
or anecdotes which, out of context, cast reflection on the dignity of
the office of President or which might, without purpose, have injured
the feelings of personal friends of President Kennedy"—a patriotic
and benevolent censorship policy with built-in conveniences. Mrs.
Kennedy, he added, insisted on protecting more feelings—that is,
removing more material—than he thought strictly necessary. One
noticeable excision from all the books, just for openers: the name of
any woman Kennedy ever had the slightest interest in other than
his wife, unless you count Mrs. Lincoln's passing reference to a few
anonymous girls so unimportant to Kennedy in his premarital years
that he usually took them to the movies once apiece and had his
secretary set up the dates at that. One of Fay's unforgiven transgressions, according to rumor, is his casual mention of the presence
at the inaugural festivities, presumably with Kennedy's approval,
of a young actress the President is said to have admired. Other
evidence in the Fay book makes it obvious that Grand Old Lovable
saw a great deal of his old Navy friend in the decade between the
PT-boat episode and Kennedy's marriage at the rather advanced age
of thirty-six, but virtually everything that went on in that unencum-
bered time is apparently among the thousands of words that Fay was
persuaded to sacrifice in the vain hope of staying in the family
favor. His book was published by Harper and Row, which had
brought out *Profiles in Courage* and at the time was hoping to publish

Manchester's *Death of a President* without legal incident. Clearly, if the present keepers of the eternal flame can prevent it, there will be no Ann Rutledge chapter in the Kennedy legend.

Lincoln once found a life of Edmund Burke "so lavish in praise of his every act that one is almost driven to believe that Burke never made a mistake or a failure in his life." Most biographies, he grumbled, "commemorate a lie, and cheat posterity out of the truth." Kennedy had a similar complaint after reading the first volume of Eisenhower's autobiography. "Apparently Ike never did anything wrong," he said. "When we come to writing the memoirs of this administration, we'll do it differently." Whatever blocking tactics Kennedy tried to use on books about himself during his long campaign for the Presidency, once that was won and then irrevocably lost, it was his remark about biography and infallibility that his personal historians tried to keep in mind. Despite all their excuses for him vis-à-vis McCarthy, they felt free to conclude that in many respects he was "insensitive" and "wrong" on this issue. After all the many alibis for the Bay of Pigs, his performance there is labelled essentially "stupid"—and, as is often the case in these books, the harsh judgment is his own.

Kennedy's part in the Vietnam war is not glossed over: it was "his great failure in foreign policy." The influence of his humor and instinct for self-mockery is consistently present, as when Sorensen points out that in his chapter on the 1960 fight for the nomination he finds that he has referred to powerful Kennedy supporters as "political leaders" while those in the opposition camp are "bosses," who are then converted to "political leaders" when they come over to the right side. And though Ambassador Kennedy gets the specified respectful treatment, his son Jack made a telling remark that is also available for balance. It came after a Georgia court had sent Dr. Martin Luther King, Jr., to jail and Kennedy had made a sympathy call to King's pregnant wife. On learning of the call, King's father announced that it had persuaded him to support Kennedy, whom he had planned to vote against on strictly religious grounds. The candidate's comment was, "Imagine Martin Luther King having a bigot for a father. . . . Well, we all have fathers, don't we?"

Soon after he took office, Kennedy directed the Voice of America to broadcast the nation's story "with all our blemishes and warts, all those things about us that may not be so immediately attractive." If certain of his own blemishes are still considered unmentionable, the authorized accounts are not without authorized warts. They don't hesitate to mention his crankiness, his scorching sarcasm and quick temper, his lack of consideration for those working for him, and his impatience with anyone, no matter how worthy, who bored him. Although only an infrequent "son of a bitch" or "kicked in the can" is quoted, there is no pretense that his language in private was in keeping with his posthumous saintlike image. Even the White House nannie tells of an occasion when Caroline left behind in Kennedy's office a large doll whose special accomplishment was that it would repeat whatever was said to it. The feat involved a tape recorder, and the next day when Caroline retrieved the doll and pressed the proper button, there emerged from its rosebud plastic lips Daddy's angriest voice, using, said Miss Shaw, "a very naughty word." Not knowing how to erase the tape, she hastily called a Secret Service agent to perform a disembowelment.*

The books by Kennedy's three White House assistants are, of course, the memoirs that will be of serious interest to future historians. Of these the gracefully written *A Thousand Days* is much the best job. After all, Schlesinger has been arranging presidential crises into orderly chapters for two decades. Moreover, most of his White House years were spent not in Kennedy's West Wing wheelhouse but in the East Wing writing voluminous memos, from which task he would be summoned now and then for advice or for a bit of political legwork. His engagement in Kennedy's program was not the roll-call-by-roll-call affair that it was to Sorensen and Salinger, and he was able to view it with some perspective against a background of what had gone before and what was happening elsewhere and was thus able to write a book that is more the history of an exhilarating national interval than the biography of one man. Sorensen's *Kennedy* is shorter than the Schlesinger book (758 pages *vs.* 1,031) but it gives the impression of being far longer, since it covers in dense detail the last eleven years of Kennedy's life (Schlesinger was involved only in the last four) from a vantage point rarely more than a centimeter from Kennedy's elbow. Salinger's *With Kennedy* is a slighter book than either of these; yet it has a certain long-range interest, especially in its accounts of the vast preparations for total war in October, 1962, the problems confronting the American press during the two Cuban crises, and his own comparative intimacy with individual Russians, including Khrushchev.

Before joining Kennedy's staff, reports Schlesinger, he was warned that he would be plunging into "a ruthless scramble for access and power." He found instead that "the Kennedy White House remained to the end remarkably free of the rancor which has so often welled up in Presidential households." Although the three members of the brotherhood whose memories of Kennedy are now in print often deal with the same event, in which each played some part, little jockeying for historical position clutters their books. Their put-downs and waspish digs are generally reserved for others, usually those not wearing a PT-boat tie clasp. Here also the influence of Kennedy as editor-*in-absentia* is apparent. "Nor would he tolerate from his

---

* Curiously, Miss Shaw's account of the day of the assassination omits Caroline's harrowing ride through the Washington streets with a Secret Service man just after the news from Dallas began to come in, the episode that *Death of a President* relates in such detail. Caroline and John, she says, had just had lunch at the White House with Teddy Kennedy's children and were about to be put down for their naps when the word came. Thus, as in so many aspects of the Kennedy saga, historians are reminded of how variable is the human memory of events even so soon after the fact.

staff the slightest disparagement of the Vice President," notes Schlesinger, and although it may have taken some self-control, there are no swipes at the Vice President by these witnesses. All three, in fact, write with sympathy of Johnson's understandable discomfort in his diminished role. Kennedy's biographers feel freer to let their disparagement show, however, in reporting the 1960 convention when the two politicians were sworn enemies and, as Schlesinger puts it with historical detachment, Johnson was "laying about with heavy saber strokes, Kennedy mastering him with an urbane and deadly rapier." As for Rusk, since Kennedy's commitment to him was no longer total by 1963, Sorensen and Schlesinger permit themselves to write of him with less than total Saint Crispin's Day loyalty. He was "almost too amiably cautious," "bland," "colorless," "Buddha-like," and so circumspect that during any given crisis "no one knew quite where he stood."

There have been complaints, of course, that it was unseemly for Kennedy confidants to rush into print—and then off to the bank— with their versions of events that were so recent and that in some cases involved men still in office. But some historians will presumably be grateful that these reports were published while the memories of the impassioned participants were fresh and feisty rather than, like the biography by Lincoln's secretaries, written decades later when the excitements of the age were measured from a stately distance. As for their lack of neutrality and occasional discreet excision, perhaps their degree of candor should be compared to that of accounts of the Eisenhower administration that Sherman Adams or George Humphrey might have written if *their* President had died in office— whether or not the testimonials had been cleared with his survivors.

History, like the news, has always been subject to some management, but the stage directions should be out of earshot. The question is how far the Kennedys and company propose to carry their by now conspicuous presumption. Only three of Kennedy's ten White House assistants and none of his Cabinet have so far been heard from. But nearly all of them, it now appears, scurried directly home from the West Wing each night to write in their diaries, and the next wave of memoirs should start rolling from the typewriters soon. The planned collaboration by the Irish Mafia—Ken O'Donnell, Dave Powers, and Larry O'Brien—will apparently be a mere tandem affair. O'Brien, unlike the rest of the old gang, is still welcomed in the redecorated West Wing where augmenting the J.F.K. mythology is not politically healthy. But doubtless O'Brien's version will not be permanently withheld from us.

Will the heirs and tenders of the Kennedy mystique continue to assert editorial rights over each new volume, and will the authors acknowledge their eminent domain? No doubt it will depend on whether the authors firmly believe that a new Saint Crispin's Day lies ahead and care to keep their place among the happy brotherhood around the new Henry V. If so, they will probably see the merit of not tampering with the legend. After all, the saintly-Lincoln myth that flourished after 1865 was of prodigious value to the then-new Republican party, whose dubious political caracoles in the next decades often took place behind a blown-up poster image of a much-loved President dead by an assassin's hand.

Kennedy's inaugural message was written after Sorensen, at the President-elect's direction, made a searching study of the Gettysburg Address, trying to discover its magic formula for immortality. To White House gratification, Sam Rayburn announced after hearing the result of this effort that Kennedy was "better than Lincoln" ("I think—I really think—he's a man of destiny"). But in *Portrait of a President*, his first book on Kennedy, published before he became a true, genuflecting believer, William Manchester wrote: "Certainly John Kennedy is not as lovable as Abe. He has a weaker grasp on the nation's heartstrings, and the reason isn't that he hasn't been shot." It was, of course, after he was shot that the two names began to be linked in an incessant litany. (The other two assassinated Presidents, Garfield and McKinley, were way out of it.) Reams were written about their common vein of humor, their similar fatalism about the danger of assassination, their century-apart (and equally gingerly) enlistment of the authority of the Presidency to help the Negro cause. Jim Bishop, who had written *The Day Lincoln Was Shot* and was soon making plans to give the same treatment to November 22, 1963, played a macabre game in the Hearst papers, listing numerous other similarities—from the fact that both men were succeeded by Vice Presidents named Johnson to the discovery that the names John Wilkes Booth and Lee Harvey Oswald had fifteen letters each. And right after the murder, Bill Mauldin's cartoon in the Chicago *Sun-Times* showed the statue in the Lincoln Memorial covering its face with its hands.

"Find out how Lincoln was buried," were Jacqueline Kennedy's words to Chief of Protocol Angier Biddle Duke a few moments after Air Force One landed at the Washington airport on the tragic flight from Dallas. It was not a precedent that was desirable to follow in all details. After the Washington rites, Lincoln's body was borne on a dead march through a dozen cities before finally being laid to rest in Springfield on May 4, nearly three harrowing weeks after the murder. The Lincoln funeral arrangements were in the hands of Secretary of War Stanton, the widow being bedfast and only half-lucid. Fortunately for the nation, Mrs. Kennedy was of a different mettle. Indeed it seems probable that the memory of her strength and heartbreaking dignity and the part she played in getting the American people through that terrible weekend will make it impossible for most of them to find serious fault with anything she does for the rest of her days (unless, as she herself shrewdly put it three years later, "I do something silly like run away with Eddie Fisher"). At her direction, Kennedy's coffin, like Lincoln's, stood in the candlelit East Room of the White House beneath chandeliers draped in black, and then in the great rotunda of the Capitol on the same catafalque, covered in black velvet, that had held Lincoln's coffin.

Following the ninety-eight-year-old scenario, six gray horses drew it down Pennsylvania Avenue to the same muffled roll of drums. Behind the wooden caisson walked, as in 1865, a riderless gelding with boots reversed in the stirrups, the military symbol of the fallen warrior. Two weeks later when Mrs. Kennedy and her children left the White House, the new tenants found that, in case anyone had missed the point, the names of the two murdered Presidents were now permanently linked in stone. The words "In this room lived John Fitzgerald Kennedy with his wife Jacqueline during the two years, ten months, and two days he was President of the United States, January 20, 1961–November 22, 1963" had been carved in the white marble fireplace of what had been Kennedy's bedroom, directly below those that had long read: "In this room Abraham Lincoln slept during his occupancy of the White House as President of the United States, March 4, 1861—April 13, 1865." It is doubtful if A. Philip Randolph, who a few days earlier had said that Kennedy's "place in history will be next to Abraham Lincoln," expected his words to be followed so literally, or so soon. But what seems most remarkable of all is that Abraham Lincoln found his place—in history, graven in stone, enshrined in legend—although at the time of his death his widow was the kind of woman no one paid any attention to, and he hadn't a father, mother, sister, or brother to his name.

Picture Credits

11, Library of Congress. 35, Library of Congress. 40, Free Library of Philadelphia. 45, Library of Congress. 46, *Harper's Weekly*, April 17, 1875. 48, Culver Pictures, Inc. 51, Library of Congress. 59, Library of Congress. 60, Culver Pictures, Inc. 64, Library of Congress. 70, Mississippi Department of Archives and History. 76, Harvard College Library. 83, Brown Brothers. 87, Culver Pictures, Inc. 93, National Steel Corporation, Pittsburgh, Pa. 97, Library of Congress. 98, New York *World*, July 1, 1892. 99, Culver Pictures, Inc. 103, Culver Pictures, Inc. 107, Culver Pictures, Inc. 109, Library of Congress. 111, Brown Brothers. 118, Photo by Margaret Bourke-White, *Life* Magazine, © Time Inc. 119, 1958 Time Inc. 125, Drawn by Michael Ramus for *American Heritage*. 128, Library of Congress. 129, Harvard University Library. 131, Harvard University Library. 141, Library of Congress. 149, Library of Congress. 153, Brown Brothers. 156, *Puck*, January 13, 1904. 158, Wide World Photos. 163, Library of Congress. 164, State Historical Society of Wisconsin. 167, State Historical Society of Wisconsin. 171, Library of Congress. 172, Culver Pictures, Inc. 176, Photo by Wallace Kirkland. 177, Chicago Historical Society. 179, Chicago Historical Society. 181 (top), Photo by Wallace Kirkland.

181 (middle), Photo by Wallace Kirkland. 181 (bottom), Chicago *Tribune* Library. 195, Warshaw Collection of Business Americana. 199, Official U. S. Navy Photograph. 203, Culver Pictures, Inc. 205, New York *Journal*. 208, Chicago Historical Society. 214, State of Vermont. 217, *Leslie's Official History of the Spanish-American War*. 223, *Puck*, March 22, 1899. 229, Library of Congress. 231, Garraty, *Henry Cabot Lodge*, 1953. 232, Library of Congress. 235, The San Francisco *Chronicle*. 238, Wide World Photos. 241, UPI. 260, National Archives. 261, National Archives. 263, National Archives. 267, National Archives. 273, Wide World Photos. 276, *Arizona Republic*. 278, UPI. 281, Photo by Cornell Capa, Magnum. 287, *Judge*, November, 1929. 291, Wide World Photos. 293, Collection of Rita and Daniel Fraad. 296, Wide World Photos. 299, Evans, in the Columbus *Dispatch*, November, 1938. 312, Courtesy of the New-York Historical Society. 313, Wide World Photos. 316, Ewing Galloway. 324, UPI. 325, UPI. 330, Brown Brothers. 332, Brown Brothers. 333, Brown Brothers. 336, James Reagan and HARYOU-ACT Commercial Workshop. 337, Jeff McDonald and HARYOU-ACT Commercial Workshop. 341, Drawn by Michael Ramus for *American Heritage*. 343, Photo by Fred Ward, Black Star.